Burial in Later Anglo-Saxon England

STUDIES IN FUNERARY ARCHAEOLOGY

Vol. 1 *Social Archaeology of Funerary Remains*
Edited by Rebecca Gowland and Christopher Knüsel

Vol. 2 *Deviant Burial in the Archaeological Record*
Edited by Eileen M. Murphy

Vol. 3 *The Archaeology of the Dead*
Henri Duday

Burial in Later Anglo-Saxon England *c.* 650–1100 AD

Edited by
Jo Buckberry and Annia Cherryson

OXBOW BOOKS
Oxford and Oakville

First published in the United Kingdom in 2010. Reprinted in 2016 by
OXBOW BOOKS
The Old Music Hall, 106–108 Cowley Road, Oxford OX4 1JE

and in the United States by
OXBOW BOOKS
1950 Lawrence Road, Havertown, PA 19083

Paperback Edition: ISBN 978-1-78570-549-6
Digital Edition: ISBN 978-1-84217-819-5

A CIP record for this book is available from the British Library

Library of Congress Cataloging-in-Publication Data

Burial in later Anglo-Saxon England c. 650-1100 ad / edited by Jo Buckberry and Annia Cherryson.
p. cm.
ISBN 978-1-84217-965-9
1. Funeral rites and ceremonies, Medieval--England. 2. Burial--England--History. 3. Civilization, Anglo-Saxon. 4. Human remains (Archaeology)--England. 5. Anglo-Saxons--England--Antiquities. 6. Great Britain--Civilization--To 1066 I. Buckberry, Jo. II. Cherryson, Annia.
GT3243.B87 2010 393.90942--dc22

For a complete list of Oxbow titles, please contact:

UNITED KINGDOM
Oxbow Books
Telephone (01865) 241249, Fax (01865) 794449
Email: oxbow@oxbowbooks.com
www.oxbowbooks.com

UNITED STATES OF AMERICA
Oxbow Books
Telephone (800) 791-9354, Fax (610) 853-9146
Email: queries@casemateacademic.com
www.casemateacademic.com/oxbow

Oxbow Books is part of the Casemate Group

Front cover: Burial in a lead coffin, Staple Gardens, Winchester. Courtesy of Winchester Museums Service

Contents

List of Contributors

JO BUCKBERRY
Biological Anthropology Research Centre
Archaeological Sciences
University of Bradford
Bradford, BD7 1DP
Email: J.Buckberry@bradford.ac.uk

ANNIA CHERRYSON
45 Horseshoe Drive
Romsey
Hants, S051 7TP
Email: annia.cherryson@ntlworld.com

ELIZABETH CRAIG
Department of Archaeology
University of Sheffield
Westcourt
2 Mappin Street
Sheffield, S1 4DT
Email: lizzyfloracraig@hotmail.co.uk

SALLY CRAWFORD
The Institute of Archaeology
36 Beaumont Street
Oxford, OX1 2PG
Email: sally.crawford@arch.ox.ac.uk

SARAH GROVES
Department of Archaeology
Durham University
South Road
Durham, DH1 3LE
Email: s.e.groves@durham.ac.uk

CHRISTOPHER GUY
Chapter Office
8 College Yard
Worcester, WR1 2LA
Email: ChrisGuy@worcestercathedral.org.uk

D. M. HADLEY
Department of Archaeology
University of Sheffield
Northgate House
West Street
Sheffield, S1 4ET
Email: D.M.Hadley@sheffield.ac.uk

JAMES HOLLOWAY
76 Milton Road
Cambridge, CB4 1LA
Email: james.holloway@cantab.net

NICK STOODLEY
Department of Archaeology
University of Winchester
Winchester
Hants, SO22 4NR
Email: Nick.Stoodley@winchester.ac.uk

HOWARD WILLIAMS
Department of History and Archaeology
University of Chester
Parkgate Road
Chester, CH1 4BJ
Email: howard.williams@chester.ac.uk

Introduction

Annia Cherryson and Jo Buckberry

The last ten to fifteen years have seen major breakthroughs in the way later Anglo-Saxon cemeteries are studied. These developments follow the publication of several important cemeteries (Phillips and Heywood 1995; Boddington 1996; Heighway and Bryant 1999; Rodwell 2001; Cramp 2005; Mays *et al.* 2007), but more importantly a number of synthetic works that draw together this wealth of primary archaeological data (Hadley 2000a; Hadley 2001; Blair 2005; Reynolds 2009). This book aims to bring together a range of papers that give an overview of current research on later Anglo-Saxon cemeteries from a number of different perspectives. The overarching theme of the book is differential treatment in death, which is examined at the site-specific, settlement, regional and national level.

Twenty years ago, later Anglo-Saxon funerary archaeology was the poor relation to the study of earlier cemeteries, which contain a high proportion of individuals accompanied by grave or pyre goods. The seminal volume 'Anglo Saxon Cemeteries, 1979' (Rahtz *et al.* 1980) contained 25 papers. Just three of these papers considered later cemeteries. The chronological imbalance seen in the earliest studies can be attributed in part to the absence of grave goods in later Anglo-Saxon burials but perhaps even more so to the traditional view that the conversion of the Anglo-Saxon kingdoms to Christianity during the seventh century led to the rapid abandonment of furnished burial and ushered in an era of homogenous churchyard burial (Meaney and Hawkes 1970, 51). Christian cemeteries and the burial practices within them were viewed, at least nominally, as comparable to that of modern society (Watts and Rahtz 1985, 128), in which (Christian) burial expresses 'an ideal of equality, humility and non-materialism which is blatantly in contrast with the way we live our lives in practice' (Hodder 1980, 168). This sentiment has led to the view that later Anglo-Saxon burials were uniform and egalitarian, following the Christian ideal, despite the evident stratification in society at that time (Geake 1997, 127; Tarlow 1997, 139; Carver 1999, 8). These views meant that Christian burials were perceived as having a lower research potential and significance than earlier accompanied burials.

Recent work has questioned many of the assumptions that had underpinned the study of later Anglo-Saxon cemeteries by demonstrating that the transition to churchyard burial was far from rapid or straightforward (Hadley 2000a, 199; Hadley 2000b, 160; Blair 2005, 245). Furthermore, the decline in the use of grave goods did not lead to a uniformity of burial practices but instead the expression of individuality through other aspects of the burial rite, such as the use of funerary furnishing and above-ground markers (Hadley 2000a; Buckberry 2007; Hadley 2007). It is no coincidence that the increasing interest in burials of the later Anglo-Saxon period, and indeed the dead of the medieval and post medieval period, came at time when an increasingly holistic approach is being taken to the study of mortuary behaviour. Grave goods dominated many of the early studies of early medieval burials and still remain an important aspect of any analysis, yet the last few decades has seen the scope of enquiry widen to encompass personal and group identity, the body, the grave and the placement of the dead within the landscape (for example see Pader 1982; Stoodley 1999; Gowland 2006; Williams 2006).

Several broad themes run through the papers in this volume. The development of churchyard burial and the impact of the church on mortuary practice is key to any study of later Anglo-Saxon burial, however recent work has demonstrated that mortuary behaviour during this period was shaped by a multiplicity of factors including social structure, status and political developments, as well as religion. This variability is addressed directly by Buckberry, in her study of cemetery variation in the northern Danelaw (Chapter 1) and by Cherryson in her analysis of burial in early medieval Southampton (Chapter 4). The use of grave goods in the seventh and eighth centuries is discussed by Williams (Chapter 2), who stress the biography of objects and their role in constructing a commemorative identity, and by Stoodley (Chapter 3), who discusses the unusually well furnished weapon graves at St Mary's Stadium, Southampton, and the importance of these objects as symbols of status and identity. Many authors discuss variation in grave type; in particular, Holloway (Chapter 6) discusses the meaning of charcoal burials at a national level, whereas Guy (Chapter 5) discusses the range of variation in burial practice seen within a partially excavated cemetery at Worcester Cathedral. Several papers use a biocultural approach to cemetery analysis: Groves (Chapter 9) and Craig and Buckberry (Chapter 10) use primary osteological data to investigate health, status and identity at the Bamburgh Bowl Hole and Raunds Furnells cemeteries respectively; Hadley (Chapter 8) synthesises osteological data from a number of sites to investigate the differential treatment of individuals buried both within and outside churchyards; whereas Crawford (Chapter 7) applies a biocultural approach to documentary evidence to better understand the social meaning of physical deformity. Common to many papers is the issue of independent dating evidence and the need for more extensive and rigorous radiocarbon dating programmes to fully understand the chronology of the changes seen in burial location and form throughout this period. This volume was conceived as a means of demonstrating the vitality and diversity of the research currently being undertaken on the burials of the later Anglo-Saxon period. By drawing together these papers, it demonstrates the potential for further study of the burials of this period and the importance of examining old questions and assumptions using new methods and approaches.

The editors thank all of the individual authors for their contributions to this volume, and for many engaging discussions on the subject. We also thank the many reviewers who commented on papers in this volume and Edward Faber for acting as a sounding board throughout this project. Winchester Museums Service granted permission to use the picture of the burial in the lead coffin from Staple Gardens, Winchester on the cover of this volume. Finally we thank Oxbow Books for all their assistance in the production of this volume.

References

Blair, J. (2005) *The Church in Anglo-Saxon society*. Oxford, Oxford University Press.

Boddington, A. (1996) *Raunds Furnells. The Anglo-Saxon church and churchyard.* English Heritage Archaeological Report 7. London, English Heritage.

Buckberry, J. L. (2007) On sacred ground: social identity and churchyard burial in Lincolnshire and Yorkshire, c.700–1100 AD. In: Williams, H. and Semple, S. (eds.) *Early medieval mortuary practices. Anglo-Saxon Studies in Archaeology and History 14,* 120–132. Oxford, Oxbow.

Carver, M. (1999) Cemetery and society at Sutton Hoo: five awkward questions and four contradictory answers. In: Karkov, C., Wickham-Crowley, K. and Young, B. (eds.) *Spaces of the living and the dead: an archaeological dialogue,* 1–14. American Early Medieval Studies 3. Oxford, Oxbow.

Cramp, R. J. (2005) *Wearmouth and Jarrow monastic sites. Volume 1.* Swindon, English Heritage.

Geake, H. (1997) *The use of grave-goods in Conversion-period England c.600–c.850.* British Archaeological Reports British Series 261. Oxford, British Archaeological Reports.

Gowland, R. (2006) Ageing the past: examining age identity from funerary evidence. In: Gowland, R. and Knüsel, C. (eds.) *The social archaeology of funerary remains,* 143–154. Oxford, Oxbow.

Hadley, D. M. (2000a) Burial practices in the northern Danelaw, c.650–1100. *Northern History* 36, 199–216.

Hadley, D. M. (2000b) Equality, humility and non-materialism? Christianity and Anglo-Saxon burial practices. *Archaeological Review from Cambridge* 17, 149–178.

Hadley, D. M. (2001) *Death in medieval England.* Stroud, Tempus.

Hadley, D. M. (2007) The garden gives up its secrets: the developing relationship between rural settlements and cemeteries, c. 750–1100. In: Williams, H. and Semple, S. (eds.) *Early medieval mortuary practices. Anglo-Saxon Studies in Archaeology and History 14,* 194–203. Oxford, Oxbow.

Heighway, C. and Bryant, R. (1999) *The golden Minster. The Anglo-Saxon Minster and later medieval priory of St Oswald at Gloucester.* Council for British Archaeology Research Report 117. London, Council for British Archaeology.

Hodder, I. (1980) Social structure and cemeteries: a critical appraisal. In: Rahtz, P., Dickinson, T. and Watts, L. (eds.) *Anglo-Saxon cemeteries 1979,* 161–169. British Archaeological Reports British Series 82. Oxford, British Archaeological Reports.

Mays, S., Harding, C. and Heighway, C. (2007) *Wharram. A study of settlement on the Yorkshire Wolds, XI. The churchyard.* York University Archaeological Publications 13. York, University of York.

Meaney, A. L. and Hawkes, S. C. (1970) *Two Anglo-Saxon cemeteries at Winnall, Winchester, Hampshire.* The Society for Medieval Archaeology Monograph 4. London, Society for Medieval Archaeology.

Pader, E. J. (1982) *Symbolism, social relations and the interpretation of mortuary remains.* British Archaeological Reports International Series 130. Oxford, British Archaeological Reports.

Phillips, D. and Heywood, B. (1995) *Excavations at York Minster volume 1: from Roman fortress to Norman cathedral.* London, HMSO.

Rahtz, P., Dickinson, T. and Watts, L. (eds.) (1980) *Anglo-Saxon cemeteries 1979.* British Archaeological Reports British Series 82. Oxford, British Archaeological Reports.

Reynolds, A. (2009) *Anglo-Saxon deviant burial customs.* Oxford, Oxford University Press.

Rodwell, W. (2001) *Wells Cathedral: excavations and structural studies, 1978–93.* English Heritage Archaeological Report 21. London, English Heritage.

Stoodley, N. (1999) *The spindle and the spear: a critical enquiry into the construction and meaning of gender in the early Anglo-Saxon burial rite.* British Archaeological Reports British Series 288. Oxford, British Archaeological Reports.

Tarlow, S. (1997) The dread of something after death: violation and desecration on the Isle of Man in the tenth century. In: Carman, J. (ed.) *Material harm. Archaeological studies of war and violence,* 133–142. Glasgow, Cruinthne Press.

Watts, L. and Rahtz, P. (1985) *Mary-le-Port, Bristol: Excavations 1962–1963.* Bristol Museum and Art Gallery Monograph 7. Bristol, Bristol Museum and Art Gallery.

Williams, H. (2006) *Death and Memory in Early Medieval Britain.* Cambridge, Cambridge University Press.

1. Cemetery Diversity in the Mid to Late Anglo-Saxon Period in Lincolnshire and Yorkshire

Jo Buckberry

It has long been assumed that, following the foundation of Minsters in the seventh and eighth centuries (Blair 1988; Blair 2005), all late Anglo-Saxon cemeteries were situated next to churches and are now located under medieval churchyards (Meaney and Hawkes 1970; Biddle 1976, 69). However, over the last decade this model has been questioned, following the excavation and publication of a number of late Anglo-Saxon cemeteries not perpetuated by a later medieval churchyard (Hadley 2000; Lucy and Reynolds 2002). Moreover, the identification of increasing numbers of late Anglo-Saxon execution cemeteries, isolated burials and Scandinavian burials demonstrates the diversity of burial location during this period (Reynolds 1997; Richards 2002; Cherryson 2008; Reynolds 2009). The suggestion that from the eighth century all individuals were buried in Minster-controlled cemeteries, adjacent to a church, can no longer be sustained (Hadley 2000; Blair 2005, 245). During the last decade, work has highlighted diversity in funerary provision, shattering traditional concepts of a uniform mortuary practice, both in terms of cemetery type and grave form (Hadley 2001; Blair 2005; Cherryson 2005; Buckberry 2007; Hadley 2007; Cherryson 2008, and this volume). This paper seeks to consider diversity in cemetery location in detail by discussing the wide variety of cemetery types that have now been identified for the later Anglo-Saxon period in the northern Danelaw, within the modern counties of Lincolnshire and Yorkshire.

Lincolnshire and Yorkshire: a case study

Between 1999 and 2004, a comprehensive survey of later Anglo-Saxon cemeteries in Lincolnshire and Yorkshire was undertaken by the author (Buckberry 2004) and additional sites have been added to the dataset subsequently. All local Historic Environment Records (HERs) and the National Monuments Record (NMR) were consulted, as were published excavation summaries in journals including Medieval Archaeology, Yorkshire Archaeological Journal and Lincolnshire History and Archaeology and relevant published gazetteers (Meaney 1964; Magilton 1977; Eagles 1979; Faull 1979; Loughlin and Miller 1979; Faull and Moorhouse 1981; Morris 1983; Leahy 1993; Geake 1997; Leahy 1998; Lucy 1998). The resulting dataset was compared with data on early Anglo-Saxon cemeteries, to establish the extent to which later Anglo-Saxon cemeteries are archaeologically less visible compared with the artefact-rich cemeteries of the fifth and sixth centuries. In addition, data were collected on all ostensibly undated burials recorded in the two counties, in an attempt to identify further later Anglo-Saxon cemeteries.

A total of 470 burial sites were identified in the survey, of which 301 were dated (with varying degrees of certainty) to the Anglo-Saxon period (see Table 1.1, below). Just over one third of the records related to undated burials (n=165). A further four sites noted as being only possibly of Anglo-Saxon date on the HER or other data source were recorded, however all of these were thought unlikely to be Anglo-Saxon following more detailed investigation. Eighty-five sites were dated to the fifth to sixth centuries (18% of all sites; 28.2% of dated sites). Only a small number of cemeteries (30; 6.4% of all sites; 10% of dated sites) were identified as being middle Anglo-Saxon in date, however 51 early Anglo-Saxon cemeteries (10.9% of all sites; 16.9% of dated sites) continued to be used into the seventh century, and 29 cemeteries founded in the middle Anglo-Saxon period continued in use beyond the end of the eighth century (6.2% of all sites; 9.6% of dated sites). Just 40 cemeteries were founded in the late Anglo-Saxon period (8.5% of all sites; 13.3% of dated sites), of which 17 continued in use after the Conquest. Twenty-five sites (5.3% of all sites;

Period	No. sites	% of dated sites (n=301)	Number of sites with reasonable evidence for date	% of dated sites (n=301)	Number of sites with tentative evidence for date	% of dated sites (n=301)
Anglo-Saxon	25	8.3	7	2.3	18	6.0
Early Anglo-Saxon	85	28.2	59	19.6	26	8.6
Early to mid Anglo-Saxon	51	16.9	40	13.3	11	3.7
Early to mid grave goods, but no burial	41	13.6	41	13.6	-	-
Mid Anglo-Saxon	30	10.0	28	9.3	2	0.7
Mid to late Anglo-Saxon	29	9.6	20	6.6	9	3.0
Late Anglo-Saxon	23	7.7	15	5.0	8	2.7
Late Anglo-Saxon to medieval (or later)	17	5.7	16	5.3	1	0.3
Total	301	100%	226	75%	75	25%

Table 1.1: Results of a survey of Anglo-Saxon burial sites in Lincolnshire and Yorkshire

8.3% of dated sites) were recorded as merely 'Anglo-Saxon' – these were predominantly identified from antiquarian reports and were mainly dated on the basis of grave goods, therefore they are likely to be early to mid in date. Overall this shows, as expected, that far more sites are known for the early/early to middle Anglo-Saxon period, however later cemeteries are perhaps not as under-represented in the archaeological record as expected. A similar pattern has been noted in Wessex, but, in contrast in the counties of Dorset, Somerset and Devon – where grave goods were not deposited – this pattern is less obvious, indicating that where dating of cemeteries is entirely dependent on radiocarbon or stratigraphic evidence earlier sites do not predominate (Cherryson 2005). This paper will focus on those cemeteries founded in the middle Anglo-Saxon period or later, including those with tentative dating evidence (see Table 1.1, n=99), to highlight the variability in cemetery types within this apparently small group.

Cemeteries without churches

The mid-seventh and eighth centuries witnessed the foundation of a large number of new cemeteries. Initially, many of these contained furnished burials; the proportion of furnished to unfurnished burials within a cemetery is highly variable, but is generally lower than is the case in the early Anglo-Saxon period. Mid Anglo-Saxon cemeteries with many furnished graves are often referred to as 'final phase' cemeteries (*i.e.* the final phase of furnished burial), but broadly contemporary cemeteries containing few or no accompanied burials have also been excavated, and there is no clear dividing line in terms of the percentage of accompanied burials within a cemetery to separate 'final phase' cemeteries from cemeteries of (largely) unaccompanied burials. It is far more useful to categorise individual burials of the conversion period as accompanied or unaccompanied, rather than try to categorise the cemeteries as being largely furnished or unfurnished (Geake 1992, 89).

Burials accompanied by conversion period grave goods are found in cemeteries founded in the fifth and sixth centuries, as well as in the newly founded cemeteries dating to the late seventh and early eighth centuries, clearly showing that a simple transition from one type of cemetery to another did not occur (Stoodley 2007). Conversion-period cemeteries were more highly organised than earlier cemeteries, with burials arranged regularly, sometimes in rows, and the bodies positioned in a more uniform manner, usually supine and extended, and often west-east aligned (throughout this paper, the first orientation will refer to the head end of the grave). For those cemeteries containing higher proportions of accompanied burials, there was a visible decrease in both the number of grave goods deposited, and also in the range and type of artefacts deposited, and many burials were accompanied by just a buckle and/or a knife (Geake 1992, 85). However, many of the artefacts were of a superior quality compared with those commonly deposited during the sixth century, and cruciform items became more common (Lethbridge 1936, 47–9; Evison 1956; Hyslop 1963, 162; Meaney and Hawkes 1970; Boddington 1990, 181; Geake 1992, 84–5). Margaret Faull suggested that 'final phase' cemeteries were located closer to settlements than the early cemeteries, whereas by the late Anglo-Saxon period churchyards were located within the settlement itself (Faull 1976). More recent surveys of cemetery and settlement evidence, however, have shown that cemeteries did not move towards settlements (which were also moving in the landscape), although there is evidence for 'paired' pagan and conversion-period cemeteries, as seen at Sancton (Yorks.) and Sheffield's Hill (Lincs.) (Hadley 2007; Stoodley 2007). The decline in grave goods and the shift towards more organised cemeteries was traditionally attributed to the conversion process, with the Church seen as the instigator of these changes (Hyslop 1963, 192). However, there is little evidence that the Anglo-Saxon Church was especially concerned with the manner in which people were buried (Bullough 1983), and therefore it has alternatively been suggested that economic, political and social reasons explain the change in burial style (Arnold 1982; Boddington 1990; Geake 1992), with personal choice,

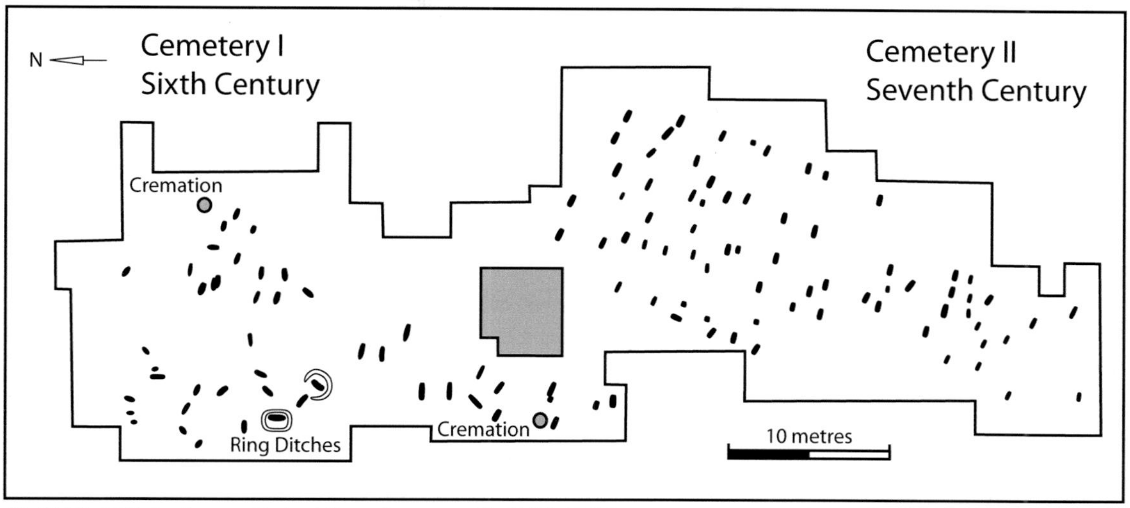

Figure 1.1: Sheffield's Hill, Roxby-cum-Risby. The sixth-century Sheffield's Hill I cemetery is 10m to the north of the seventh- century Sheffield's Hill II cemetery (drawn by Dan Bashford).

either by the individual or the community, often playing an important role in cemetery and burial diversity.

Of the 29 mid-Anglo-Saxon sites identified in Lincolnshire and Yorkshire, twenty had graves containing conversion-period grave goods (Table 1.2 and Table 1.3). This includes twelve cemeteries, one barrow burial and seven isolated burials. Isolated and barrow burials are discussed in more detail below.

In Yorkshire, several cemeteries of accompanied burials were inserted into, or located around, prehistoric earthworks, including the Iron Age square barrow cemetery at Garton Station (Stead 1991, 17–24), the barrow and linear earthwork at Garton Green Lane Crossing (Mortimer 1905, 247–257) and the Bronze Age barrow at Uncleby (Smith 1912), following a pattern commonly seen for early Anglo-Saxon cemeteries in this region (Lucy 1998) and elsewhere (Williams 1997; Cherryson 2005). The re-use of prehistoric sites was observed less frequently in Lincolnshire, however some examples were noted, including the seventh-century cemetery at Kirkby-la-Thorpe, which overlay two prehistoric ring ditches (Bonnor and Allen 2000) and a disturbed burial inserted into a Bronze Age barrow at West Halton (Dawn Hadley, *pers. comm.*). In some cases, the seventh-century cemetery could be shown to be located a short distance away from an earlier cemetery, following the pattern first noted at Sancton (Faull 1976). For example, the seventh-century Sheffield's Hill II in Roxby-cum-Risby parish, was located just 10m to the south of the sixth-century Sheffield's Hill I (Figure 1.1) (Leahy and Williams 2001); however in most cases this kind of relationship could not be demonstrated.

Traditional models saw the so-called 'final phase' cemeteries as a fairly short-lived and transitional phase, disappearing in the early-mid eighth century as churchyard burial became universal (Meaney and Hawkes 1970; Biddle 1976). Similarly, non-churchyard cemeteries are also often seen as a largely late seventh- to eighth-century phenomenon. These burial grounds are, in many ways, identical to churchyard cemeteries, with west-east aligned supine burials often arranged into rows, but without a church. The biggest difficulty encountered when studying non-churchyard cemeteries is establishing if they were merely partially excavated churchyards with any archaeological evidence of a church either destroyed by later activity or remaining outside the excavated area. This said, a growing number of non-churchyard cemeteries are being recognised. For example, non-churchyard cemeteries in Wessex include the long-lived seventh-century foundations at Bevis Grave, Bedhampton and SOU 862 in Southampton (both Hants), Wembdon and Templecombe (both Somerset); and the later cemeteries of Six Dials (Hants) and Staple Gardens in Winchester (Cherryson 2008). Clearly, burial persisted away from churches into the eighth century and beyond, both within existing seventh-century cemeteries and in later foundations, but to what extent were these non-churchyard cemeteries nonetheless under ecclesiastical control? At Chimney (Oxon), the non-churchyard cemetery was located on land granted to the clergy of Bampton Minster (located three miles away) in the mid-tenth century (Crawford 1989; Blair 2005, 467). Other examples of satellite lay cemeteries have not been securely identified, but often the absence of good documentary evidence makes this kind of connection difficult to substantiate. However, monasteries sometimes had multiple cemeteries, including satellite cemeteries; for example Ailcy Hill in Ripon (Yorks) has been interpreted as a satellite cemetery of Ripon Minster, although in this case the cemetery was just 200m from the Minster (Hall and Whyman 1996).

Unfortunately, independent dating evidence is rarely obtained for middle Anglo-Saxon cemeteries, and this makes it difficult to assess their origins and longevity. Cemeteries

Cemetery name(s)	Date	Dating evidence	Associated features	References
Burton Pidsea EY	Conversion period	Grave goods		Poulson 1841, 44; Geake 1997, 157
Howe Hill (Carthorpe parish) NY	Conversion period	Grave goods	Inserted into a natural mound	Lukis 1870; Geake 1997, 189
Garton Green Lane Crossing (Garton II, Garton Gate House) – first group EY	Conversion period	Grave goods	Bronze Age barrow. First of two groups of burials to the north of barrow number C34. The second group of burials was located approximately 46 feet to the east of the first group and are treated as a separate cemetery here	Mortimer 1905, 247–57; Geake 1997, 158
Garton on the Wolds (Garton Slack I, Sledmere) EY	8C	Grave goods, 8 sceattas (720–725)	Linear earthwork (the 'Double Dyke')	Mortimer 1905, 624–70; Grantham and Grantham 1965; Geake 1997, 158
Garton Station EY	Conversion period	Grave goods	Iron Age square barrow cemetery	Stead 1987; Stead 1991, 17–24; Geake 1997, 158
Painsthorpe Wold I (Kirkby Underdale parish) EY	7C	Grave goods	Bronze Age barrow	Mortimer 1905, 113–7; Geake 1997, 158
Uncleby (Kelleythorpe) (Kirkby Underdale parish) EY	7C	Grave goods	Bronze Age barrow	Greenwell 1877, 135–6; Mortimer 1905, 118; Smith 1912; Geake 1997, 159; Harrison 1997
Kirkby-la-Thorpe L	7C	Grave goods	Two prehistoric ring ditches (either Bronze Age or Iron Age)	Network Archaeology Ltd 1999; Bonnor and Allen 2000
Chapel Lane, Navenby L	Mid Anglo-Saxon	Grave goods including 7C beaker	Bronze Age and Romano-British cremations	Palmer-Brown 1996
Seamer NY	Conversion period	Grave goods		Wright 1865; Geake 1997, 190
Tetford Hill L	Conversion period	Grave goods		Wilson and Hurst 1959, 297; Petch 1960, 19–20; Geake 1997, 168
Sheffield's Hill II (Roxby-cum-Risby) L	Conversion period	Grave goods	10m to south of 6C cemetery	Leahy and Williams 2001

Table 1.2: Cemeteries with accompanied burials. Grave goods were identified as merely 'conversion-period' (following Geake 1997) unless further details are given. Counties are given in this and all subsequent tables as follows: L=Lincolnshire, EY=East Yorkshire, NY=North Yorkshire, SY=South Yorkshire, WY=West Yorkshire.

Cemetery name(s)	Date	Dating evidence	Associated features	References
Caenby L	Conversion period	Grave goods	7C barrow	Jarvis 1850; Geake 1997, 167
West Halton L	600–670 cal AD	C14	Bronze Age barrow	Dawn Hadley, *pers. comm.*
Occaney Beck (Occaney) (Walkingham Hill with Occaney parish) NY	7C	Annular brooches		Waterman 1951; Meaney 1964, 295; Geake 1997, 190
Womersley SY	7C	Pendant		Bateman 1860, 289; Meaney 1964, 303; Geake 1997, 191
Burton Fields (Stamford Bridge parish) EY	Conversion period	Grave goods		Kitson Clark 1942; Meaney 1964; Eagles 1979; Loughlin and Miller 1979; Geake 1997; Lucy 1998
Hambleton Moor (Byland with Wass parish) NY	Conversion period	Grave goods		Geake 1997, 189
White Hart Farm, North Elmsall WY	7C	Grave goods	Located 'some 10 yds from the west wall of the church'	Bellamy 1963–6, 9; Wilson and Hurst 1964, 238; Faull and Moorhouse 1981, 180; Geake 1997, 191
Dalton Parlours (Collingham parish) WY	?7C	Brooch	Overlying a Roman villa	Moorhouse 1977, 8; Moorhouse 1978, 11; Webster and Cherry 1978, 150–1; Moorhouse 1979, 6; Faull and Moorhouse 1981, 180; Wrathmell and Nicholson 1990, 285–7; Geake 1997, 191
Kettlewell NY	660–780 cal AD	C14		HER records
Ash Hill long barrow (Swinhope) L	730–1149 cal AD	C14	Neolithic barrow	Phillips 1985, 72–73; Phillips 1989
Tattershall Thorpe L	7C or later	Artefacts	Overlying a Neolithic settlement	Hinton and White 1993; Geake 1997, 168
Wharram Percy NY	600–760 cal AD	C14	Associated with SFB	Milne and Richards 1992, 20, 79, 84–5; Geake 1997, 190
Blue Bridge Lane, York	Probably late Anglo-Saxon or medieval period	Circumstantial	Interpreted as outliers of the St Andrew's Fishergate cemetery	York Archaeological Trust 1994
Coppergate, York	9C	Stratigraphy	Coppergate settlement	Hall 1994, 43
Carr Farm, Arncliffe NY	Probably middle Anglo-Saxon	Reliquary box		Cale 2000
Sheep Wash Farm, Little Bytham L	Probably late Anglo-Saxon	Circumstantial		Hurley 1992

Table 1.3: Isolated burials. Unless otherwise stated, all radiocarbon dates are calibrated to 2 sigma (in this and all subsequent tables).

with accompanied burials are assumed to date to the seventh and eighth centuries (and not continue any later) and those without any grave goods (or a church) are assumed to date to the eighth and possibly early ninth centuries. Where radiocarbon dates are obtained, only a small number of burials are usually sampled, which makes it difficult to assess when cemeteries were founded, how long they were in use for and, crucially, when during the period of cemetery use the most burial occurred. At the Dixon Keld burial ground in Masham (Yorks), dated to AD 679–868, AD 784–983 and AD 872–1011 (all cal 2 sigma) (Buckberry *et al.* 2009) and Thornton Steward (Yorks), dated to AD 660–810, AD 680–900 and AD 810–1020 (all cal 2 sigma) (Adamson and Abramson 1997), multiple radiocarbon dates revealed that both cemeteries were in use for several centuries, and in both cases beyond the ninth century. At Riccall (Yorks), initially three radiocarbon dates were obtained, giving a date range spanning the eighth to late eleventh/early twelfth centuries, but centred on the tenth century (Buckberry 2004), showing that the cemetery was in use far later than anyone would have expected. A further six burials were radiocarbon dated prior to publication and these indicated that the cemetery was is use from the seventh until the twelfth century (Hall *et al.* 2008) – a wider range than the initial three dates indicated. Beyond issues of dating, the biggest difficulty encountered when studying non-churchyard cemeteries is establishing if they were merely partially excavated churchyards with any archaeological evidence of a church either destroyed by later activity or remaining outside the excavated area. Indeed, at Riccall, Masham and Thornton Steward it is possible that evidence for a church lay beyond the limits of the excavations.

Cemeteries without churches have been commonly referred to as 'field cemeteries' by a number of archaeologists (for example Lucy and Reynolds 2002; Cherryson 2008). This definition is, however, somewhat problematic, as the word 'field' could imply an open rural location away from contemporary settlement. In many cases cemeteries without churches contain burials that cut through earlier occupation layers, indicating that some, at least, were contained within settlements, often being founded or falling into disuse as part of the regular reorganisation of space within villages (Hadley 2007). The extent to which non-churchyard cemeteries were present within towns is much less well established, as in most cases partial excavation has left it impossible to ascertain whether a church was actually present, although several cemeteries without churches have been excavated in Southampton (Morton 1992b; Morton 1992a; Andrews 1997, Cherryson, this volume).

The survey of Lincolnshire and Yorkshire identified nineteen cemeteries without strong evidence for a church (Table 1.4). It is notable that all of these cemeteries appear to have been founded in the middle Anglo-Saxon period, even though many were used into the late Anglo-Saxon period and occasionally after the Conquest. This probably relates to a change in practice in the tenth and eleventh centuries, when burial became more centralised. The boom in church building seen at this time (Morris 1983, 65–6; Blair 2005, 368–425) also meant that newly-founded cemeteries were likely to have a church. Several non-church cemeteries were located within a settlement, but between 70 and 250m from the parish church – indicating that burial location within the settlement was not static (Hadley 2007). Cemeteries excavated at some distance from the medieval parish church include those at Fillingham (250m, Buckberry and Hadley 2001b), Great Hale (70m, Buckberry and Hadley 2001c) (both Lincs), Thornton Steward (100m, Adamson and Abramson 1997) and Ripon Ailcy Hill (200m, Hall and Whyman 1996). This pattern could be due to various scenarios. In some cases, the location of the cemetery (and possibly a church) might have moved within a settlement at some point during the later Anglo-Saxon or medieval period. Alternatively, settlements may have contained two cemeteries during the later Anglo-Saxon period, one of which went out of use and the other continuing as the burial ground of the medieval parish church. As Dawn Hadley notes, relocation of cemeteries often took place during the reorganisation of settlements, and was likely to be influenced by both lords and the Church (Hadley 2007, 200).

Churchyard cemeteries

The most commonly encountered type of late Anglo-Saxon cemetery is the churchyard. Indeed, such is the expectation that a church should be associated with a late Anglo-Saxon cemetery that excavators frequently speculate where the church was probably located even if archaeological evidence is absent. This begs the question; just how much archaeological evidence is needed to establish that a cemetery had a church? It is often difficult to assess the quality of evidence for the presence of a church, especially from older excavation reports and small-scale excavations. Early timber churches leave little archaeological trace beyond post holes – how many post holes are needed to indicate the presence of a church? When walls, and especially west-east aligned walls, are encountered in cemeteries they are often attributed to churches. This is problematic when only a small-scale excavation has taken place. More recent excavation reports tend to err on the side of caution – for example at Whitton (Lincs), excavated between 2001 and 2002 by Dawn Hadley, a wall and an area of more dense burial were identified within the cemetery, however the excavator clearly states that they could not establish if the wall was from a church (Hadley 2003; 2004).

The issue of the quality of evidence for churches is crucial when trying to establish if a cemetery was a churchyard or a non-church cemetery. If the cemetery and church continued to be used during the medieval period and later, successive churches are likely to have destroyed or concealed any evidence of the earliest buildings, especially if they were timber. Indeed, the building of later churches and successive grave digging can

Cemetery	Date	Evidence for date	Number of graves/ burials	Relationship to known church/associated features	References
North Frodingham L		Location in village (*c.*100m from church), on church land	'many human bones'	100m to the south of parish church	Data from HER
North Kelsey L		Saxon pottery	*c.*30	*c.*100m from parish church	Lindsey Archaeological Services 1995
Fillingham L	660–885, 895–1025 and 900–1160 cal AD	C14	1953: 1 1982: 12 2000: 6		Field 1983; Buckberry and Hadley 2001b
Normanby-le-Wold L	Mid Anglo-Saxon	Ceramics found in vicinity	Not specified		Addyman and Whitwell 1970, 96–8
Kemp Howe (Cowlam) EY	Early-mid 8C	C14	1878: 6 1967/8: 12		Mortimer 1905, 336–8; Wilson and Hurst 1969, 285
Flixborough (southern group) L	8C	Sceat	11		Field 1989, 53; Geake *et al.* 2007
Garton Green Lane Crossing (Garton II). East group EY	Mid Anglo-Saxon	Location and coffin hinges	32	Bronze Age barrow. Second of two groups of burials to the north of barrow number C34. (see Table 1.2)	Mortimer 1905, 247–57
Great Hale L	655–765 cal AD	C14	8	70m to the east of the parish church	White 1982, 76; Youngs *et al.* 1987, 150; Buckberry and Hadley 2001c
Middle Street, Kilham EY	720–980 and 690–940 cal AD	C14	10+	Many burials and a lead coffin reported prior to 1928. Excavations revealed intercutting west-east aligned burials	Buckberry 2004, 89; Dave Evans, *pers. comm.*
York Road, Kilham EY	Late Anglo-Saxon	Circumstantial	6	Some in coffins	Eagles 1979, 219, 438; Loughlin and Miller 1979, 109; Lucy 1998, 129
Saltergate, Lincoln	660–1020 cal AD	Knife blade, late Saxon pottery. C14 of animal bone	4		Reynolds 1979; Geake 1997, 169; Jen Mann, *pers. comm.*
Riccall Landing NY	7–12C	C14: 9 dates	61		Wenham 1960, 301–7; Brinklow 1986; Hall *et al.* 2008
Ailcy Hill, Ripon NY	Phase 1: 560–660 cal AD; Phase 2: 660–810 cal AD & 680–880 cal AD; Phase 3: 780–990 cal AD & 660–860 cal AD	C14	37+		Hall and Whyman 1996

Table 1.4: Cemeteries with no evidence of a church (continued over the next page).

Cemetery	Date	Evidence for date	Number of graves/ burials	Relationship to known church/associated features	References
Scampton L	Believed to be late Anglo-Saxon	? stratigraphy and orientation	'upwards of 20' (11 shown on plan)	Overlying Roman villa	Illingworth 1810; Marjoram 1974, 21
Thornton Steward NY	660–810, 680–900 & 810–1020 cal AD	C14	17 inhumations and 1 cremation	100m to west of St Oswald's church	Adamson and Abramson 1997
Grantham Rd, Waddington L	7C	2 coffin nails and copper-alloy staining on one skeleton. Could be later	3 graves, 2 unexcavated grave cuts	Eleven 6C burials were found nearby in 1947	Lindsey Archaeological Services 1999
Lamel Hill/Belle Vue House, Heslington Rd, York	Mid to late Anglo-Saxon	Coffin fittings	1849: 20–30 1983: 38		Thurnam 1849; Briden 1983; Briden 1984
Dixon Keld, Masham NY	679–868, 872–1011 and 784–983 cal AD	C14	58		Anon 1989; Neale and Buckberry 2008; Buckberry *et al.* 2009
Castle Yard, York	9–11C	Under 11C rampart. Styca 840–867	2; further burials left *in situ*		Meaney 1964, 303; York Archaeological Trust 1998

Table 1.4: Cemeteries with no evidence of a church (continued from the previous page).

obscure much of the evidence of late Anglo-Saxon cemeteries and churches. Another complication is establishing which came first, the church or the cemetery. Whereas many churches and cemeteries appear to have been founded contemporaneously, others have clear evidence that the first known church post-dated burials (Hadley 2000), as church walls cut through and disturb earlier burials, indicating that churches were sometimes built within previously founded cemeteries.

The present study identified 27 cemeteries with good evidence of a church (see Table 1.5). At sixteen sites a church is still standing today. At six of these sites significant excavation has taken place, revealing evidence of the Anglo-Saxon church(es). For those sites where more limited excavation took place, it is generally assumed that the earliest burials must have been associated with a pre-Conquest church, however this does not necessarily mean that the cemetery was founded before or at the same time as the first church on the site. At St Peter's Holton-le-Clay, Barrow-on-Humber (both Lincs; see Figure 1.2) and Pontefract Tanners Row (Yorks), burials were cut by church foundations, showing that burials had taken place before the church was constructed. However, at other sites it was difficult to ascertain if the burials were disturbed by the earliest church, or by later rebuilding exercises. The latter was the case at St Mary's Stow (Lincs) and Holton-le-Clay, where pre-Conquest burials were cut by eleventh-century walls. Ten of the churchyards identified no longer have a standing church, but excavations revealed church foundations, including Thwing (Yorks), Pontefract Tanners Row and Barrow-on-Humber. Most of the churches went out of use in the Anglo-Saxon or medieval period, although St Mary Bishophill Senior, York, was not demolished until 1963.

A further nineteen cemeteries were identified where, although there is no primary evidence for a church, there is an assumption that they were churchyards (Table 1.6). However the strength of the argument for the presence of a church varies greatly. Although the location of York Minster has been a subject of ongoing debate (Carver 1995; Norton 1998), there is little doubt that the burials excavated from underneath the present Minster originated from the cemetery associated with the Anglo-Saxon Minster (Phillips and Heywood 1995). In many cases, excavated cemeteries were in very close proximity to the known locations of churches that have been identified during excavation and/or watching briefs prior to construction work, or that are still extant. These burials are usually attributed to the known church, even if this church can be securely dated to no earlier than the later medieval period. For example, the burials at St Marygate in Ripon (Yorks) are located just 12m from the excavated ?eighth- to tenth-century Ladykirk (Hall and Whyman 1996, 124–30); and the Swinegate cemetery in York which is close to the suspected location of St Benet's church, first recorded in AD 1154 when the church was granted by the king to the monks of Pontefract (Pearson 1989; Pearson 1990; Wilson and Mee 1998, 60). Burials from Cornhill Square, Lincoln, are close to the suspected location

Cemetery	Date	Date and evidence for date	Number of graves/burials	Evidence for church	References
Addingham WY	660–1020 cal AD	C14: 4 dates	56 graves (some empty)	Standing church. 6m to east of excavated area	Adams 1996
Barrow-on-Humber L	10–12C	C14, two coins dated *c.*870 AD	Approximately 75 partial and complete skeletons	Excavated 11th to 12th-century apsidal church. Initially incorrectly identified as Æt Bæruwe/St Chad's monastery	Boden and Whitwell 1979; Foreman n.d.
St Peter's Barton-on-Humber L	Phase E, *c.*950–1150	C14, dendrochronology and stratigraphy	Phase E: 446 burials	Standing church. First church: three-celled, late 10C /early 11C, pre-existing cemetery	Rodwell and Rodwell 1981; 1982; Rodwell 2007
Conisborough SY	Probably pre-Conquest	Stratigraphy	1	Standing church	Miller 1804, 262
St Helen's, Cumberworth L	9–11C	Tweezers, lead plaque, pottery, stratigraphy	26	Standing medieval church. Excavated 2-celled stone church 10/11C. Earlier posthole structure may be first church	Green 1997
Hessle I (Haltemprice parish) EY		Dated as Anglo-Saxon by Meaney	1	Standing church	Meaney 1964, 291; Lucy 1998, 129
St Peter's, Holton-le-Clay L	10–12C	Stratigraphy, grave cover fragment, artefacts	14	Standing church	Sills 1982
Hickleton SY	Late Anglo-Saxon to 19C	Stratigraphy		Standing church	Stroud n.d.
Kellington NY	10–11C	Stratigraphy		Excavated churches under standing church	Mytum 1994
St Mark's, Lincoln	10–19C. Phase VIII: 9–11C	Stratigraphy, burial practices. Phase VIII C14: 9–11C	Phases VIII and IX (*c.*950–1150): 127	Excavated church	Gilmour and Stocker 1986; Steane *et al.* 2001, 252–8
St Paul-in-the-Bail, Lincoln	Late Roman/early Anglo-Saxon to post-medieval	Stratigraphy and C14 dates. 7C hanging bowl	Phase I (pre-church): 14. Phase 2 (very late Roman to middle/late Saxon): 242	Excavated churches date from the late Roman/Anglo-Saxon to Georgian period	Gilmour 1979, Jen Mann *pers. comm.*; Jones *et al.* 2003
Tanners Row Pontefract (The Booths) WY	Pre-10C	Stratigraphy. Site A sealed by 10–12C settlement	Site A: between 24 and 26 burials. Site B: 197	Excavated churches. First timber, later single-celled then double-celled stone churches	Wilmott 1986; 1987; Tony Wilmott *pers. comm.*
Ladykirk, Ripon NY	8–11C	Bone combs, sculpture	36	Excavated two-celled stone church (?12C)	Ryder 1990; Hall and Whyman 1996, 124–30
Castle Hill, Scarborough NY	8/9–11C	Church early 11C. 11C coin, artefacts	*c.*400	Excavated two-celled stone church. Possible earlier timber church	Rowntree 1931; Bell 1998, 308–11
St Giles' Avenue, Sleaford L	Late Anglo-Saxon	Stratigraphy. 10–11C grave cover found nearby	17 graves or grave cuts identified, 1 stratigraphically pre-Conquest	Excavated late Anglo-Saxon church	Trimble 1997
Stow L		Stratigraphy – burials cut by 11C wall.	At least 17	Standing church. 11C foundations may be from pre-Conquest church	Field 1984

Table 1.5: Churchyards (continued over the next page).

Cemetery	Date	Date and evidence for date	Number of graves/burials	Evidence for church	References
St Lawrence, Burnham (Thornton Curtis) L	10C	Stratigraphy	Infant burial found within timber church. No other burials noted	Sequence of churches excavated	White 1978, 81–2
Wakefield Cathedral WY	9–11C	9C ring. Sealed by foundations *c.*1100	6 pre-Conquest burials	Standing church	Thorp 1975, 9; Webster and Cherry 1975, 230
Kildale NY	Anglo-Scandinavian	Grave goods	7 or 8	Standing church	See Table 1.7: Scandinavian burials
Kirkdale NY		8/9C pottery in cemetery layers. Stratigraphy. 10C cross fragments and 8/9C box shrine fragments built into church	Unspecified number of burials	Standing church	Rahtz and Watts 1997; Watts *et al.* 1997; Jemmeson 1998
St Martin's, Welton-le-Wold L	10–11C	Pottery	11	Standing church	Field 2002
Wensley NY	Anglo-Scandinavian	Scandinavian burials	1	Standing church	See Table 1.7: Scandinavian burials
St Martin's, Wharram Percy NY	*c.*950–1850	Stratigraphy, C14. Churches: Phase I: mid/late 10C Phase II: early/mid 11C	10 pre-Conquest; 167 *c.*950–*c.*1348	Standing church with excavated sequence of churches. Phase I: postholes, possible timber church Phase II: 2 celled church	Bell and Beresford 1987; Mays *et al.* 2007
St Andrew's Fishergate, York	10–12C	Stratigraphy	Total number of burials 412 Phase 4 (pre-12C): 130	Excavated sequence of churches. Wooden structure interpreted as an early church	Stroud and Kemp 1993
St Helen-on-the-Walls, York	Founded 10C	Stratigraphy	800 burials. Late Anglo-Saxon to medieval	Excavated sequence of five churches. First church single-celled, 10/11C	Dawes and Magilton 1980; Magilton 1980
St Mary Bishophill Junior, York	9–10C	Grave goods	8	Standing church	See Table 1.7: Scandinavian burials
St Mary Bishophill Senior, York	10–11C	10C strap end, stratigraphy	Unspecified	Church demolished 1963	Ramm 1965, 334; Wilson and Hurst 1965, 176; Hall 1994, 45; Richards 2000, 151

Table 1.5: Churchyards (continued from the previous page).

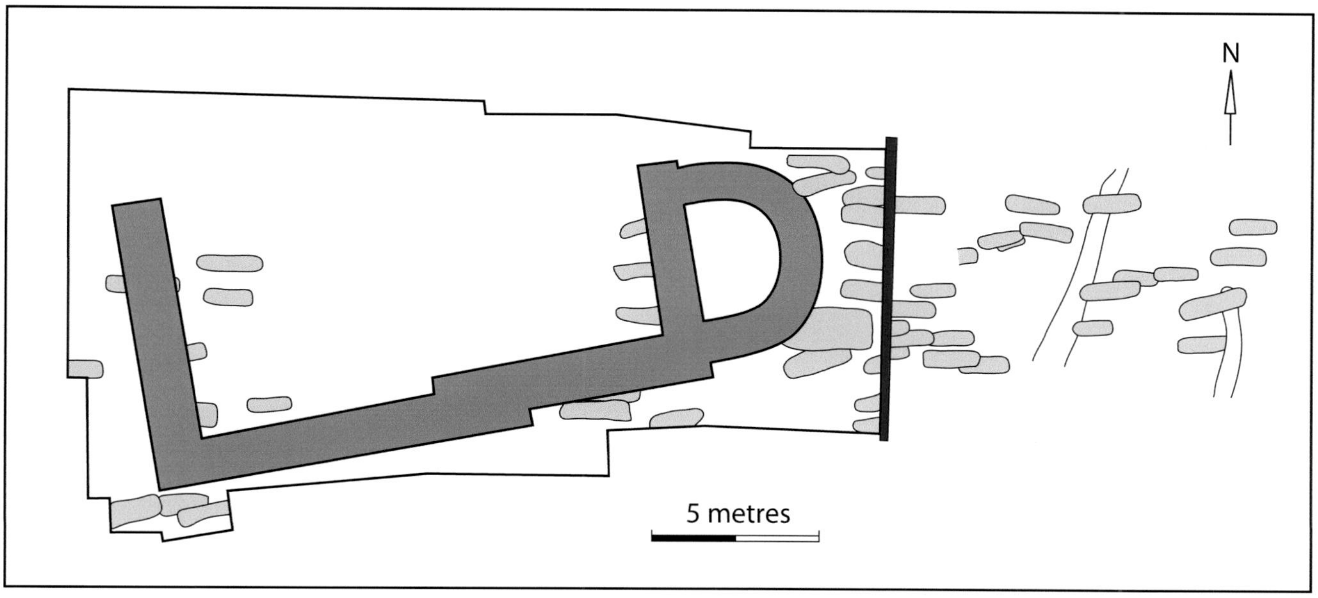

Figure 1.2: The tenth- to twelfth-century cemetery at Barrow-on-Humber, Lincs. Several burials pre-dated the eleventh to twelfth-century apsidal church (drawn by Dan Bashford).

of the church of St John the Evangelist, founded in the tenth century (City of Lincoln Archaeology Unit 1999), although it is likely that most, if not all, of the excavated graves were post-Conquest in date.

In many cases, these possible churchyards were only partially excavated, which makes it impossible to ascertain if a church was present or not. However there is a tendency to assume that they were churchyards if we cannot prove otherwise – is this because of the (usually eighth-century or later) date of the cemeteries or the location of the cemeteries (especially if they are associated with a settlement)? In most cases it is because churchyards fit our perception of later Anglo-Saxon cemeteries more than non-church cemeteries – despite the growing evidence for long-lived cemeteries that either never had a church, or only gained a church some time after their foundation. At Fillingham, the small-scale excavation made it impossible to establish if a church was present, and larger scale excavations would not provide the answer, as a large area surrounding the excavated articulated burials had been quarried in the post-medieval period (Buckberry and Hadley 2001b). However, it would be easy to assume that a church was present: some burials dated to the tenth to twelfth centuries (although the cemetery was founded in the seventh or eighth), it was associated with settlement activity and Domesday Book refers to a church at Fillingham. But was the Domesday church associated with the excavated cemetery, or is it located under the parish church, some 250m to the east? Essentially there is no simple way of determining if cemeteries without archaeological evidence of a church, like the one at Fillingham, actually had a church, yet there is a general assumption that they did. Clearly we need to think about cemetery types with more open minds if we are to fully appreciate the variety that existed – essentially there are four kinds of cemetery excavated: those with primary evidence for a church, those with secondary evidence for a church, those that clearly did not have a church, and those where we cannot tell for certain. Date does seem to play a part here – cemeteries founded in the tenth century or later all appear to be churchyards, however there is growing evidence that church-less cemeteries founded in the middle Anglo-Saxon continued to be used beyond the tenth century without necessarily obtaining a church. This is probably connected to the introduction of consecration rites (Gittos 2002) and the increase in the rate of the foundation of proprietary churches in the tenth century.

It should also be noted that not all churches, and therefore churchyards, were the same. The differences between royal foundations, Minster churches and proprietary churches are clear from documentary sources and it is likely that these different establishments catered for different groups of society. Indeed, previous research has shown that high-status and urban churchyards contained greater variation in grave elaboration, sometimes in a higher proportion of graves, than their lower status or rural counterparts (Buckberry 2007), and often had more stone sculpture (Stocker 2000). Scandinavian burials, although frequently isolated from settlements, have also been found within churchyards, as at Repton (Derbs) and St Mary Bishophill Junior in York.

Execution cemeteries

Cemeteries containing high proportions of 'deviant' burials,

Cemetery	Date	Evidence for date	Number of graves/ burials	Evidence for church	References
Former Gas House, Barrow-on-Humber L	Possibly late Anglo-Saxon	Circumstantial. No evidence the rings have been dated securely	Not specified	Initially interpreted as the lost monastery of *Æt Bæruwe* (but see below)	White 1856; Webster and Cherry 1978, 255; Loughlin and Miller 1979, 184
The Island, Barrow-on-Humber L	650–810 cal AD	C14	30–40	The HER reports all the skeletons were adult males, but only two crania were analysed. This is a good contender for the lost monastery of *Æt Bæruwe*	Loughlin and Miller 1979, 184; Dawn Hadley, *pers. comm.*
Crayke NY	770–1020 cal AD	C14	16 in 1956, 'further' graves in 1983	Probably St Cuthbert's monastery	Hildyard 1960; Adams 1984; Adams 1990
Flixborough (northern group) L	8–9C		5	Associated with building which may have been a church	Loveluck 1998; Geake *et al.* 2007
Cornhill Square Lincoln	Late Saxon or medieval	Circumstantial	Not specified	Cemetery, believed to be that of St John the Evangelist	City of Lincoln Archaeology Unit 1999
Pontefract Castle WY	Predates 11C castle	Stratigraphy	8	Outliers to church excavated on The Booths/Tanners Row	Youngs *et al.* 1985, 208; Abramson 1987, 198; Youngs *et al.* 1987, 172–3
Deanery Gardens, Ripon NY	*c.*600–850 AD	Stratigraphy, 7C Ripon Jewel from unstratified deposit	3	60m south of the Ladykirk site and 80m north of Ripon Cathedral. Possible outliers of these cemeteries	Ryder 1990; Hall and Whyman 1996, 130–6
St Marygate, Ripon NY	8–11C	Assumed to relate to Ladykirk	8	Outliers Ladykirk cemetery (12m to west)	Hall and Whyman 1996, 124–30
St Germanus' Chapel, Selby NY	Pre- 1265–79	Circumstantial – assumed to be St Germanus' Chapel	14	Building foundations and burials uncovered	Wright 1857, 118–9; Hodges 1893, 344–5
Winghale Priory Farm, South Kelsey L	Mid to late Anglo-Saxon	Mid Saxon pottery, late Saxon metal artefacts	Not specified	Domesday Book indicates there was a pre-Conquest religious foundation at Wingale, which was refounded by the 13th century	Wilson 1971, 14; Everson *et al.* 1991, 170–1; Kevin Leahy, *pers. comm.*
Thwing EY	8–9C	Artefacts	132	Rubble platform may have provided the foundations for a timber church	Manby 1988; Geake 1997, 159
Castle Farm, Torksey L	11C	Hoard of 11C pennies	10+	May be cemetery of lost church of All Saints	Field 1990; Palmer-Brown 1995
Kirkham Priory NY	996–1254 and 997–1268 cal AD	C14	19 graves containing 20 individuals	Interpreted as pre-monastic village churchyard	Coppack *et al.* 1995

including evidence for peri-mortem trauma have been interpreted as both battlefield cemeteries, for example Ocklynge Hill (Sussex), (Meaney 1964, 252) and execution cemeteries, for example Sutton Hoo (Suff), Cuddesdon (Oxon) and South Acre (Norf) (Dickinson 1974; Wymer 1996; Carver 2005). In the light of recent research by Andrew Reynolds (2009), the latter interpretation seems more plausible for most of these cemeteries, however the recently excavated mass grave at Heronbridge, Chester, appears to relate to the Battle of Chester AD 616 (Mason 2006).

Execution cemeteries have been defined as having several of the following characteristics: varied burial alignments; unusual burial positions; prone burials; evidence of decapitation or other trauma (for example amputation of hands or feet); evidence of tied hands; shallow and undersized graves; evidence of inter-cutting graves; multiple interments; the presence of low status dress fittings; predominantly adult male populations; association with pre-existing earthworks, especially prehistoric barrows; location close to boundaries, especially of hundreds; and proximity to routeways (Wymer 1996, 89; Reynolds 1997; Reynolds 2009).

Separate execution cemeteries were first founded in the seventh century, and continued to be used throughout the later Anglo-Saxon period (Reynolds 1997), as seen at Walkington Wold (Yorks) (Buckberry and Hadley 2007) and sometimes continued to be used as late as the twelfth century, for example at Staines (Surrey) (Hayman and Reynolds 2006). As with most late Anglo-Saxon cemeteries, the dates of foundation and abandonment of execution cemeteries are often unclear, as many were discovered before the advent of radiocarbon dating. More recently, when radiocarbon dates have been obtained, this is frequently restricted to only one or two dates per site, making it impossible to get a full picture of the duration of cemetery use.

The introduction of separate execution cemeteries, often in peripheral locations, during the seventh and eighth centuries has been linked to conversion to Christianity in the seventh century and the rise of churchyard burial from the eighth century onwards (Reynolds 1997, 37). This shift in burial location for wrongdoers does not appear to have been imposed by the Church, which showed little interest in enforcing churchyard burial, at least in the centuries immediately following the conversion (Bullough 1983, 186; Morris 1983, 50; Geake 2002, 153; Gittos 2002, 202). Indeed, the first law code referring to the exclusion of criminals from burial in consecrated ground (II Æthelstan 26) dates to the early tenth century (Wormald 1999, 307–8, 339–40; Gittos 2002, 201). Churchyards appear to have been consecrated systematically from the tenth century onwards (Gittos 2002, 208), and from this date it is legitimate to argue that the unbaptised, suicides and criminals were excluded from burial in consecrated ground. However, it appears that in practice they were buried away from churchyards and other community cemeteries at a much earlier date (Reynolds 1997, 38). Prior to the seventh

Cemetery	**Date**	**Evidence for date**	**Number of graves/ burials**	**Evidence for church**	**References**
Whitby Abbey NY	Possibly pre-Conquest burials	Stratigraphy, Anglo-Saxon inscribed grave markers	Unclear	May relate to Hild's 7C foundation	Peers and Radford 1943; Cramp 1976a; Cramp 1976b; Rahtz 1976
Whitby Abbey Headland NY	8C	Sceat, 700–740 AD	110	Probably relates to Hild's 7C foundation	English Heritage 1999; English Heritage 2000
Whitton L	560–960 cal AD	C14, coffin fittings 8–9C		Not possible to determine if there was a church, but there was probably a focal point (?church) to the west of the excavated area	Field 1988, 82; Hadley 2003; 2004
Florence Row, York	10C	Fragment of a silver arm ring	3	Believed to be contemporary to adjacent St Mary Bishophill Junior	Wenham 1963; Wenham *et al.* 1987, 75–83
York Minster	Pre 11C	Sealed by 11C cobbled surface and 11C apsidal church. Grave goods	118	No archaeological evidence of a church, however assumed to be the cemetery of St Peter's	Phillips and Heywood 1995
Swinegate, York	Very late 9C to early 11C	Dendrochronology. Areas sealed by 11C surface	100	Associated with lost church of St Benet	Pearson 1989; Pearson 1990; Bagwell and Tyers 2001

Table 1.6: Probable churchyards.

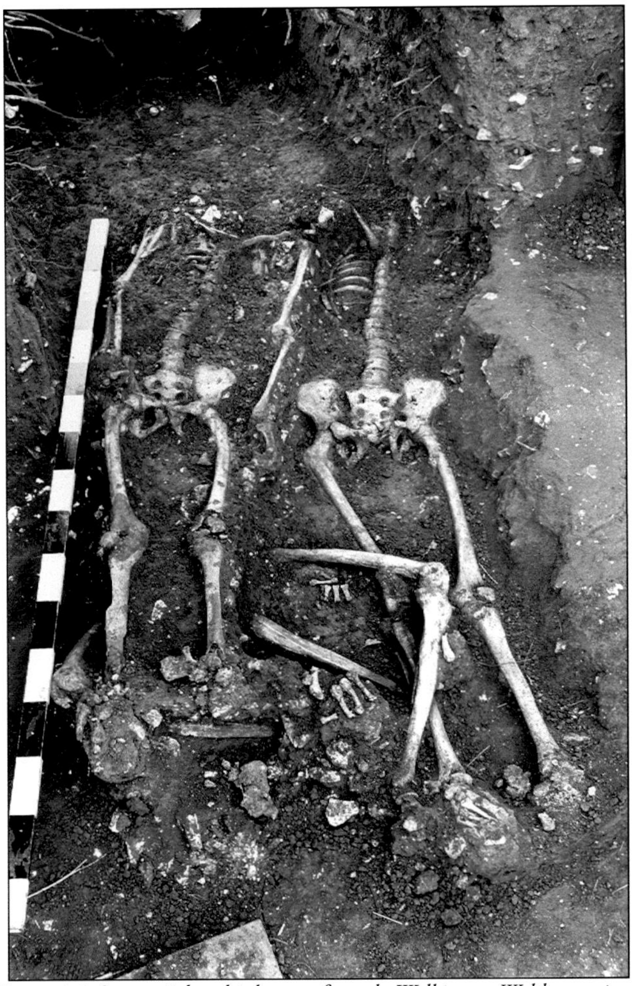

Figure 1.3: Sequential multiple grave from the Walkington Wold execution cemetery. Skeleton 8 (left, radiocarbon dated to AD 900–1030) was interred generations after skeletons 11 (AD 640–775; underneath skeleton 8) and skeleton 12 (right), which disturbed an earlier burial (skeleton 13). Skeleton 11 had peri-mortem trauma consistent with decapitation, and the other individuals were buried without their crania (copyright Hull and East Riding Museum).

century, deviant burials were usually found within community cemeteries – there are no cemeteries that contain primarily deviant burials dating to the fifth and sixth centuries (Geake 1992, 87; Reynolds 1997, 37).

Execution cemeteries are a largely southern England phenomenon. The recently reassessed execution cemetery at Walkington Wold is notable as the most northern execution cemetery identified to date (Buckberry and Hadley 2007). An isolated cranium from a pit in the Anglo-Scandinavian settlement at Cottam (Yorks) may also have been from an execution victim, as the radiocarbon date for the cranium (AD 647 to 877 cal 2 sigma) suggests that it was probably of some antiquity before it was deposited in a pit that has been dated to the late ninth century. This deduction is reinforced by the presence of weathering on the cranium which indicates that it may have been displayed, possibly on a *heafod stoccan*, or 'head stake' before its deposition in the pit (Richards 1999).

At Walkington Wold, most of the burials were apparently decapitated (Figure 1.3) – although osteological evidence of decapitation could only be securely identified for six individuals, just two individuals were buried with their skulls articulated with the remainder of the body, and clearly the individual from Cottam must have been decapitated to enable the cranium to be displayed on a head stake. Hanging has been suggested as an alternative manner of dispatch in the southern counties, although decapitations are also present in most southern execution cemeteries, such as Old Dairy Cottage, Stockbridge Down and Meon Hill (all Hants) (Liddell 1933; Hill 1937; McCulloch 1990; Cherryson 2005, 234; Wessex Archaeology 2007, Winchester Museum Archive ODC89).

Isolated and other unusual burials

A small but growing number of isolated burials have been assigned to the later Anglo-Saxon period (Reynolds 2002; Cherryson 2008). These are rather varied, and can only be grouped together due to the fact that they appear to be isolated burials, rather than part of a larger cemetery. These have been found both within settlements and away from settlements, and if unaccompanied were often something of a mystery until a radiocarbon date was obtained. In addition, historical evidence gives tantalising clues to the presence of other potential isolated burials: Andrew Reynolds has drawn attention to the burials of named individuals appearing in charter bounds, and has argued that these burials are more likely to be contemporary with the bounds (and therefore date to the later Anglo-Saxon period) then record the burials of long-dead pagans (Reynolds 2002, 181). Clearly, isolated burials are not a cohesive group, and multiple meanings behind these burials should be expected.

Sixteen isolated burials (or small groups of burials) were identified in this study (Table 1.3). Nine of these dated to the mid Anglo-Saxon period, two dated to the ninth to eleventh centuries and two were probably late Anglo-Saxon in date, but could not be dated securely. Given that this is a fairly small corpus, each will be discussed here. Seven of these were accompanied by typical conversion period grave goods: a single burial accompanied by a seventh-century pendant was discovered at Womersley (Yorks) in 1860 (Bateman 1860). Two seventh-century annular brooches accompanied the Occaney Beck burial (Yorks), discovered *c.*1947 to 1949 (Waterman 1951). One accompanied burial was found at Burton Fields gravel pit, Stamford Bridge (Yorks) in 1937 (Kitson Clark 1942). The single inhumation overlying part of a Roman villa at Dalton Parlours, Collingham (Yorks), was first recorded in 1977 (Moorhouse 1977; Wrathmell and Nicholson 1990, 285–7), but it is difficult to ascertain when it was discovered; the accompanied burial from Hambleton

Moor (Yorks) was found prior to 1912 (Geake 1997, 189). Finally, a seventh-century burial accompanied by a spearhead and a gilt-bronze belt fitting was found at White Hart Farm, North Elmsall (Yorks) in 1962 (Bellamy 1963–6, 9). The early dates of discovery for Womersley, Occaney Beck, Burton Fields and Hambleton Moor, in particular, make it difficult to be certain that these burials were really isolated or whether they were merely a single discovery from a larger unexcavated or unrecorded cemetery; indeed, the HER records that the White Hall Farm burial is in an extensive area of mid to late Anglo-Saxon finds (West Yorkshire HER record 4481).

Seventh-century barrow burials are comparatively rare in this region – only two seventh-century barrow burials were identified during this survey. At Caenby (Lincs), excavations in 1849 uncovered a central grave containing various elaborate grave goods including a shield with silver mounts, a sword, a bronze buckle and possible fragments of a helmet (Jarvis 1850). The grave goods have been dated to the seventh century (Geake 1997, 167). At West Halton, a Bronze Age barrow was reused for burial in the seventh century; however the burial was heavily disturbed so it was impossible to determine if the burial was furnished or unfurnished (Dawn Hadley, *pers. comm.*). Unaccompanied seventh- and eighth-century barrow burials have been identified in Wessex (Cherryson, *pers. comm.*) and it is possible that more unfurnished middle Anglo-Saxon barrow burials would be identified in Lincolnshire and Yorkshire, were radiocarbon dating to be used more frequently.

Radiocarbon dates are needed for most unaccompanied burials, if we are to understand their frequency and significance fully. An unaccompanied crouched burial, dated to AD 660–780 (cal 2 sigma), found in a pylon trench at Kettlewell (Yorks) in 1997, may have come from a larger cemetery, as a second individual, assumed to be contemporary, was identified in the baulk of a trench further along the electricity line (Cale 2004). The disturbed remains of at least two individuals were found close to the findspot of a copper-alloy reliquary box at Carr Farm, Arncliffe (Yorks). The burials were disturbed and it is impossible to determine if this discovery represents a larger cemetery (Cale 2000). Two burials, an adult female and an adolescent, the former dated to AD 885–1010 (cal 2 sigma), were found in the north-west end of Ash Hill Long Barrow, Swinhope (Lincs) (Garland 1989; Phillips and Walker 1989). In this case, the burials clearly did not come from a larger cemetery and therefore they must have been deliberately buried away from the community cemetery. It is tempting to assume that these individuals fall into the groups denied burial in consecrated ground – criminals, strangers and the unbaptised – however we cannot assume that these were the only reasons behind isolated burial in this period. Accidental deaths and illicit disposal of murder victims have been postulated for unusual isolated burials dating to the post-medieval period (Cherryson *et al.* forthcoming) and were also likely to have taken place in the Anglo-Saxon period (see Hadley, this volume).

The 'travelling tinker/smith' burial from Tattershall Thorpe (Lincs) is another convincing example of an isolated burial. This single inhumation, accompanied by metalworking tools and scrap metal, was dated to the seventh century or later (Hinton and White 1993). This individual might have been buried away from the local community cemetery because, as a 'travelling smith', he was a stranger.

The remains of a neonate, dated to AD 600–760 (cal 2 sigma) were found in the upcast of a building at Wharram Percy (Yorks) (Milne and Richards 1992, 20, 79, 84–5), and this burial is also likely to have been deliberately isolated from the community cemetery, even though it was found within a settlement. This may be a continuation of an early Anglo-Saxon practice of alternative disposal of some infant remains, for example the burial of infants within the settlement at West Heslerton (Yorks) (Powlesland 1997; Buckberry 2000). Indeed, two infant burials probably dating to the eighth or ninth century have been found in rubbish pits in Hamwic (Morton 1992b; Andrews 1997, Cherryson, this volume).

Only two examples of isolated burials securely dated to the ninth century and later were identified – two individuals from Ash Hill long barrow (radiocarbon dated, see above) and two or possibly three individuals found during the excavation of the Anglo-Scandinavian settlement at Coppergate, York. Two of the Coppergate skeletons were largely articulated and were in pits dated stratigraphically to the ninth century (Figure 1.4). A third ninth-century pit contained a disarticulated skeleton; however it is unclear if this individual and other disarticulated skeletal material excavated in the vicinity were also Anglo-Scandinavian in date, or rather were redeposited from the small Roman cemetery also excavated at Coppergate (Richard Hall, *pers. comm.*). The deposition of the remains within the settlement, at a time when York was well endowed with churchyard cemeteries, is striking. Clearly they do not derive from a previously unknown churchyard or non-church cemetery, as so few individuals were recovered from an area that was extensively excavated to a high standard. Deposition in pits rather than graves is also unusual for this period. Given that these burials were found within the Anglo-Scandinavian settlement, it is tempting to deduce that they were Scandinavians, although there is no evidence to support this. They may have been clandestine burials; however this would seem unlikely within a busy settlement. The burial of these individuals was evidently a deliberate act, decided upon by an individual or a group of people, indicating that the location of burial was chosen rather than necessarily being dictated by the Church or state.

Given that most of the middle Anglo-Saxon isolated burials have been dated using grave goods, it is likely that most late Anglo-Saxon isolated burials would remain undated unless radiocarbon dates were obtained. Indeed, the final two isolated burials identified in the survey were assumed by the excavators to be late Anglo-Saxon based on fairly circumstantial evidence. Two west-east aligned burials recoded during an evaluation in

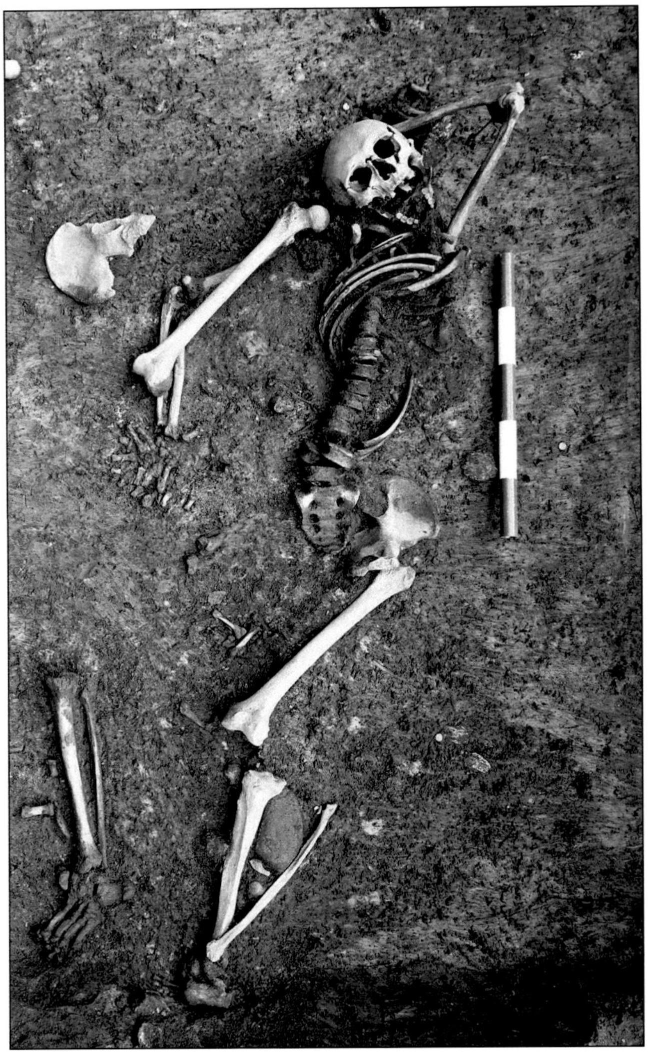

Figure 1.4: Ninth-century burial from the Coppergate excavation in York. The right femur and os coxae have been disturbed post-mortem, however the position of the upper limbs indicate an unceremonial burial (copyright York Archaeological Trust).

Blue Bridge Lane, York were assumed to be outliers of the St Andrew's Fishergate cemetery and therefore are probably late Anglo-Saxon or medieval in date (York Archaeological Trust 1994). A pair of inhumations, an adult aligned west-east, and a child aligned east-west, were found in a pipe trench at Sheep Wash Farm, Castle Bytham (Lincs). These were assumed to be late Anglo-Saxon by the excavator (Hurley 1992), however no evidence was given to support this date. Ideally, both of these sites should be radiocarbon dated, although it is unclear if the skeletal remains were retained.

Overall this is quite a mixed bag of certainly and potentially isolated burials. The larger number of middle Anglo-Saxon isolated burials is probably due to the presence of artefacts that could be used to date them. However, many isolated skeletons without grave goods remain undated, and it remains possible that many more later Anglo-Saxon isolated burials may be included within the large corpus of undated burials recorded in HERs. It is also notable that many of the examples of isolated burials reported here might have been from a larger cemetery, as only very small-scale excavation was undertaken. The most convincing examples of isolated burial – Tattershall Thorpe, Wharram Percy, Coppergate and Ash Hill Long Barrow – were all uncovered during larger scale excavations, which have allowed better insight into their context and stratigraphy.

Scandinavian burials

Despite the historical and archaeological evidence of the extent of Scandinavian settlement in eastern England, very few ninth- and tenth-century graves have been confidently identified as those of Scandinavians (Halsall 2000, 259; Richards 2000, 142). The clearest evidence of Scandinavian burial in the Danelaw is from Heath Wood, Ingleby (Derbs), where a cemetery of 59 barrows containing cremation burials and animal offerings has been excavated (Richards *et al.* 1995; Richards 2004). The use of an intrusive burial rite (cremation) and the presence of two broken swords, a ring headed pin and some wire embroidery, similar to items found in graves at Birka in Sweden, identified this as a Viking cemetery (Richards *et al.* 1995; Richards 2000; Richards 2004).

In Yorkshire, seven sites with good evidence for Scandinavian burial have been identified (Table 1.7). Three apparently isolated barrow burials containing Scandinavian artefacts such as tortoise brooches and swords rings, identified as the graves of Scandinavians, have been found around Northallerton (Yorks). At Camphill (also known as Bedale) in Carthorpe parish, a burial in a natural mound accompanied by a sword and a spear has been identified as a possible Scandinavian. A pair of tenth-century tortoise brooches has also been found at Bedale (this time in Northallerton parish), which may have come from a second Scandinavian burial in the area (Bjørn and Shetelig 1940, 77, 105–6). In addition, a pair of tortoise brooches from Romanby (close to Northallerton) were reported by Bjørn and Shetelig (Bjørn and Shetelig 1940, 15, 19). More recently, a Scandinavian burial was excavated at Adwick-le-Street (Yorks). Isotopic analysis showed that the woman, buried with Scandinavian artefacts, including a non-matching pair of tortoise brooches, probably grew up in Norway (Speed and Walton Rogers 2004). The use of burial practices that were uncommon in England but typical of Scandinavia at this time (*i.e.* barrow burial with grave goods) strongly identifies such burials to be those of migrants, something confirmed in the recent analysis of the Adwick-le-Street burial. However, the handful of examples excavated to date cannot account for the numbers of immigrants that appear to have settled in the Danelaw (Halsall 2000; Richards 2002).

Many other supposed Scandinavian burials are rather less

distinctive. These burials, both isolated and in churchyards, generally contain grave goods, which has been taken as evidence that these were the burials of pagans (and hence Scandinavian) at a time when accompanied burial had largely ceased (Halsall 2000, 263). However, as the deposition of items in graves continued into the late Anglo-Saxon period, the presence of grave goods (particularly those of Anglo-Saxon manufacture) does not necessarily indicate that the deceased was of Scandinavian origin (Halsall 2000, 262–8). It appears that many individuals of Scandinavian descent were buried in the established cemeteries in Christian-style graves (Halsall 2000, 270; Richards 2000, 151), suggesting a quick integration into some aspects of local traditions. A small number of Scandinavian burials within churchyards *were* accompanied by Scandinavian grave goods, for example those buried at Repton (Biddle and Kjølbye-Biddle 1992), however it is likely that many more were buried in a manner indistinguishable from the burial rites of local inhabitants.

Three cases of churchyard burials accompanied with Scandinavian artefacts have been excavated in Yorkshire. A single burial accompanied by a sword, spearhead, sickle and a knife found in Wensley churchyard in 1915 has been interpreted as that of a Scandinavian, despite the fact the sword is probably of Anglo-Saxon manufacture (Richards 2000, 150). Seven or eight burials found under the church at Kildale in the nineteenth century were west-east aligned but were accompanied by grave goods including three swords, several daggers, an axe, a set of scales and spurs (Atkinson 1868). Sadly these artefacts were stolen, however an illustration of the grave goods has been used to suggest that they were, indeed, of Scandinavian character (Richards 2000, 150). Two burials from a group of eight excavated at St Mary Bishophill Junior, York, have also been identified as Scandinavians on the basis of grave goods. The first burial was accompanied by a silver penannular arm-ring and the second burial was accompanied by a tenth-century silver penny, an iron knife, a whetstone and a copper-alloy buckle (Wenham *et al.* 1987, 75–83). There is no evidence for furnished Scandinavian burial in Lincolnshire, although there are many Scandinavian-style stone monuments, which probably marked graves (Everson and Stocker 1999). The extent to which these sculptures marked the graves of Scandinavian immigrants or indigenous individuals adopting a new Anglo-Scandinavian fashion is difficult to ascertain (Stocker 2000, 180), and remains outside the scope of this paper.

The presence of Scandinavian artefacts within later Anglo-Saxon cemeteries, or the use of Scandinavian-style stone sculpture probably represents a Scandinavian presence within the local population, and both targeted and random isotopic analysis of individuals both within these cemeteries and in contemporary cemeteries nearby may help to identify more first generation Scandinavian immigrants. To date this method has been applied sparingly, with limited success, (but see Macpherson 2005, and Groves, this volume) however it

Cemetery name(s)	**Date**	**Dating evidence**	**Church-yard?**	**Why Scandinavian?**	**Grave goods**	**References**
Adwick-le-Street SY	Late 9C	Brooches	N	Grave goods, isotope evidence	Tortoise brooches, bowl, knife, latch-lifter	Speed and Walton Rogers 2004
Camphill (Bedale) Carthorpe parish NY	Anglo-Scandinavian	Grave goods	N	Grave goods	Sword and spear	Richards 2000, 145
Bedale (Northallerton parish) NY	10C	Grave goods	N	Grave goods	Tortoise brooches	Bjørn and Shetelig 1940, 77, 105–6; Richards 2000, 151
Romanby (Northallerton parish) NY	10C	Grave goods	N	Grave goods	Tortoise brooches	Bjørn and Shetelig 1940, 15, 19
Wensley NY	Anglo-Scandinavian	Grave goods	Y	Grave goods	Iron sword, spearhead, sickle and knife. Sword was of Anglo-Saxon manufacture	Richards 2000, 150
St Mary Bishophill Junior, York	9–10C	Grave goods including 10C penny	Y	Grave goods	Arm-ring, silver penny, iron knife, whetstone and copper-alloy buckle	Wenham *et al.* 1987, 75–83
Kildale NY	Anglo-Scandinavian	Grave goods	Y	Grave goods stolen, but illustration indicates Scandinavian in character	3 swords, 3 or 4 daggers, axe, tweezers, scales, spurs, whetstone, buckles, and iron knife	Atkinson 1868; Richards 2000, 150

Table 1.7: Scandinavian burials

probably offers the best opportunity to identify Scandinavian (and other) settlers in the British Isles.

Several individuals from the non-church cemetery at Riccall have been subjected to isotope analysis. Initially believed to be the defeated Scandinavian army from the Battle of Stamford Bridge in 1066 (Wenham 1960; Hall 2002), recent analysis has revealed that the cemetery contained a lay population with little evidence of peri-mortem trauma and that the cemetery was long-lived (see above and Table 1.4) (Hall *et al.* 2008). Although initial oxygen isotope analysis had suggested that some individuals buried at Riccall were from western Norway or areas around the Baltic (Hall 2002), further analysis showed that the individuals buried at Riccall were probably local to the area (Hall *et al.* 2008). A small Anglo-Scandinavian non-churchyard cemetery at Dixon Keld, Masham was excavated in 1988–9. The cemetery is located *c.*10 miles away from the cluster of Scandinavian barrow burials around Northallerton. A current project, coordinated by Harrogate Museums and Arts and funded by Harrogate Borough Council, has enabled analysis of the skeletal population (Neale and Buckberry 2008). Further work includes strontium and oxygen isotope analyses to determine if first generation Scandinavian migrants were present in the population; however these analyses have not yet been completed.

Overall, it is notable that all of the potential Scandinavian burials identified in this survey were located in Yorkshire, the heart of the Danelaw. Clearly many Scandinavians must have been buried in their administrative centre, York, however very few can be identified archaeologically. Historical evidence is also lacking – of the 14 burials recorded for York, just three were of Scandinavians – King Swein (d. 1014), Earl Siward (d. 1055) and Earl Tostig (d. 1066) (Buckberry 2007, 119) – none of whom were among the first wave of Scandinavian settlers in the late ninth century.

Undated Burials

As stated at the beginning of this paper, data were also collected about undated burials in Lincolnshire and Yorkshire, with a total of 165 burial sites recorded, although presumably many more burials have gone unrecorded. Overall it was difficult to see any strong patterns within the undated burials data, mostly because the vast majority were reports dating from the 1940s and earlier, noting the presence of human bone during construction or landscaping, but providing little or no contextual information. However, careful consideration of the data gathered about later Anglo-Saxon cemeteries in the area has allowed the identification among this group of a small number of sites, which may well date to the later Anglo-Saxon period, each of which will be discussed below.

The following criteria could be used to propose a later Anglo-Saxon date for burials without clear dating evidence and in the absence of radiocarbon dates. It should be noted that few of these characteristics offer conclusive dating evidence, and it is the combination of these criteria that help to narrow down the date of cemeteries.

The criteria identified are as follows (with caveats expressed in brackets):

- Burials are typically (but not always) supine and extended.
- Burials tend to be west-east aligned.
- Cemeteries tend to be planned, with burials arranged in rows and care taken to avoid inter-cutting (in cemeteries that were not in use for several generations).
- Carved grave markers, grave covers, crosses *etc.* may be present or have been found locally.
- Occasional artefacts, in particular finger rings, knives and buckles, may be present in burials post-dating the eighth century.
- Charcoal burials, stones arrangements around the head or feet (sometimes referred to as 'pillow stones', 'ear muffs', or 'head cists') and the deposition of white quartz pebbles all strongly suggest a late Anglo-Saxon date (although these practices may have continued into the twelfth century). These grave variations are more common in, but are not confined to, urban cemeteries.
- Evidence of coffins, and coffin brackets in particular, is common in cemeteries from the seventh century onwards.
- Stone lined graves (or cists) are also common in later Anglo-Saxon cemeteries (however these are also present in late Roman and later Medieval cemeteries).
- Late Anglo-Saxon pottery or artefacts may be found in close proximity to the cemetery.
- Many cemeteries are located within 50 to 250m of a known Anglo-Saxon or medieval church. This is particularly true for rural cemeteries.

Many cemeteries are difficult to identify as later Anglo-Saxon, due to the similarities in the form of burial that exist between these and later medieval, early modern and late Roman cemeteries. However, evidence of coffin fittings, in particular coffin brackets, as found at Ripon Ailcy Hill and Whitton, and 'pillow stones' strongly indicate a later Anglo-Saxon date for such a cemetery, although twelfth-century 'pillow stones' were reported at St Mary's, Stow (Field 1984). The presence of stone-lined graves could also be used as an indicator of later Anglo-Saxon date, however stone-lined graves were also used during the Roman and later medieval periods. It should, however, be noted that cemeteries that conform to several of the above characteristics, and especially those that are located between 50 and 250m from a medieval church, have been consistently found to be of mid to late Anglo-Saxon date. Indeed, a series of nine cemeteries, selected by the present author and Dawn Hadley, which conformed to the criteria outlined above to varying degrees, were selected for radiocarbon dating. Of these, seven were shown to be later Anglo-Saxon in date: Fillingham (Buckberry and Hadley 2001b), Great Hale (Buckberry and Hadley 2001c), Whitton (Hadley 2003), and Kilham (Yorks) (Buckberry 2004, 89) all conformed to several criteria, whereas The Island, Barrow (Lincs) (Hadley *pers. comm.*) and Riccall (Buckberry 2004, 91; Hall *et al.* 2008) fit the criteria less well but were still shown to date to the later Anglo-Saxon period. Walkington Wold did not fit the criteria given here for community cemeteries, but rather had many features consistent with an Anglo-Saxon execution cemetery (Buckberry and Hadley 2007), as discussed above. On this basis it was included in the radiocarbon dating programme, and was shown to date to the seventh to eleventh centuries.

Two further cemeteries, which met only a small number of the criteria listed above, were also radiocarbon dated; however these did not date to the Anglo-Saxon period. A single west-east aligned supine burial with a coffin bracket from Green Lane, Belton (Lincs) was dated to the late fourteenth to early fifteenth century (Buckberry and Hadley 2001a). The burials from Wold Newton were disturbed burials and recovered during construction work in the village. Little contextual information could be gleaned from the builders; however they were described as west-east aligned and supine with lower limbs slightly flexed. Two samples were dated to 1783 ± 33 and 3330 ± 120 BP – prehistoric and Roman to early Anglo-Saxon respectively (Buckberry 2004). Unfortunately the two samples were later found to have been contaminated during the ultra filtration process, giving rise to a slightly older dates being estimated and therefore the radiocarbon dates were withdrawn. The dates provided were estimated to be incorrect by 300 years and 50 years, but as this contamination led to the production of dates that were probably more recent, neither of the samples date to the later Anglo-Saxon period.

It is hoped that the criteria given here above can be used in the future to identify further later Anglo-Saxon cemeteries. Indeed, there were several 'undated' burial sites identified in the present survey which fit them well. Probably the best example is North Kelsey (Lincs), where approximately thirty burials were excavated prior to construction work. The burials were west-east aligned and were arranged in rows. One of the graves contained nails and a second contained wood fragments, indicating that some of the burials were coffined. Inter-cutting burials revealed that at least three phases of burial activity were present, suggesting a long period of cemetery use. A robbed west-east aligned mortared wall had burials on either side and post-dated the cemetery, however two sherds of Saxon pottery were found in the backfill of this wall trench. The excavators interpreted these as later medieval, possibly connected with the parish church, which lies 100m to the southeast (Lindsey Archaeological Services 1995). Given the location of this cemetery, 100m from the parish church, the character of the burials and the presence of both Anglo-Saxon pottery and evidence of coffins, it seems likely that these burials were late Anglo-Saxon in date. The robbed wall may have been from an early church, although this is purely speculation. Unfortunately all of the human remains from the site were reburied, so it is not possible to obtain a radiocarbon date for the cemetery.

Conclusions

Overall this study has demonstrated that variety in burial location was characteristic of the later Anglo-Saxon period. While the evidence for non-churchyard burial has been growing, and is becoming widely accepted, the full extent of this phenomenon is only just beginning to be understood. The evidence for Lincolnshire and Yorkshire has shown that, although 27 cemeteries had good evidence for a church and a further 19 cemeteries may well have had a church; at 14 sites it was impossible to be certain. It is perhaps significant that all of these 14 cemeteries were founded in the middle Anglo-Saxon period. It should also be noted that it is also possible that several of the 19 cemeteries that may have had a church actually did not; indeed in many cases these cemeteries have been assumed to be churchyards with little hard evidence to support that deduction. It is also apparent that many of the non-churchyard cemeteries, including execution cemeteries, were used throughout the Anglo-Saxon period. The longevity of non-churchyard cemeteries is an issue that needs to be addressed more fully, an aim that can only be achieved via more extensive radiocarbon dating programmes. Evidence for the late foundation of a non-churchyard cemetery is much rarer, however satellite cemeteries attached to local churches (which archaeologically are identical to non-churchyard cemeteries) could be founded quite late – for example the mid-tenth to mid-eleventh-century cemetery at Chimney, located on land granted to Bampton Minster, was founded in the 950s (Crawford 1989; Blair 2005).

The huge variation in cemetery types and burial forms throughout the later Anglo-Saxon period is now gaining wider acceptance (Hadley 2007, 194); however the reasons for this variety are little understood. Undoubtedly, the Church had a huge impact on burial location throughout this period, from the conversion and the foundation of Minster churches in the seventh century to the explosion in proprietary churches and more widespread use of churchyards by the tenth century. But it is also evident that some people, and not just those who were interred in so-called execution cemeteries, continued to be buried away from churches into the tenth century and beyond – although to what extent this was taking place outside the parochial system by this time is unclear. The nobility no doubt also played a role, by choosing to be buried in high-status locations within important churches or in 'princely' barrows in the seventh century, to founding their own churches in later centuries, to reorganising settlements, landscapes and funerary landscapes throughout the period. It is difficult to ascertain to what extent the common people were able to influence the manner of their burial, but it is likely that there was far more choice available than we have previously realised.

Acknowledgements

There are many individuals and organisations who assisted in this research. First I thank all of the SMR, HER and NMR officers for assisting with very unwieldy search questions, followed by endless chasing up of small details within their archives. Without their knowledge and assistance this research would have failed at the first hurdle. Many museum curators, archivists and archaeologists graciously provided information, site plans and draft reports, for which I am very grateful. Particular thanks are extended to Kevin Leahy, Richard Hall, Chris Loveluck, Andrew Reynolds, Dave Evans, Ian Roberts, Jen Mann, Warwick Rodwell and Caroline Atkins for enlightening discussions about various excavations. I thank Hull and East Riding Museum, Humber Archaeology Partnership, York Archaeological Trust, York Museum and The Collection Lincoln for allowing me to sample skeletons for radiocarbon dating. Dawn Hadley, Julian Richards and Annia Cherryson kindly commented on earlier drafts of this paper, their criticisms and suggestions were gratefully received; however any errors and omissions are mine.

This research was funded by a White Rose Studentship awarded by the Universities of Sheffield, Leeds and York. Radiocarbon dates were funded by NERC.

References

Abramson, P. (1987) The Yorkshire archaeological register: 1986. *The Yorkshire Archaeological Journal* 59, 193–187.

Adams, K. A. (1984) Excavation and fieldwork at Crayke. *Bulletin of the Council for British Archaeology Churches Committee* 21, 3–6.

Adams, K. A. (1990) Monastery and village at Crayke, North Yorkshire. *The Yorkshire Archaeological Journal* 62, 29–50.

Adams, M. (1996) Excavation of a pre-conquest cemetery at Addingham, West Yorkshire. *Medieval Archaeology* 40, 151–191.

Adamson, C. H. and Abramson, P. (1997) *Thornton Steward to Sowden Beck water pipeline. Archaeological excavation and watching brief for Yorkshire Water Services Ltd.* Unpublished excavation report. Available at Northallerton SMR. Northern Archaeological Associates.

Addyman, P. V. and Whitwell, J. B. (1970) Some middle Saxon pottery types in Lincolnshire. *The Antiquaries Journal* 50, 96–102.

Andrews, P. (ed.) (1997) *Excavations at Hamwic. Volume 2: excavations at Six Dials.* Council for British Archaeology Research Report 109. York, Council for British Archaeology.

Anon (1989) *Dixon Keld burial ground Masham. Archaeological watching brief/excavation March 6th–27th April 1989.* Unpublished archaeological report supplied by Harrogate Museums and Arts.

Arnold, C. J. (1982) Stress as a stimulus for socio-economic change: Anglo-Saxon England in the seventh century. In: Renfrew, A. C. and Shennan, S. (eds.) *Ranking, resource and exchange,* 124–131. Cambridge, Cambridge University Press.

Atkinson, J. C. (1868) Account of discoveries recently made in the parish church of Kildale in Yorkshire. *Proceedings of the Society of Antiquaries* 4, 52–54.

Bagwell, T. and Tyers, I. (2001) *Dendrochronological analysis of a coffin assemblage from Swinegate, York, North Yorkshire.* Project Report 575p. Unpublished dendrochronology report. Supplied by ARCUS Dendrochronology. Sheffield, ARCUS Dendrochronology.

Bateman, T. (1860) Comment in 'Proceedings of the Association'. *Journal of the British Archaeological Association* 16, 286–363.

Bell, R. D. and Beresford, M. W. (1987) *Wharram Percy: the church of St Martin.* Wharram: a Study of Settlement of the Yorkshire Wolds Volume III. The Society for Medieval Archaeology Monograph 11. London, Society for Medieval Archaeology.

Bell, T. W. (1998) A Roman signal station at Whitby. *Archaeological Journal* 155, 303–322.

Bellamy, C. V. (1963–6) 'North Elmsall' in the Yorkshire archaeological register 1962. *The Yorkshire Archaeological Journal* 41, 9.

Biddle, M. (1976) The archaeology of the Church: a widening horizon. In: Addyman, P. and Morris, R. (eds.) *The archaeological study of churches,* 65–71. Council for British Archaeology Research Report 13. London, Council for British Archaeology.

Biddle, M. and Kjølbye-Biddle, B. (1992) Repton and the Vikings. *Antiquity* 66, 36–51.

Bjørn, A. and Shetelig, H. (1940) *Viking antiquities in Great Britain and Ireland. Part IV: Viking antiquities in England.* Oslo, H. Aschehoug and Co.

Blair, J. (1988) Minster churches in the landscape. In: Hooke, D. (ed.) *Anglo-Saxon settlements,* 35–58. Oxford, Basil Blackwell.

Blair, J. (2005) *The Church in Anglo-Saxon society.* Oxford, Oxford University Press.

Boddington, A. (1990) Models of burial, settlement and worship: the final phase reviewed. In: Southworth, E. (ed.) *Anglo-Saxon cemeteries: a reappraisal,* 177–199. Stroud, Sutton.

Boden, J. M. and Whitwell, J. B. (1979) Barrow-upon-Humber. *Lincolnshire History and Archaeology* 14, 66–67.

Bonnor, L. and Allen, M. (2000) A possible Iron Age barrow monument and Anglo-Saxon cemetery site at Kirkby-la-Thorpe. *Lincolnshire History and Archaeology* 35, 21–34.

Briden, C. (1983) Belle Vue House. *Interim* 9, 11–13.

Briden, C. (1984) Belle Vue House. *Interim* 9, 5–8.

Brinklow, D. A. (1986) 'Riccall' in the Yorkshire archaeological register: 1985. *The Yorkshire Archaeological Journal* 58, 201.

Buckberry, J. L. (2000) Missing, presumed buried? Bone diagenesis and the under-representation of Anglo-Saxon children. *Assemblage* 5, www.shef.ac.uk/~assem/5.

Buckberry, J. L. (2004) *A social and anthropological analysis of conversion period and later Anglo-Saxon cemeteries in Lincolnshire and Yorkshire.* Unpublished PhD Thesis, University of Sheffield.

Buckberry, J. L. (2007) On sacred ground: social identity and churchyard burial in Lincolnshire and Yorkshire, c.700–1100 AD. In: Williams, H. and Semple, S. (eds.) *Early medieval mortuary practices. Anglo-Saxon Studies in Archaeology and History 14,* 120–132. Oxford, Oxbow.

Buckberry, J. L. and Hadley, D. M. (2001a) Belton: Green Lane. *Lincolnshire History and Archaeology* 36, 58–9.

Buckberry, J. L. and Hadley, D. M. (2001b) Excavations at Chapel Road, Fillingham. *Lincolnshire History and Archaeology* 36, 11–18.

Buckberry, J. L. and Hadley, D. M. (2001c) Great Hale. *Lincolnshire History and Archaeology* 36, 59.

Buckberry, J. L. and Hadley, D. M. (2007) An Anglo-Saxon execution cemetery at Walkington Wold, Yorkshire. *Oxford Journal of Archaeology* 26, 309–329.

Buckberry, J. L., Lee-Thorp, J. A. and Montgomery, J. M. (2009) *Isotope analyses and radiocarbon dates for the human skeletal remains from Dixon Keld, Masham, North Yorkshire (MSM 88 and MSM 89).* Unpublished report. Bradford, Biological Anthropology Research Centre, Archaeological Sciences, University of Bradford.

Bullough, D. (1983) Burial community and belief in the early medieval West. In: Wormald, P. (ed.) *Ideal and reality in Frankish and Anglo-Saxon society,* 177–201. Oxford, Basil Blackwell.

Cale, K. J. (2000) *Archaeological investigation, Carr Farm, Arncliffe, North Yorkshire*. Unpublished interim statement. Available at Yorkshire Dales National Park SMR.

Cale, K. J. (2004) "Was the skeleton lady dead?" In: White, R. F. and Wilson, P. R. (eds.) *Archaeology and historic landscapes of the Yorkshire Dales,* 105–110. Leeds, Yorkshire Archaeological Society.

Carver, M. O. H. (1995) Roman to Norman at York Minster. In: Phillips, D. and Heywood, B. (eds.) *Excavations at York Minster volume 1: from Roman fortress to Norman cathedral,* 177–221. London, HMSO.

Carver, M. O. H. (2005) *Sutton Hoo: a seventh-century princely burial ground and its context.* London, British Museum Press.

Cherryson, A. K. (2005) *In the shadow of the church: burial practices in the Wessex heartlands, c.600–1100AD.* Unpublished PhD Thesis, University of Sheffield.

Cherryson, A. K. (2008) Normal, deviant and atypical: burial variation in late Saxon Wessex. In: Murphy, E. M. (ed.) *Deviant burial in the archaeological record,* 115–130. Oxford, Oxbow.

Cherryson, A. K., Crossland, Z. and Tarlow, S. (forthcoming) *A fine and private place: The archaeology of death and burial in post-medieval Britain and Ireland.* Leicester Archaeology Monograph. Leicester: University of Leicester Press.

City of Lincoln Archaeology Unit (1999) *Tourist information centre, Cornhill Square, Lincoln. Archaeological Recording.* Unpublished watching brief report. Available at Lincoln SMR. Lincoln, City of Lincoln Archaeology Unit.

Coppack, G., Harrison, S. and Hayfield, C. (1995) Kirkham Priory: The architecture and archaeology of an Augustinian house. *Journal of the British Archaeological Association* 148, 55–136.

Cramp, R. J. (1976a) Analysis of the finds register and location plan of Whitby Abbey. In: Wilson, D. M. (ed.) *The archaeology of Anglo-Saxon England,* 453–457. Cambridge, Cambridge University Press.

Cramp, R. J. (1976b) Monastic sites. In: Wilson, D. M. (ed.) *The archaeology of Anglo-Saxon England,* 201–252. Cambridge, Cambridge University Press.

Crawford, S. (1989) The Anglo-Saxon cemetery at Chimney, Oxfordshire. *Oxoniensia* 54, 45–56.

Dawes, J. D. and Magilton, J. R. (1980) *The cemetery of St Helen-on-the-Walls, Aldwark.* The archaeology of York 12/1. The medieval cemeteries. York, Council for British Archaeology.

Dickinson, T. M. (1974) *Cuddesdon and Dorchester-on-Thames, Oxfordshire: two early Anglo-Saxon 'princely' sites in Wessex.* British Archaeological Reports 1. Oxford, British Archaeological Reports.

Eagles, B. N. (1979) *The Anglo-Saxon settlement of Humberside.* British Archaeological Reports British Series 68. Oxford, British Archaeological Reports.

English Heritage (1999) Whitby Abbey Headland Project – Southern Anglian Enclosure. *http://www.eng-h.gov.uk/projects/whitby/wahpsae/* (consulted 05/03/2009).

English Heritage (2000) *Whitby Abbey southern Anglian enclosure. Project design 2000.* Unpublished Project Design. Available at Northallerton SMR. English Heritage.

Everson, P. L. and Stocker, D. (1999) *Corpus of Anglo-Saxon stone sculpture volume V: Lincolnshire.* Oxford, Oxford University Press.

Everson, P. L., Taylor, C. C. and Dunn, C. J. (1991) *Change and continuity. Rural settlement in North-West Lincolnshire.* London, HMSO.

Evison, V. I. (1956) An Anglo-Saxon cemetery at Holborough, Kent. *Archaeologia Cantiana* 70, 84–141.

Faull, M. L. (1976) The location and relationship of the Sancton Anglo-Saxon cemeteries. *Antiquaries Journal* 56, 277–233.

Faull, M. L. (1979) *British Survival in Anglo-Saxon Yorkshire.* Unpublished PhD thesis, University of Leeds.

Faull, M. L. and Moorhouse, S. A. (eds.) (1981) *West Yorkshire: an archaeological survey to AD 1500. Volume 1.* Wakefield, West Yorkshire Metropolitan County Council.

Field, N. (1983) Fillingham. *Lincolnshire History and Archaeology* 18, 96–97.

Field, N. (1984) Stow Church. *Lincolnshire History and Archaeology* 19, 105–106.

Field, N. (1988) Archaeology in Lincolnshire and South Humberside 1987. *Lincolnshire History and Archaeology* 23, 81–88.

Field, N. (1989) Archaeology in Lincolnshire and South Humberside. *Lincolnshire History and Archaeology* 24, 53–63.

Field, N. (1990) *Castle Farm Torksey: exploratory excavations.* Unpublished excavation report. Available at Lincoln SMR. Lincoln, Lindsey Archaeological Services.

Field, N. (2002) *St. Martin's Church, Welton le Wold. Archaeological watching brief.* Unpublished watching brief report. Available at Lincoln SMR. Lincoln, Lindsey Archaeological Services.

Foreman, M. (ed.) (n.d.) *Excavations at St Chads, Barrow-on-Humber, 1977–78.* Draft of unpublished excavation report. Provided by Humber Archaeology Partnership in advance of publication.

Garland, N. (1989) Human skeletal remains from Ash Hill. In: Phillips, P. (ed.) *Archaeology and landscape studies in North Lincolnshire. Part 1: excavations at North Lincolnshire long barrows,* 149–160. British Archaeological Reports British Series 208. Oxford, British Archaeological Reports.

Geake, H. (1992) Burial practice in 7th and 8th century England. In: Carver, M. (ed.) *The age of Sutton Hoo,* 83–94. Woodbridge, The Boydell Press.

Geake, H. (1997) *The use of grave-goods in Conversion-period England c.600–c.850.* British Archaeological Reports British Series 261. Oxford, British Archaeological Reports.

Geake, H. (2002) Persistent problems in the study of conversion-period burials in England. In: Lucy, S. J. and Reynolds, A. (eds.) *Burial in early medieval England and Wales,* 144–155. The Society for Medieval Archaeology Monograph 17. London, Society for Medieval Archaeology.

Geake, H., Mays, S. and Ottaway, P. (2007) The inhabitants. In: Loveluck, C. and Atkinson, D. (eds.) *The early medieval settlement remains from Flixborough, Lincolnshire. The occupation sequence, c. AD 600–1000,* 113–124. Oxford, Oxbow.

Gilmour, B. J. J. (1979) The Anglo-Saxon church at St. Paul-in-the-Bail, Lincoln. *Medieval Archaeology* 23, 214–218.

Gilmour, B. J. J. and Stocker, D. A. (1986) *St. Mark's church and cemetery*. The Archaeology of Lincoln xiii–i. London, Council for British Archaeology.

Gittos, H. (2002) Creating the sacred: Anglo-Saxon rites for consecrating cemeteries. In: Lucy, S. J. and Reynolds, A. (eds.) *Burial in early medieval England and Wales,* 195–208. The Society for Medieval Archaeology Monograph 17. London, Society for Medieval Archaeology.

Grantham, C. and Grantham, E. (1965) An earthwork and Anglian cemetery at Garton-on-the-Wolds, East Riding, Yorkshire. *The Yorkshire Archaeological Journal* 41, 355–360.

Green, F. J. (1997) *St Helen's, Cumberworth. Assessment report.* Unpublished excavation report. Available at Lincoln SMR. Romsey, Hampshire Archaeology/Test Valley Archaeological Trust.

Greenwell, W. (1877) *British barrows. A record of the examination of sepulchral mounds in various parts of England.* London, Macmillan and Co.

Hadley, D. M. (2000) Burial practices in the northern Danelaw, c.650–1100. *Northern History* 36, 199–216.

Hadley, D. M. (2001) *Death in medieval England.* Stroud, Tempus.

Hadley, D. M. (2003) Whitton, Lincolnshire. *Current Archaeology* 186, 234–237.

Hadley, D. M. (2004) Excavations at Whitton, Lincolnshire. *Church Archaeology* 5–6, 108–109.

Hadley, D. M. (2007) The garden gives up its secrets: the developing relationship between rural settlements and cemeteries, c.750–1100. In: Williams, H. and Semple, S. (eds.) *Early medieval mortuary practices. Anglo-Saxon Studies in Archaeology and History 14,* 194–203. Oxford, Oxbow.

Hall, R. A. (1994) *Viking age York.* London, Batsford.

Hall, R. A. (2002) Blood of the Vikings – the riddle at Riccall. *Yorkshire Archaeology Today* 2, 5.

Hall, R. A., Buckberry, J., Storm, R., Budd, P., Hamilton, W. D. and McCormac, G. (2008) The medieval cemetery at Riccall Landing: a reappraisal. *Yorkshire Archaeological Journal* 80, 55–92.

Hall, R. A. and Whyman, M. (1996) Settlement and monasticism at Ripon, North Yorkshire, from the 7th to the 11th centuries A.D. *Medieval Archaeology* 40, 62–150.

Halsall, G. (2000) The Viking presence in England? The burial evidence reconsidered. In: Hadley, D. M. and Richards, J. D. (eds.) *Cultures in contact: Scandinavian settlement in England in the ninth and tenth centuries,* 259–276. Turnhout, Brepols.

Harrison, S. (1997) William Greenwell and Uncleby I: a recently discovered contemporary account. *East Riding Archaeologist* 9, 1–6.

Hayman, G. and Reynolds, A. (2006) A Saxon and Saxo-Norman execution cemetery at 42–54 London Road, Staines. *Archaeological Journal* 162, 215–255.

Hildyard, E. J. W. (1960) Romano-British discoveries at Crayke, N. R. Yorks. ii: the trial excavation. *The Yorkshire Archaeological Journal* 40, 99–111.

Hill, N. G. (1937) Excavations on Stockbridge Down 1935–36. *Proceedings of the Hampshire Field Club and Archaeological Society* 13, 247–259.

Hinton, D. A. and White, R. (1993) A smith's hoard from Tattershall Thorpe, Lincolnshire: a synopsis. *Anglo-Saxon England* 22, 147–166.

Hodges, C. C. (1893) The architectural history of Selby Abbey. *The Yorkshire Archaeological Journal* 12, 344–394.

Hurley, T. (1992) *Skeleton, Sheep Wash Farm, Little Bytham.* Unpublished excavation archive. Available at South Lincolnshire SMR. Sleaford, Heritage Trust of Lincolnshire.

Hyslop, M. (1963) Two Anglo-Saxon cemeteries at Chamberlains Barn, Leighton Buzzard, Bedfordshire. *Archaeological Journal* 120, 161–200.

Illingworth, C. (1810) *A topographical account of the parish of Scampton.* London, T. Cadell and W. Davies.

Jarvis, E. (1850) Account of the discovery of ornaments and remains, supposed to be of Danish origin, in the parish of Caenby, Lincolnshire. *Archaeological Journal* 7, 36–44.

Jemmeson, S. (1998) *A taphonomic, demographic and pathological study of the excavated human remains from St. Gregory's Minster, Kirkdale.* Unpublished MSc Dissertation, University of York.

Jones, M. J., Stocker, D. and Vince, A. (eds.) (2003) *The city by the pool.* Lincoln Archaeological Studies 10. Oxford, Oxbow.

Kitson Clark, M. (1942) Bracelet and toilet set from Burton Fields Gravel Pit. *Proceedings of the Leeds Philosophical and Literary Society* 5, 339–343.

Leahy, K. (1993) The Anglo-Saxon settlement of Lindsey. In: Vince, A. (ed.) *Pre-Viking Lindsey,* 29–44. Lincoln Archaeological Studies 1. Lincoln, City of Lincoln Archaeology Unit.

Leahy, K. (1998) The early Saxon context. In: Drinkall, G. and Foreman, H. (eds.) *The Anglo-Saxon cemetery at Castledyke South, Barton-on-Humber,* 6–17. Sheffield Excavation Reports 6, Sheffield, Sheffield Academic Press.

Leahy, K. and Williams, D. (2001) Sheffield's Hill: two Anglo-Saxon cemeteries. *Current Archaeology* 15, 310–313.

Lethbridge, T. C. (1936) *A cemetery at Shudy Camps, Cambridgeshire.* Cambridge Antiquarian Society Quarto Publications New Series 5. Cambridge, Bowes for Cambridge Antiquarian Society.

Liddell, D. M. (1933) Excavations at Meon Hill. *Papers and Proceedings of the Hampshire Field Club and Archaeological Society* 12, 127–162.

Lindsey Archaeological Services (1995) *Churchview, North Kelsey: archaeological report on the human remains.* Unpublished excavation report. Available at Lincoln SMR. Lincoln, Lindsey Archaeological Services.

Lindsey Archaeological Services (1999) *Waddington replacements. Grantham Road water main archaeological watching brief.* Unpublished excavation report. Available at Lincoln SMR. Lincoln, Lindsey Archaeological Services.

Loughlin, N. and Miller, K. R. (1979) *A survey of archaeological sites in Humberside.* Hull, Humberside Libraries and Amenities.

Loveluck, C. P. (1998) A high-status Anglo-Saxon settlement at Flixborough, Lincolnshire. *Antiquity* 72, 146–161.

Lucy, S. J. (1998) *The early Anglo-Saxon cemeteries of East Yorkshire: an analysis and reinterpretation.* British Archaeological Reports British Series 272. Oxford, British Archaeological Reports.

Lucy, S. J. and Reynolds, A. (2002) Burial in early medieval England and Wales: past, present and future. In: Lucy, S. J. and Reynolds, A. (eds.) *Burial in early medieval England and Wales,* 1–23. The

Society for Medieval Archaeology Monograph 17. London, Society for Medieval Archaeology.

Lukis, W. C. (1870) On some Anglo-Saxon graves on Howe Hill, near Carthorpe, in the parish of Burneston, North Riding of Yorlshire. *The Yorkshire Archaeological Journal* 1, 175–181.

Macpherson, P. M. (2005) *Tracing change. An isotopic investigation of Anglo-Saxon childhood diet.* Unpublished PhD Thesis, University of Sheffield.

Magilton, J. R. (1977) *The Doncaster district: an archaeological survey.* Doncaster, Museums and Arts Services.

Magilton, J. R. (1980) *The church of St Helen-on-the-Walls, Aldwark.* The archaeology of York AY 10/1. The medieval walled city north-west of the Ouse. York, Council for British Archaeology.

Manby, T. G. (1988) Excavation and Field Archaeology in Eastern Yorkshire: The Thwing Project 1973–1987. *CBA Forum* 1988, 16–18.

Marjoram, J. (1974) Archaeological Notes, 1973. *Lincolnshire History and Archaeology* 9, 17–34.

Mason, D. (2006) AD 616: the battle of Chester. *Current Archaeology* 202, 516–524.

Mays, S., Harding, C. and Heighway, C. (2007) *Wharram. A study of settlement on the Yorkshire Wolds, XI. The churchyard.* York University Archaeological Publications 13. York, University of York.

McCulloch, P. (1990) *Archaeology in Hampshire. Annual Report for 1990.* Winchester, Hampshire County Council.

Meaney, A. L. (1964) *A gazetteer of early Anglo-Saxon burial sites.* London, George Allen and Unwin.

Meaney, A. L. and Hawkes, S. C. (1970) *Two Anglo-Saxon cemeteries at Winnall, Winchester, Hampshire.* The Society for Medieval Archaeology Monograph 4. London, Society for Medieval Archaeology.

Miller, E. (1804) *History and antiquities of Doncaster and its vicinity, with anecdotes of eminent men.* London, W. Sheardown.

Milne, G. and Richards, J. D. (1992) *Wharram. A study of settlement on the Yorkshire Wolds, VII. Two Anglo-Saxon buildings and associated finds.* York University Archaeological Publications. York, York University.

Moorhouse, S. (1977) The Yorkshire archaeological register: 1976. *The Yorkshire Archaeological Journal* 49, 1–18.

Moorhouse, S. (1978) The Yorkshire archaeological register: 1977. *The Yorkshire Archaeological Journal* 50, 7–19.

Moorhouse, S. (1979) The Yorkshire archaeological register: 1979. *The Yorkshire Archaeological Journal* 51, 1–13.

Morris, R. K. (1983) *The church in British archaeology.* Council for British Archaeology Research Report 47. London, Council for British Archaeology.

Mortimer, J. R. (1905) *Forty years' researches in British and Saxon burial mounds of East Yorkshire.* London, A. Brown and Sons.

Morton, A. (1992a) Burial in middle Saxon Southampton. In: Bassett, S. (ed.) *Death in towns,* 68–77. Leicester, Leicester University Press.

Morton, A. (1992b) *Excavations at Hamwic: Volume 1: excavations 1946–83, excluding Six Dials and Melbourne Street.* Council for British Archaeology Research Report 84. York, Council for British Archaeology.

Mytum, H. (1994) Parish and people: excavations at Kellington church. *Medieval Life* 1, 19–22.

Neale, N. and Buckberry, J. L. (2008) *Osteological analysis of the human skeletal remains from Dixon Keld, Masham, North Yorkshire (MSM 88 and MSM 89).* Unpublished osteological report. Bradford, Biological Anthropology Research Centre, Archaeological Sciences, University of Bradford.

Network Archaeology Ltd (1999) *Hatton to Silk Willoughby 1050mm natural gas pipeline. Archaeological evaluation, excavation and watching brief 1998.* Unpublished excavation report. Available at Lincoln SMR. Buckingham, Network Archaeology.

Norton, C. (1998) The Anglo-Saxon cathedral at York and the topography of the Anglian City. *Journal of the British Archaeological Association* 151, 1–42.

Palmer-Brown, C. (1995) *Castle Farm Torksey. An archaeological excavation report for Mantle and Bartlet Architects.* Unpublished excavation report. Available at Lincoln SMR. Sleaford, Pre-Construct Archaeology.

Palmer-Brown, C. (1996) *Chapel Lane, Navenby.* Unpublished excavation report. Available at Lincoln SMR. Sleaford, Pre-Construct Archaeology.

Pearson, N. F. (1989) Swinegate excavation. *Interim* 14, 2–9.

Pearson, N. F. (1990) Swinegate excavation. *Interim* 15, 2–10.

Peers, C. and Radford, C. A. R. (1943) The Saxon monastery at Whitby. *Archaeologia* 89, 27–88.

Petch, D. F. (1960) Archaeological Notes for 1958. *Lincolnshire Architectural and Archaeological Society Reports and Papers* 8, 1–25.

Phillips, D. and Heywood, B. (1995) *Excavations at York Minster volume 1: from Roman fortress to Norman cathedral.* London, HMSO.

Phillips, P. (1985) Excavation and survey at Swinhope. *Lincolnshire History and Archaeology* 20, 72–73.

Phillips, P. (1989) *Archaeology and landscape studies in North Lincolnshire. Part 1: excavations at North Lincolnshire long barrows.* British Archaeological Report British Series 208(i). Oxford, British Archaeological Report.

Phillips, P. and Walker, J. (1989) Radiocarbon dating. In: Phillips, P. (ed.) *Archaeology and landscape studies in North Lincolnshire. Part 1: excavations at North Lincolnshire long barrows,* 169–171. British Archaeological Reports British Series 208. Oxford, British Archaeological Reports.

Poulson, G. (1841) *The history and antiquities of the seignniory of Holderness.* Hull, Robert Brown.

Powlesland, D. (1997) Discussion. In: Hines, J. (ed.) *The Anglo-Saxons from the migration period to the eighth century,* 160–169. Woodbridge, Boydell.

Rahtz, P. (1976) The building plan of the Anglo-Saxon monastery of Whitby Abbey. In: Wilson, D. M. (ed.) *The archaeology of Anglo-Saxon England,* 459–462. Cambridge, Cambridge University Press.

Rahtz, P. and Watts, L. (1997) Kirkdale Anglo-Saxon Minster. *Current Archaeology* 155, 419–422.

Ramm, H. G. (1965) The Yorkshire archaeological register 1964. *The Yorkshire Archaeological Journal* 41, 315–337.

Reynolds, A. (1997) The definition and ideology of Anglo-Saxon execution sites and cemeteries. In: De Boe, G. and Verhaege, F. (eds.) *Death and Burial in Medieval Europe,* 33–41. Papers of the 'Medieval Europe Brugge 1997' Conference 2. Zellick, I. A. P. Rapporten.

Reynolds, A. (2002) Burials, boundaries and charters in Anglo-Saxon England: a reassessment. In: Lucy, S. J. and Reynolds, A. (eds.)

Burial in early medieval England and Wales, 171–194. The Society for Medieval Archaeology Monograph 17. London, Society for Medieval Archaeology.

Reynolds, A. (2009) *Anglo-Saxon deviant burial customs.* Oxford, Oxford University Press.

Reynolds, N. M. (1979) Saltergate In: C. Colyer and M. J. Jones (eds.) Excavations at Lincoln. *Antiquaries Journal* 59, 84–89.

Richards, J. D. (1999) Cottam: an Anglian and Anglo-Scandinavian settlement on the Yorkshire Wolds. *Archaeological Journal* 156, 1–110.

Richards, J. D. (2000) *Viking Age England.* (2nd edition). Stroud, Tempus.

Richards, J. D. (2002) The case of the missing Vikings: Scandinavian burial in the Danelaw. In: Lucy, S. J. and Reynolds, A. (eds.) *Burial in early medieval England and Wales,* 156–170. The Society for Medieval Archaeology Monograph 17. London, Society for Medieval Archaeology.

Richards, J. D. (2004) Excavations at the Viking Barrow Cemetery at Heath Wood, Ingleby, Derbyshire. *Antiquaries Journal* 84, 23–116.

Richards, J. D., Jecock, M., Richmond, L. and Tuck, C. (1995) The Viking barrow cemetery at Heath Wood, Ingleby, Derbyshire. *Medieval Archaeology* 39, 51–70.

Rodwell, W. (2007) Burial archaeology. In: Waldron, T. (ed.) *St Peter's Barton-upon-Humber, Lincolnshire. A parish church and its community. Volume 2: the human remains,* 14–32. Oxford, Oxbow.

Rodwell, W. and Rodwell, K. (1981) Barton on Humber. *Current Archaeology* 78, 209–215.

Rodwell, W. and Rodwell, K. (1982) St. Peter's Church, Barton-upon-Humber: excavation and structural study 1978–1981. *Antiquaries Journal* 62, 283–513.

Rowntree, A. (1931) The castle. In: Rowntree, A. (ed.) *The history of Scarborough,* 141–149. London, J. M. Dent & Sons Ltd.

Ryder, P. (1990) *Monuments protection plan. Cathedral Close reports, Ripon.* Unpublished Report. Available at Northallerton SMR. English Heritage.

Sills, J. (1982) St. Peter's Church, Holton-le-Clay, Lincolnshire. *Lincolnshire History and Archaeology* 17, 29–44.

Smith, R. (1912) An Anglo-Saxon cemetery at Uncleby, East Riding of Yorkshire. *Proceedings of the Society of Antiquaries* 24, 146–158.

Speed, G. and Walton Rogers, P. (2004) A burial of a Viking woman at Adwick-le-Street, South Yorkshire. *Medieval Archaeology* 48, 51–90.

Stead, I. (1987) Garton Station. *Current Archaeology* 103, 234–237.

Stead, I. (1991) *Iron Age cemeteries in East Yorkshire.* London, English Heritage in association with British Museum Press.

Steane, K., Darling, M. J., Mann, J., Vince, A. and Young, J. (eds.) (2001) *The Archaeology of Wigford and the Brayford Pool.* Lincoln Archaeological Studies 2. Oxford, Oxbow.

Stocker, D. (2000) Monuments and merchants: irregularities in the distribution of stone sculpture in Lincolnshire and Yorkshire in the tenth century. In: Hadley, D. M. and Richards, J. D. (eds.) *Cultures in contact: Scandinavian settlement in England in the ninth and tenth centuries,* 179–212. Turnhout, Brepols.

Stoodley, N. (2007) New perspectives on cemetery reloaction in the seventh century AD: the example of Portway, Andover. In: Williams, H. and Semple, S. (eds.) *Early medieval mortuary practices. Anglo-Saxon Studies in Archaeology and History 14,* 154–162. Oxford, Oxbow.

Stroud, G. (n.d.) *The human skeletal remains from Hickleton, South Yorkshire.* Unpublished skeletal report, held at the Biological Anthropology Research Centre, Department of Archaeological Sciences, University of Bradford.

Stroud, G. and Kemp, R. L. (1993) *Cemeteries of St Andrew, Fishergate.* The archaeology of York 12/2. The medieval cemeteries. York, Council for British Archaeology.

Thorp, F. (1975) The Yorkshire archaeological register: 1974. *The Yorkshire Archaeological Journal* 47, 1–11.

Thurnam, J. (1849) Description of an ancient tumular cemetery, probably of the Anglo-Saxon period, at Lamel Hill, near York. *Archaeological Journal* 6, 27–39, 123–136.

Trimble, G. (1997) *Archaeological investigation of a pipeline along St Giles' Avenue, Sleaford, Lincolnshire.* Unpublished excavation report. Available at Lincoln SMR. Heckington, Archaeological Project Services.

Waterman, D. M. (1951) Anglian burial at Occaney, W.R. Yorks. *The Yorkshire Archaeological Journal* 37, 440–441.

Watts, L., Rahtz, P., Okasha, E., Bradley, S. A. J. and Higgitt, J. (1997) Kirkdale – the inscriptions. *Medieval Archaeology* 41, 51–99.

Webster, L. E. and Cherry, J. (1975) Medieval Britain in 1974. *Medieval Archaeology* 19, 220–260.

Webster, L. E. and Cherry, J. (1978) Medieval Britain in 1977. *Medieval Archaeology* 22, 142–188.

Wenham, L. P. (1960) Seven archaeological discoveries in Yorkshire. *The Yorkshire Archaeological Journal* 40, 298–328.

Wenham, L. P. (1963) 'York' in the Yorkshire archaeological register 1962. *The Yorkshire Archaeological Journal* 41, 13.

Wenham, L. P., Hall, R. A., Briden, C. M. and Stocker, D. A. (1987) *St Mary Bishophill Junior and St Mary Castlegate.* The Archaeology of York 8/2. Anglo-Scandinavian York. York, Council for British Archaeology.

Wessex Archaeology (2007) *Archaeological excavations at Berwick Field and Old Dairy Cottage, west of Andover Road, Winchester, Hampshire, 1989–1994. Post-excavation assessment report and project design for analysis and publication.* Unpublished report. Salisbury, Wessex Archaeology.

White, A. J. (1978) Archaeology in Lincolnshire and South Humberside, 1977. *Lincolnshire History and Archaeology* 13, 75–90.

White, A. J. (1982) Archaeology in Lincolnshire and South Humberside, 1981. *Lincolnshire History and Archaeology* 17, 71–86.

White, W. (1856) *History, gazetteer, and directory of Lincolnshire, and the city and diocese of Lincoln.* (2nd edition). Sheffield, William White.

Williams, H. (1997) Ancient landscapes and the dead: the reuse of prehistoric and Roman monuments as early Anglo-Saxon burial sites. *Medieval Archaeology* 41, 1–32.

Wilmott, T. (1986) Excavations at Tanners Row, Pontefract: second interim report. *CBA Forum* 1986, 20–21.

Wilmott, T. (1987) Pontefract. *Current Archaeology* 9, 340–344.

Wilson, B. and Mee, F. (1998) *The medieval parish churches of York: the pictorial evidence.* The Archaeology of York Vol.1. York, York Archaeological Trust.

Wilson, C. M. (1971) Archaeological Notes 1970. *Lincolnshire History and Archaeology* 6, 3–17.

Wilson, D. M. and Hurst, D. G. (1964) Medieval Britain in 1962 and 1963. *Medieval Archaeology* 8, 231–299.

Wilson, D. M. and Hurst, D. G. (1965) Medieval Britain in 1964. *Medieval Archaeology* 9, 170–220.

Wilson, D. M. and Hurst, D. G. (1969) Medieval Britain in 1968. *Medieval Archaeology* 13, 230–287.

Wilson, D. M. and Hurst, J. G. (1959) Medieval Britain in 1958. *Medieval Archaeology* 3, 295–326.

Wormald, P. (1999) *The making of English law. Volume I: King Alfred to the twelfth century*. Oxford, Blackwell.

Wrathmell, S. and Nicholson, A. (eds.) (1990) *Dalton Parlours. Iron Age settlement and Roman villa*. Yorkshire Archaeology 3. Wakefield, West Yorkshire Archaeology Service.

Wright, T. (1857) On some curious forms of sepulchral interment found in East Yorkshire. *Gentleman's Magazine* 3, 114–119.

Wright, T. (1865) Account of Anglo-Saxon jewellery etc. found at Seamer in the East Riding of Yorkshire. *Journal of the British Archaeological Association* 21, 329–332.

Wymer, J. J. (1996) The excavation of a ring ditch at South Acre. In: Wymer, J. J. (ed.) *Barrow Excavations in Norfolk, 1984–88*, 58–89. East Anglian Archaeology Report 77. Dereham, East Anglian Archaeology.

York Archaeological Trust (1994) *An archaeological evaluation at Blue Bridge Lane, York*. Unpublished evaluation report. Available at York SMR. York, York Archaeological Trust.

York Archaeological Trust (1998) *Former female prison, Castle Yard, York. Report on an archaeological evaluation*. Unpublished evaluation report. Available at York SMR. York, York Archaeological Trust.

Youngs, S. M., Clark, J. and Barry, T. (1985) Medieval Britain and Ireland in 1984. *Medieval Archaeology* 29, 158–230.

Youngs, S. M., Clark, J. and Barry, T. (1987) Medieval Britain and Ireland in 1986. *Medieval Archaeology* 31, 110–191.

2. Engendered Bodies and Objects of Memory in Final Phase Graves

Howard Williams

Introduction

The grave goods within conversion-period or Final Phase burial rites of the seventh and early eighth centuries AD have received varying explanations by archaeologists. Common interpretative themes include religious conversion, kingdom formation and new ideologies connected to both of these processes. This paper presents a distinct but related perspective on the wealthy female assemblages found in some Final Phase graves. Instead of regarding them as indicative of broad social and religious changes *per se*, the paper interprets the burial of grave goods as a strategy to constitute the social memories of an idealised aristocratic female personhood. Focusing on five female-gendered wealthy grave assemblages from two burial plots excavated at Harford Farm, Norfolk, the paper highlights the biographical qualities of certain artefacts. Meanwhile other artefacts are related to the engendering of the female aristocratic body including its management, adornment and magical protection. Further artefacts are connected to key feminine bodily practices associated with household activities and ritual practices.

The paper argues that artefact deposition was made effective both through public display and staged concealment and consignment in the grave. This has two implications for early medieval archaeology. First, artefacts were operating as mnemonic devices instrumental in the mortuary commemoration of a new conception of female-gendered aristocratic personhood in the seventh century. Second, female-gendered grave assemblages incorporated 'objects of memory'. Indeed, the long biographies of these objects hint at the increasing use of portable artefacts to commemorate the dead through their exchange among the living rather than their burial with the dead. The Final Phase is therefore not so much evidence of changing afterlife beliefs as evolving strategies of commemoration and a shift in the balance from mnemonic consignment to curation.

The Interpretation of Final Phase Grave Goods

The slow adoption of shrouds instead of clothed burial might to some extent account for the quantitative decline in grave goods in the Final Phase (see below). Yet the frequent practice of clothing and adorning the cadaver continued in the Final Phase and incorporated a qualitative shift. There is evidence for dress accessories including buckles, knives and (usually for select adult females) jewellery (see Geake 1997). Tools such as shears are sometimes found, as are female-gendered items such as combs, toilet sets and a range of objects loosely defined as 'amulets' suspended around the neck or at the waist (Meaney 1981; *e.g.* see Boyle *et al.* 1998).

When wealthy graves do occur, there is an exentuated differentiation from other graves (*e.g.* Boddington 1990, 184–7; Shephard 1979). Grave-gifts can be placed around the cadaver including the continuation of the weapon burial rite for select adult males, albeit at a reduced frequency (Härke 1992). Moreover, containers were sometimes placed in graves including buckets, drinking vessels, boxes and caskets. The Final Phase therefore encapsulated the adoption of new styles of costume and new forms of artefact previously unknown in the pagan period including examples with Christian iconography (Boddington 1990, 181, 183–7; Geake 1997). Moreover, it is increasingly clear that some items deposited in Final Phase graves had long 'life-histories', being old when interred, including jewellery and bronze hanging bowls (Geake 1999). Artefacts were clearly an important medium for expressing the identity of the deceased as perceived by mourners as they had been in the fifth and sixth centuries.

The most traditional approach has been to consider the nature of artefacts in graves as an indication of religious change, namely conversion to Christianity. From this perspective, the Final Phase was a waivering shift towards Christian religious and afterlife beliefs, the first influence of the clergy on overt pagan mortuary display or simply the influence of Christian and Continental fashions. Final Phase burials simultaneously illustrate both the tenacity of pagan Germanic religious propensities while simultaneously showing the adoption of Romanising styles of artefacts with some evidence of 'Celtic' influence (Leeds 1936, 113–4). Christian symbols and iconography on the objects have been used to illustrate the process of religious conversion (*e.g.* Meaney and Hawkes 1970; Meaney 1981). Central to this religious interpretation is the idea that the Final Phase burial rites indicate some form of 'syncretism' or 'transition' between pagan practice in the later fifth and sixth centuries AD and Christian practice from the eighth century onwards (*e.g.* Boddington 1990, 178; Hadley 2000; Hoggett 2007; Pluskowski and Patrick 2003, 35). This view is sustained by the lack of a geographical contiguity between Final Phase furnished graves and early church sites (Geake 2002; Geake 2003, 261; but see Loveluck 1996).

A religious interpretation was popular within a culture-historic framework for Anglo-Saxon archaeology and continues to be favoured by some authors, although few now accept a simple correlation between furnished graves and religious belief. The religious status of Final Phase burials is therefore generally seen as 'ambiguous' (Meaney 2003, 240–1). Hence, studies have looked beyond religion for other explanations. These include increased socio-economic differentiation and changing socio-political structures associated with kingdom formation. Social explanations for the shift in burial practices and the provision of grave goods are seen in terms of changing patterns in the social structuring of age (Crawford 1993; 2000), gender (Stoodley 1999), status (Arnold 1997; Shephard 1979), kinship structures and ethnicity (Boddington 1990; Härke 1992; Sayer 2009) as well as territoriality and regionality (Loveluck 1996; Lucy 1998; Semple 2003; Stoodley 2007). Socio-economic and socio-political changes in this period included patterns of taxation (Carver 1989), changes in law, inheritance patterns and concepts of land tenure (Shephard 1979). These perspectives have been inspired by a realisation that the church was likely to have had only a slow and superficial influence over burial rites that remained for families and communities to preside over (Bullough 1983; Geake 2003; Hadley 2000; 2001; 2002). Indeed, explanations for the changes and decline in grave goods might even be seen as somewhat disconnected from socio-economic or religious change, related to broader cycles of competitive expenditure in the mortuary realm (Cannon 1989). A further social context is to regard the decline and subsequent cessation of artefact deposition as part of a long-term shift towards above-ground monumental display, whether through burial mounds or church-burial (Boddington 1990, 197; Effros 2003; Hadley 2000).

While useful in explaining overall processes of change, these socio-economic approaches do not adequately deal with the qualitative and contextual changes evident in Final Phase mortuary practices and the persistent roles of portable artefacts in certain graves. To counter this challenge, some studies have adopted a symbolic and ideological perspective including attempts to analyse the meanings of artefacts and the political contexts within which these meanings were deployed via the mortuary context (Carver 2000; Halsall 2003). It has long been recognised through a combination of archaeological and later written sources that many items of jewellery in Final Phase graves may have had an amuletic or apotropaic functions that span the traditional perception of a clear pagan/Christian divide (Meaney 1981). Indeed, the deposition of amulets and crosses seems to increase in this period, suggesting both continuity and adaptation to the new symbols of the Christian faith to protect both the living and the dead (Blair 2005, 173–5; Crawford 2004).

Notably, Helen Geake (1997; 2003) defined the Final Phase as a shift in mentality and ideology rather than either exclusively religious or social in nature. The adaptation of influences from the Frankish (and more indirectly) the Roman and Byzantine worlds shows competitive networks of ideas and ideals linking church and state and permeating Anglo-Saxon culture (Geake 1997; Marzinzik 2003). Artefacts in graves might assert political affiliations as well as new worldviews. Equally, the final decline in frequent artefact provision can be regarded as related in part to a new ideology of humility in treating the body in death. This could represent the secular utilisation of Christian monastic ideals as they were adopted and promulgated in aristocratic and royal circles rather than any direct influence from the clergy (Bazelmans 2002; Effros 2002). The artefacts found in select graves could indicate the continued use of a grave as medium for social display but also a new conception of the body in life and in death as a medium for expressing and constituting personhood (see Karkov 2003). In this regard the Anglo-Saxon evidence can be best seen as a part of a broader phenomenon of changing relationships between ideology and mortuary practice found across north-west Europe and Scandinavia in the later first millennium AD (see also Effros 2002; 2003; Halsall 2003; Marzinzik 2000; Theuws 1999).

The three interpretative themes of religion, socio-politics and symbolism/ideology are not fully satisfactory in isolation nor need they be seen as mutually exclusive. In combination rather than separately, they bring us closer to appreciate the significance of Final Phase grave goods. In particular, they encourage a contextual interpretation of mortuary artefact as more than 'pagan survivals' or as manifestations of 'popular superstitions' but the results of conscious and strategic mortuary decisions by the living about the identities of the dead (Crawford 2004; Hadley 2000; 2002).

The Exchange of Final Phase Mortuary Artefacts

These arguments have built a more sophisticated understanding of the complex interactions of society, economy, politics and religion in addressing the changing burial rites of the seventh century. Yet while serving to frame and contextualise the use of grave goods in the Final Phase, most previous work has ignored the precise ways in which selected artefacts were deployed within the mortuary process and the burial context as well as the potential commemorative significance of artefact burial. Early medieval mortuary practices were most certainly a process mediated by religious and social concepts of dying, death and the dead. Yet archaeologists have only begun to consider the static remains left in graves in terms of the complex sequence of procedures and performances that both preceded and succeeded the interment of the corpse and how even mundane and prosaic artefacts can bring powerful memories to the fore through their association with the deceased (*e.g.* Williams 2005).

To develop such an approach, the most useful starting-point is a recent paper by Sally Crawford (2004) which focuses on the jewellery found in wealthy female graves of the seventh century. Crawford argues that the jewellery with Christian motifs placed within containers and on the bodies in such graves can best be described as 'votive' offerings. This is a crucial and significant argument. Rather than seeing mortuary artefacts as personal possessions placed simply to display the deceased's social identity, she suggests that the manner of their placement and their Christian iconography indicate an adaptation of earlier pre-Christian dedicatory and cultic practices associated with the dead and the cemetery. The principal and valuable argument that can be taken from Crawford's study is that Final Phase artefacts cannot be simplistically defined as 'grave goods' nor 'pagan survivals' but a new manifestation of traditional relationships between the living, the dead and the sacred.

Crawford re-positions the debate away from the precise identity of the deceased reflected in the choice of mortuary artefacts as well as challenging traditional associations of grave goods with afterlife beliefs. The emphasis is instead upon the relationship between the living and the dead negotiated through the deployment of selected items in the mortuary process. In this regard, artefacts in graves can be considered as exchange items between the living and the dead. Placing artefacts with the dead defined the social and religious identities of living people. Meanwhile, as gifts to the dead, they set up obligations of reciprocity and continued bonds across the divide of death. These relationships may have drawn upon both pre-Christian concepts of ancestors as sources of social and religious power as well as new, Christian, concepts of intercessory prayer by the living over the fate of the soul mediated by material culture. Crawford therefore provides us with a basis for rethinking the significance of Final Phase mortuary artefacts (see also Effros 2002; 2003).

A fuller exploration of Crawford's approach requires putting these 'votive' wealthy objects in a wider context. This will include their association with other items of costume, materials and artefacts placed with the dead, mortuary process as well as their particular positioning in relation to the dead body. In doing so, we are able to see these acts as more than elements of social display but equally as more than acts of religious devotion, but as having implications for the construction of social memories.

Final Phase Mortuary Artefacts and Social Memory

How did artefact deposition affect social memory in seventh-century England? A useful starting point is to regard artefacts as operating within funerals as 'technologies of remembrance' (see Jones 2003). By this it is meant that rather than a representation of afterlife belief, a symbolic statement or a social display, mortuary practices were strategies for mediating the selective remembering and forgetting of the dead. This was undoubtedly a lengthy process that focused upon, and involved the careful management of, the cadaver. From death-bed to the grave and beyond, artefacts mediated this transition in commemorating an idealised vision of the person in death. Regarding the deployment of material culture in mortuary practices as technologies of remembrance enables scrutiny to be fixed upon the mnemonic efficacy of objects rather than their precise meanings of things or the manifold registers upon which social memory may have been materialised within any single artefact. This involves considering the contribution objects made to the creation of a burial 'tableau' that would have been employed in the creation of a memorable scene during the funeral (Carver 2000; Geake 2003, 260) but also the roles of artefacts and materials in the sequential removal of the cadaver from the senses of the survivors as the grave was covered over (Halsall 2003; Williams 2006).

This approach also provides new insights into the overall explanation for the end of the frequent provision of artefacts in graves. By considering material culture as contributing to the commemorative significance of the dead, the decline and final cessation of regular grave-good provision during this period can be reinterpreted in mnemonic terms. The move in focus from artefact deposition in the grave to giving artefacts to the church and circulating them among the living can be seen as enhancing, rather than diminishing, the significance of artefacts in the commemoration of the dead. The wealthy female assemblages of the Final Phase may provide clues to this transition in artefact-use between deposition and circulation by regarding them as gifts intended to commemorate the dead.

Final Phase Graves from Harford Farm, Norfolk

A full review of seventh and early eighth-century burial sites is beyond the scope of this discussion. This paper will instead focus upon one recently-published and carefully-excavated cemetery of the Final Phase from Harford Farm, near Caistor St. Edmund, Norfolk to provide the basis for building a wider argument about the significance of portable artefacts in the commemoration of the dead (Penn 2000). The excavation in question was conducted ahead of road construction south

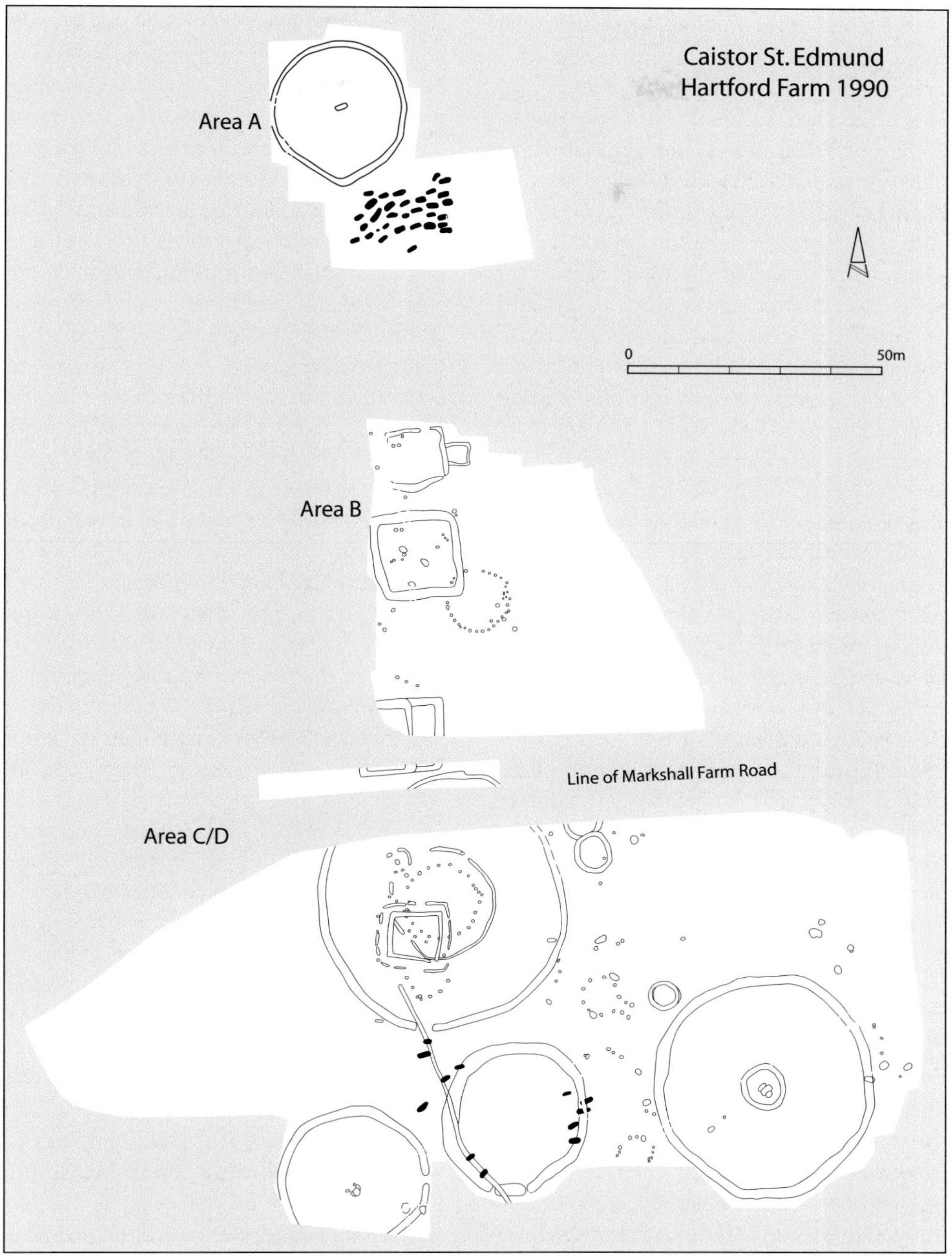

Figure 2.1: Plan of the excavations at Harford Farm, Caistor St Edmund, Norfolk showing two groups of seventh/early eighth century burials focusing upon a Bronze Age barrow cemetery (Redrawn by Seán Goddard after Penn 2000).

of Norwich. In total, 47 burials in 46 west-east orientated graves were revealed. They were located in two discrete burial plots, each focusing seemingly intentionally upon a series of prehistoric burial mounds (Figure 2.1). Disappointingly, preservation within the graves was poor with the presence of human bodies only revealed through stains in the soil. This provided evidence that most graves were those of adults, positioned supine and extended in most instances (Penn 2000, 74). Organic grave goods were absent and inorganic artefacts were often poorly preserved. Despite this, the soil-stains provided valuable evidence, hinting at the provision of coffins and other organic linings and coverings in many graves.

Concerning the portable artefacts from the Harford Farm graves, only 13 out of 47 (28%) had no grave goods at all. Of the remaining 34 graves (72%), 18 (38%) had knives or knives together with buckles. Eleven (23%) were regarded as 'modestly equipped' with knives, buckles and sometimes chatelaines. Of these there was one instance of 'weapon burial', grave 25 interred with a seax. Five (11%) of the graves stand out as exceptionally rich and are the focus of the subsequent discussion.

Bearing in mind the caveat that many more artefacts may have been present but yielded no trace upon excavation, wealthy graves 11, 18, 22, 28 and 33 stand out from the rest of the burials. All date to the late seventh or very early eighth centuries and were distinguished from the rest of the graves on the basis of the number and quality of the artefacts deposited. Interestingly these burials are not set apart in terms of location, orientation or grave-size. In these aspects they seem typical. Therefore it appears that these individuals were afforded a comparable burial rite to their lesser-furnished companions, but the choice was made to distinguish them through the inclusion of a range of portable artefacts on and around the body.

It is of considerable importance that all of the five rich burials from Harford Farm are female-gender assemblages although because of the poor bone-preservation, the determination of the osteological sex of these individuals was not possible. Of equal note, the artefacts were not always located as one might expect if they were elements of the deceased's mortuary costume. This suggests that many of the artefacts had other roles in the composition of the burial assemblage than simply costume accessories. It is argued that the assemblages can be understood less in terms of the display and commemoration of the deceased's individual identity, political allegiance or religious beliefs. Instead these furnished graves were a distinctive 'technology of remembrance', they were concerned with strategies for the selective commemoration of idealised concepts of the social person. Let us explore each grave in turn to see how the artefacts were deployed in this regard.

The Five Wealthy Graves from Harford Farm

Grave 11 (Figure 2.2) revealed traces of a coffin-stain surrounding a semi-flexed body with a costume consisting of elaborate precious metal accessories suspended around the corpse's neck. They comprised of a gold, silver and garnet composite disc brooch, three silver-wire rings, eight to ten silver-wire knot rings and a silver toilet set of three items (a perforated spoon and two picks). Between the right arm and the chest were placed a knife and shears, while at the belt were three iron suspension rings and a key. Another key and a comb were placed beside the cadaver's feet and copper-alloy fragments hint that further objects were placed towards the foot end of the grave (Penn 2000, 14). The grave goods appear to consist of a mortuary costume and artefacts placed into the grave by the mourners. Some of the objects might be described as heirlooms. For instance, the disc brooch had a long life-history. It was a product of Kent from the early seventh century (*c*.610–650) and on its back-plate was a runic inscription commemorating its repair sometime prior to deposition towards the end of the seventh century (Hines 2000, 80; Penn 2000, 45–9; see below).

Grave 18 (Figure 2.2) was another encoffined burial. An iron barrel-lock and key fragment found at the far west end of the grave suggest that a wooden box had been placed adjacent to the head containing an iron awl (Penn 2000, 65). Also found in the grave were a gold and garnet pendant, shears, a copper-alloy bracelet used as a suspension ring, an iron purse-mount and a collection of suspended objects of unknown function (possibly an inkpot and pen-case). Of special note is a suspended bronze cylinder of a type often described as 'relic-boxes'. It contained a silver pin-set and linking chain (Penn 2000, 66–7). In stark contrast to grave 11, none of these items were situated on the body as elements of costume. The body may indeed have been clothed but with some modesty, or else the cadaver may have been loosely wrapped within a shroud. Instead of adorning the dead, the artefacts were all located alongside the northern edge of the grave in the area of the left-side of the waist and left thigh, all seemingly beside or upon the coffin. The final item is one of only two pin-sets characteristic of Final Phase Byzantine-style jewellery from the cemetery. Its position shows that it was not placed on the body as an element of costume but concealed within the relic-box. It appears that two sceattas (silver coins) were added to the grave, possibly placed on the coffin to the right and above the head. These diagnostic items date the grave to the very early years of the eighth century (Penn 2000, 75).

The three other wealthy female-gendered graves contained artefacts deployed in a mixture between the two patterns found in graves 11 and 18. Grave 22 (Figure 2.2) contained the surviving stains of an extended supine body encoffined with two groups of artefacts. The first group consisted of the remains of a necklace or festoon at the neck comprising of silver-wire knot-rings, silver bullae and glass beads (as in grave 11). There was also a concentration along the left side of the waist (as in grave 18); a chatelaine of copper-alloy rings, beads, a buckle, a knife, a tool (possibly a pair of tweezers) and two keys (Penn 2000, 27–9).

Grave 28 (Figure 2.3) was also encoffined and contained a further division between objects located by the neck and two groups of objects by the waist. A festoon of 15 silver-wire rings and a single silver bucket-shaped pendant was found at the neck. However, other items of jewellery were found in a cluster situated outside of the coffin on the north side adjacent to the waist and left forearm of the skeleton. These included eleven bullae of a silver necklace as well as an open-work gold pendant. Also placed outside the left forearm were two spindle-whorls, two silver decorated discs, five iron rivets that may indicate the presence of a comb, and knife. Placed upon the left hip was a chatelaine consisting of an iron ring, shears, a steel, a key and a series of other undiagnosed iron objects. Evidence that the cadaver had been dressed for burial is evident from a copper-alloy shoelace tag found by the left foot, suggesting the presence of footwear (Penn 2000, 25–7).

Grave 33 (Figure 2.3) was interred without evidence of a coffin and the only one of the five to be found in the southern,

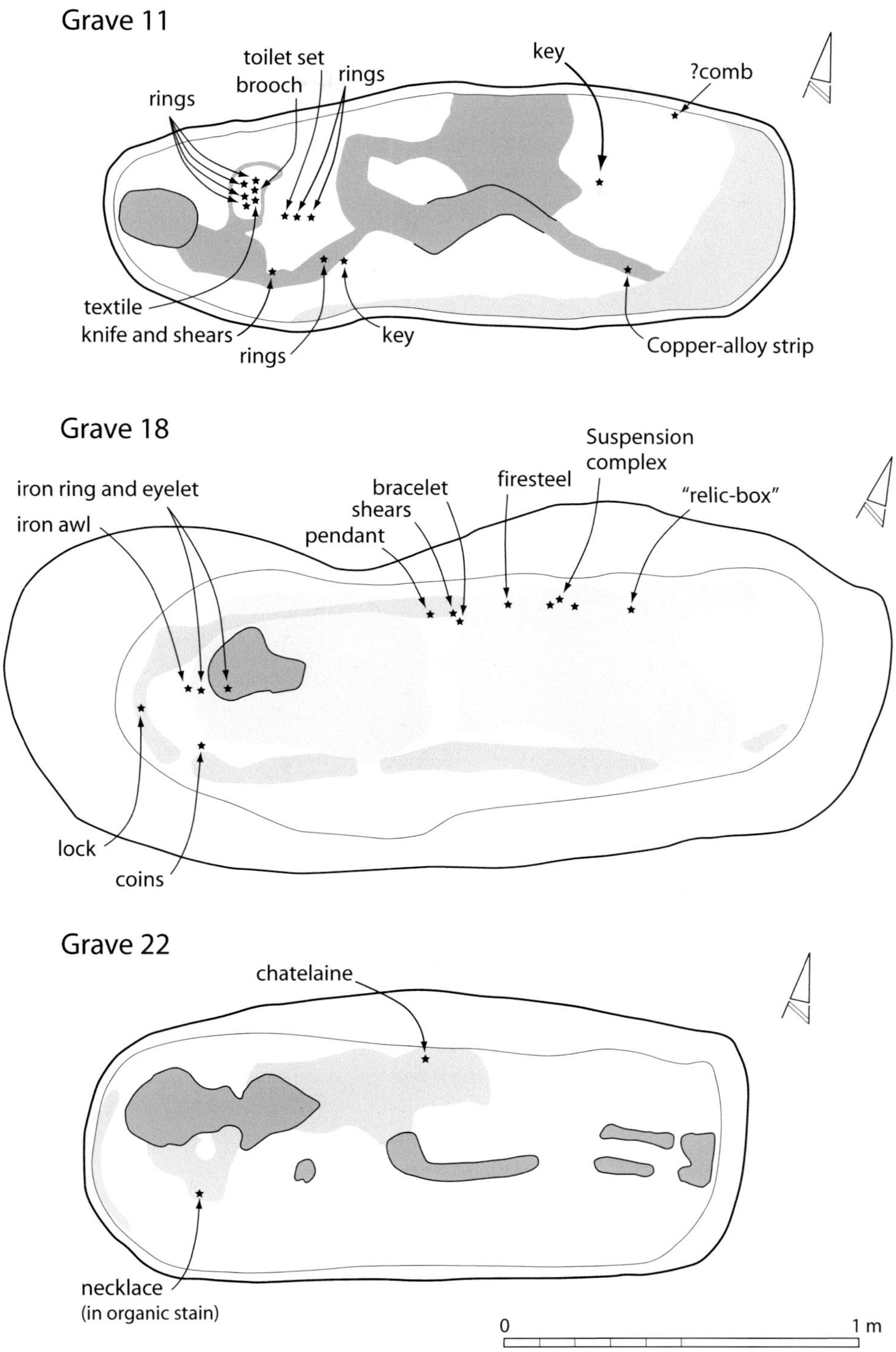

Figure 2.2: Plans of graves 11, 18 and 22 from the Harford Farm cemetery (Redrawn by Seán Goddard after Penn 2000).

more dispersed, burial group. The body seems to have been positioned in a semi-flexed posture. By the neck was a Roman intaglio mounted in a frame of twisted and beaded gold wire and showing signs of wear. Again this might be regarded as an heirloom of some kind. On the right side of the body were found two gold discs with garnets that may have adorned the outside of an adjacent leather or textile bag. Had a bag been present, its contents consisted of a necklace of silver-wire knot-rings with seventeen beads of either glass or amethyst. Also in the hypothesised bag was a silver toilet set of three

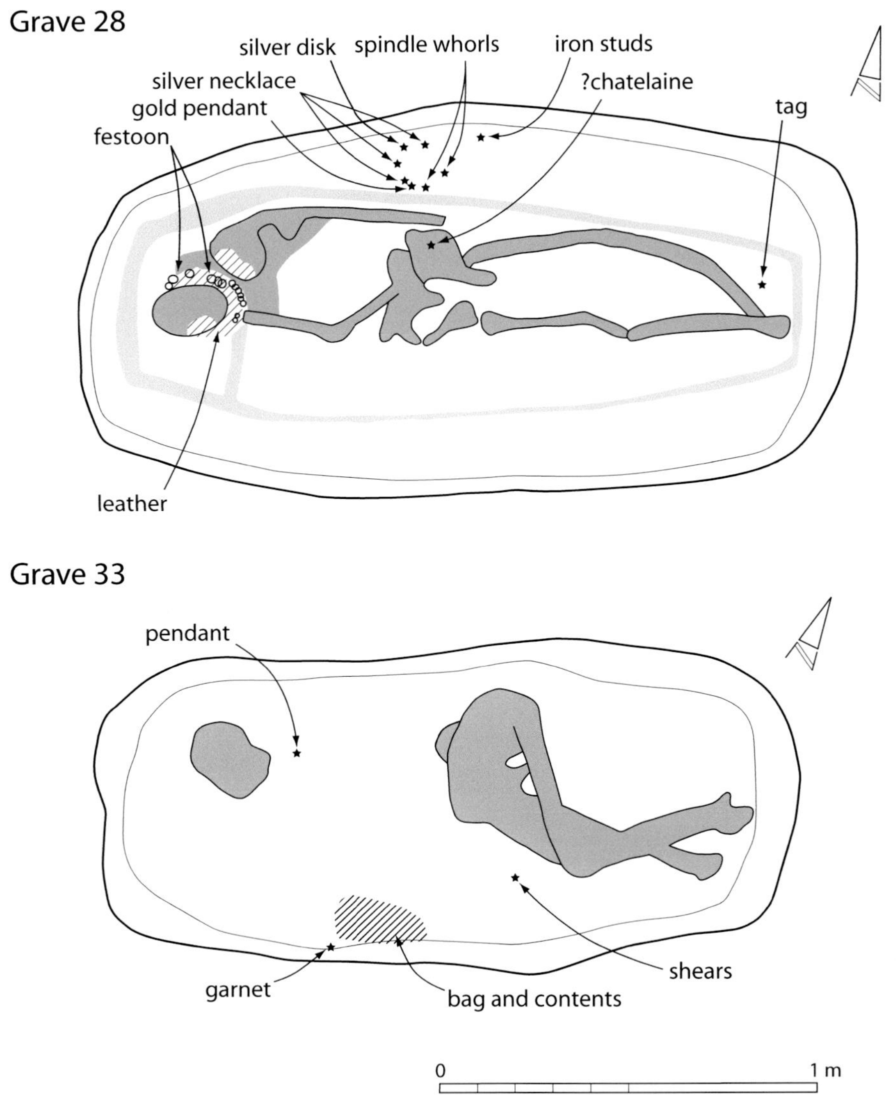

Figure 2.3: Plans of graves 28 and 33 from the Harford Farm cemetery (Redrawn by Seán Goddard after Penn 2000).

implements (one of which was a perforated spoon) like those suspended from the neck of grave 11, and the remains of a chatelaine consisting of an iron ring and key. By the right leg was a pair of shears. Therefore, once again we have artefacts that *could* have been worn on the body but were instead interred within a bag.

A clear distinction between mortuary costume and grave gifts is not apparent at Harford Farm. This is because comparable artefact-types could be placed both on and with the body including keys, pendants and necklaces and toilet implements. Equally, regarding the artefacts as a burial tableau is somewhat misleading. Certainly the cadaver was dressed for death in at least four out of five cases. In some cases, the mourners had placed jewellery upon the body. These artefacts may have accompanied the body through the funeral from the preparation of the body to the graveside. Yet they may have only been on view a short time before the body was encoffined and wrapped in textiles. This suggests that an appreciation of mortuary display should also consider the mnemonic efficacy of consignment. Moreover, many of the objects were contained within bags and caskets (including items of jewellery and costume) or only placed in the grave once the coffin was in place and possibly after it was closed over, suggesting they would not have been juxtaposed with the body as part of a tableau.

The same observations apply to other prestigious objects placed in the Harford Farm graves. The one certain weapon-burial from the cemetery (grave 25) had a seax enclosed in a leather sheath placed on the north side of the grave, possibly over the left side of the corpse's torso. As well as this position suggesting the blade was lain on the corpse, the seax was placed upside-down from a conventional location had it been placed as an element of 'dress'. In grave 25, the blade faced the head of the corpse (Penn 2000, 25). Furthermore, many of the basic elements of burial 'costume' at Harford Farm are not present in these five wealthy graves. Only two of the five have knives, and none of the five have belt-buckles. Therefore, despite overall similarities in grave orientation and structure, in terms of artefact provision it is difficult to see these graves as augmenting a common repertoire. They were a distinctive practice in the duration of this burying community. The artefacts were connected to discrete practices linked to the composition and consignment of the grave.

Harford Farm in Context

Much remains unclear about the mortuary process at Harford Farm and other Final Phase cemeteries. Not only are interpretations impeded by the limited bone and artefact preservation but it is unclear when in the funeral the cadaver was concealed from view (*i.e.* was it when the body was lain in-state after which the coffin remained closed, or else was the coffin only finally closed within the grave itself). Despite these many uncertainties, some broad points can be made from the available evidence.

The interaction between material culture in both mortuary display and mortuary consignment can be recognised at Harford Farm as well as in other wealthy female-gendered burial assemblages of the later seventh and early eighth centuries. For instance, grave 93 from the Boss Hall cemetery from Ipswich in Essex produced a composite brooch with evidence of repair and of some antiquity when buried. Over fifty years old when buried in the early eighth century, the brooch was placed together with a gold and silver necklace and a silver toilet set in a box and not as a visible part of the burial costume (Webster and Backhouse 1991, 51–3; Scull 2009, 120). In grave 4275 at the nearby Buttermarket cemetery, a necklet was enclosed within a pouch at the waist of an adult female (Scull 2009, 152–154, 283). Meanwhile, grave 14 at Lechlade in Gloucestershire contained a female aged between 14 and 16 years. A silver pin-suite and a necklace of silver-wire rings, silver pendants on silver-wire rings and beads together with a mounted beaver tooth pendant were all found at the neck forming a part of the mortuary costume. However the other items including iron shears, a cowrie shell, fragments of a glass vessel, glass beads and a 'relic-box' were hidden from view within a wooden box left of the lower legs of the internment (Boyle *et. al.* 1998, 58–9, 156). A further example is the isolated adult female from the Eton Rowing Lake site. Suspended from her neck was an heirloom (an old and broken silver ring). Meanwhile a broken amethyst pendant formed part of a 'bag collection' together with two bronze discs, an iron nail, a lead object, bone rod and bronze strap (Boyle *et al.* 2002, 31–3). These items were found underneath the left pelvis, perhaps suggesting a deliberate element of concealment within the grave. The same 'concealed' location of a bag collection was noticed in a late seventh or early eighth century female grave from Orsett, Essex (Webster 1985). This theme appears even among the wealthiest female graves of the period, as with the Swallowcliffe Down bed-burial inserted into a prehistoric burial mound high on the downland of southern Wiltshire. This disturbed grave lacks a complete assemblage, yet we can recognise that many of the artefacts were contained within vessels and boxes, themselves possibly covered with textiles during the sequence of the burial rituals (Speake 1989; see Williams 2006, 28–30).

Set against this wider context, the review of the five wealthy female graves at Harford Farm shows a more complex and layered relationship between the cadaver and artefacts in the mortuary process. The selection of objects were not simply 'personal possessions and jewellery' linked to 'mundane' associations (Penn 2000, 98) nor simply offerings indicative of Christian devotion (Crawford 2004). Moreover, it is the contention that reducing the objects to define the graves' occupants' social or religious identity overlooks the commemorative significance of staging both display and consignment in early medieval mortuary practices. In this regard, artefacts were displayed and disposed of to create specific menmonic connections to the dead among the living. For example, locking objects in caskets and sealing them in bags and containers may have defined an intimate engagement between the living and the dead through gift-giving.

A focus on the 'meaning' of the artefacts found in the wealthy graves from Harford Farm is only partially successful. The artefacts selected did not compose a single message. Instead, it appears that artefacts were associated with a constellation of practices and the display and management of the female body (*e.g.* jewellery and toilet implements). Moreover, we have seen the importance of the artefacts selected for their amuletic properties (including crosses) that may perhaps have been intended to protect the body in life and in death through magic (whether pagan or Christian). There are objects that may have had significant biographical histories (some were very old when interred like the pin-set inside the relic box in grave 18) as well as apotropaic and symbolic qualities. Finally there are objects connected with the household and household activities, including the casket with lock and key in grave 18 and the shears in graves 22 and 28. The burial of the key with the box may have in itself been a statement of consignment and dedication; only the dead person could access its contents in the grave (Buckberry *pers. comm.*). Perhaps most importantly, only those allowed to engage with the cadaver at close quarters during the mortuary practices leading up to the burial would have known what was interred within.

Engendered Bodies

What connects this diverse material culture is an association with the social construction of the body and the body's use to mediate the relational identities of the living and the deceased. Moreover the artefacts deployed were significant because of their use, not simply through their design and form. They were associated with bodily management but also ways of doing things, what Connerton refers to as 'bodily practices' (see Connerton 1989). The placing and consignment of these objects within the grave may have been intended to evoke a wider set of ideals and metaphors concerning the identity of selected female adults in life and upon their death. These may have concerned with the household and agricultural production as well as concerns over spiritual protection. Gender construction and commemoration is also a powerful theme. In other words, an idealised concept of the social person was constructed and rendered memorable within the grave through its composition and subsequent consignment (see Fowler 2004; Williams 2006).

Why were rich collections of artefacts only afforded to selected adult females? Certainly it would be problematic to 'read-off' the social status of the graves' occupants directly from the wealth afforded to them in death. However, it may be possible to suggest a specific significance for certain adult females in a community's social structure and commemorative strategies that meant their deaths demanded particular mortuary practices of this kind. As custodians of the future in their roles as potential or real mothers, female-members of households may have been regarded as a particular loss for the community if they died untimely or 'bad' deaths. Similarly, given the prominent role envisaged for certain women in early medieval mourning rituals, these were individuals who may have had a special role as custodians of the past, mediating and configuring social memory for families as well as the wider community (see Innes 2001). This dual function for particular women may have drawn upon traditional pre-Christian perceptions of the continuity-crisis instigated by adult-female deaths (see Williams 2007) and the roles of particular women as practitioners of magic and possibly control over funerary and mourning rituals (*e.g.* Dickinson 1993; see also Geake 2003; Price 2002). It may have also been enhanced by the particular status afforded to certain women in the earliest stages of the conversion process as envisaged for both Anglo-Saxon England and Scandinavia (Blair 2005; Gräslund 2003; Staecker 2003). The commemorative role of early Christian women in Anglo-Saxon England and their subsequent prominent mortuary commemoration has tended to focus on those women that took up the monastic life and the cults that developed around their graves (*e.g.* Karkov 2003). Yet this may have been only one facet in the role of women in mortuary commemoration. The deaths of these particular aristocratic women may have equally mediated the identities and social memories of secular communities. The strategic deployment of selected artefacts could have defined such group histories through mortuary commemoration, marking both the end of artefact circulation and inheritance and new beginnings for the community and family (see also Sayer 2009).

Therefore, these individuals were not necessarily any more 'high status' or 'less Christian' because of the presence of grave goods in comparison with other contemporary inhumations with no or few artefacts. Instead, the investment in wealth was intended to promote social memory through the gendered cadaver by the survivors. What is becoming increasingly clear to archaeologists is that while the deployment of artefacts became sporadic and varied in later Anglo-Saxon England (Hadley 2000; 2002) and persisted intermittently throughout the later Middle Ages (Williams 2003; Gilchrist and Sloane 2005, 228–30), it remained a deliberate choice in mortuary commemoration used at particular times to protect the dead physically and spiritually but also to mediate their commemoration. In other words, these rich female grave assemblages reflected the influence of Christian conversion and kingdom formation in broad terms but more specifically they indicate new concepts of the female aristocratic body as a medium for constituting gendered and elite identities. Material culture connected to the body's appearance, management and protection as well as bodily practices mediated these embodied identities in the mortuary context when consigned to the grave with the cadaver.

Objects of Memory

The contextual evidence from the Harford Farm therefore allows a more qualified perspective on the commemorative significance of Final Phase grave goods. Moreover, indirectly, this encourages an alternate perspective on the mnemonics of objects with biographies like those found at the Harford Farm cemetery. The traditional view of the end of grave goods regards their absence from graves as evidence that they were instead paid to the king as tax or replaced by elite gifts to the church and/or investment in more effective and enduring above-ground commemorative media including mausolea and chapels (*e.g.* Bullough 1983). This argument remains important. However, middle Anglo-Saxon England between the late seventh and early ninth century is renowned for a set of well-preserved but poorly-provenanced high-status sets of jewellery and other items of treasure from the Witham Pins to the Coppergate Helmet (Webster and Backhouse 1991). Dawn Hadley (2001, 108–9) and Sally Crawford (2004) have both recognised the continued importance of portable artefacts in ritual exchanges into the Christian era. In this light, although these items are no longer placed in graves, they were prestige objects that were commissioned and displayed by elites, circulated among the living, given to the Church and disposed of in watery places (Stocker and Everson 2003) and within settlements (Thomas 2008). Detached from a secure mortuary context, the evidence is patchy and ambiguous. Yet it is tempting, drawing upon contemporary written and archaeological sources, to consider an enduring and complex set of practices by which portable artefacts retained a mnemonic efficacy through circulation and disposal. These uses of portable artefacts can be understood in terms of new Christian commemorative media as well as in terms of an aristocratic class sustaining their social relations and inventing group histories through the use of material culture in complex patterns of gift-giving and ritual practices (see Bazelmans 2000; Hadley 2001, 108–9). For example, Heinrich Härke (2000) has developed this argument using both later Anglo-Saxon written sources and archaeological evidence to show the ritual circulation of weapons in particular may have served in social reproduction and political legitimisation in which ritual deposition and exchange were constituent elements. It is not difficult to extend this argument to envisage parallel cycles of circulation related other artefacts such as jewellery, amulets and vessels focusing on the aristocratic hall (see Bazelmans 2000). Through their production/acquisition, exchange as gifts, display within treasuries and ritual deposition, these exchanges made them objects of memory (Llilios 1999); artefacts that through their decoration, form, inscriptions and the stories attached to them, recorded and commemorated the alliances and identities of those associated with their 'life-histories'. These relationships could have incorporated the commemoration of the dead if they were inherited and if they were gifted to the church in exchange for prayers for the dead. In such an environment, we can suggest that selected artefacts – including both weapons and jewellery – were more than repositories of economic wealth, but valued mnemonic tools that connected the living and the dead through their use and circulation (see also Devlin 2009). Indeed, we might view this ritual and commemorative exchange of artefacts instigated by elites in the Christian early Middle Ages as the secular basis upon which the circulation of saint's relics was able to thrive (Geary 1986).

In this light, the deposition of objects of considerable value and age in graves at sites like Harford Farm might be regarded less as the tail-end of furnished burial and more as evidence for increasingly sophisticated strategies in which portable artefacts were selectively deployed in mortuary and commemorative exchanges. It is therefore possible to regard the decline in grave-goods deposition as heralding an enhanced commemorative role for jewellery and weapons as *objects of memory* – accruing prestige and associations through their circulation among the living rather than their deposition with the dead.

Conclusion

Portable artefacts served in the commemoration of the dead through *both* their transformation and burial with the cadaver *and* their circulation among the living in the later fifth and sixth centuries AD in southern and eastern England (Williams 2005). Here, the argument has been extended to suggest that artefacts in Final Phase graves retained their commemorative significance but were deployed in novel ways. In the later seventh and eighth centuries, certain female-gendered artefacts used in regimes of body management and adornment accrued a mnemonic significance through their mortuary display and consignment through staged and sequential association with the cadaver. Moreover, the development of kingdoms and Christian-influenced aristocratic concepts of the body and material culture provided the potential for select artefacts to take on even more complex mnemonic roles. Rather than the replacement of portable artefacts with monuments as a medium for early medieval commemoration (*e.g.* Effros 2003, 200–18), this evidence instead suggests that the final end of furnished burial marked a new significance of jewellery and weapons in mortuary commemoration through their display and gift-giving among the living. The aristocratic hall and the church both provided important settings in which portable material culture mediated social memories and identities. In this sense, the Final Phase female assemblages from Harford Farm illustrate both the commemorative use of artefacts in the construction of the aristocratic engendered body and an enhanced role for artefacts as objects of memory in the seventh century and beyond.

Acknowledgements

This paper reflects the development of arguments originally made in Williams 2006: 65–78. Thanks to East Anglian Archaeology for permission to reproduce the illustrations and to Seán Goddard for re-drawing them. Thanks to Jo Buckberry, Annia Cherryson, Elizabeth Williams and the anonymous referee for commenting on earlier versions of the paper.

References

Arnold, C. J. (1997) *An Archaeology of the Early Anglo-Saxon Kingdoms.* (2nd edition). London, Routledge.

Bazelmans, J. (2000) Beyond Power. Ceremonial Exchanges in *Beowulf.* In: Theuws, F. and Nelson, J. L. (eds.) *Rituals of Power from Late Antiquity to the Early Middle Ages*, 311–375. Leiden, Brill.

Bazelmans, J. (2002) Moralities of dress and the dress of the dead in early medieval Europe. In: Hamilakis, Y. Pluciennik, M. and Tarlow, S. (eds.) *Thinking through the Body: Archaeologies of Corporeality*, 71–84. New York: Kluwer/Plenum.

Blair, J. (2005) *The Church in Anglo-Saxon Society.* Oxford, Oxford University Press.

Boddington, A. (1990) Models of Burial, Settlement and Worship: The Final Phase Reviewed. In: Southworth, E. (ed.) *Anglo-Saxon Cemeteries: A Reappraisal*, 177–199. Stroud, Sutton.

Boyle, A., Hacking, P., Allen, T. and Ambers, J. (2002) The Anglo-Saxon grave from Boveney. In: Foreman, S., Hiller, J. and Petts, D. (eds.) *Gathering the people, settling the land: The Archaeology of a middle Thames landscape: Anglo-Saxon to post-medieval*, 28–34. Thames Valley Landscapes Monograph 14. Oxford, Oxford Archaeology.

Boyle, A., Jennings, D., Miles, D. and Palmer, S. (1998) *The Anglo-Saxon Cemetery at Butler's Field, Lechlade, Gloucestershire*. Thames Valley Landscapes Monograph 10. Oxford, Oxford Archaeological Unit.

Bullough, D. A. (1983) Burial, Community and Belief in the Early Medieval West. In: Wormald, P. (ed.) *Ideal and Reality in Frankish and Anglo-Saxon Society*, 175–201. Oxford: Clarendon.

Cannon, A. (1989) The Historical Dimension in Mortuary Expressions of Status and Sentiment. *Current Anthropology* 30(4), 4–58.

Carver, M. (1989) Kingship and material culture in early Anglo-Saxon East Anglia. In: Bassett, S. (ed.) *The Origins of the Anglo-Saxon kingdoms*, 141–158. Leicester, Leicester University Press.

Carver, M. (2000) Burial as Poetry: The Context of Treasure in Anglo-Saxon Graves. In: Tyler, E. (ed.) *Treasure in the Medieval West*, 25–48. York, York Medieval Press.

Connerton, P. (1989) *How Societies Remember*. Cambridge, Cambridge University Press.

Crawford, S. (1993) Children, death and the afterlife in Anglo-Saxon England. In: Filmer-Sankey, W. (ed.) *Anglo-Saxon Studies in Archaeology and History* 6, 83–91. Oxford: Oxbow.

Crawford, S. (2004) Votive deposition, religion and the Anglo-Saxon furnished burial ritual. *World Archaeology* 36(1), 83–102.

Devlin, Z. (2009) The end of Anglo-Saxon furnished burial: an interdisciplinary perspective. In: Devlin, Z. L. and Holas-Clark, C. N. J. (eds) *Approaching Interdisciplinarity: Archaeology, History and the Study of Early Medieval Britain, c. 400-1100*, 28-37. British Archaeological Reports British Series 486. Oxford, Archaeopress.

Dickinson, T. (1993) An Anglo-Saxon 'Cunning Woman' from Bidford-upon-Avon. In: Carver, M. (ed.) *In Search of Cult: Archaeological Investigations in Honour of Philip Rahtz*, 45–54. Woodbridge, Boydell.

Effros, B. (2002) *Caring for Body and Soul*. Pennsylvania, Pennsylvania State University Press.

Effros, B. (2003) *Merovingian Mortuary Archaeology and the Making of the Early Middle Ages*. Berkeley, University of California Press.

Fowler, C. (2004) *The Archaeology of Personhood*. London, Routledge.

Geake, H. (1997) *The Use of Grave-Goods in Conversion-Period England*. British Archaeological Reports British Series 261. Oxford, British Archaeological Reports.

Geake, H. (1999) When were Hanging Bowls deposited in Anglo-Saxon graves? *Medieval Archaeology* 43, 1–18.

Geake, H. (2002) Persistent problems in the study of Conversion-Period burials in England. In: Lucy, S. and Reynolds, A. (eds.) *Burial in Early Medieval England and Wales*, 144–155. The Society for Medieval Archaeology Monograph 17. Leeds, Society for Medieval Archaeology.

Geake, H. (2003) The Control of Burial Practice in middle Anglo-Saxon England. In: Carver, M. (ed.) *The Cross Goes North: Processes of Conversion in Northern Europe, AD 300–1300*, 259–270. Woodbridge, Boydell.

Geary, P. (1986) Sacred commodities: the circulation of medieval relics. In: Appadurai, A. (ed.) *The Social Life of Things: Commodities in Cultural Perspective*, 169–191. Cambridge, Cambridge University Press.

Gilchrist, R. and Sloane, B. (2005) *Requiem: The Medieval Monastic Cemetery in Britain*. London, Museum of London.

Gräslund (2003) The Role of Scandinavian Women in Christianisation: the Neglected Evidence. In: Carver, M. (ed.) *The Cross Goes North: Processes of Conversion in Northern Europe, AD 300–1300*, 483–496. Woodbridge, Boydell.

Hadley, D. M. (2000) Burial practice in the Northern Danelaw, *c.* 650–1100, *Northern History* 36, 199–216.

Hadley, D. M. (2001) *Death in Medieval England*. Stroud, Tempus.

Hadley, D. M. (2002) Burial Practices in Northern England in the Later Anglo-Saxon Period. In: Lucy, S. and Reynolds, A. (eds.) *Burial in Early Medieval England and Wales*, 209–228. The Society for Medieval Archaeology Monograph 17. Leeds, Society for Medieval Archaeology.

Halsall, G. (2003) Burial Writes: Graves, Texts and Time in Early Merovingian Northern Gaul. In: Jarnut, J. and Wemhoff, M. (eds.) *Erinnerungskultur im Bestattungsritual*, 61–74. Munich, Wilhelm Fink.

Härke, H. (1992) Changing Symbols in a Changing Society: the Anglo-Saxon weapon burial rite in the seventh century. In: Carver, M. (ed.) *The Age of Sutton Hoo*, 149–166. Woodbridge, Boydell.

Härke, H. (2000) The Circulation of Weapons in Anglo-Saxon Society. In: Theuws, F. and Nelson, J. L. (eds.) *Rituals of Power From Late Antiquity to the Early Middle Ages*, 377–399. Leiden, Brill.

Hines, J. (2000) The runic inscription on the composite brooch from grave 11. In: Penn, K. (ed.) *Excavations on the Norwich Southern Bypass, 1989–91 Part II: The Anglo-Saxon Cemetery at Harford Farm, Caistor St Edmund, Norfolk*, 81–82. East Anglian Archaeology Report 92. Gressenhall, East Anglian Archaeology.

Hoggett, R. (2007) Charting Conversion: Burial as a Barometer of Belief? In: Semple, S. and Williams, H. (eds.) *Early Medieval Mortuary Practices. Anglo-Saxon Studies in Archaeology and History* 14, 27–37. Oxford, Oxford University School for Archaeology.

Innes, M. (2001) Keeping it in the family: women and aristocratic memory, 700–1200. In: van Houts, E. (ed.) *Medieval Memories: Men, Women and the Past, 700–1300*, 17–35. London, Longman.

Jones, A. (2003) Technologies of Remembrance. In: Williams, H. (ed.) *Archaeologies of Remembrance: death and memory in past societies*, 65–88. New York, Kluwer/Plenum.

Karkov, C. E. (2003) The Body of St Æthelthryth: Desire, Conversion and Reform in Anglo-Saxon England. In: Carver, M. (ed.) *The Cross Goes North*, 397–411. Woodbridge, Boydell.

Leeds, E. T. (1936) *Early Anglo-Saxon Art and Archaeology*. Oxford, Clarendon.

Llilios, K. T. (1999) Objects of Memory: The Ethnography and Archaeology of Heirlooms. *Journal of Archaeological Method and Theory* 6(3), 235–62.

Loveluck, C. (1996) The Development of the Anglo-Saxon Landscape: Economy and Society 'On Driffield', East Yorkshire, 400–750 AD. In: Griffiths, D. (ed.) *Anglo-Saxon Studies in Archaeology and History* 9, 25–48. Oxford, Oxford University Committee for Archaeology.

Lucy, S. J. (1998) *The Early Anglo-Saxon Cemeteries of East Yorkshire: An Analysis and Re-interpretation*. British Archaeological Reports British Series 272. Oxford, Archaeopress.

Marzinzik, S. (2000) Grave goods in Conversion Period and later burials – a case of early medieval religious double standards? In: Pollmann, K. (ed.) *Double Standards in the Ancient and Medieval World*, 149–166. Göttingen, Göttinger Forum für Altertumswissenschaften, Beihefte 1.

Marzinzik, S. (2003) *Early Anglo-Saxon Belt Buckles (late 5th to early 8th centuries AD): Their classification and context.* British Archaeological Reports British Series 357. Oxford, Archaeopress.

Meaney, A. (1981) *Anglo-Saxon Amulets and Curing Stones*, British Archaeological Reports British Series 96. Oxford, British Archaeological Reports.

Meaney, A. (2003) Anglo-Saxon Pagan and Early Christian Attitudes to the Dead. In: Carver, M. (ed.) *The Cross Goes North,* 229–242. Woodbridge, Boydell.

Meaney, A. L. and Hawkes, S. C. (1970) *Two Anglo-Saxon Cemeteries at Winnall.* The Society for Medieval Archaeology Monograph 4. London, Society for Medieval Archaeology.

Penn, K. (2000) *Excavations on the Norwich Southern Bypas, 1989–91 Part II: The Anglo-Saxon Cemetery at Harford Farm, Caistor St Edmund, Norfolk.* East Anglian Archaeology Report 92. Gressenhall, East Anglian Archaeology.

Pluskowski, A. and Patrick, P. (2003) How do you pray to God?' Fragmentation and Variety in Early Medieval Christianity. In: Carver, M. (ed.) *The Cross Goes North,* 29–57. Woodbridge, Boydell.

Price, N. (2002) *The Viking Way: Religion and War in Late Iron Age Scandinavia.* Uppsala, University of Uppsala.

Sayer, D. (2009) Laws, funerals and cemetery organisation: the seventh-century Kentish family. In: Sayer, D. and Williams, H. (eds) *Mortuary Practices and Social Identities in the Middle Ages*, 141-69, Exeter, University of Exeter Press.

Scull, C. (2009) *Early Medieval (Late 5th- Early 8th Centuries AD) Cemeteries at Boss Hall and Buttermarket, Ipswich, Suffolk*, The Society for Medieval Archaeology Monograph 27. London, Society for Medieval Archaeology.

Semple, S. (2003) Burials and Political Boundaries in the Avebury Region, North Wiltshire. In: Griffiths, D., Reynolds, A. and Semple, S. (eds.) *Anglo-Saxon Studies in Archaeology and History* 12, 72–91. Oxford, Oxbow.

Shephard, J. (1979) The Social Identity of the Individual in Isolated Barrows and Barrow Cemeteries in Anglo-Saxon England. In: Burnham, B. C. and Kingsbury, J. (eds.) *Space, Hierarchy and Society. Interdisciplinary Studies in Social Area Analysis*, 47–79. British Archaeological Reports International Series 59. Oxford, British Archaeological Reports.

Speake, G. (1989) *A Saxon Bed Burial on Swallowcliffe Down.* English Heritage Archaeological Report 10. London, Historic Buildings and Monuments Commission for England.

Staecker, J. (2003) The Cross Goes North: Christian Symbols and Scandinavian Women. In: Carver, M. (ed.) *The Cross Goes North,* 463–482. York, York Medieval Press.

Stocker, D. and Everson, P. 2003. The Straight and Narrow Way: Fenland Causeways and the Conversion of the Landscape in the Witham Valley, Lincolnshire. In: Carver, M. (ed.) *The Cross Goes North*, 271–288. York, York Medieval Press.

Stoodley, N. (1999) Burial rites, Gender and the Creation of Kingdoms: the Evidence from seventh-century Wessex. In: Dickinson, T. and Griffiths, D. (eds.) *The Making of Kingdoms: Anglo-Saxon Studies in Archaeology and History 10*, 99–108. Oxford: Oxford University Committee for Archaeology.

Stoodley, N. (2007) New Perspectives on Cemetery Relocation in the Seventh Century AD: the Example of Portway, Andover. In: Semple, S. and Williams, H. (eds.) *Early Medieval Mortuary Practices. Anglo-Saxon Studies in Archaeology and History* 14, 154–162. Oxford, Oxford School of Archaeology.

Theuws, F. (1999) Changing settlement patterns, burial grounds and the symbolic construction of ancestors and communities in the late Merovingian southern Netherlands. In Fabech, C. and Ringtved, J. (eds.) *Settlement and Landscape*, 337–349. Moesgård, Jutland Archaeological Society.

Thomas, G. (2008) The symbolic lives of Late Anglo-Saxon settlements: a cellared structure and iron hoard from Bishopstone, East Sussex, *Archaeological Journal* 165: 334–398.

Webster, L. (1985) The grave goods. In Hedges, J. and Buckley, D. Anglo-Saxon burials and later features excavated at Orsett, Essex, 1975, *Medieval Archaeology* 29: 9–14 (1–24).

Webster, L. and Backhouse, J. (eds.) (1991) *The Making of England: Anglo-Saxon Art and Culture AD 600–900.* Toronto, University of Toronto Press.

Williams, H. (2003) Remembering and Forgetting the Medieval Dead. In: Williams, H. (ed.) *Archaeologies of Remembrance. Death and Memory in Past Societies*, 227–254. New York, Kluwer/Plenum.

Williams, H. (2005) Keeping the dead at arms length: Memory, weaponry and early medieval mortuary technologies. *Journal of Social Archaeology* 5(2), 253–275.

Williams, H. (2006) *Death and Memory in Early Medieval Britain.* Cambridge, Cambridge University Press.

Williams, H. (2007) Depicting Gender & Genealogy: cists, cairns and symbols in early medieval northern Britain. *Cambridge Archaeological Journal* 17(2), 145–164.

3. Burial Practice in Seventh-Century Hampshire: St Mary's Stadium in Context

Nick Stoodley

Introduction – The Saints Come Home

In August 2001 Southampton Football Club (a.k.a. The Saints) played the first match in their new stadium. The site chosen was in the St Mary's area of the city, an appropriate location because the club was formed by members of St Mary's Church in 1885. It was known however to overlap with the mainly eighth- to ninth-century mercantile settlement of Hamwic (Andrews 1997; Morton 1992), and the potential for disturbing archaeological deposits was high. This was confirmed by an evaluation in late 1998 and early 1999 and the subsequent excavation by Wessex Archaeology revealed and recorded a complex range of burials and settlement features (Birbeck 2005).

The focus of this article is an assessment of the burial archaeology from these excavations. In the first half the range and variety of practices at St Mary's will be described and discussed while in the second half the information will be evaluated by comparing it to contemporary practice both locally in Southampton and in the wider context of Hampshire. The enquiry will also include Bargates, Christchurch (Dorset) (Jarvis 1983), originally in the historic county boundaries of Hampshire and the two cemeteries investigated at Apple Down (West Sussex) (Down and Welch 1990) which are located close to the Hampshire border and demonstrate very similar practices to the southern Hampshire group of cemeteries (Stoodley *forthcoming*).

It will be argued that during the seventh and early eighth-century mortuary behaviour in Hampshire is characterised by a hitherto unexpected degree of diversity. This is witnessed in the type of rite, the form of the cemetery and its location in the landscape, and is a finding that is in contrast to the traditional image presented by the final-phase model. Explanations for this diverse range of mortuary strategies will be sought in the specific political and cultural circumstances affecting Hampshire at this time.

Accommodating the Ancestors

The new home of Southampton F.C. covers an area of 4.5 ha, lying one km east of the city centre and about 100 m to the west of the River Itchen (Figure 3.1); although in Saxon times the site would have been very close to the shore of the Itchen and the waterfront area of the middle Saxon Emporium. Intervention took place in those areas that were directly affected by the development *i.e.* the stands. Archaeology in the areas of the football pitch and the car parks surrounding the stadium was preserved *in situ*, a strategy that has made the interpretation of the site problematic – the presence of further burials and other deposits underneath the pitch is strongly suspected.

An interesting aside is that it took Southampton six games before they recorded their first home win at St Mary's and in some quarters the disturbance of the Saxon dead was held responsible for this dismal performance!

The Early Cemetery

The following details have been kept brief and are intended to highlight the main points. A full description and discussion can be found in the report published by Wessex Archaeology (Birbeck 2005). Two separate burial grounds were excavated. In the north (Northam) stand a group of unaccompanied inhumations were discovered that exhibit a very similar rite to burials from Hamwic. In addition, a single radiocarbon date (burial 7381) gave a calibrated date of AD 650–950 (expressed at the 95% confidence level) supporting the notion that the inhumations belonged to a cemetery of the later eighth and ninth century. In the west (Kingsland) stand part of a mixed rite cemetery was discovered (Figure 3.2). And a possible outlier to this group consisting of a double inhumation of two adults with weapons was found in the south (Chapel) stand.

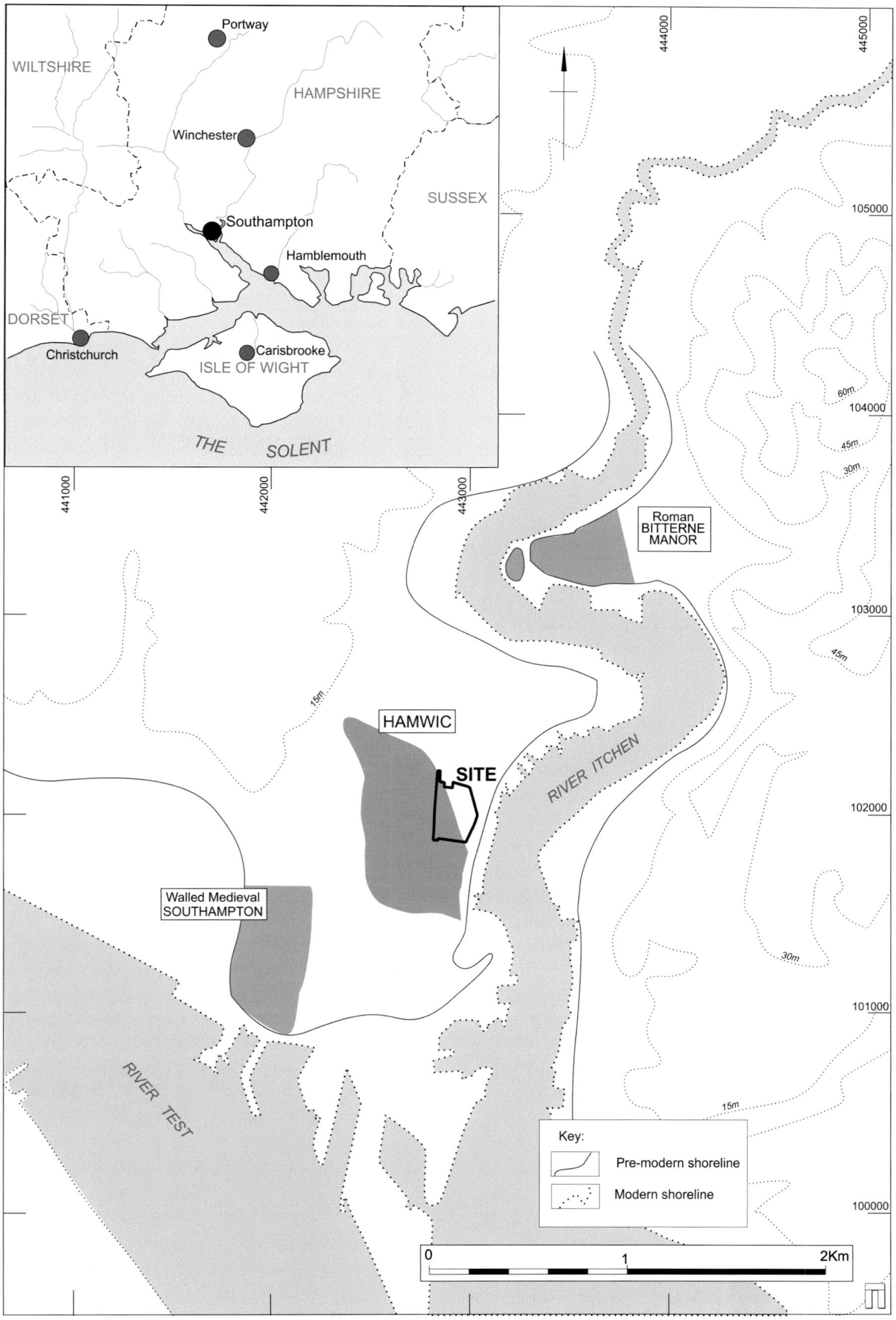

Figure 3.1: Location of St Mary's cemetery (Birbeck 2005, fig. 1).

Grave	Material	Context/urn	Result BP	Calibrated result (2 sigma)
7138	charcoal *Corylus*	7140	1245 ± 40	cal AD 670–880
7138	cremated human bone	7140	1510 ± 45	cal AD 430–630
5106	charcoal *Corylus*	5107	1350 ± 40	cal AD 610–770
5114	charcoal *Corylus*	5115	1420 ± 45	cal AD 550–680
5134	cremated human bone	5135	1540 ± 45	cal AD 420–610
7381	human bone	7381	1245 ± 70	cal AD 650–95

Table 3.1: Radiocarbon dates (after Allen 2005, table 1).

It is the group of graves in the west stand that is the main focus of this article. Before turning to examine these graves it should be mentioned that in 1975 at SOU 20, just to the west of the Kingsland stand, two weapon burials of probable late seventh-century date were found (Holdsworth 1980) and given their proximity they almost certainly indicate the continuance of the St Mary's cemetery in this direction.

In total the investigations produced 26 inhumations in 25 graves and 18 cremations. An examination of the arrangement of the main group of graves demonstrates little evidence for any coherent organisation. The two rites are to a certain extent separate which incidentally is similar to what is found in some sixth-century burial grounds in Hampshire, *e.g.* Portway East (Cook and Dacre 1985), although different spatial relationships are also noted, for example at Worthy Park (Hawkes and Grainger 2003) the two rites are intermingled. It is possible that at St Mary's the graves may have been placed in rough rows, but on the available evidence it does not appear to have been a managed cemetery in the same way that some of the final-phase burial grounds are. Burials belonging to different ages and sexes are interspersed throughout the excavated area. It should be cautioned that because of the incompleteness of the excavation and the poor bone preservation, which has resulted in a lack of sex and age determinations for some burials, we cannot be certain of this, however. Overall, it is interesting that the layout and organisation of St Mary's has more in common with the rural sixth-century cemeteries in Hampshire, than the later final-phase grounds, a suggestion that has also been made for the earlier of the Hamwic cemeteries (Scull 2001, 71–2).

The dating of the inhumation graves is dependent on the associated artefacts and allows several to be placed in the period of the later seventh to early eighth century. Determining the date of the cremations was somewhat more problematic because of the lack of diagnostic artefacts and vessel forms and fabrics, although the predominance of organic-tempered wares may point to a date as early as the sixth century for some of the vessels (Mepham 2005, 26–27). To help clarify the picture a series of radiocarbon dates were taken from calcined bone and samples of charcoal (Table 3.1). The results from the charcoal are considered more accurate because the radiocarbon dating of cremated bone is still in an experimental stage and has produced dates considerably earlier than that returned by independently dated material (Allen 2005, 11–13). A similar finding was returned by St Mary's burial 7138.

Overall, the combined information from both burial traditions strongly indicates that the cemetery was founded before the establishment of Hamwic, possibly as early as the sixth century, but that for a time during the seventh century the two rites were contemporary. The presence of cremation taking place during the seventh century, although relatively rare, is not without parallels: the cemeteries of Apple Down I (Down and Welch 1990) and Weston Colley, Micheldever, (Fern and Stoodley 2005) have both produced late cremations (see below). At St Mary's the radiocarbon dates from the charcoal provided a date range from the late sixth to late ninth century, although the survival of this rite post 700 is considered unlikely. Its decline during the seventh century has traditionally been seen as resulting from Christian belief and ideas about how the dead should be treated (Boddington 1990, 179–82). Strong archaeological evidence is provided by the absence of such deposits in final-phase cemeteries. Moreover there is a lack of associations between cremated remains and later types of pottery fabrics, although it is possible that less visible forms, such as unurned deposits may have outlived the seventh century. The important point is that for a time during the seventh century both practices were being followed at St Mary's – there was a choice of methods of disposal available to this community.

The Graves

Let us turn to survey the different rites starting with the cremations. All the excavated remains were found urned and were mainly contained within simple rounded jar/bowl forms, although two had been buried in biconical jars (Figure 3.3). Seven of the urns were burnished and six had decoration that including tooling, stamps and bosses (Mepham 2005, 24). Twelve of the burials sustained damage through later cultivation and building activity (Mepham 2005, 23) and it is possible that evidence for any unurned deposits may have been lost altogether. A few fragmentary pyre goods were retrieved from the deposits, such as the ivory bag ring from grave 5126. The most notable is a circular bone or antler object decorated with a ring and dot motif from grave 7138. The lack of accompanying artefacts is generally typical of cremation in Hampshire (Table 3.2) and is clearly illustrated by the examples from Portway East: most of the identified objects are the remains of heat-distorted dress accessories. Similar findings are

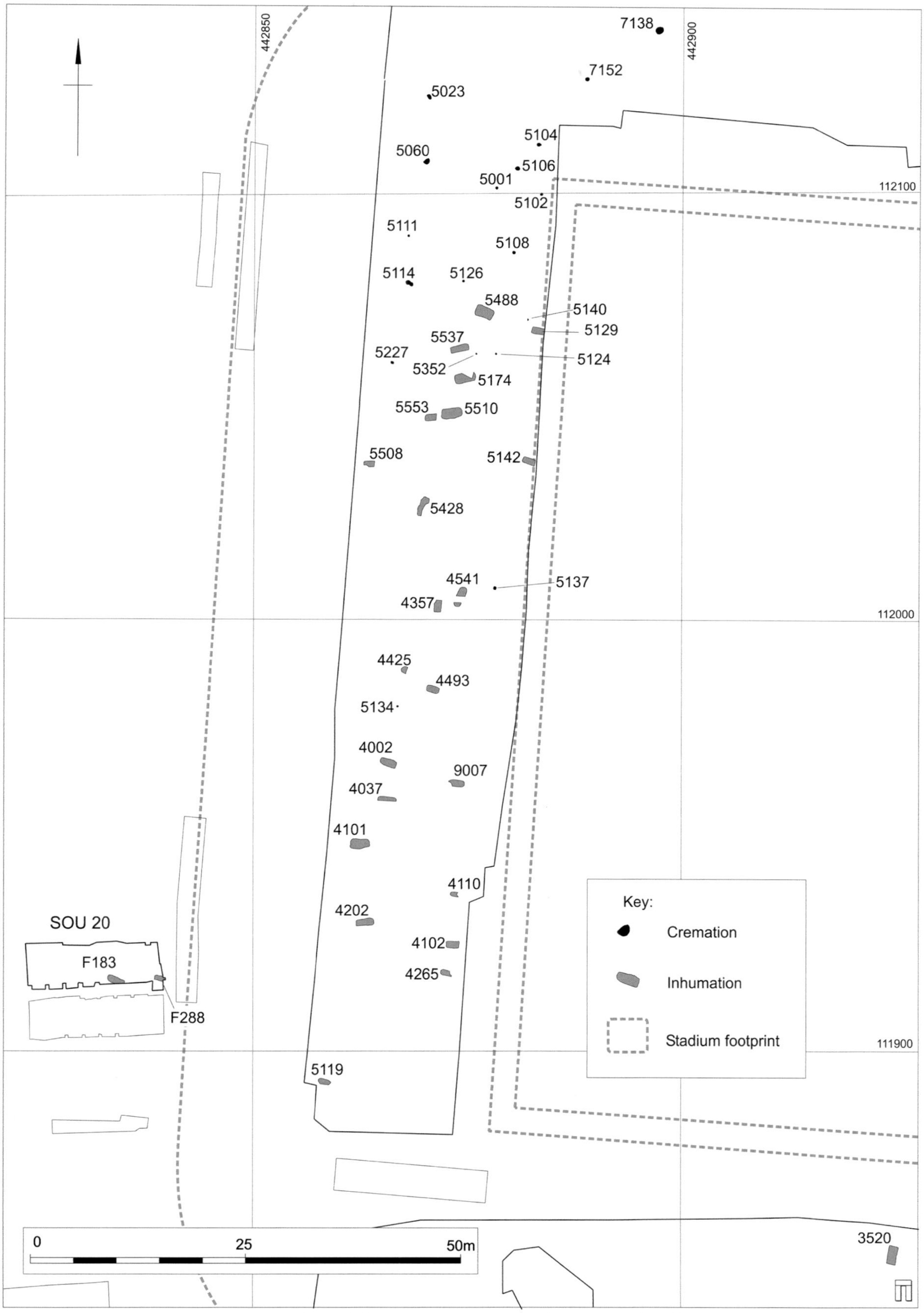

Figure 3.2: Seventh- to earlier eighth-century cemetery under the West Stand (Birbeck 2005, fig. 9).

Cemetery	No. cremations	No. urned cremations	No. with grave/pyre goods
Alton	46	*c*.27	13
Apple Down I	*c*.63	34	18
Portway East	*c*.87	65	17
Worthy Park	46	46	9

Table 3.2: Fifth- to sixth-century cremations in Hampshire (note: Apple Down I also includes several seventh-century cremations).

true of Apple Down and Worthy Park (Hawkes and Grainger 2003), although for the latter the objects tend to consist of toilet items. The St Mary's burials exhibit other features that are typical of cremation in Hampshire. The first point of interest is the generally low quantity of cremated bone in the deposits: at St Mary's the weight varies considerably with an overall range of 7.9–697.3g, and a mean for the adult deposits of 301.8g (McKinley 2005, 21–22). This is very different to the situation in Anglian areas where a greater quantity of material is found, but is similar to the situation in other south of England cemeteries (McKinley 2005, 22). Likewise, a regional distinction in mortuary behaviour is evidenced by the lack of additional individuals found in the urns from St Mary's and elsewhere in southern England (McKinley 2005). And finally, the examples from St Mary's and Hampshire typically have a low percentage of cremated animals and pyre debris, which again differs to the north and east of the country (McKinley 2005). The St Mary's cremations seem to belong to a distinctive practice that was established in Hampshire probably sometime during the fifth century and represents a real regional difference within southern England. To illustrate this we can take a quick look at the evidence provided by the Upper Thames Valley cemetery at Abingdon (Oxfordshire) (Leeds and Harden 1936). This was a mixed rite burial ground that produced 82 cremations and makes for a particularly good example because of the extensiveness of the excavations and, for its time, the careful recording of deposits. Of the cremations, 38 were contained within vessels displaying decorative motifs and 34 were discovered to have had pyre goods. The majority of the objects were toilet implements, but a wide range of other objects were also recovered, such as items of jewellery, personal equipment, such as four knives, and the fragmentary remains of vessels.

It is now time to briefly survey the evidence provided by the inhumations. Grave structure is generally standardised and unspectacular: sub-rectangular pits, several individuals were encoffined and a couple also had their location marked with posts. All the burials were laid out extended supine and all but the grave in the south stand contained a single interment: G3520 of two individuals both with weapons (a poorly preserved unsexed adult of 18 years or older and another unsexed adult judged to be between 25 and 35 years of age). The author's analysis of the multiple burial rite has shown that pairings of two adults of the same sex is rare, especially if both are accompanied by weapons (Stoodley 2002b, 112–14). Given the unusual nature of this grave it is tempting to view it as an outlier and spatially separate from the other interments, although this idea has to remain conjectural because of the large expanse of unexcavated ground beneath the football pitch. The majority of the pits were orientated west-east (n=19), although a small group recorded a north-south (n=4) alignment and this variation is more typical of early Anglo-Saxon burial practice (Stoodley 1999a, 63–4; fig. 54) and contrasts with the standardised layout typical of final-phase cemeteries.

The evidence is starting to demonstrate that within the context of the seventh and eighth century St Mary's is unusual and this is reinforced by the grave goods. In the excavated sample, 21 of the 26 interments (*c.*80%), were provided with artefacts and this is surprisingly high given the cemetery's date (Figure 3.4). The majority of the burials produced simple assemblages, such as a knife and buckle, and is generally typical of the time, but several burials clearly stand out. Two of the females illustrate this: grave 4202 (a possible female adult of 18–25 years) interred with a wooden box containing amongst other objects a decorated silver disc, two silver sceattas and a necklace made up of four silver *bullae* pendants, four glass beads and a gold pendant; and 5508 (a female of late adolescence or young adult age) accompanied with a necklace comprising a gold pendant inland with garnets, a silver intaglio ring and two glass beads. At the time of their discovery, the presence of gold jewellery grabbed the headlines and claims about the high status of the occupants were made, although it should be noted that such wealth is not out of step with some of the better furnished females from final-phase cemeteries (Stoodley 2002a, 323–24) (see below). The quantity of individuals interred with weapons (n=10/42%) is genuinely noteworthy, however. As a percentage of the adult sample this is a comparable figure to that recorded by the male populations in Hampshire's early Anglo-Saxon cemeteries: Andover (60%), Worthy Park (56%) and Alton (40%). It is not only the quantity of weapon burials that requires comment, but also the character of several of the assemblages. Grave 5352 produced a pair of spears, a seax and a shield, while 5537 was accompanied by a sword, seax, two spears and a shield (Figure 3.5). The latter is a very unusual combination indeed and such complexity is rare outside the tier of seventh-century princely and aristocratic burials. This pair easily ranks amongst the most complex and wealthy that Hampshire has so far had to offer.

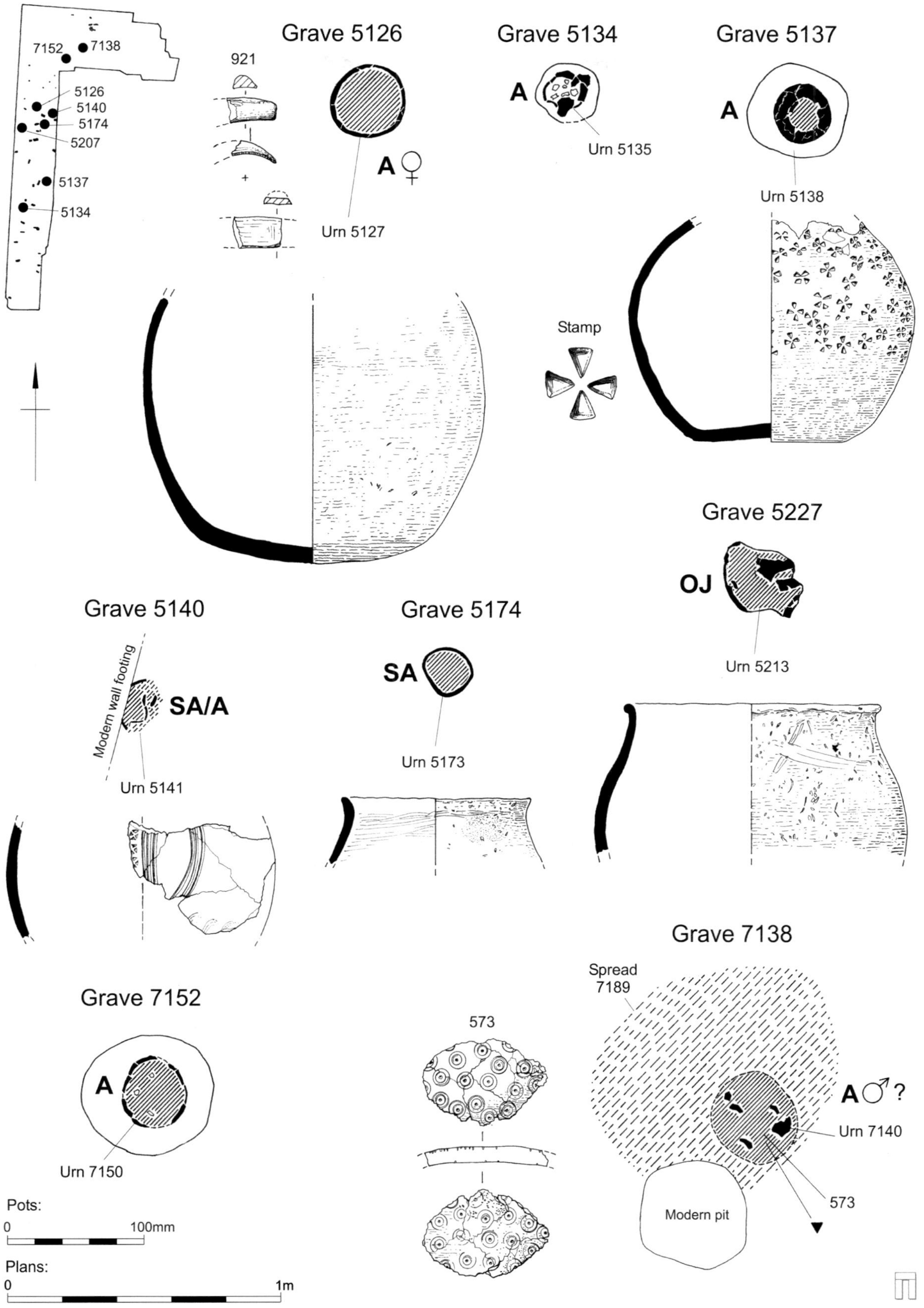

Figure 3.3: Cremation burials 5126–7152 (Birbeck 2005, fig. 11).

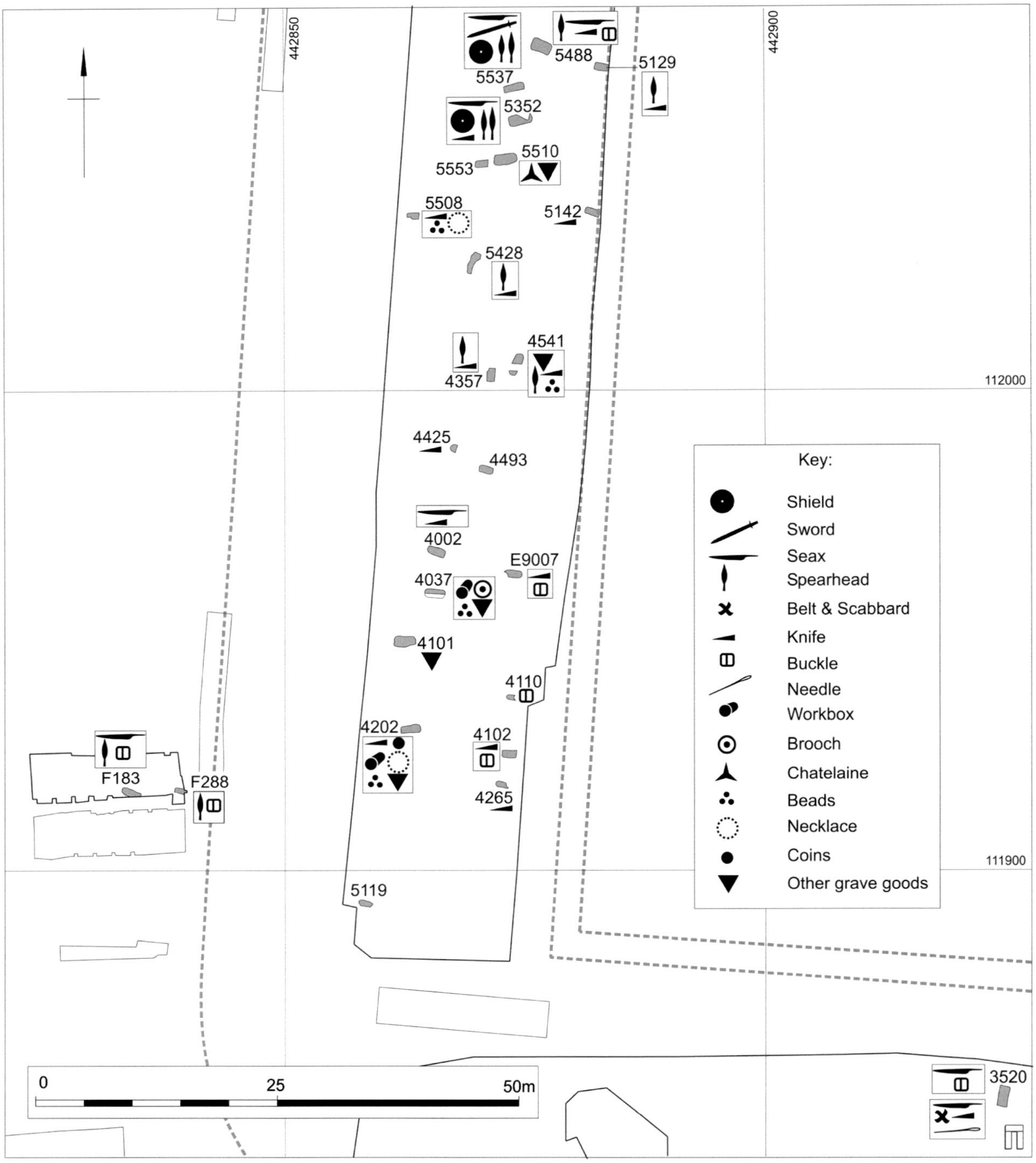

Figure 3.4: Distribution and composition of grave good assemblages (inhumations) (Birbeck 2005, fig. 31).

St Mary's and Southampton

The burials from St Mary's will probably always enjoy a high profile in the archaeological literature, but it is quite probable that this was not the only location available for burial in the immediate area. Excavations in the St Mary's area of the city have produced evidence for several cemeteries that have been dated to the earliest phase of Hamwic's occupation. But on closer inspection a number of the burials do not look out of place in the later seventh century. For example 200m west of the stadium at SOU 32/47 a grave with beads and one with a glass vessel was excavated. Moreover evidence of a penannular ditch was found (Morton 1992, 171–176) and a sample of human bone gave a radiocarbon date of the late seventh to eighth century for one of the burials. At a similar distance,

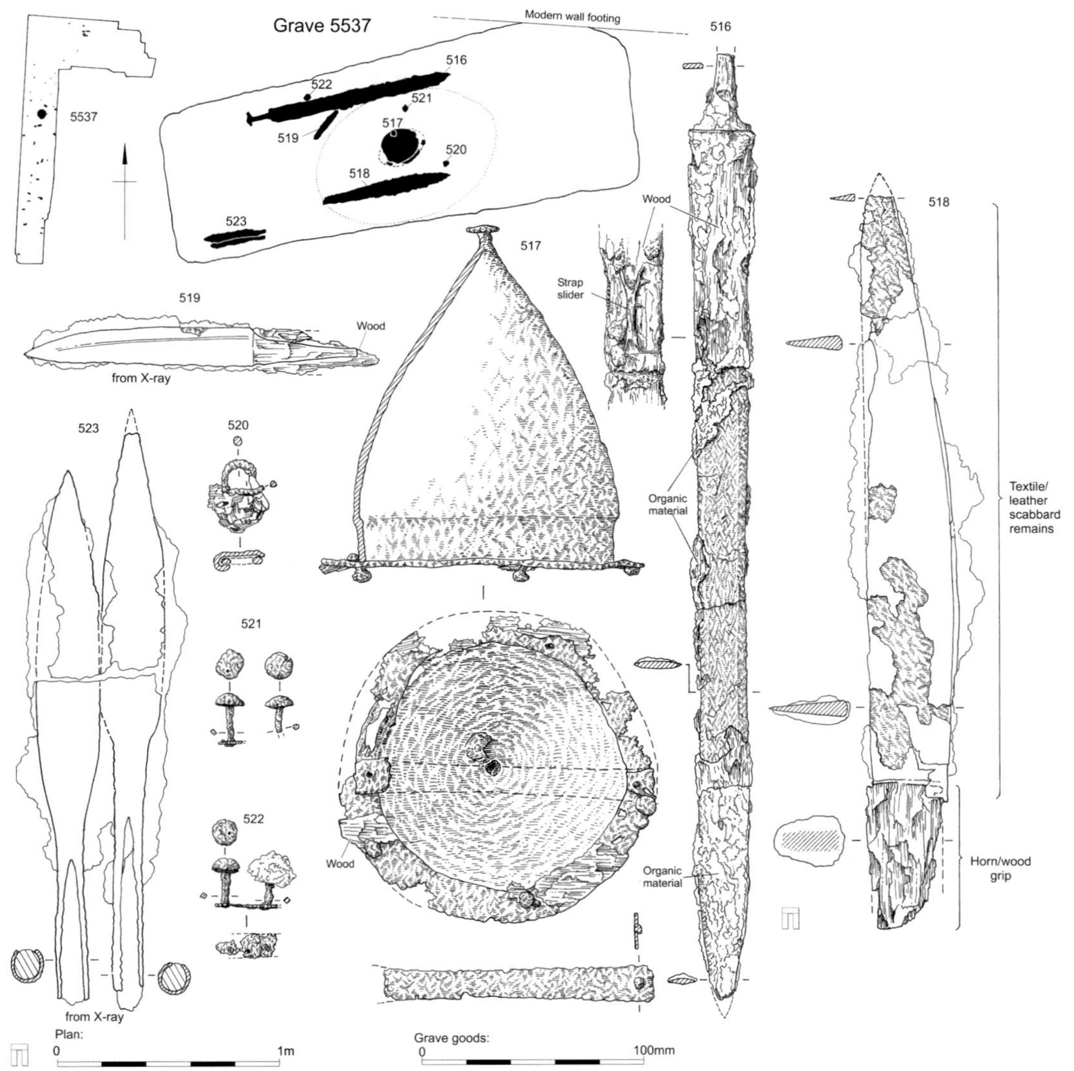

Figure 3.5: Grave goods accompanying G5537 (Birbeck 2005, figs 27 and 28).

but to the south-west, at SOU 34/43/48 an interment with keys, pin and a glass vessel was investigated (Morton 1992, 51), while *c.*500m to the south-west at the cemetery focussing on Cook Street (SOU 254/823), several graves were enclosed by annular and penannular ditches (Garner 1994; Garner and Vincent 1997; Garner 2001). One burial was accompanied by a knife and set of linked pins and along with several unstratified pins, knives and a chain suggest a point of origin in the later seventh century.

Before we leave Southampton we should not overlook the very intriguing discoveries made in the Roman site at Bitterne Manor. Over the years numerous graves have been encountered and at least some of them are contemporary with St Mary's. For example, a burial was found with a Swanton Type C2 spearhead (found predominantly in the seventh century) from a group of at least six interments excavated at the corner of Hawkeswood Road and Bitterne Road (SOU 414) (Stoodley 2004), while 15 skeletons were recorded at Bitterne road in 1998 (SOU 862), two producing radiocarbon dates of AD 640–687 and AD 564–775 (SAS108/SOU862) (Southern Archaeological Services 1998).

Another important issue is the landscape context of St Mary's and the Bitterne cemetery. We have already noted that St Mary's would have been close to the Saxon waterfront and was not occupying an elevated location typical of Hampshire's early cemeteries. In addition, the graves are relatively well spaced and all could have been covered by small earthen barrows, although it should be cautioned that no evidence for such features was found. In several instances there is enough room to permit a larger earthwork, for example graves 4202 and 5428 both have an area of about 10m separating them from their closest neighbours. These putative features would have increased the visibility of the cemetery within the context of the mouth of the Itchen and the immediately surrounding

Cemetery	Predominant orientation	No. of graves with multiple burial and no. with consecutive burials
Bargates	south west-north east	0/0
Bedhampton	west-east	13/3
Apple Down I	south-north	0/0
Apple Down II	west-east	2/2
Ports Down I	west-east	6/6
Portway West	south-north	2/1
Snell's Corner	south-north	1/1
Winnall II	west-east	2/0

Table 3.3: Hampshire cemeteries in the sample (note Apple Down I = identified seventh-century burials only).

area. St Mary's was very close to the shoreline and it can be suggested that it was deliberately sited in order to be in clear view of traffic coming in and out of the mouth of the Itchen. This was an important river and appears to have been home to numerous agricultural communities by the seventh century (Stoodley 2005, 190), in addition to the old civitas capital of Venta Belgarum (Winchester) that was to emerge as an important religious centre with the founding of the Old Minster in the later seventh century (Yorke 1982). The spatial relationship of St Mary's to the river and the later settlement is different to the pattern exhibited at both Ipswich and London. Like at Hamwic the sites of these important middle Saxon wics produced an early phase of burial, but it is interesting that at both the dead were located on the edge of settlement activity in a location that placed them away from the waterfront (Scull 2002, 308, fig. 4).

The cemetery located in the Roman settlement of Bitterne raises many interesting questions, but in a different way. In particular, what was the site's relationship to the community burying downriver on the opposite side of the river at St Mary's? Was it just another suitable location for burial, or given its location on the east side of the Itchen, did it serve a separate and independent community? It is notable that the cemetery was again in a strategically important position: on a promontory on a bend of the Itchen (Fig. 3.1). But it is also enclosed within the old Roman walls and would presumably have been screened from view. Are we seeing evidence for a different burial tradition whereby the presence of physical boundaries was more important than visual prominence, or alternatively did it result from a deliberate strategy imposed on the group, perhaps by the elite of St Mary's, who wished to conceal the memory and also political significance of other groups in the area? It is in this context that the distinctively different burial customs at St Mary's can perhaps be explained: a strategy whereby the group articulated their separateness to the surrounding communities by way of the long-lasting visibility afforded by the inhumation graves and the short-lived, but impressive, spectacle of cremation (for the latter see Williams 2006, 90–93).

St Mary's and Burial in Seventh – Eighth Century Hampshire

The article will now consider how the evidence from St Mary's compares to contemporary practice in the county. Hampshire is relatively well served by cemeteries of the seventh- to earlier eighth-century date. The most famous is Winnall II (Meaney and Hawkes 1970) – an archetype final-phase cemetery, yet there are others and each demonstrates distinctive features, which along with St Mary's reveals a scene that was both dynamic and multifaceted.

In order to facilitate a comparison the same themes that were examined at St Mary's will now be considered beginning with the method of disposal. Inhumation is the predominant rite, although cremation is present in several of the sites. It has been identified at Apple Down I (West Sussex) by several unstratified artefacts, and by cremations 159 and 43A and B that are dated to the seventh century (Down and Welch 1990, 108). The latter (43A) was cut into a ring-ditch surrounding an unurned cremation deposit. It produced a garnet stud of seventh-century date and was in turn overlaid by an unurned cremation (43B) thus demonstrating a sequence of late cremations. At Weston Colley, Micheldever (Hampshire), the ring-ditch surrounding a seventh-century female inhumation was closely associated with a number of disturbed cremation deposits (Fern and Stoodley 2005, 17) (Figure 3.6). The pit of at least one of these was overlying the ditch and the sherds are of a stylistically late organic fabric originally in the form of a long necked bag-shaped pot (Jacobs 2006). It is intriguing that Apple Down I and Weston Colley are both cemeteries that pre-date the seventh century. The careful reanalysis of other cemeteries, coupled with a programme of selective radiocarbon dating, might reveal the presence of late cremations in other long-lived sites. Overall, what is important here is that St Mary's was not the only community in seventh-century Hampshire for which a choice of burial was available.

The next topic to discuss is cemetery layout and organisation. At St Mary's two separate alignments are observed and across Hampshire a variety of orientations are also noted (Table 3.3). Grave direction may have been determined by several different factors such as local topographic features serving as boundary markers (Stoodley 2006, 67) and alignment on

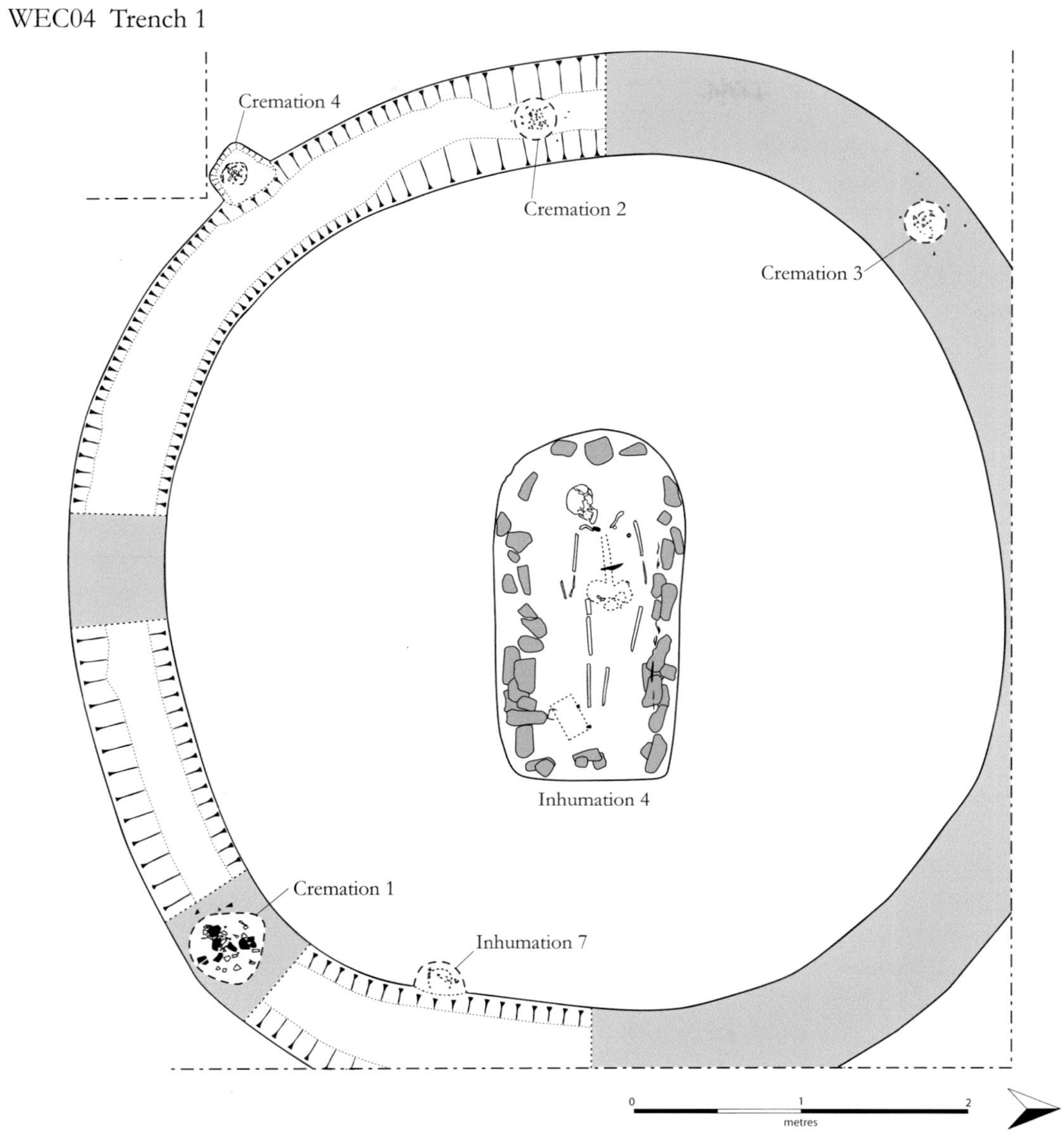

Figure 3.6: Weston Colley Grave 4 (drawn by Chris Fern).

earlier monuments (Williams 1998). The important point in respect of this enquiry is that communities seem to have been able to decide on their own policies governing the laying out and use of burial grounds. Only in the classic final-phase cemeteries, such as Winnall II and Apple Down II, do we encounter anything that can be interpreted as a standard practice with rows of (roughly) aligned west-east graves (Figure 3.7). In some cases it may be that a tradition continues, for example at Portway, Andover: the majority of interments in the migration-period cemetery were south-north following a prehistoric ditch running down the east side of the cemetery that probably served as a boundary (Stoodley 2007). In its successor 800m to the west, the majority of burials also follow this direction. There is no obvious reason for this, although a possible boundary to the Portway land-unit that may have existed in the area could have been responsible (Stoodley 2006, 67). Local concerns and traditions were more important than general notions about how the body should be orientated.

Let us now consider some of the other aspects of the burial rite. St Mary's produced the aforementioned unusual double burial (G3520). It has already been stated that multiple burial during the fifth to seventh century is rare and the examples that we have consist mostly of contemporary interments. It was therefore intriguing that the majority of the cases from the Hampshire sample involved consecutive burials – a grave pit being used over a period of time for burial, often with the earlier interment(s) being badly disturbed during the event (Table 3.3). A particularly good example of the practice is Ports Down I (Corney *et al.* 1969) where five graves produced evidence of consecutive reuse, see especially grave 9 which

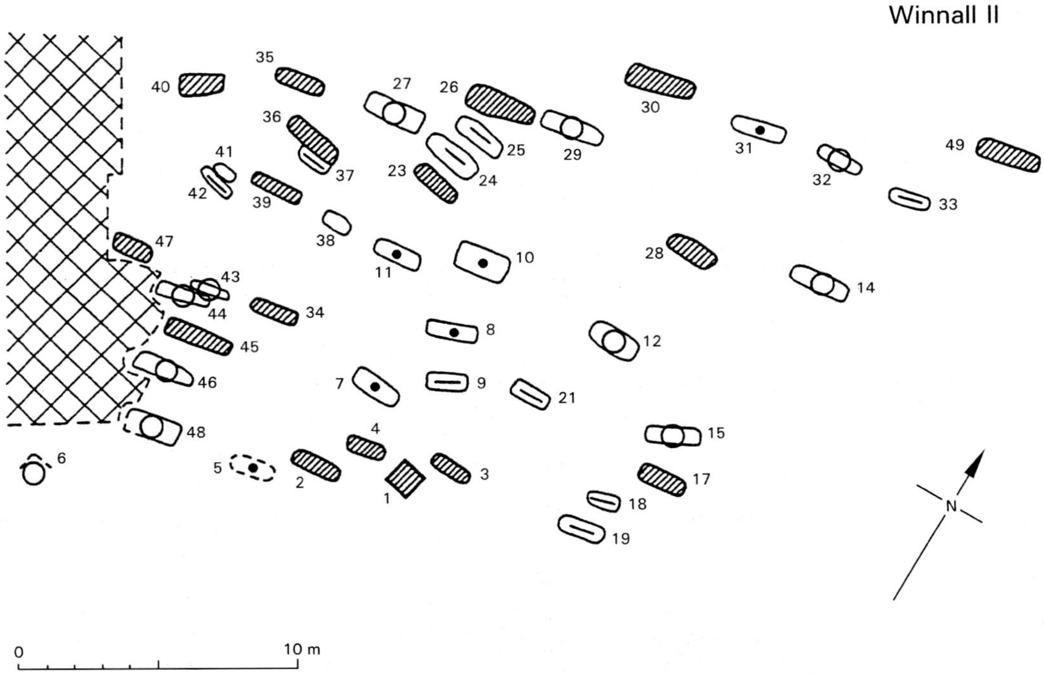

Figure 3.7: Plan of Winnall II. (Key:- Black: weapon burial; shaded: male without weapons; black circle: jewellery burial; open circle: female without jewellery; line: subadult; no symbol: unidentified; black dot: cremation).

contained the remains of three males: the bones of two had been pushed to the edges of the pit in order to accommodate the third interment. At Portway West, grave 3, is a genuine double burial of two (probable) adult males (Stoodley 2006, 67, fig. 3), but in accommodating these two, a primary individual, represented by fragments of clavicles and scapulae, was almost totally destroyed. Not only does this diversity conflict with what we understand to be typical of burial at this time, but it is also an action encountered in the later Saxon period. For example, at Bevis Grave, Bedhampton, a cemetery stretching from the seventh to tenth century a mix of contemporary and consecutive multiple burials are found and two of the latter (graves 48 and 49) involved disturbance to earlier burials (Stoodley 2002b, 109, fig. 1).

Diversity can also be observed in attitudes to the laying out of the corpse and how it was treated. An example illustrating this is the aforementioned multiple burial from Portway West. Both the males were headless and they were also located a short distance away from another, possibly, headless male who had been interred in a barrow ditch on his side (grave 17) (Stoodley 2006, 67). Investigations at a multiperiod site at Portsdown (George Inn) recovered two inhumations close to a probable long barrow and Iron Age settlement (Bradley and Lewis 1968). Grave 1 is of a seventh- to eighth-century date, while grave 2 is unaccompanied, but the immature occupant appears to have been decapitated (Bradley and Lewis 1968, 41). Earlier discoveries in the area indicate that these interments might have belonged to a larger cemetery that was focussed on the barrow (Bradley and Lewis 1968, 28–30). With these examples we are once again reminded of behaviour more commonly encountered in the late Saxon period – but this time execution cemeteries. It is interesting that at Portway West the individuals may have been buried on the extremities of the cemetery and it can be suggested that they were being marked out, not only by mutilation to the body, but by the spatial location of the graves. Are we observing a strategy by local communities to deal with individuals who had transgressed? If so we might be evidencing an early stage in the development of execution burial. During the early Anglo-Saxon period deviant burials were interred within community cemeteries and a detailed spatial analysis of a number of sites has demonstrated that a conscious decision was made to locate these burials either on the edges of the cemeteries or on the periphery of household burial plots (Reynolds 2009). During the later sixth and seventh century isolated deviant burials start to appear some of which are associated with prehistoric monuments (Reynolds 2009). The above cases from Portway West are therefore intriguing and potentially important especially within the context of the development of execution burial because they seem to represent a synthesis of traditions. On the one hand we have deviants being restricted to the periphery of a community cemetery, while on the other they demonstrate a deliberate association with an earlier monument. It can be argued that Portway presents a local response to the treatment of deviants, but one that was, in the context of seventh- and earlier eighth-century Hampshire, relatively sophisticated.

The final topic that needs to be tackled is perhaps the most complex – the grave goods. We have already noted the unusually wealthy character of several of the St Mary's weapon burials and in Hampshire few burials can compare in complexity to graves 5352 and 5537. There are several seventh-century burials that were well provided for in terms of weapons and other accompanying goods, for example, Alton grave 16 with its sword, shield and pair of spears but this is dated to the first half of the seventh century. In addition, no Hampshire cemeteries have so far produced weapon burials in such quantities. The Bargates cemetery does have an unusually high proportion of weapon burials although none of them are particularly outstanding and it appears to start earlier than St Mary's. In addition, the overall scarcity of barrow burials in Hampshire is interesting especially the lack of examples containing complex weapon assemblages. For example, the famous burial inserted into the earthwork at Oliver's Battery that produced the (Winchester) hanging bowl was only accompanied with a spear and seax (Andrews 1932).

The other side of the coin involves female burials and once again variation is the defining feature of this group. It is noted that women are in the minority in several burial grounds, such as Ports Down I, Snell's Corner (Knocker 1956) and Bargates (Stoodley 1999b) (Figure 3.8). This is a new type of cemetery and one that can be considered to have had strong masculine overtones. Moreover, the provision of female-linked grave goods differs locally. At one end of the scale, the women that do get into the 'masculine' type cemeteries tend not to have jewellery and dress accessories. For example at Bargates and Ports Down I no jewellery was recovered from the graves. At St Mary's in contrast to the weapon burials the investigation only produced four individuals with objects usually associated with females. The difference could however be chronological and the results of the project, *Anglo-Saxon England c.580–720: the Chronological Basis*, should help to clarify this. On the basis of albeit one cemetery, Winnall II, the opposite is true of cemeteries in which weapon burials are unknown or very scarce and where the more even proportion of sexes indicates a burial ground used by a community (Stoodley 1999b). Although it is not an exclusive pattern it seems like a division has taken place with separate locales being used for categories of burial that previously would have been accommodated within the same community ground.

Moreover, when the composition of the jewellery assemblages is studied it is noted that they are rather modest, consisting of a small number of pieces. St Mary's produced the two aforementioned gold pendants, but it is intriguing that these are not accompanied by other artefacts typical of final-phase female costume. Elsewhere in the region a similar finding is observed (Table 3.4) and it can be argued that the burials do not compare well to contemporary interments from other regions, for example at Harford Farm (Norfolk) grave 18

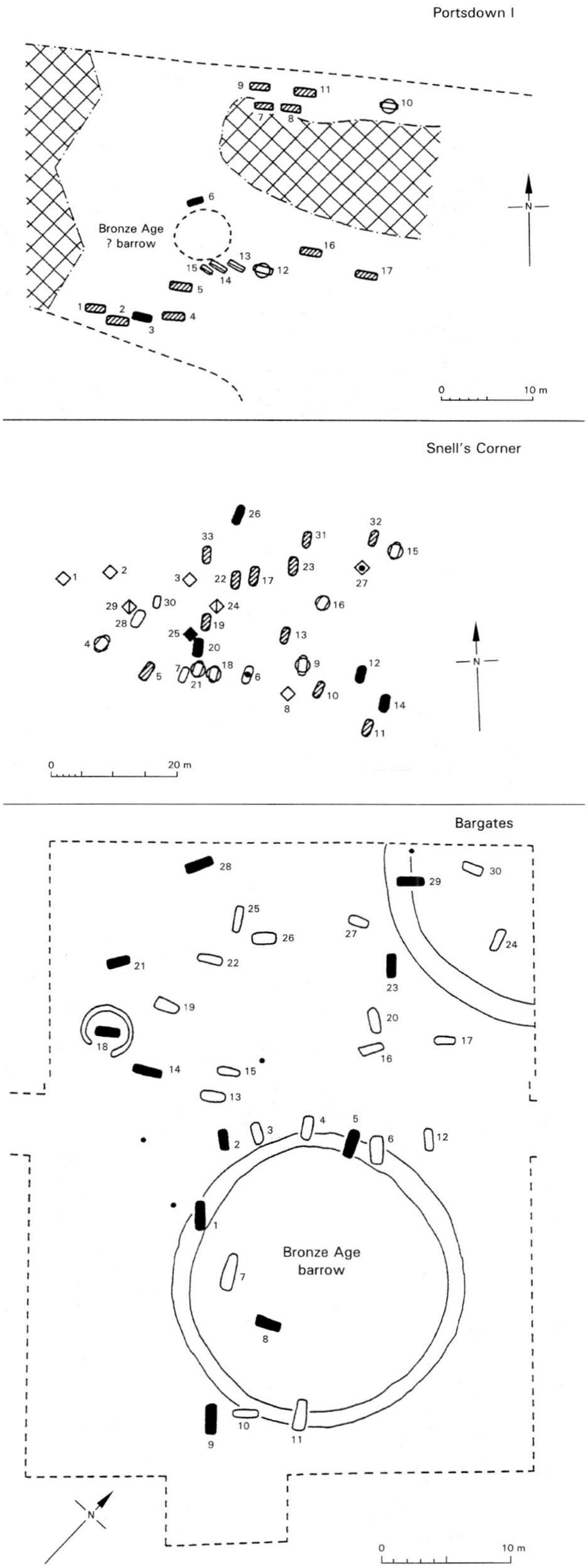

Figure 3.8: Plans of Ports Down I, Snell's Corner and Bargates. (Key:- Black: weapon burial; shaded: male without weapons; black circle: jewellery burial; open circle: female without jewellery; line: subadult; no symbol: unidentified; black dot: cremation).

Cemetery/burial	Jewellery and associated dress items
Apple Down I 48	penannular brooch, knife
Apple Down I 151	pin, bead
Portway West 6	pin, chatelaine
Portway West 11	2 beads
St Mary's 4037	2 beads, bag (ring, brooch, work box), ?key
St Mary's 4202	box (disc), 3 sceattas, necklace inc pendant
St Mary's 5508	necklace inc pendant, intaglio ring
St Mary's 5510	chatelaine
Snell's Corner 6	2 × knife, steel, finger ring, 2 × bracelet, chain, pin, ring, necklet
Snell's Corner 28	knife, bead, tags
Winnall II 5	pendant, tags, beads
Winnall II 7	2 × pin, necklet
Winnall II 8	linked pins, 2 × penannular brooches
Winnall II 10	pin, 2 × rings, key
Winnall II 21	disc brooch

Table 3.4: Female assemblages from Hampshire cemeteries.

with amongst other artefacts a wooden vessel, gold and garnet pendant, shears and threadbox (Penn 2000, 18–19) and from Lechlade (Gloucestershire) grave 14 of the numerous grave goods we can highlight the pair of linked silver pins, wooden vessel, combs and necklace of beads and rings (Boyle *et al.* 1998, 58–9). Unlike these, the adult females from Hampshire were not sent to their graves displaying the full ensemble of costume accessories and jewellery. Incidentally on close inspection some of the jewellery is old, worn or consisting of repaired pieces. For example, Winnall II grave 21 produced a broken garnet disc brooch, while the examination of the pendant from grave 5508 at St Mary's has revealed that it was made of garnets that were probably reused from another artefact.

It is possible that this reflects changing attitudes to the deposition of jewellery and the interment now of 'second best' rather than the most treasured pieces in a burial context. Crawford (2004, 91) argues that damaged and repaired objects may not necessarily have had any less value, however; in fact their longevity may have bestowed a greater significance upon them. In a similar manner, artefacts that were mended or created by recycling parts of old objects, such as the aforementioned pendant from St Mary's, could perhaps be seen in the same light. Generally it is wealthier female interments that contain such objects, which Crawford (2004) interprets as the deliberate removal of wealth from circulation, all part of a long-standing practice of votive deposition – a method of conveying religious belief which continued into the seventh century. In seventh-century Hampshire, the deposition of jewellery does become increasingly selective, with certain items remaining in circulation for many years. And if Crawford is correct about the votive aspects of grave good deposition then this represents further evidence for diversity. The general rarity of the practice, however, indicates that it was only a minority of the Hampshire women who may have followed such traditional customs and by implication other ways of signalling religious devotion and adherence were perhaps taking hold.

Discussion and Conclusion

The overriding aim of this article has been to describe and explain how burial practice in seventh- and earlier eighth-century Hampshire was one of complexity. It has established that this existed at several different levels: the type of cemetery available for the disposal of the dead, the option of whether to cremate or inhume, the principles on which a cemetery was organised and certain specific aspects of the ritual. In addition, the evidence demonstrates that burial experiences a period of transition which encompasses much more than changes to the quantity and styles of the grave goods. Hampshire demonstrates a synthesis of traditions some that demonstrate the continuance of earlier traditions, while in others we seem to be observing the origins of practices that were to become typical of the late Saxon period. It is a dynamic scene with little overall standardization and is opposite to the traditional picture of burial outlined in the final-phase model. Yet by its very nature this complexity makes interpretation problematic. The fact that it is happening concomitantly on several different societal levels may help us to break it down and offer some tentative explanations however.

For a start burial communities appear to have had a certain degree of control over how they organised their cemeteries and structured the burial practices that took place within them. This is similar to the early period and is seen by the continuance of practices such as the presence of both the rites of inhumation and cremation and the range of orientations. This might be interpreted as evidence for communities that were looking to the past and creating identities through retrospective behaviour. Yet, alongside this, and often within the same burial ground, practices appear that were rarely encountered before the seventh century and indicate a change in direction. For example, the increasing use that some communities made of multiple burial and in particular the reuse of earlier grave pits seems to mark a change in attitudes to the dead, perhaps new responses to how kin, or other, relationships were preserved, while the disturbance of earlier interments also demonstrates changing views on the sanctity of the dead. The presence of deviant burials and their deliberate restriction to the edge of a burial ground may reflect the development of legal concepts and methods of punishment by some local groups which was to find its ultimate expression in the execution cemeteries of the late Saxon period.

Close analysis of the type of female-linked assemblages reveals a fashion among women for costumes that did not require metal fasteners and other accessories and the apparent lack of a distinctive final-phase costume in Hampshire could be taken as evidence for the emergence of a regional identity centred on female costume, but one that is characterised by its modesty. The small number of women with final-phase dress accessories does seem to indicate that these influences were not being fully embraced in Hampshire. This has implications for any religious interpretations that are placed on the grave goods, especially as we heard earlier, the deposition of jewellery. Can we go a stage further and interpret it as a strategy by which the region signalled its difference to surrounding areas? Hampshire may have been making a deliberate attempt not to connect with the new styles current at this time and the classical associations that they encompass (Geake 1997, 129–136). If this is correct it has implications for the idea that there is a standard female burial costume throughout the country.

The existence of cemeteries of different statuses complicates matters. It is possible to identify three different types of cemetery each with their own distinctive features. Community cemeteries exhibiting a demographic profile made up of different age and gender groups, sites with a bias towards males, and burial grounds in which burial wealth indicates an elite. The community cemeteries are the easiest to deal with in the context of this article because they represent places where individual rural groups buried their dead. It represents a continuation of the field cemetery – a survival from the early period that would also continue into the later Saxon period (Hadley 2001, 36–8). The second type of site can be easily confused with the community cemetery except for the greater proportion of males and weapon burials which marks it out as a separate category. Examples of this type are strategically located, demonstrate a close relationship with harbours and waterways and consequently benefit from a high degree of intervisibility. The distinctive martial nature shared by these cemeteries and their locations in the landscape may suggest that they mark important boundaries and belong to an early stage in the formation of Hampshire. The county's creation can be reconstructed from documentary evidence and is a particularly complex process resulting from the amalgamation of several different groups by the West Saxon kings (Yorke 1989). This process must have been accompanied by a significant degree of political and militarily unrest. Is this the context for the complexity witnessed in the archaeological record? Furthermore, the decision to locate several of the cemeteries around an ancient monument can be seen as a deliberate strategy by which the Saxon dead were portrayed as the rightful descendants of the ancient inhabitants of the land in order to legitimise claims to the territory by linking with a mythical past (Williams 1997, 26). Although women and children are not absent they are in a minority and are buried with less grave wealth. It is the males that benefit from above average wealth both in terms of grave goods and labour expended on the monument. The form of social organisation underlying the establishment and management of such places appears to be different: the emphasis is on commemorating the male and the masculine roles that were important within these contexts.

A similar type of cemetery in terms of its landscape context and high proportion of weapon burials is the St Mary's cemetery. It differs, however, by the greater quantity and quality of the grave goods deposited with several burials. Although wealthy pieces of jewellery were found, it is once again the weapon burials that draw attention to this site. Several burials were accompanied by complex and sophisticated weapon assemblages, which are of a different character altogether to the sets observed in the other Hampshire sites. In fact a good case can be made for its association with a high status settlement, such as a royal estate that was involved in controlling trade in the lower Itchen (Scull 2001, 72; Stoodley 2005, 190; Yorke 1982). In addition to portable wealth its location in a highly visible location by the waterfront must have been intentional to signal the authority of the group to traders and travellers visiting this part of Hampshire.

It is intriguing, however, that wealthy seventh-century barrow burials involving a single or small group of interments are largely absent from the county, especially south of Winchester. These monuments are usually interpreted as representing archaeologically the increasing stratification in society that accompanied the establishment of territory (Scull 1993) and their presence is to be expected in southern Hampshire. It is suggested that isolated barrow burials were not necessarily the only strategy employed in the expression of elite power. In certain locations where a clear sign of authority and power is required, such as at an important point of entry to a territory, alternative methods were chosen: the cemetery becoming intimately linked to the expression of elite power and authority. A similar situation has been suggested for the Avebury region by Sarah Semple (2003) where the spatial and chronological changes that take place have been associated with the development of elite power and the marking out of territory. But it might also find parallels in Scandinavia at places such as Kaupang and Birka and their cemeteries of closely packed mounds that were highly visible to visiting traders and other individuals.

Overall these burial grounds indicate the appearance during the seventh century of new social hierarchies and identities, and a range of different ways in which they were articulated. Is Hampshire unique in this respect? Were regionally distinct mortuary practices also developing in other areas? An obvious point of comparison that bears certain similarities but also some notable differences is Ipswich and its range of cemeteries (Scull 2002). Research may demonstrate that at the beginning of the later Saxon period England was considerably more diverse in terms of burial practice than previously believed. But in order to investigate this detailed analysis is required that considers not only the artefactual evidence but the other aspects of the rite, the organisation of the cemetery and mortuary landscapes.

Acknowledgements

I would like to thank the following for their assistance during the preparation of this article: Annia Cherryson for making available the radiocarbon dates for several Hampshire burials; Andrew Reynolds for sharing his corpus of deviant burials; Andy Russel for providing information about the Bitterne and Hawkeswood road burials and Wessex Archaeology, especially Roland Smith, Jackie McKinley and Lorraine Mepham for valuable information and discussions about the St Mary's Stadium excavations and Julie Gardiner for granting permission to reproduce several figures from the St Mary's monograph. Chris Fern is thanked for giving permission to use Fig. 3.6. Finally I am grateful to Annia Cherryson for her insightful comments on this paper and the anonymous referee's helpful and constructive suggestions and ideas.

References

Allen, M. J. (2005) Radiocarbon dating. In: Birbeck, V. (ed.) *The Origins of Mid-Saxon Southampton: Excavations at the Friends Provident St Mary's Stadium 1998–2000*, 11–13. Wessex Archaeology Report 20. Salisbury, Wessex Archaeology.

Andrews, P. (ed.) (1997) *Excavations at Hamwic: Volume 2, Excavations at Six Dials.* CBA Research Report 109. York, Council for British Archaeology.

Andrews, W. J. (1932) The Winchester Anglo-Saxon bowl and bowl-burial. *Proceedings of the Hampshire Field Club and Archaeological Society* 12(1), 11–19.

Birbeck, V. (ed.) (2005) *The Origins of Mid-Saxon Southampton: Excavations at the Friends Provident St Mary's Stadium 1998–2000.* Wessex Archaeology Report 20. Salisbury, Wessex Archaeology.

Boddington, A. (1990) Models of burial, settlement and worship: the final phase reviewed. In: Southworth, E. (ed.) *Anglo-Saxon Cemeteries: a reappraisal*, 177–199. Slough, Alan Sutton.

Boyle, A., Jennings, D., Miles, D. and Palmer, S. (1998) *The Anglo-Saxon Cemetery at Butler's Field, Lechlade, Gloucestershire.* Thames Valley Landscape Monographs, 10. London, Thames Valley Landscape Monographs.

Bradley, R. and Lewis, E. (1968) Excavations at the George Inn, Portsdown. *Proceedings of the Hampshire Field Club and Archaeological Society* 25, 27–50.

Cook, A. M. and Dacre, M. (1985) *Excavations at Portway, Andover, 1973–1975.* University Committee for Archaeology Monograph 4. Oxford, University Committee for Archaeology.

Corney, A, Ashbee, P, Evison, V. I. and Brothwell, D. (1969) A prehistoric and Anglo-Saxon burial ground, Ports Down, Portsmouth. *Proceedings of the Hampshire Field Club and Archaeological Society* 24, 20–41.

Crawford, S. (2004) Votive deposition, religion and the Anglo-Saxon furnished burial ritual. *World Archaeology*, 36 (1), 87–102.

Down, A. and Welch, M. (1990) *Chichester Excavations 7: Apple Down and the Mardens.* Chichester, Phillmore.

Fern, C. and Stoodley, N. (2005) *The Early Anglo-Saxon Cemetery at Weston Colley, Micheldever, Hampshire: An interim report on excavations and fieldwork undertaken in 2004 and a project design for the 2005 program of investigations.* Unpublished interim report.

Garner, M. F. (1994) Middle Saxon Evidence at Cook Street, Southampton (SOU 254). *Proceedings of the Hampshire Field Club and Archaeological Society* 49, 77–127.

Garner, M. F. (2001) A Middle Saxon cemetery at Cook Street, Southampton. *Proceedings of the Hampshire Field Club and Archaeological Society* 56, 170–191.

Garner, M. F. and Vincent, J. (1997) Further Middle Saxon Evidence at Cook Street, Southampton (SOU 567). *Proceedings of the Hampshire Field Club and Archaeological Society* 52, 77–87.

Geake, H. (1997) *The Use of Grave Goods in Conversion Period England, c.600–850.* British Archaeological Reports British Series 261. Oxford, British Archaeological Reports.

Hadley, D. M. (2001) *Death in Medieval England.* Stroud, Tempus.

Hawkes, S. C. and Grainger, G. (2003) *The Anglo-Saxon Cemetery at Worthy Park, Kingsworthy, near Winchester, Hampshire.* Oxford University School of Archaeology Monograph 59. Oxford, Oxford University School of Archaeology.

Holdsworth, P. (1980) *Excavations at Melbourne Street, Southampton, 1971–6.* Council for British Archaeology Research Report 33. Hertford, Council for British Archaeology.

Jacobs, A. (2006) *The Pottery from Weston Colley, Micheldever.* Unpublished report.

Jarvis, K. (1983) *Excavation in Christchurch, 1969–1980.* Dorset Natural History and Archaeology Society Monograph 5. Dorchester, Dorset Natural History and Archaeology Society.

Knocker, G. M. (1956) Early burials and an Anglo-Saxon cemetery at Snell's Corner, near Horndean, Hampshire. *Proceedings of the Hampshire Field Club and Archaeological Society* 19, 117–171.

Leeds, E. T. and Harden, D. B. (1936) *The Anglo-Saxon cemetery at Abingdon, Berkshire.* Oxford, Ashmolean Museum.

McKinley, J. (2005) The cremated human remains. In: Birbeck, V. (ed.) *The Origins of Mid-Saxon Southampton: Excavations at the Friends Provident St Mary's Stadium 1998–2000*, 17–23. Wessex Archaeology Report 20. Salisbury, Wessex Archaeology.

Meaney, A. L. and Hawkes, S. C. (1970) *Two Anglo-Saxon Cemeteries at Winnall, Winchester, Hampshire.* The Society for Medieval Archaeology Monograph 4. London, Society for Medieval Archaeology.

Mepham, L. (2005) Pottery. In: Birbeck, V. (ed.) *The Origins of Mid-Saxon Southampton: Excavations at the Friends Provident St Mary's Stadium 1998–2000*, 23–27. Wessex Archaeology Report 20. Salisbury, Wessex Archaeology.

Morton, A. (ed.) (1992) *Excavations in Hamwic: Volume 1.* Council for British Archaeology Research Report 84. London, Council for British Archaeology.

Penn, K. (2000) *The Anglo-Saxon cemetery at Harford Farm, Caistor St Edmund, Norfolk.* East Anglian Archaeology Report 92. Dereham, East Anglian Archaeology.

Reynolds, A. (2009) *Anglo-Saxon deviant burial customs.* Oxford, Oxford University Press.

(SAS) Southern Archaeological Services, (1998) *Interim Report on an Archaeological Watching Brief at 75, Bitterne Road, Southampton.* Unpublished client report.

Scull, C. (1993) Archaeology, early Anglo-Saxon society and the origins of Anglo-Saxon Kingdoms. *Anglo-Saxon Studies in Archaeology and History* 6, 65–82.

Scull, C. (2001) Burials at Emporia in England. In: Hill, D. and Cowie, R. (eds.) *Wics. The Early Mediaeval Trading Centres of Northern Europe*, 67–74. Sheffield Archaeological Monographs 14. Sheffield, Sheffield Academic Press.

Scull, C. (2002) Ipswich: development and contacts of an urban precursor in the seventh century. In: Hårdh, B. and Larsson, L. (eds.) *Central Places in the Migration and Merovingian Periods*, 303–316. Lund, Acta Archaeologica Lundensia 8.39.

Semple, S. (2003) Burials and political boundaries in the Avebury Region, North Wiltshire. *Anglo-Saxon Studies in Archaeology and History* 12, 72–91.

Stoodley, N. (1999a) *The Spindle and the Spear: a Critical Enquiry into the Construction and Meaning of Gender in the Early Anglo-Saxon Burial Rite.* British Archaeological Reports British Series 288, Oxford, British Archaeological Reports.

Stoodley, N. (1999b) Burial rites, gender and the creation of kingdoms: the evidence from seventh-century Wessex. *Anglo-Saxon Studies in Archaeology and History* 10, 101–109.

Stoodley, N. (2002a) The origins of Hamwic and its central role in the 7th century as revealed by recent archaeological discoveries. In: Hårdh, B and Larsson, L (eds.), *Central Places in the Migration and Merovingian Periods*, 317–31. Acta Archaeologica Lundensia 8,39, Lund.

Stoodley, N. (2002b) Multiple Burials, Multiple Meanings? Interpreting the early Anglo-Saxon multiple interment? In: Lucy, S. and Reynolds, A. (eds.), *Burial in Early Medieval England,* 103–121. The Society for Medieval Archaeology 17. London, Society for Medieval Archaeology.

Stoodley, N. (2004) *An Anglo-Saxon Spearhead from Bitterne Road, Southampton.* Unpublished client report (Southampton Archaeology).

Stoodley, N. (2005) The early cemetery and its place within southern England. In Birbeck, V. (ed.) 2005 *The Origins of Mid-Saxon Southampton: Excavations at the Friends Provident St Mary's Stadium 1998–2000*, 75–81. Wessex Archaeology Report 20. Salisbury, Wessex Archaeology.

Stoodley, N. (2006) Changing burial practice in seventh-century Hampshire: the Anglo-Saxon cemetery at Portway West, Andover. *Proceedings of the Hampshire Field Club and Archaeological Society* 60, 63–80.

Stoodley, N. (2007) New perspectives in cemetery relocation in the seventh century AD: the example of Portway, Andover. *Anglo-Saxon Studies in Archaeology and History* 14, 154–162.

Stoodley, N. (*forthcoming*) Costume groups in Hampshire and their bearing on the question of Jutish settlement in the sixth century AD.

Williams, H. M. R. (1997) Ancient landscapes and the dead: the reuse of Roman and prehistoric monuments as early Anglo-Saxon burial sites. *Medieval Archaeology* 41, 1–32.

Williams, H. M. R. (1998) Monuments and the past in early Anglo-Saxon England. *World Archaeology* 30 (1), 90–108.

Williams, H. M. R. (2006) *Death and Memory in Early Medieval Britain.* Cambridge, Cambridge University Press.

Yorke, B. A. E. (1982) The foundation of the Old Minster and the status of Winchester in the seventh and eighth centuries. *Proceedings of the Hampshire Field Club and Archaeological Society* 38, 75–84.

Yorke, B. A. E. (1989) The Jutes of Hampshire and Wight and the origins of Wessex. In: Bassett, S. (ed.), *The Origins of Anglo-Saxon Kingdoms*, 84–96. Leicester, Leicester University Press.

4. *'Such a resting-place as is necessary for us in God's sight and fitting in the eyes of the world'*: Saxon Southampton and the Development of Churchyard Burial

Annia Kristina Cherryson

The late Saxon bequest of an estate by Ordnoth and his wife to the Old Minster, Winchester requests that 'on the day of our death they (members of the monastic community) will fetch us with the minster's resources and provide for us such a resting-place as is necessary for us in God's sight and fitting in the eyes of the world' (Whitelock 1930, 19). By the end of the Saxon period, a suitable resting place was perceived to be in consecrated ground either within or adjacent to a church. Few, if any, chose to be interred away from sacred ground and the prospect of the Church's intercession on behalf of their souls. Just as five hundred years earlier in the sixth century, burial as either inhumations or cremations, usually with grave goods, in a field cemetery was an appropriate final resting place. This change from field cemetery to churchyard was a fundamental shift in burial location – one which continues to affect where the dead are interred over 1000 years later and in many ways represents the Church's greatest impact on funerary behaviour during the Anglo-Saxon period. Traditionally, the transition to churchyard burial was thought to have been relatively rapid, occurring over a few generations in the seventh and eighth centuries (Meaney and Hawkes 1970, 51). The validity of this assumption is now increasingly questioned, with recent work suggesting that the transition to churchyard burial was far more complex and protracted than traditionally envisioned (Hadley 2000a, 160; 2000b, 199; 2007; Blair 2005, 245). This paper uses the evidence from early medieval Southampton in Hampshire as a case study to examine the rate at which churchyard burial was adopted and the variation in burial location during the later Anglo-Saxon period.

The origins and development of churchyard burial in the Southampton area

Documentary sources indicate that the first churches appeared in what would become the late Saxon shire of Hampshire during the seventh century. Churches known to have been founded near Southampton included the Old Minster within Winchester's Roman walls some 15 miles away while the abbot of a monastery at Redbridge, approximately 3.5 miles away, interceded in the fate of the last two princes of the Isle of Wight's royal house in AD 686 (ASC F 648 – Swanton 2000, 28; HE III:7 – Sherley-Price 1990, 154; HE IV:16 – Sherley-Price 1990, 231; Hase 1988, 45). These early churches presumably had some form of associated churchyard, probably catering for members of the ecclesiastical community and perhaps a few members of the laity. The conversion process was known to have initially targeted royalty and the nobility (Morris 1989, 91) and it seems probable that at least a few of the newly converted elite may have been interred adjacent to churches. According to the twelfth-century *Annales monasterii de Wintonia,* the seventh-century West Saxon kings Cenwalh, Aescwine and Centwine were interred at the Old Minster in Winchester (Deliyannis 1995, 119). However there is no evidence that the seventh-century Church demanded that the newly converted were interred in churchyards (Geake 1992, 89; Blair 2005, 229). Indeed, there is no evidence to suggest that the early Church was overly concerned where the dead were buried (Bullough 1983, 186). Moreover in the first century of its existence, the Anglo-Saxon church was not in a position to enforce a shift in burial location (Morris 1983, 54). Archaeologically, the evidence for seventh-century churchyard burial in Hampshire is sparse. Burials dating to the late seventh century have been excavated from the churchyard of the Old Minster in Winchester (Kjølbye-Biddle 1992, 222) and it is possible that some of the churchyard burials at SOU13 in Southampton date to the seventh century (see below). Yet while there is paucity of examples of churchyard burial, there is substantial archaeological evidence for burial in Hampshire during this period, in non-churchyard cemeteries such as Winnall II, Ports Down, Snell's Corner, Bevis Grave, and Portway West (Meaney and Hawkes 1970; Corney 1967; Knocker 1955; Rudkin 2001; Stoodley 2006). The archaeological data suggests that lay interment in churchyards was very much a minority rite in seventh- and early eighth-century Hampshire, probably limited to those with close connections to ecclesiastical establishments such as patrons and possibly tenants (Blair 2005, 241). The Church had provided a new alternative location for the population of Hampshire to inter their dead (Hadley 2000a, 160), but at least in the seventh and early-eighth centuries, it was one with a limited appeal. Traditional burial locations, containing the remains of ancestors were not easily discarded for Christian burial in the vicinity of a church (Blair 2005, 58).

So if there was no immediate transition to churchyard burial, how rapidly was churchyard burial adopted by the wider community? Traditional models have viewed the non-churchyard cemeteries of the late seventh and early eighth century as representing the final flourish of pagan burial prior to the rapid adoption of churchyard burial (Meaney and Hawkes 1970, 50–51). The archaeological evidence could be perceived as supporting this hypothesis as the vast majority of early medieval burials known to post-date *c.*AD 800 in Hampshire and Wessex are associated with ecclesiastical buildings (Cherryson 2005, 222–4). Yet this does not necessarily mean that there was a rapid transition to churchyard burial during the eighth century. Most late Saxon churchyards are dated using either radiocarbon dating or stratigraphy, methods which tend to provide a relatively wide chronological range. Moreover, stratigraphic dating usually provides a general date range for the entire cemetery, while cost means only a few burials are radiocarbon dated. Thus, while the period of use of a churchyard can be determined, detecting changes in the level of use is problematic, making it difficult to determine whether churchyard burial was rapidly adopted by the laity in the eighth century or only became commonplace in the tenth and eleventh centuries.

Another way to examine the rate of adoption of churchyard burial is to consider the increasing evidence for the persistence of non-churchyard burial into the late Saxon period, which suggests a slower transition to universal inhumation adjacent to or within a church than traditionally envisioned (Hadley and Buckberry 2005, 127; Hadley 2000a, 160; 2000b, 199; 2007; Blair 2005, 245). In some cases the burials lie in cemeteries that were founded in the seventh century and continued in use into the ninth and tenth centuries, such as Bevis Grave in Hampshire (Rudkin 2001; Cherryson 2005, 228). While other cemeteries, such as the tenth- and eleventh-century cemetery at Chimney and the ninth-century cemetery at Yarnton, both in Oxfordshire, were founded away from any known church, centuries after the introduction of Christianity (Crawford 1989, 54; Hey 2004, 75). The incidence of such burial grounds may be much higher, as demonstrating the presence or absence of associated religious buildings is not always simple if only the part of the sites has been excavated and the timber churches of the middle Saxon period do not leave substantive evidence (Buckberry this volume). Nor were all the non-churchyard burials interred in cemeteries, with increasing numbers of single inhumations or small groups of burials dating to the late Saxon period being identified (Cherryson 2005; Cherryson 2008; Buckberry this volume). Examples in the Wessex area include the two late ninth- or tenth-century burials found at the Brooks in Winchester (Scobie *et al.* 1991, 37) and the three eighth- or ninth-century burials from Shepton Mallet in Somerset (Leach 2001, 31). This evidence for the persistence of non-churchyard burial argues against a rapid adoption of churchyard burial and points to greater diversity in burial location during the later Saxon period, although it should be noted that separation in distance from ecclesiastical buildings does not necessarily equate with freedom from church control. It could be argued that examples of the later Saxon non-churchyard burial are the exceptions that prove the rule. This could be true but such burials are likely to be under-represented in the archaeological record. Recent surveys of Sites and Monuments Records in Wessex (Cherryson 2005) and in Lincolnshire and Yorkshire (Buckberry 2004 and this volume) identified large numbers of undated unaccompanied burials, many not associated with any ecclesiastical structures, some of which are likely to date to the later Saxon period. In addition, poorly furnished field cemeteries with predominately extended west-east burials have tended to be dated to the seventh and early eighth centuries, either on the basis of datable grave goods or, if the grave goods cannot be closely dated, assumed to be of that date. In many cases such assumptions are valid but, as the later field cemetery at Chimney demonstrates, this is not always the case. Moreover, even if some of the burials in a cemetery date to the seventh and early eighth century, do all the burials? Sites like Bevis Grave raise the possibility that other seventh- and eighth-century cemeteries, such as Winnall II, may contain later burials that can only be identified using radiocarbon dating. Further investigation of the continued use of these seventh-century cemeteries, many of which are only partially excavated, is of particular relevance to the understanding of the development of churchyard burial.

One way of illustrating the diversity of burial location and the evolution of churchyard burial during the later Saxon period is by the use of a case study. The city of Southampton lies at the junction of the Rivers Test and Itchen at the top of Southampton Water in Southern Hampshire and contains the sites of the middle Saxon emporium of Hamwic, the Roman settlement of Clausentum and the later Saxon town (Figure 4.1). There has been much debate about the extent to which middle Saxon emporia should be considered urban or whether they were simply some form of proto-urban settlement or urban precursor (Biddle 1976, 114–6; Scull 1997; Morton 1999). Yet whether urban or not, Hamwic represents a settlement of greater size, complexity and, to a degree, density

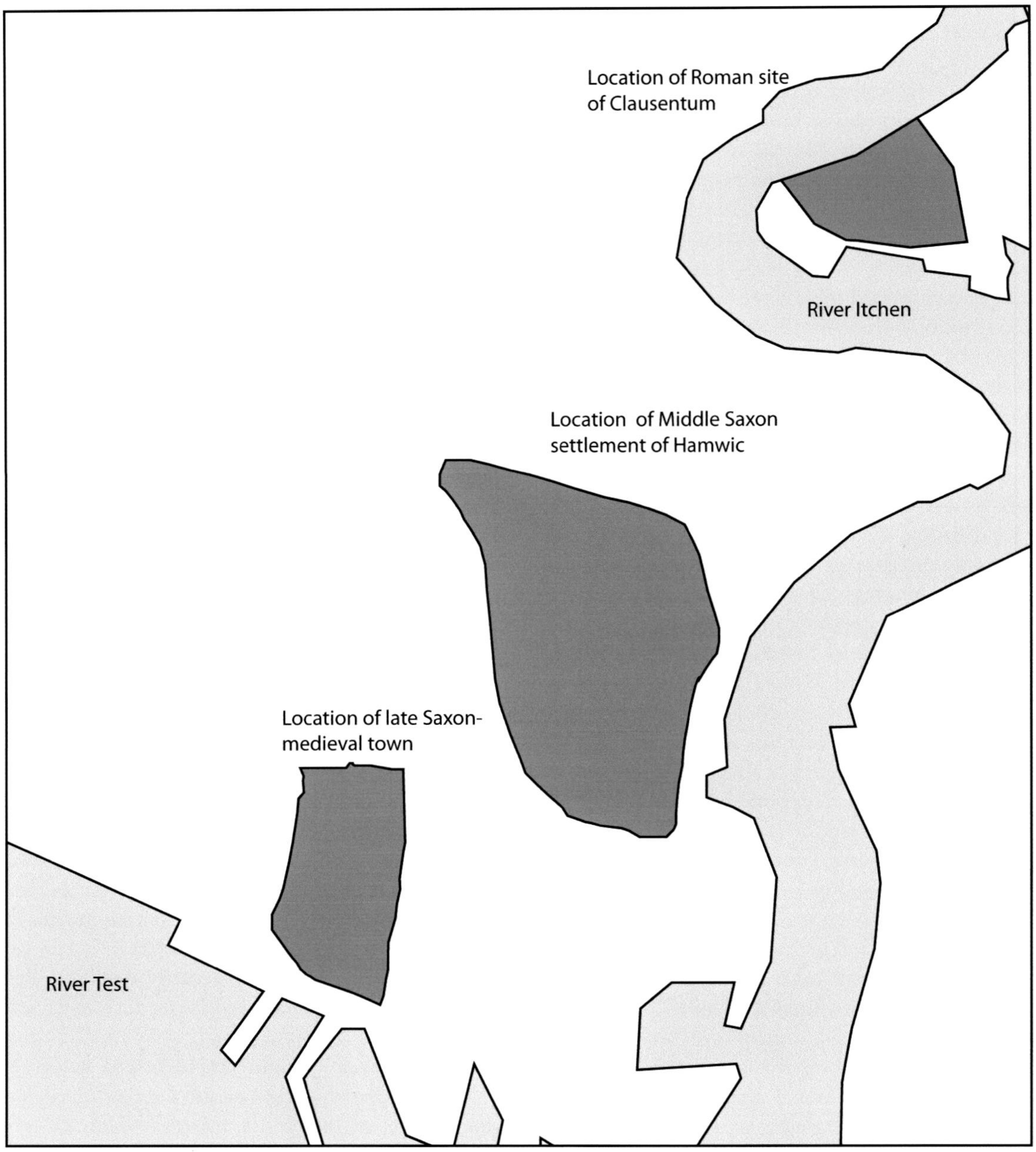

Figure 4.1: Map of the Southampton area showing the location of Roman, middle Saxon and late Saxon settlements (adapted from Birbeck 2005, 2).

than had been seen in Wessex since the Roman period, offering a different physical and social context for burial. The modern city has been subject to large-scale excavations due to post-war development, which has produced substantial settlement and burial evidence of early medieval date (Holdsworth 1980; Morton 1992a; Andrews 1997; Garner 1993; 2001; Garner and Vincent 1997; Birbeck 2005). Not only are there multiple cemeteries, but there is a complete sequence of burials between the late seventh and eleventh centuries, although it should be noted that some centuries are better represented than others. Burials of the late eighth and ninth century are central to understanding the evolution of churchyard burial, yet interments of this period tend to be under-represented within the archaeological record in Wessex (Cherryson 2005). The Southampton area is blessed with a wealth of cemeteries of mid to late Saxon date, making it a particularly useful case study of the transition to churchyard burial in the emerging non-rural settlements of the later Saxon period.

Burial in late seventh- and early eighth-century Southampton

There is little evidence for early medieval burial in the Southampton area prior to the appearance of a number of late-seventh century and early-eighth century cemeteries. These cemeteries are discussed in detail elsewhere in this volume by Nick Stoodley and therefore only an abbreviated summary is included below and in Table 4.1, to provide sufficient information to understand later developments. Southampton's late seventh- to early eighth-century cemeteries occur in two distinct clusters; one within the site of the middle Saxon emporium of Hamwic and the other lying approximately a mile to the north on the other side of the River Itchen in the vicinity of the Roman settlement of Clausentum. At least three distinct cemeteries were founded in Hamwic just prior to its foundation or during the early phases of the settlement's existence. The earliest of these is the larger of the two cemeteries uncovered during the excavations at St. Mary's Stadium in the north east of the settlement, which has been dated to *c.*AD 650–720 (Birbeck 2005; Stoodley this volume) (Figure 4.2; Tables 4.1 and 4.2). Two furnished burials recovered from the adjacent site of SOU 20 in 1975 are considered to be part of the same cemetery, giving a total of 26 inhumations and 18 cremations (Holdsworth 1980; Birbeck 2005, 11). Some 300 metres to the north-west of the St. Mary's Stadium cemetery lies the small burial ground at SOU 32 (Figure 4.2; Table 4.1). An early eighth-century sceatta found in the fill of one of the ten graves and a radiocarbon date from one of the burials suggests a late seventh- or early eighth-century date for the cemetery (Morton 1992a, 179) (Tables 4.1 and 4.2). Five hundred metres to the south of SOU 32 lies another cemetery of similar date and with analogous features. The Cook Street cemetery (SOU 254, 567 and 823) consists of twenty-one burials as well as disarticulated human remains (Figure 4.2, Table 4.1) (Garner 1993 and 2001; Garner and Vincent 1997). Eighteen burials lie to the east of a ditch, which appears to demark the boundary of either the cemetery or the settlement of Hamwic (Garner 2001, 188). Grave goods in the form of a knife and linked pins of silver and bronze were found with only one burial (Garner 1993, 86). A radiocarbon date from one of the burials within a penannular ditch suggests that the main part of the cemetery was in use during the late seventh or early eighth century (Garner 2001, 177) (Table 4.2). The subject of the burials within the boundary ditch will be considered later.

The second group of late seventh- and early eighth-century cemeteries in the Southampton area lie approximately a mile to the north of the area of the Hamwic settlement, in the vicinity of the Roman settlement of Clausentum (Figure 4.1). Large quantities of human bone have been uncovered in this area over the last two centuries with burials from three sites known to date to the late seventh or eighth century (Figure 4.3). The largest of these sites, SOU 862, contained the

Cemetery	Date	Basis of dating	Number of inhumations	Number of burials with				References
				Grave goods	Coffins/ wooden linings	Evidence for above ground markers	Penannular ditches	
St. Mary's Stadium and SOU 20	*c.*AD 650–720	C14 grave goods	26 +18 cremations	20 inhumations, 2 of cremations	4	2	0	Birbeck 2005; Holdsworth 1980
SOU 32	Late 7–early 8C	C14 sceatta	10 + 6 grave-like features	1	4	2	1	Morton 1992a and b
Cook Street (SOU 254, 567 and 823)	Late 7–early 8C	C14	18 + 3 north south burials in ditch	1	4	0	3	Garner 1993 and 2001; Garner and Vincent 1997
SOU 862	Late 7–early 8C	C14	15+	0	0	0	0	Southern Archaeological Services 1998
SOU 414	Late 7–early 8C	C14	6	1	0	0	0	Smith 1991
SOU 207	Late 7–early 8C	C14	9	0	0	0	0	SCM Archive 207

Table 4.1: Summary of funerary provision in the late seventh- and early eight-century cemeteries in the Southampton area.

Site Name	SOU Number	Grave Number	Laboratory Number Reference	Uncalibrated date	Calibrated age ranges		Reference
					68.2% probability	95.4% probability	
St Mary's Stadium cemetery I	-	7138	GU-9322	1245±40 BP	690–860AD	680–890AD	Birbeck 2005
		7138	GrA-18295	1510±45 BP	440–620AD	430–640AD	
		5106	GU-9324	1350±40 BP	640–770AD	610–780AD	
		5114	GU-9323	1420±45 BP	600–665AD	540–690AD	
		5134	GrA-18294	1540±45 BP	430–600AD	420–620AD	
Cook Street	SOU 254, 567 and 823	5663	AA-35544	980±55 BP	990–1160AD	970–1210AD	Garner 1993; 2001; Garner and Vincent 1997
		201	AA-40364	1250±45 BP	680–850AD	680–890AD	
		5690	AA-35543	1330±45 BP	650–770AD	620–780AD	
Clifford Street	SOU 32	428	Wk-14450	132639 BP	650–770 AD	640–780 AD	Cherryson 2005
-	SOU 862	Context 22	GU-7595	1160±70	770–980AD	690–1020AD	A. Morton *pers. comm.*
		Context 20	GU-7594	1405±45 BP	600–665AD	540–700AD	
Bitterne Road	SOU 414	Context 546	OxA-12078	1336±22 BP	660–690AD	650–770AD	Southampton City Museum Archive SOU 414; Cherryson 2005
			RCD-3357	1255±75 BP	680–870AD	650–970AD	
-	SOU 207	N/A	OxA-12077	1267±22 BP	690–780AD	675–805AD	Southampton City Museum Archive SOU 207; Cherryson 2005
St Mary's Church	SOU 630	106	OxA-5447	1065±45 BP	900–1020AD	880–1040AD	Smith 1995
		113	OxA-5548	1215±45 BP	720–890AD	680–950AD	
	SOU 184	-	OxA-12075	965±22 BP	1020–1155AD	1015–1160AD	Cherryson 2005
	SOU 753	-	OxA-7187	885±60 BP	1040–1220AD	1020–1260AD	Garner 2004a, 5
Marine Parade	SOU 13	31	OxA-12041	1260±26 BP	690–780AD	675–865AD	Cherryson 2005
		40	OxA-12042	1475±26 BP	560–640AD	540–645AD	
		59	OxA-12043	1239±26 BP	690–860AD	685–885AD	
		64	OxA-12044	1290±25 BP	685–770AD	665–780AD	
St Mary's Stadium cemetery II	-	7380	NZA-14941	1245±70 BP	680–880AD	650–950AD	Birbeck 2005
Six Dials	SOU 31/258	6004	Wk-14449	1410±49 BP	600–665 AD	550–690 AD	Cherryson 2005
Upper Bugle Street	SOU 124		OxA-12076	1169±22 BP	780–940AD	775–960AD	Cherryson 2005
Westgate	SOU 25	3558	OxA-12115	1075±24 BP	900–1000AD	895–1020AD	Cherryson 2005
		3425	OxA-12195	1066±32 BP	900–1020AD	895–1025AD	
Lower High Street	SOU 161	31	OxA-5941	1135±26 BP	780–990AD	770–1020AD	Andy Russel *pers. comm.*

Table 4.2: Radiocarbon dates obtained from burials in Hamwic or late Saxon Southampton (all dates calibrated using OxCal v. 3.9).

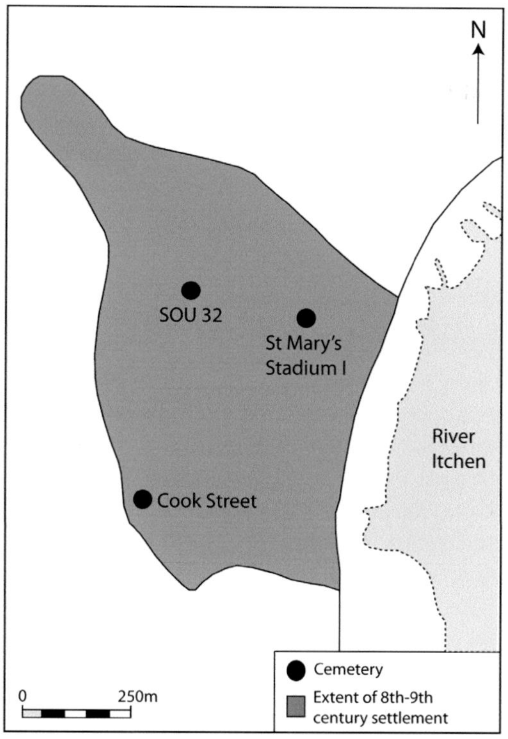

Figure 4.2: Plan of Hamwic showing the location of the securely dated late seventh- to early eighth-century cemeteries (adapted from Birbeck 2005, 196).

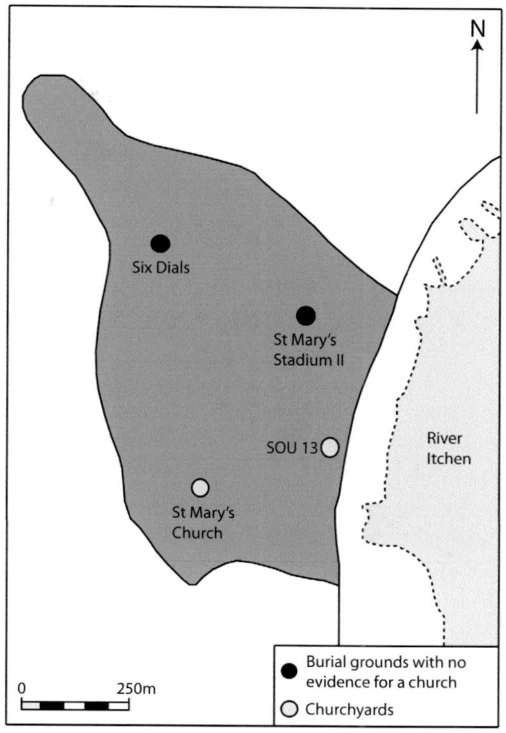

Figure 4.4: Plan of Hamwic showing the location of the post mid-eighth-century cemeteries (adapted from Birbeck 2005, 196).

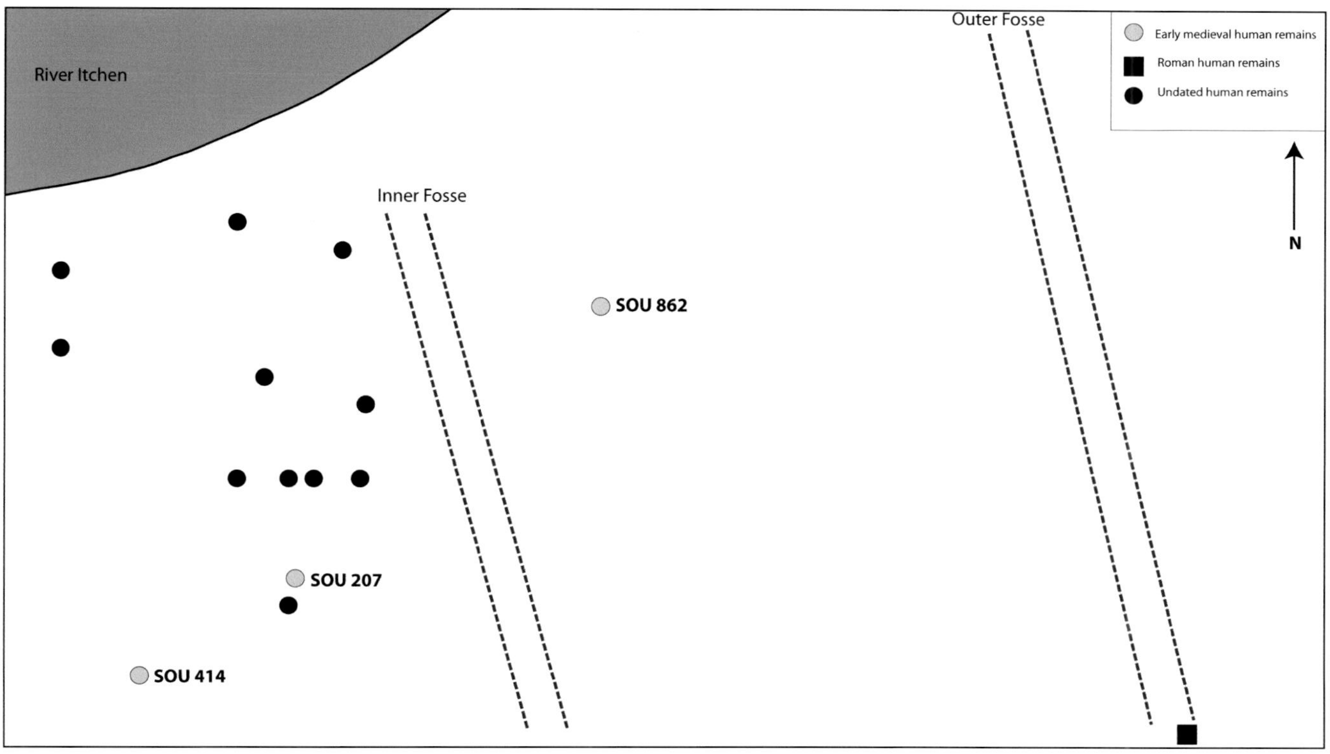

Figure 4.3: Location plan of the cemeteries and finds of human bone around the defences of the Roman settlement at Clausentum (adapted from Southern Archaeological Services 1998).

remains of at least fifteen individuals (Southern Archaeological Services 1998). The burials were unfurnished and, with the exception of a single southwest-northeast grave, all orientated approximately west-east (Table 4.1) (Southern Archaeological Services 1998, 25, 30). Radiocarbon dates from three of the skeletons produced a rather wide date range (Table 4.2), but a date of seventh through to eighth century seems likely with a possibility that the cemetery continued into the ninth or tenth century. The other two sites, SOU 207 and SOU 414, lie some 500m to the south-west of SOU 862. The remains of six individuals were excavated at SOU 414 (Table 4.1) (Smith 1991 15, 20). The burials were supine and orientated west-east. All the graves were unfurnished with one exception, which contained a spearhead. Radiocarbon dating suggests a late seventh- or eighth-century date for these burials (Table 4.2). At least nine unfurnished inhumations were recovered from the site of SOU 207, which lies some 100m west-south-west of SOU 414 (Table 4.1) (Southampton City Museum SOU 207 archive). Radiocarbon dating of one of the burial suggests a late seventh- or early eighth-century date (Table 4.2). The proximity of the burials from SOU 414 and SOU 207 suggest they may well form part of the same cemetery, particularly as undated human remains have been found between the two sites (Englefield 1841, 69). While it is possible that the burials from SOU 862 may also be part of the same cemetery it seems unlikely as these burials lie on the other side of Clausentum's inner fosse and excavations between the two areas have not yielded any human remains (Alan Morton *pers. comm*).

Churchyard burial in Hamwic

The church offered an alternative location for burial from the seventh century onwards and Hamwic contains one of the earliest excavated churchyards in the Wessex region. Excavations at SOU 13 in 1973 uncovered the remains of at least 81 burials, laying either side of a trench and post-hole structure (Figures 4.4 and 4.5) (Morton 1992a, 121–2). The structure was approximately 4.2 meters wide and at least 12.94 metres long with the spacing of the post holes suggesting a door was present in the south wall (Morton 1992a, 122). A fragment of window glass recovered during the excavations

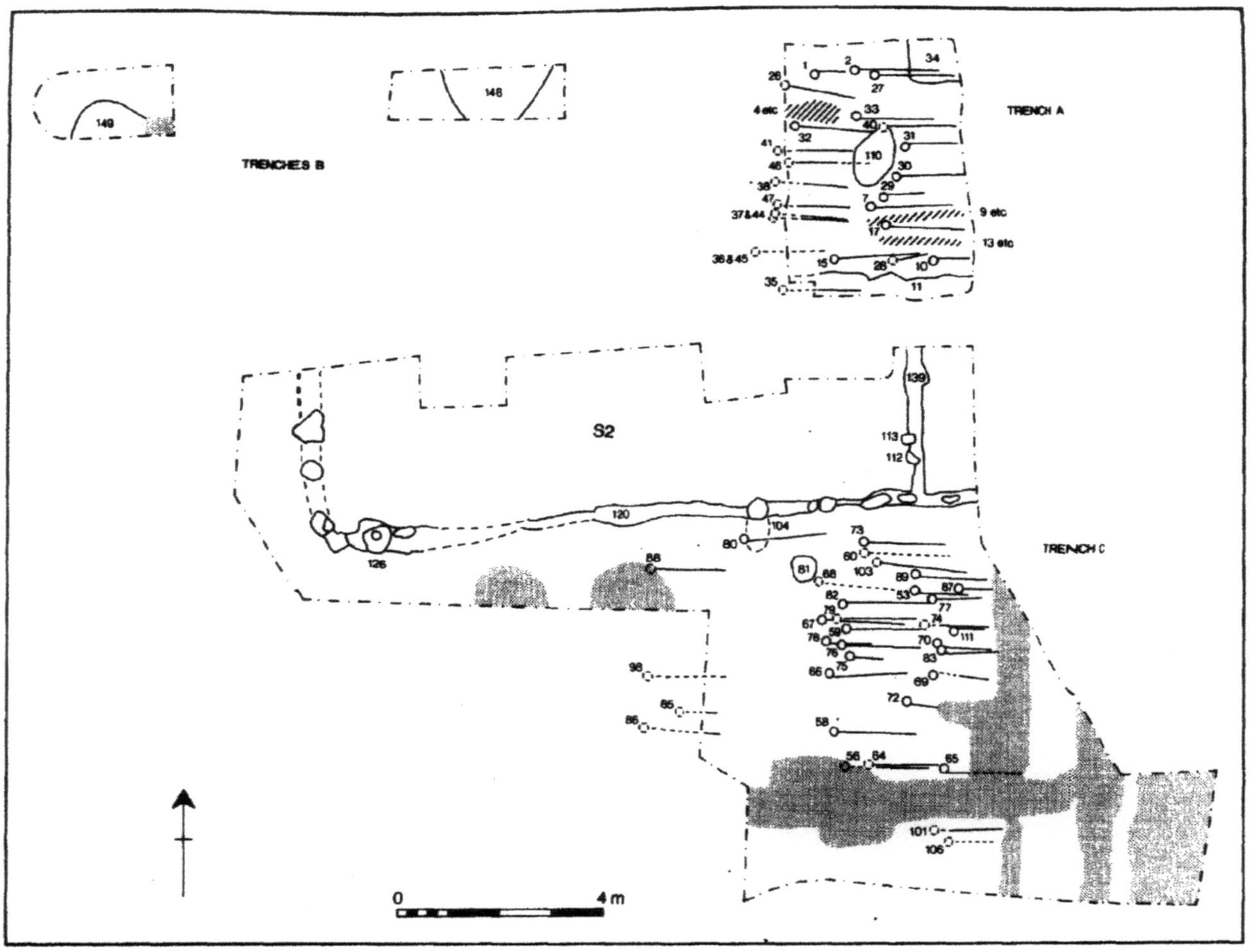

Figure 4.5: Plan of the eighth- and ninth-century cemetery at SOU 13, Southampton (permission of Southampton City Council Arts and Heritage).

indicates the building was at least partly glazed (Morton 1992a, 124). Burials, orientated west-east and organised in rows set approximately at right angles to the structure, were recovered from either side of the building, with at least 45 individuals to the north and a minimum of 36 to the south (Morton 1992a, 123, 134). The association between the burials and the structure suggests that the building is likely to have been a double-celled church, which usually date to the eighth century or later (Morton 1992a, 123, 136). Grave goods were only found with two burials, one accompanied by a knife and the other an iron object, although the two knives, three pin shafts, three possible tags and an copper-alloy object, possibly part of a chatelaine, recovered from the site may have initially been deposited in graves (Morton 1992a, 133–4). Wood stains, indicative of the use of a coffin or wooden grave linings, were found in only one grave. There was no other evidence for the use of grave structures or above ground markers observed in the cemetery. Radiocarbon dating suggests that the burial ground was likely to have been in use between the late seventh and ninth centuries, most probably during the eighth and ninth century (Table 4.2). One of the burials radiocarbon dated was from one of the earlier levels in one of the trenches. It produced a mid-sixth to mid-seventh century date, raising the possibility that the cemetery had its origins in a small seventh-century field churchyard. While not common, the construction of ecclesiastical buildings over or near earlier graves of seventh-century date has been noted elsewhere (Blair 2005, 237).

The SOU 13 cemetery exhibited many features characteristic of churchyards of the late Saxon and medieval period with a higher density of burials, considerable post-burial disturbance and greater levels of intercutting of graves than has been seen in other contemporary cemeteries (Scull 2001, 71). The rows of burials within the cemetery were reworked five times with approximately a third of all skeletons being redeposited (Morton 1992b, 72). There is evidence for post-burial disturbance of the dead in Wessex throughout the early medieval period, but it is much more pronounced in the churchyard cemeteries of the late Saxon period (Cherryson 2007, 136). The late Saxon period saw the increasing enclosure of churchyards, separating the sacred from secular, and establishing them as distinct places within the landscape, contained within boundaries (Thompson 2002, 232). Enclosing churchyards restricted the space available for burial resulting in higher level of intercutting and post-burial disturbance (Cherryson 2007, 137). Yet the churchyard at SOU 13 is not late Saxon, but middle Saxon, so why does this much earlier burial ground exhibit levels of post-burial disturbance characteristic of later cemeteries? The activities of the Church were not the only factor that affected the levels of post-burial disturbance. Middle Saxon emporium possessed larger populations and greater limitations on the space available for burial than contemporary rural settlements. SOU 13, one of the earliest examples of a cemetery with high levels of post-burial disturbance in Wessex, lies within one of the earliest non-rural settlements in the West Saxon Kingdom. The cemetery at SOU 13 was in use after the major expansion of the settlement of Hamwic in the mid-eighth century (Morton 1992a, 54). With this expansion came increased pressure on space within the settlement, placing the living and dead in direct competition for land – and the living were always going to have the upper hand. The resulting pressure on space meant that the cemetery at SOU 13 rapidly exceeded its capacity (Morton 1992b, 75), leading to high levels of post-burial disturbance as existing rows of burials were reworked to make space for later burials (Morton 1992b, 74). Thus, SOU 13 exhibits features more synonymous with later churchyards because the space for burial was restricted in early non-rural settlements due to competition over land much earlier than seen elsewhere (Cherryson 2007, 138).

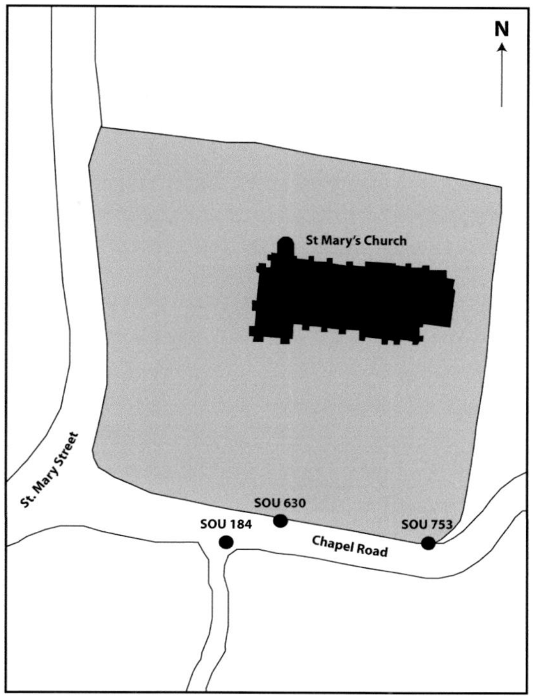

Figure 4.6: Location of early medieval burials in relation to the modern church and churchyard (adapted from Garner 2004a).

St Mary's Church has been long considered to be Southampton's mother church (Figure 4.4) (Hase 1994, 45). It was known to be the mother church for the entire lower part of the Itchen Valley during the eleventh and twelfth centuries and was the main church for the later medieval town, despite lying outside the city walls. Indeed, the fact that the church lies within the site of middle Saxon Hamwic rather than being in the medieval town seemed suggestive of a middle Saxon origin, but until recently there was little archaeological evidence to support this supposition. A series 49 sceatta was found in the churchyard in the first half of the nineteenth century (Addyman and Hill 1969, 67) and a lead cross of early medieval date was found accompanying a burial in 1884 (Morton 1992a, 50). Fortunately, the last decade has seen a number of skeletons excavated within and immediately adjacent to St Mary's churchyard mainly as small scale excavations prior to repairing the churchyard wall, installing parking meters or laying pipes or cables (Figure 4.6) (Smith 1995; 1996; Garner 1998, 2004a and b). Several of the burials recovered have been radiocarbon dated to the early medieval period (Table 4.2), providing more substantive evidence that St Mary's was in use as a burial ground during the early medieval period (Smith 1995, 259). The earliest radiocarbon dates from one of these burials gave a range of AD 680–950 at a 2σ level of confidence, suggesting that the churchyard was in use by at least the ninth century and possibly earlier (Smith 1995, 258). All of the burials that were radiocarbon dated lie on the periphery of the current churchyard, and, assuming that burial commenced closer to the church, it is possible that the core of the burial ground is considerably earlier, possibly of seventh- or eighth-century date (Smith 1995, 259). With only a few fragmented skeletons recovered from the edge of the churchyard, it is virtually impossible to determine anything of the funerary practices being used except that the burials are supine and orientated west-east.

The late seventh and early eighth centuries saw the establishment of a network of minister churches in the Wessex heartlands (Blair 1994, 56). Consequently it is not surprising that there should have been a church within the Hamwic settlement. Yet the settlement was home to two churches, lying some 200m apart – so what was the relationship between the two churches? The radiocarbon dating evidence indicates that the churchyard in SOU 13 was in use during the eighth and ninth centuries, while burial was occurring around St Mary's Church by at least the ninth century, and possibly as early as the seventh or eighth century. The evidence currently available makes it impossible to determine which of the two churches is earlier. St Mary's Church held a monopoly over burial rights in the city during the medieval period and also served as a mother church in the eleventh and twelfth centuries (Hase 1994, 45). Thus it could be argued that St Mary's Church was a minster during the middle Saxon period. This in turn may indicate an early foundation date, predating the church at SOU 13. While it is possible that the two churches were used successively, it seems highly probable that burial was occurring concurrently in both churchyards for at least part of the eighth and ninth centuries.

The Hamwic area is thought to have been the location of Hamtun (Yorke 1995, 306). The suffix 'tun' has multiple meanings but in many early place names it often seems to denote a royal residence or centre of authority (Yorke 1982, 80). Hamtun was also called a *villa regalis* in a charter dated to the ninth century issued by King Aethelwulf while in residence there (Yorke 1982, 80; Yorke 1995, 307). While the presence of the earlier of the two cemeteries from St Mary's Stadium does not necessarily prove the existence of a royal centre in Hamwic, it does indicate the presence of a distinct and elite group in the vicinity (Stoodley 2005, 81). In addition, the concentration of imported pottery in one part of Hamwic has led to suggestions of a possible foreign enclave (Timby 1988, 117). Given the possibility of distinctive communities within the settlement, it is possible that the two churchyards in Hamwic represented two discrete ecclesiastical foci, perhaps serving different communities.

Minsters of the eighth and ninth century were not compact enclosed units, but rather were composed of dispersed elements including multiple churches, chapels, holy wells and cemeteries (Blair 1992, 239, 257; 2005, 199). Thus, St Mary's Church and the church at SOU 13 may well have been components of a single ecclesiastical complex. Two churches are known to have lain at the core of most minster complexes and perhaps this was the case in Hamwic (Blair 2005, 199). Yet usually these multiple central churches were aligned approximately linearly along a west-east axis (Blair 2005, 199; Blair 1992, 249–50), as at Hexham (Bailey 1991) and Jarrow (Cramp 2005), although there are a few examples where the buildings lie with their long sides parallel to each other aligned north-south, as suggested at Nazeingbury in Essex (Huggins 1978). The Hamwic churches are not arranged in anything approaching a straight line and in addition they lie some 200m apart. While irregularities in the layout of multiple churches are not unknown – for example at Bywell, Carlisle and Coldringham (Blair 1992, 250) – they are unusual. Moreover, the 200m distance between the two churches is much larger than usually seen between groups of central churches, thus reducing the likelihood that both churches were part of the central core of an ecclesiastical complex. Some minster complexes are known to have possessed subsidiary chapels and oratories, which lay away from the central churches. In some cases, these structures may have had associated burial grounds. For example, the nun's cemetery at Barking was associated with an oratory which lay in the southern part of the monastic precinct (HE IV:7 – Sherley-Price 1990, 217). As such, it may be that the timber church structure found at SOU 13 was a mortuary chapel or a small outlying church linked to the minster complex. Excavations at Whithorn have uncovered two distinct religious foci, one a church at the core of the ecclesiastical complex and the second consisting of a church and mortuary chapel on the periphery of the monastic precinct (Blair 2005, 202; Hill 1997, 31). It has been suggested that there may have been a degree of zoning within the precinct, with restricted access to the central monastic core with many confined to the periphery (Blair 2005, 202; Hill 1997, 41). While the minsters of the West Saxon kingdom are unlikely to be subject to the same influences as those in Northumbria, perhaps the underlying principle can be applied to the Hamwic data. Burial adjacent to St Mary's Church may initially have been restricted to certain elements of the Hamwic community, possibly members of the ecclesiastical community and selected members of the laity, with all others desiring a burial *ad sanctos* being interred at the churchyard at SOU 13.

Figure 4.7: Burials from the Six Dials Cemetery cut through the surface of an earlier road (permission of Southampton City Council Arts and Heritage).

The churchyard at SOU 13 appears to have gone out of use prior to the decline in the population in Hamwic, with pits cut into layers above the burials indicating a change in the function of the site (Morton 1992a, 136, 138). The abandonment of one or more of the multiple burial foci associated with minster complexes of middle Saxon origin is known from elsewhere with changes in population and parish size being among the contributory factors (Hadley 2007, 195–7). The abandonment of the churchyard at SOU 13 pre-dates the decline of the settlement and it seems unlikely to be the result of population change. Instead the end of interment at SOU 13 may be linked to burial in the churchyard around St Mary's Church becoming more inclusive. As greater numbers were allowed to be interred adjacent to the church at the heart of Hamwic's ecclesiastical core, burial by the subsidiary chapel at SOU 13 became less desirable and thus this second churchyard was no longer necessary.

Non-churchyard burial in Hamwic

The two churchyards were not the only cemeteries in Hamwic in use during the eighth and ninth centuries. Although their use may have overlapped with the churchyards for a short time, the late seventh- and early eighth-century cemeteries at Cook Street, St Mary's Stadium and SOU 32 were probably abandoned and subsumed when the settlement expanded in the mid-eighth century (Scull 2001, 74; Birbeck 2005, 77). However, there are at least two cemeteries, which appear to post-date the mid-eighth century, both without any apparent evidence for associated ecclesiastical structures. The earliest of these is the later of the two cemeteries uncovered during the excavations at St Mary's Stadium (Birbeck 2005, 107). The cemetery, referred to as St Mary's Stadium cemetery II in this paper, contained eight unfurnished inhumations, orientated approximately west-east with their heads to the west (Figure 4.4). All the burials were supine with extended or slightly flexed legs. There was no evidence for the use of grave structures or above-ground markers, although the base of one grave was lined with a three-centimetre layer of gravel. A radiocarbon date from one of the graves seems to indicate a later eighth-century date for the cemetery (Table 4.2). It has been suggested that the cemetery may have been a small family burial ground (Birbeck 2005, 107).

The second Hamwic cemetery, post-dating the mid-eighth century, was uncovered during excavations at Six Dials (Figures 4.4 and 4.7) (Andrews 1997, 198). The cemetery consisted of a total of eleven articulated burials and three groups of disarticulated bone representing at least 19 individuals. No evidence for the use of grave goods, above-ground markers or any form of grave furniture was observed, although iron nails recovered from the area around the graves are possibly indicative of the use of coffins (Andrews 1997, 203). The graves were all oriented approximately west-east and, where it could be observed, all the burials were supine and extended, with the exception of one burial where the legs were flexed. A number of the burials were cut into large deposits of slag and charcoal, containing pottery dated to *c.*AD 750–850, while others had sunk into rubbish pits thought to have been in use between *c.*AD 750–850, suggesting little time had elapsed between the filling of the pits and the deposition of the burials. Two burials from the cemetery were cut into one of the last extant surfaces of one of Hamwic's roads (Figure 4.7) (Andrews 1997, 202). Overall, the stratigraphic evidence suggests a late ninth century date for the burials. However, a recent radiocarbon analysis of one of the burials has produced a date of AD 550–690 at a 2σ level of confidence (Table 4.2). This date is difficult to reconcile with the stratigraphic evidence, particularly as the burial used in the analysis was cut into a pit containing pottery dated to *c.*AD 750–850. Results on a second skeleton are currently awaited and until receipt of this result, the stratigraphic evidence will be used to date these burials

It seems unlikely, although not impossible, that the short-lived cemeteries at Six Dials and the later of the two at St Mary's Stadium were in use at the same time. However, both cemeteries were in use at the same time as the burial grounds at St Mary's Church and/or SOU 13. There is increasing evidence for small, short-lived non-churchyard cemeteries both within and around settlements during in the eighth, ninth and tenth centuries, even when a church and churchyard is present (Hadley 2007, 194; Zadora-Rio 2003, 3). Where there is an ecclesiastical presence in the settlement, non-churchyard cemeteries, such as those in Hamwic, may lie under the control of the Church and form some of the more diffuse elements of a minster complex despite the absence of any associated buildings (Blair 1988, 54). In some cases, these cemeteries may have had free-standing crosses. Indeed, it has been suggested that one of the post-holes lying on the south side of the church at SOU 13 may have held a free standing cross (Morton 1992a, 123), which may have predated the church or have been a feature within the churchyard (Morton 1992b, 52). The post-settings for standing crosses leave little distinctive evidence within the archaeological record and it is possible that standing crosses may have been present in the non-churchyard cemeteries in Hamwic. Thus the church may have influenced the way these individuals were interred, but they were not necessarily all being interred adjacent to the church. Finally although it seems probable that the non-churchyard cemeteries were part of a minster complex, the possibility that some or all of these groups of non-churchyard burials are completely independent of any ecclesiastical presence within the settlement, and may represent the persistence of an alternative non-ecclesiastical funerary practice, cannot be excluded (Zadora-Rio 2003, 3).

Not all of Hamwic's dead received formal burial in one of the settlement's burial grounds. The remains of two neonates have been found buried in middle Saxon rubbish pits at SOU 36 (Morton 1992a, 198) and Six Dials (Andrews 1997, 204). Occasional isolated burials of infants have been found in the early Saxon settlements, often in sunken-featured buildings (Hamerow 2006, 4–5). In a survey of special deposits of human bone found in early Anglo-Saxon settlements one-third were of infants (Hamerow 2006, 13). This is significantly higher proportion than the *c.*6% found in early Anglo-Saxon cemeteries. The differential treatment of infants in death has been used to explain the comparative lack of infant burials observed in early Anglo-Saxon burial grounds, perhaps the very young were not necessarily interred within community burial grounds (Crawford 1993, 84–5; Crawford 1999, 75–6). It is possible that the Hamwic infant burials represent some form of continuation of this tradition, perhaps rubbish pits close to domestic occupation were considered an appropriate place to dispose of the bodies of neonates and the stillborn in middle Saxon Southampton in certain circumstances (Andrews 1997, 204; Morton 1992b, 52). Another possibility is that perhaps the two infants found in rubbish pits were unbaptised and thus excluded from community burial grounds (Morton 1992b, 52), while illicit disposal away from unusual burial locations, for whatever reason, cannot be excluded.

Illicit disposal may also provide an explanation for the isolated west-east burial of an adult male found in a ditch at SOU 124 on the site of the later Saxon town, some 500 meters to the south-west of Hamwic (Figure 4.8) (Shaw n.d.). The burial has been radiocarbon dated to AD 775–960 at a 2σ level of confidence (Table 4.2), suggesting the burial occurred before the site became the main focus of settlement in the Southampton area or during the early days of the late Saxon town. The disorganised body position suggests that this individual was not accorded a formal interment. Another burial worth mentioning in this context is burial 5663 from the boundary ditch associated with the Cook Street cemetery. This has been radiocarbon dated to the tenth to early thirteenth centuries (Garner 2001, 175) (Table 4.2), and was deposited several centuries later than the burials in the late seventh- and early eighth-century cemetery. Another of the three skeletons and two skulls that were found in the ditch (burial 201) has produced a seventh- to ninth-century radiocarbon date (Garner 2001, 177). While the latter burial could have been contemporary to the burials in the rest of the cemetery, there is a possibility that it too could post-date the Cook Street cemetery, possibly also representing the use of the boundary ditch for burial after the cemetery had passed out of general use. The evidence is far from clear, but it is worth noting that both burials were north-south aligned (following the alignment of the ditch) and have one or both legs flexed in an era where west-east aligned, supine and extended burial was increasingly universal. Thus, the possibility that these burials represent a later and perhaps less formal phase of burial at Cook Street must at least be entertained. Formal and informal inhumations have been found within ditches within a number of settlements sites, including Yarnton in Oxfordshire (Reynolds 2009, 219; Hey 2004, 163). While the informal interments carry connotations of illicit disposal and exclusion, the formal interments may simply be a reflection of the comparatively unregulated nature of burial during this period or the continuation of earlier traditions.

Burial in the Southampton area after the decline of Hamwic

The ninth century saw a change in the pattern of settlement in the Southampton area. The archaeological evidence suggests that by AD 900 the settlement of Hamwic was largely deserted, although scattered occupation, possibly centred around key foci, may have persisted into the tenth century (Morton 1992a, 70, 72; Andrews 1997, 255). This did not mark the end of non-rural settlement in the Southampton area and by the early tenth century settlement had begun on the site of what was to be the late Saxon and medieval town (Figure 4.1), lying some 500 metres to the south-west of Hamwic on higher and more defensible land alongside the River Test (Morton 1992a, 73).

Hamwic's decline seems likely to have been the result of multiple factors. Hamwic appears to have owed much of its existence to trade. Consequently, the vicissitudes of trade were always likely to impact on the settlement and a number of factors combined to disrupt commerce, as well as Hamwic's position in trading networks, during the ninth century. Trade and the collection of tolls required a level of social stability and this is likely to have been absent, at times, on both sides of the channel during the ninth century. On the continent there was the general instability caused by the civil wars between Charlemagne's heirs in the first half of the ninth century, as well as the anarchic conditions within the Empire in the later part of the century and the disruption caused by Viking activities (Hodges 1982, 156–7; Morton 1992a, 76). Similarly, in England there were numerous incursions by Viking armies in the ninth century, with Hamwic, itself, directly experiencing this turbulence when it was raided by Vikings in AD 840 (ASC A and E. s.a. 837(840) – Swanton 2000, 62–3; Morton 1992a, 75–6). This may have served to reduce trade at the settlement although it should be noted that raids on Quentovic in AD 842 did not result in the end of that settlement (Morton 1992a, 76–7). In addition, it has been suggested that much of Hamwic's trade was based on agricultural goods and the Viking incursions in Wessex may have also resulted in a reduction in levels of agricultural surplus, leading to a dearth of goods to export (Hinton 1999, 29). Finally, it is possible that Hamwic's position on the edge of the north-west European trading network contributed to its decline. The settlement's peripheral location may have meant that when the West Saxons established control over the Kent ports in the first half of the ninth century, their more central location within the trading network may have resulted in the relocation of much of Hamwic's trade to the east.

By the time settlement had been largely abandoned at Hamwic, burial had ceased at three of its four post-mid-eighth century burial grounds. However, establishing exactly when burial ceased is more problematic. St Mary's Cemetery II has been dated to the late eighth century, but it may have been in use during the ninth century and exactly when interment finished is unknown. As has been discussed earlier, the presence of rubbish pits above the burials at SOU 13 suggests that the cemetery had been abandoned before the decline of the Hamwic settlement. The cemetery at Six Dials is thought to date to the later part of the ninth century, making it the last known burial ground founded within the settlement (Andrews 1997, 203). The cemetery was short-lived and appears to have gone out of use by the end of the ninth century. In contrast, the radiocarbon dates from three interments from St Mary's churchyard demonstrate that burial continued at the church between the tenth and twelfth centuries (Table 4.2) (Smith 1995, 259), after Hamwic had to all intents and purposes ceased to exist. It is possible that all those interred at St Mary's were members of the religious community or dwelt in those parts of Hamwic where occupation had persisted in some form. However, St Mary's Church was known to hold a monopoly over the burial rights for Southampton in the post-Conquest period (Hase 1988, 45), until this was contested from the thirteenth century by the Augustinian Friary (Ruddock 1947, 140–1). Hence it seems likely that many of the occupants of the late Saxon town were laid to rest in St Mary's Churchyard (Morton 1992a, 50).

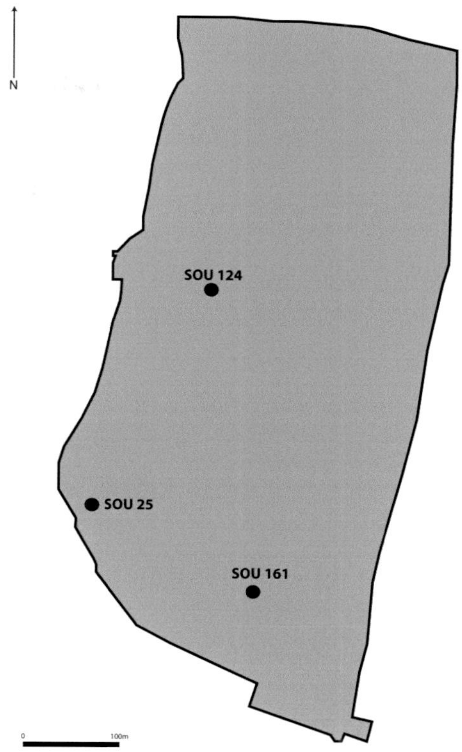

Figure 4.8: Outline of walled area of Medieval Southampton showing location of late Saxon burials (adapted from Holdsworth 1984, 338)

The recent identification of late Saxon burials from two sites within the medieval town suggests the St Mary's Church did not hold a monopoly over burial in the tenth and early eleventh century. At the first site, SOU 161/266, which lies adjacent to the High Street, the disturbed partial remains of at least three individuals were uncovered (Figure 4.8). The burials were found during excavations in the late 1960s and had been disturbed by the construction of later medieval stone houses, which suggested a possible late Saxon date for the burials (Platt 1975, 232–69; McKinley 1995, 3). Indeed, radiocarbon dating of one of these burials gave a date of AD 770–1020 at a 2σ level of confidence (Table 4.2) (Russel and Leivers 2003), demonstrating the presence of late Saxon burials with the town. The burials were badly disturbed and little can be said about the nature of funerary provision accorded these individuals.

At the second site, SOU 25 at the Westgate, a row of three undisturbed articulated burials were uncovered in the late 1970s (Figure 4.8) (Webster and Cherry 1980, 251). These burials lay on the edge of the excavated area and it has been suggested by the excavator that they formed the edge of a cemetery, which extended north into an unexcavated area. All three burials were orientated west-east and two of the burials were supine extended while the third lay partially crouched on its side (Webster and Cherry 1980, 251; Blackman 1979). Two of the three burials were subject to radiocarbon analysis giving dates of AD 895–1020 and AD 895–1025 at a 2σ level of confidence (Table 4.2). There was no evidence for the use of coffins, wooden linings, pillow stones or charcoal in any of the graves, although one burial was accompanied by a piece of animal bone, which may be an accidental inclusion, while another had a knife by its arm. Knives, in the absence of other grave goods, are often thought to be characteristic of late seventh and eighth century burials, yet there is increasing evidence that knives continued to be occasionally included in late Saxon burials, perhaps indicating the persistence of clothed burial as a minority rite (Hadley and Buckberry 2005, 140), with other examples in Wessex found at Bevis Grave (Hampshire) (Rudkin 2001), Lewknor (Oxfordshire) (Blair 1994, 73; Chambers 1976, 83–4) and Chimney (Oxfordshire) (Crawford 1989, 54).

The burials at SOU 25 and SOU 266 lie approximately 250 metres apart in the southern part of the medieval town. It is possible that all the burials come from a single cemetery, but this appears unlikely as no human remains have been reported from excavations in the area lying between the two sites. Instead, it appears that burial was occurring in at least two separate locations within the settlement during the late Saxon period, although the fragmentary nature of the evidence makes it difficult to say much about the precise nature of the burials. It may be that the situation at Southampton was analogous to that at Winchester during the same period. There, the churchyards of the Old Minster, New Minster and to a lesser extent Nunnaminster in the south-east corner of the walled city provided the main focus of burial (Kjølbye-Biddle 1992; Scobie and Qualmann 1993), but there was a large cemetery, Staple Gardens, some 350 metres from the minster in the western part of the walled area (Kipling and Scobie 1990). In the case of Southampton, the minster church at St Mary's provided one option for the occupants of the late Saxon town with some of the population being interred within its churchyard, while others favoured, or were only permitted, burial in satellite cemeteries within the late Saxon settlement.

Burial within the late Saxon town appears to have ceased by the early eleventh century. Although the evidence is fragmentary, it suggests the late tenth and early eleventh century saw the increased centralisation of burial around the minster church in Hamwic with the end of burial in satellite cemeteries within the Saxon town. This echoes the pattern seen elsewhere in Wessex, with the archaeological evidence suggesting that it is only in tenth and eleventh century that burial becomes completely concentrated around minster, manorial and urban churches with the virtual disappearance of scattered cemeteries and burials within settlements (Cherryson 2005, 241). This was a process driven, in part, by the minster churches, such as St Mary's, as they increasingly sought to enforce its monopoly on burial rights against the growing challenge posed by the new manorial and urban churches (Blair 2005, 463–5). A monopoly over burial also brought with it financial rewards in the form of *soulscot* – an ecclesiastical charge for burial levied at the graveside (Blair 1988, 8). *Soulscot* was an important source of revenue to religious houses and one they were, at times, over-zealous to collect. Aelfric's first pastoral letter to Archbishop Wulfstan written in *c.*AD 1006 describes how 'Some priests are glad when men die and they flock to the corpse like greedy ravens when they see a carcass in the wood or in field' (Blair 2005, 463). These comments were made in the early eleventh century, precisely where burial appears to have become increasingly centralised around minster churches and a period when the minster church's monopoly over burial was being contested by lay foundations – a fact which may have provided added incentive for the clergy to pursue any lay individuals choosing to be interred away from the church with increased vigour. It should be noted that *soulscot* may not necessarily have been for a space within a churchyard, but for ecclesiastical provision in the form of last rites and other funerary activities (Blair 2005, 437).

Another factor which may have contributed to the centralisation of burial around churches was the consecration of churchyards. The practice is first mentioned in documentary sources from the late ninth century, although references remain infrequent until the tenth century (Gittos 2002, 201). Consecration was used to separate the sacred from the secular and required a greater definition of churchyard boundaries (Gittos 2002, 202), establishing churchyard cemeteries as fixed and separate places within the landscape (Thompson 2002, 232). It would have been simpler to enclose and consecrate a single central burial ground adjacent to a church rather than a number of scattered satellite cemeteries. A final consideration is that by the eleventh century, there appears to have been an increasing expectation by the general population of a final resting place in consecrated ground near to a church, and as

8

The Parthian Language in Early Sasanian Times

Rika Gyselen
CNRS

Of semi-nomadic stock from central Asia, the Arsacid dynasty conquered north-eastern Iran and soon assimilated the native population whose language, Parthian, was adopted by the conquerors. This language was a local variety of Middle Iranian.[1] The Parthian victory during the period 148–139/8 BC over the Hellenistic dynasty of the Seleucids, who controlled western Iran and Mesopotamia, brought the Parthian dynasty into contact with Greek, a language of culture and power. Little by little, Parthian would supplant Greek. In the first century of our era, it gradually replaced Greek on coins, an outstanding tool for official propaganda.

When the Sasanian dynasty ousted the Parthian Arsacids in 224 AD, the official status of its own language, Pārsīg, usually called Pahlavi or Middle Persian (a variety of southern Middle Iranian), had already been well established. In fact, Pārsīg was the language used for inscriptions on the coins issued by Ardashir I before he became the King of Kings of Iranians and, of course, was still used for this purpose from the very start of his reign as King of Kings. It is highly probable that the Sasanian imperial administration also used Pārsīg from the start of the dynasty, although tangible proof of this is lacking.

The Parthian language, however, remained a major means of communication for Sasanian royalty. Otherwise, Shapur I (241/2–271/2 AD) would not have bothered placing his great inscription on the Ka'ba of Zoroaster in Parthian, as well as Middle Persian and Greek. In the late part of the third century, Parthian was still being used for royal inscriptions, for instance on the monument erected by Narseh (293–302 AD) in Paikuli. Thereafter, the custom of engraving inscriptions on royal monuments was lost; or at least none has yet been discovered. It is, therefore, impossible to specify when Parthian was no longer of interest to the Sasanian dynasty and vanished as a "royal" language. According to Livshits, the Parthian script was used till the fifth century AD, in particular for inscriptions on earthenware vessels found in southern Turkmenistan and in caves in Iranian Khorasan.[2]

However, we are not always sure that an inscription in Parthian actually dates from the Sasanian era in the absence of any specific evidence of this. This is the case of the Khorasan graffito *gry'rthštr/nhwdr W hštrp*, which might be interpreted either as "Gar-Ardashir [a person's name], *naxwār* and *šahrab*" or as "*naxwār* and *šahrab* of Gar-Ardashir [a place-name]" (Figure 8.1). The word Gar-Ardashir is evidence that this inscription might date from the Sasanian era,[3] since Gar-Ardashir might be a city (and province) founded by Ardashir I (224–240 AD).

When a Parthian inscription is associated with an explicitly Sasanian image, however, it necessarily dates from the Sasanian era. To make this point, I shall comment upon a silver plate and a few seals.

The silver plate, usually known as the "plate from Krasnaya Polyana", was found in 1947, and has been the subject of several publications.[4] The plate's imagery consists of a horseman who has lassoed a bear, a not very frequent motif (Figure 8.2a). The first publication on this plate recognised the inscription as Parthian (Figure 8.2b); but in 1961, Lukonin, thinking he saw there the name Wahrām, proposed for the first time an interpretation[5] attributing the plate to Wahrām II. Harmatta proposed a completely different interpretation in 1973. Harper and Meyers, in their piece on the plate in 1981, followed up on Lukonin's interpretation.[6] Harmatta's interpretation proposed not a proper name but a sort of formula: "(To be) healthy (is) the supreme (thing) ...", which is quite unusual on this sort of object.[7] For his part, Livshits saw in the inscription the name and patronymic of the plate's presumed owner, "Drust, son of Xwan ...", a reading much more in line with the usual inscriptions on silver plates.[8]

This variety of interpretations has no bearing on dating the plate however, the elementary composition in silver

Figure 8.1: After Henning 1953, pl. V.

being typical of the initial phase of the Sasanian era.[9] Furthermore, the style presents traits similar to other plates from the third century. Several aspects of the imagery are Parthian: the position of the rider who has turned backwards to lasso the bear, a position known, when the horseman is shooting an arrow, as the "Parthian shot". Furthermore, his left profile is portrayed, whereas the right profile is more common during the Sasanian era.

When Harper published her study of the plate, she likened the rider's headdress (*kulāf*) (Figure 8.3a) to that of a dignitary on a clay sealing found in Qasr-i Abu Nasr (Figure 8.3b).[10] We have since learned that the decoration around the headdress signals the person's office or rank. The palmette depicted on the *kulāf* of the horseman on the Krasnaya Polyana plate is the same as the one associated with *dar-(h)andarzbed*, "court counsellor", (Figure 8.3c) and *mogūn-handarzbed*, "counsellor of magi" (Figure 8.3b); but the number of palmettes is different. On the seals, the *kulāf* of the "court counsellor" has eight palmettes,[11] and that of the "counsellor of magi" has six – as compared with three

Figure 8.2a: Silver-gilt plate from Krasnaya Polyana. After Harper/Meyers 1981, pl. 9.

Figure 8.3a: Head of the male figure on the plate from Krasnaya Polyana. Drawing by H. Renel. Scale 1:1.

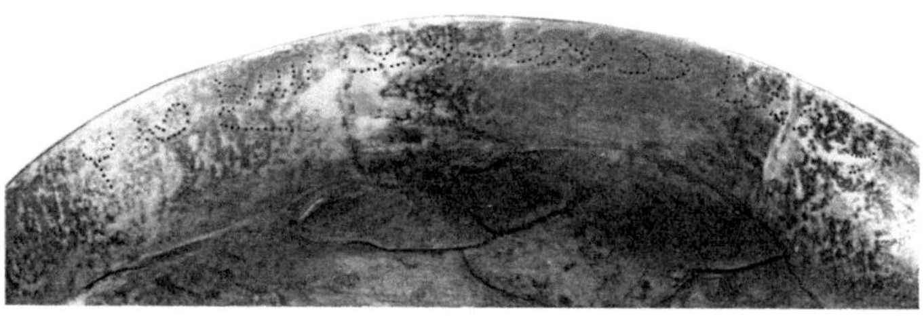

Figure 8.2b: Inscription on the plate from Krasnaya Polyana. After Lukonin 1961, pl. XII.

Figure 8.3b: Drawing of a seal impression on a clay bulla found in Qasr-i Abu Nasr. After Frye 1973: D.103. Scale 2:1(?).

on the horseman's headdress depicted on the plate. We can deduce that he, too, was a "counsellor", but we cannot determine to whom, even though the hypothesis that he might have been the king's counsellor would be compatible with such a precious object.

Although other silver vessels bear inscriptions in Parthian, few present imagery of a Sasanian type.[12] Several collections contain Sasanian seals with Parthian inscriptions.[13] In my opinion, some of these seals do not have enough clearly Sasanian traits to assign them definitively to this period.[14]

I shall comment on only four seals, each with a man's bust of a type also attested on seals with inscriptions in Pahlavi, clear evidence that they can be identified as Sasanian. The best known of the four belonged to someone named

Figure 8.3c: Seal impression (44.5 × 50.5 mm) on a clay bulla. Drawing by H. Renel. After Gyselen 2008, Seal 13. Scale 1:1.

Figure 8.4a: Seal of Agn-wist. State Hermitage Museum, St Petersburg (19 × 27 mm). Drawing by H. Renel. After Gyselen 2008, Seal 1. Scale 2:1.

Figure 8.4b: Seal impression of the šahrab of Balkh (± 21 × 31 mm). Drawing by H. David after the illustrations in Nikitin 1994. Scale 2:1.

Figure 8.4c: Seal of Rōz-būd (24 × 32.5 mm), British Museum (inv. nr. 135071). Drawing by H. Renel. After Gyselen 2008, Seal 13. Scale 2:1.

Figure 8.5a: Seal of Tiris (19 × 24 mm), British Museum (inv. nr. 120202). Bivar 1969, AA1. Drawing by H. David. Scale 2:1.

Figure 8.5b: Seal of Manučihr (15 × 20 mm), British Museum (inv. nr. 119737). Bivar 1969, AA2. Drawing by H. David. Scale 2:1.

Figure 8.5c: Glass paste found in Vietnam. After Manguin 2004, p. 299, fig. 12.14. Unknown dimensions.

Figure 8.6a: Seal with Parthian inscription ((?) × 11 × 13.5 mm), Bibliothèque nationale de France (inv. nr. Coll. Chandon de Briailles, 23.455bis (1953)). After Gyselen 1993, 20.C.1. Scale 2:1.

Figure 8.6b: Seal with Pahlavi inscription (15.5 × 17.5 mm), Musée du Louvre (inv. nr. AOD 246 (ex-coll. Dieulafoy)). After Gyselen 1993, 20.C.10. Scale 2:1.

Figure 8.7a: Seal with Parthian inscription (21 × 23.7 mm), Bibliothèque nationale de France (inv. nr. D3398 (1854)). After Gyselen 1993, 20.D.1. Scale 2:1.

Figure 8.7b: Seal with Pahlavi inscription (12.5 × 17 mm), Bibliothèque nationale de France (I 6 (ancien fonds?)). After Gyselen 1993, 20.D.2. Scale 2:1.

Agn-wist; it is in the State Hermitage Museum in St Petersburg (Figure 8.4a). The last study of its Parthian inscription was by Livshits and Xurshudjan.[15] The seal's owner was a *mardbed*, the "head of controllers, of warehousemen", "head of accountancy" or "chief accountant". The title *mardbed* is not attested elsewhere. This person's high status is evident in the imagery: the wearing of a *kulāf* (of a Parthian sort) enhanced by a device was reserved for top officials in the Sasanian empire, most of whom came from the traditional nobility. The type and style of the bust are similar to what appears on several other seals, for instance the bilingual Pahlavi-Bactrian seal of Mihrmeh *šahrab* of Balkh (Figure 8.4b)[16] or the seal of Rōz-būd with, in Pahlavi, the title *mēhārān-sālār* (Figure 8.4c).[17]

An inscription in Parthian with the name Tiris (Figure 8.5a) is engraved on the only known personal seal of an *āmārgar*, "bookkeeper, accountant".[18] On the Ka'ba of Zoroaster (ŠKZ), no courtier of Ardashir I or Shapur I was mentioned as holding this office. This is obviously not proof that this office was not held by high-ranking persons. Like the *mardbed*, the *āmārgar* is wearing a beaded *kulāf* of a Parthian type but without any device. Headdresses of this sort are attested elsewhere. A glass seal without any inscription, found in Vietnam, presents a quite similar image (Figure 8.5c),[19] as does a seal bearing in Pahlavi the name and title Manučihr, Ardašīr-šnōm (Figure 8.5b).[20] The honorary title with *šnōm* "satisfaction" and Ardashir's name (probably Ardashir I) are evidence of this person's high status. In fact, two members of the court of Shapur I had comparable honorary names: Ardašīr, Ardašīr-šnōm and Wohnām, Šābuhr-šnōm.[21] Thanks to Sebeos's history, we know that this kind of honorary title continued to exist, since Khusro II (590–628 AD) honoured Sembat Bagratuni, his Armenian general, with the title Khusrō-šnōm.[22] Ohrmazd-šnōm was the honorary name of a certain Khusrō, who was probably the lucky owner of a silver plate.[23] All these instances of a title made up of the king's name followed by *šnōm* are evidence that someone who received such an honorary title belonged to the empire's elite.

The smaller third seal bears a bust of a man with long curls (Figure 8.6a), similar to the one on a personal seal with the owner's name and patronymic in Pahlavi, "Ādur, (son of) Anāhīdag" (Figure 8.6b).[24] Father de Menasce (1962) proposed reading the Parthian inscription as *m'ny SPRA*, "the scribe Māni", whereas Gignoux read it as *[M]H mg 'spk(n)y*, "son of Mag-Aspak"[25] and Livshits as *s(?)mr 'spk(n)y*, "son of Aspak".[26] This inscription has a few reversed or erroneous letters – partly engraved in a positive instead of the customary negative manner; and its interpretation is probably not definitive.

Likewise, the inscription on the fourth seal is puzzling since part of it is in Parthian and the rest in Bactrian or Sogdian (Figure 8.7a).[27] But there are several parallels with the imagery on Sasanian seals, for instance the seal in the collection of the Bibliothèque nationale de France (henceforth BnF) with the name Gūrgēn engraved on it (Figure 8.7b).[28] This fourth seal bears the following inscriptions: from four o'clock to one o'clock the Parthian letters *ssnwn*, then from one o'clock to eleven o'clock the Sogdian letters, and then from eleven to eight o'clock, the Parthian letters *dtBRY*. The Parthian inscription reads "Sāsān, son of Vindād".[29] Livshits has suggested that this seal is a "palimpsest"; in other words, it was reused.[30] Since the Parthian inscription is interrupted by the Sogdian, the latter probably dates farther back than the former. However, it is hard to imagine how this image in a fully Sasanian style came to be associated with an inscription in Sogdian.

Apart from the motif, these four seals have several other points in common. All are convex bezels (or slightly cabochon) in materials used exclusively for flat or convex bezels but never for other shapes: amethyst for the Agn-wist seal, onyx for the seals of Tiris and the son of Mag-Aspak, almandine garnet for the Sāsān seal. Furthermore, each of the four bears its owner's name.

Let us now turn to the use of Parthian on Sasanian magic seals. In 1967, Bivar published a study of a magic seal in the shape of a thick bezel with, on one side, a motif in a Sasanian style and an inscription in Parthian (Figure 8.8a) and, on the other side, a she-wolf suckling two cubs with, in Pahlavi, a woman's name and the oft-attested formula *rāst*: "Duxt-Ādur, true" (Figure 8.8b).[31] The motif of a suckling she-wolf exists on many other magic seals, but never with two cubs — instead with a small human being and a small wolf or with two small human beings. For this reason, these scenes, though very similar at first sight, have, in fact, different meanings.[32]

According to Bivar, the side with the she-wolf might have been engraved after the side with the inscription in Parthian, the seal having been reworked to receive the second motif. Now however we also know of several other magic seals with a similar shape – a large, thick bezel with two slightly convex sides.[33] This increases the plausibility of the hypothesis that the seal was initially designed as a bezel with two sides.

The side with the Parthian inscription bears the image of a "royal" person who has caught a hybrid ithyphallic hermaphrodite with long ears (Figure 8.8a). A nearly identical image and inscription figure on a large convex seal in the Cabinet des Médailles in Paris (Figure 8.9). Livshits proposed to Gignoux that the Parthian inscription on the latter seal was: *ptgwb*[34] *ZNH* (*ssn*) with, on a second line, *mgw* i.e. *paygōy/paygōw ēn sāsān mog*, which was interpreted as "This charm (belongs to) Sasan, the Magian".[35] The name of Sasan [*sic*] in Pahlavi has been deciphered on several magic seals, in particular on one that mentions Sasan opposing a demon with the same name, Sasan-Marg *dēw* (literally: the demon Sasan's death).[36]

Figure 8.8: Magical seal (38 × 36 × 13 mm), Collection R. Falkiner. After Gyselen 1995, p. 38, fig. 37a-b. Scale 2:1.

Figure 8.9: Magical seal (15.7 × 34.4 × 34.4 mm), Bibliothèque nationale de France (inv. nr.1975.251.12). After Gyselen 1995, fig. 36. Scale 2:1.

Why does this Parthian seal qualify this guardian divinity (?) as a "magus"?

Seals with inscriptions in Pahlavi exist that have an imagery similar to the four seals with a man's bust and an inscription in Parthian. This is not the case for these magic seals with inscriptions in Parthian. Nevertheless, the style of this motif of a royal hero fighting a demon clearly seems to be Sasanian. Furthermore, nothing opposes *a priori* the idea of attributing it to the third century,[37] and this might explain the choice of Parthian for the inscription. However, the concomitance of Parthian with a motif that is never associated with an inscription in Pahlavi leads us to wonder whether we should not look for a reason other than chronology to account for this.

To end this overview, I would like to make a general comment about the use of Parthian on Sasanian objects. Nearly all the objects with Parthian inscriptions presented herein have characteristics more compatible with the first than with the last century of the Sasanian era. At first sight, the presence of an inscription in Parthian can be explained in terms of chronology. This suggests that the use of Parthian as a language for inscriptions would have ceased in the second century of the Sasanian era, in other words by the fourth/fifth century AD; and this, in turn, implies that Parthian, after losing its place as a "royal" language, also lost its place as a "common" language. We can adopt the point of view of Gilbert Lazard:

> Parthian subsisted only in the form of local dialects to the benefit of *pārsi*, Middle Persian from the south, which was the Sasanian dynasty's official language. In the north-east of the Sasanian empire, the place of origin of the Parthians, Parthian dialects were wiped out, perhaps deliberately, following the settlement of military colonies that spoke *pārsi* and that authorities had settled there to cope with invaders from the east. The Persian language that emerged in these areas would, therefore, have come from a form of colonial Middle Persian in the Parthian land.[38]

For as long as Parthian served as a "royal" and a "common" language, it was used in inscriptions on seals. When it no longer survived save in the form of dialects, it vanished as a language for inscriptions on Sasanian objects.

Notes

1 The term "Parthian", comes from Old Persian *parθava-*, "Parthia or Parthian", which, owing to the evolution in Iranian from *-rθ-* to *-hl-*, became "Pahlav", whence the confusion from the linguistic viewpoint of these two dialects (Parthian = a Middle Iranian language of the north-east and Pahlavi = the Middle Iranian language of Fārs in southern Iran), both stemming from a single Old Persian word. To avoid confusion, it is better to use Middle Persian or *Pārsīg* instead of Pahlavi.
2 Livshits and Xurshudjan 1989, p. 170.
3 Hackl, Jacobs and Weber 2010, vol. 2, p. 588.
4 Lukonin 1961, pl. XI: illustration of the plate and pl. XII: illustration of the inscription.
5 On this, see Harmatta 1973.
6 Harper and Meyers 1981, p. 50–52.
7 Harmatta 1973, p. 245–247: *drwšt bryst sng IIIIC XX X II.*
8 Livshits 1989 p. 171: *drwst BRY hwn sng IIII C M II.*
9 Harper and Meyers 1981, p. 169.
10 Harper in Harper and Meyers 1981, p. 50–51 and note 59.
11 Gyselen 2008, seals 12, 13, 14, 15 and 16.
12 Gignoux 1975, p. 271 as well as fig. 3 and 4.
13 Livshits & Xurshudjan (1989: 171–173) list a dozen or more seals with Parthian inscriptions. Several of them lack any characteristics suggesting a Sasanian style. Other seals have not been the subject of publication (for instance, two seals in the History Museum of Uzbekistan: H-159/29 and H-60/19) and it is not possible to assess whether or not they were made during the Sasanian era. The seal published by Herzfeld 1924, p. 77, no. 1 could not be traced.
14 Several Sasanian seals with inscriptions defined as Parthian in the collection of the Bibliothèque nationale de France bear, in fact, inscriptions in Hebrew: Gignoux 1976, 8.1–8. 30.L.26/8.3 (*cabochon*), 8.4, 50.B.5/8.7 (*dactyloid*), 70.68/8.8 (*dactyloid*). *Cf.* Shaked 1995: p. 242, n° 13; p. 242, n° 10; p. 242, n° 11; p. 241, n° 4. Others have Parthian inscriptions, but the style does not correspond with what we are used to calling Sasanian; and I would be inclined to attribute them instead to a "Hellenistic" rather than a Sasanian engraver: Gyselen 1993: seals 10.A.19/8.2, 10.B.23/8.9, 20.J.2/8.5.
15 Livshits and Xurshudjan 1989.
16 Nikitin 1994.
17 This title was translated by Gignoux (1977, p. 146) as *chef des buveurs (?)*. In a recent article, Bāghbidi (2011) has suggested that *mayhārān-sālār* refers to a wine merchant (*may* "wine", and *hār* < *ir.* **harH-* "engage in trade, exchange"). According to him, this office would have been placed under the *wāzārbed*. Rōz-būd was, of course, no ordinary wine merchant. The attributes of this office-holder emphasise his status. He very likely played a major role in supplying and distributing wine at the imperial court or in controlling the production of wine in the empire and trade in it.
18 Bivar 1969, AA1.
19 Manguin 2004, p. 299, fig. 12.14.
20 Bivar 1969, AA2.
21 Huyse 1999, vol. I, p. 59, §46–47.
22 Sebeos 1999, p. 49, 101.
23 Baratte, Bopearachchi, Gyselen, Sims-Williams 2012.
24 BnF 20.C.8/4.25. Gignoux 1976, p. 35, 4.25.
25 Gignoux 1976, p. 65, 8.6.
26 Livshits and Xurshudjan 1989, p. 172, note 20.
27 BnF 20.D.1/8.1. Gignoux (1976, p. 65, 8.1) reads the letters from one o'clock to eleven o'clock as Bactrian (*lao*: *λαο*), whereas Livshits sees them as a Sogdian *wsc* (Livshits and Xurshudjan, p. 172, note 20).
28 Gignoux 1976, p. 32, 4.5.
29 Gignoux 1976, p. 65, 8.1.
30 Livshits and Xurshudjan 1989, p. 172, note 20.
31 Bivar 1967.
32 See Gyselen 1995 on magic seals in general.
33 See, for example, Gyselen 1995, fig. 2a–b, 3a–b, 43a–b, 46a–b.
34 *Ptgwb* comes from **pati-gauba-* which means "word (cf. *guftan*, *guy-*) against (something)", hence "charm, incantation, and amulet".
35 Gignoux 1976, p. 76, 10.2.
36 *Cf.* Shaked 1994, p. 166.
37 However, this kind of tunic like an apron in front is not attested in 3rd-century rock reliefs and silver plates: Peck 1992.
38 Personal exchange with G. Lazard.

References

Bāghbidi, H.R. (2011/1390). "Dar bāre-ye čand mohr nevešte va sekke-nevešte-ye sāsāni va 'arab-sāsāni" [On a few inscriptions on Sasanian and Arab-Sasanian seals and coins], *Āyine-ye Mirās* 48, New Series, 9th year, n. 1: p. 73–89.

Baratte, F., Bopearachchi, O., Gyselen, R., and Sims-Williams, N. (2012). "Un plat romain inscrit en bactrien et *pārsīg*", in R. Gyselen (ed.), *Objets et documents inscrits en* pārsīg, Res Orientales XXI, Bures-sur-Yvette: p. 9–20.

Bivar, A.D.H. (1969). "A Parthian amulet", *Bulletin of the School of Oriental and African Studies* XXX, 3, 1967: p. 512–525.

Frye, R.N. (ed.) (1973). *Sasanian remains from Qasr-i Abu Nasr: Seals, sealings and coins*, Cambridge, MA.

Gignoux, Ph. (1975). "Coupes inscrites de la collection Mohsen Foroughi", *Monumentum H.S. Nyberg*, I (Acta Iranica 4), Tehran and Liège: Bibliothèque Pahlavi: p. 269–276.

——— (1976). *Catalogue des sceaux, camées et bulles sassanides de la Bibliothèque nationale et du Musée du Louvre. II. Les sceaux et bulles inscrits*, Paris.

Gyselen, R. (1993). *Catalogue des sceaux, camées et bulles sassanides de la Bibliothèque Nationale et du Musée du Louvre. I. Collection générale*, Paris.

——— (1995). *Sceaux magiques en Iran sassanide,* Cahiers de Studia Iranica 17, Paris.

——— (2008). *Great-Commander (vuzurg-framadār) and Court Counsellor (dar-andarzbed) in the Sasanian empire (224–651): The sigillographic evidence (Conferenze 19)*, Rome.

Hackl, U., Jacobs, B., and Weber, D. (eds) (2010). *Quellen zur Geschichte des Partherreiches. Textsammlung mit Übersetzungen und Kommentaren*, 3 vols (Novum Testamentum et Orbis Antiquus, Studien zur Umwelt des Neuen Testaments 83), Göttingen and Oakville.

Harmatta, J. (1973). "Inscription de vaisselle de l'époque sassanide et post-sassanide", *Acta Antiqua Academiae Scientiarum Hungaricae* 21: p. 245–266.

Harper, O., and Meyers, P. (1981). *Silver vessels of the Sasanian period, volume I: Royal imagery*, New York.

Henning, W.B. (1953). "A new Parthian inscription", *Journal of the Royal Asiatic Society* 1953: p. 132–136, pl. V.

Herzfeld, E. (1924). *Paikuli, monument and inscription on the early history of the Sasanian Empire*, vol. I–II, Forschungen zur islamischen Kunst, F. Sarre (ed.), III, Berlin.

Huyse, P. (1999). *Die dreisprachige Inschrift Šābuhrs I. an der Ka'ba-i Zardušt (ŠKZ)*, vols 1–2. (Corpus Inscriptionum Iranicarum Part III, Pahlavi Inscriptions, vol. I. Royal Inscriptions with their Parthian and Greek versions, Texts 1), London.

Livshits, V.A., and Xurshudjan, E.S. (1989). "Le titre *mrtpty* sur un sceau parthe et l'arménien *mardpet*", *Studia Iranica* 18: p. 169–191.

Lukonin, V.G. (1961). *Iran v epoxu pervyx Sasanidov*, Leningrad.

Manguin, P.Y. (2004). "The archaeology of early maritime polities of southeast Asia", in I. Glover and P. Bellwood (eds.), *Southeast Asia: From prehistory to history*, London and New York: p. 282–313.

Menasce, J.de (1962). "Un cachet parthe", *Syria* XXXIX: p. 225–230.

Nikitin, A.B. (1994). "The Sasanian Šahrab of Balkh", *Ancient Civilizations* 1, 3: p. 365–368.

Peck, E.H. (1992). "Clothing in the Sasanian Period", *Encyclopaedia Iranica* V/7: p. 739–752.

Sebeos (1999). *The Armenian history attributed to Sebeos*, translated by R.W. Thomson with historical commentary by J. Howard-Johnston and assistance from T. Greenwood, Liverpool.

Shaked, S. (1994). "Notes on the Pahlavi amulet and Sasanian courts of law", *Iranian studies in honor of A.D.H. Bivar, Bulletin of the Asia Institute* VII: p. 165–172.

9

From Aramaic to Pahlavi: Epigraphic Observations Based on the Persis Coin Series

*Khodadad Rezakhani**

Humboldt Fellow, Institut für Iranistik, Freie Universität Berlin

The post-Achaemenid coinage of Persis, starting from Baydād and ending in Ardashir V (the future Sasanian King of Kings, Ardashir I),[1] presents a continuous series issued by over twenty authorities and covering the length of the Hellenistic period in Iran.[2] The series is unique among Hellenistic coinages from the region in that, even in its earliest issues, it does not use the Greek alphabet for its inscriptions. It can therefore act as an important source for Aramaic epigraphy and its development into Middle Persian (Pahlavi) script. The present paper aims to study the inscriptions on the Persis coin series in order to understand the roots of the so-called *Inscription Pahlavi*,[3] the earliest representation of that script. The hypothesis is advanced that the Inscription Pahlavi does not in fact represent a logical continuation of the Persis script, and that the inscriptions on the coins of Shapur and Ardashir V, the two "Sasanian" rulers of Persis, in fact show influences from other, non-Persis sources.

The study of the development of Pahlavi, and its derivative and associated scripts, has been a relatively lively subject of research. Much of this, however, has been concerned with the later stages of Pahlavi and has concentrated on the development of the Avestan script,[4] as well as palaeographic remarks on the formation and use of cursive Pahlavi.[5] An important issue has been brought up with regard to this matter, and that is the naming of the script itself. Students of Middle Persian often face a puzzling situation when trying to master the language, as the associated scripts are in fact several, and each has its own characteristics, which leads many specialists to categorise even the languages on the basis of the script variations.

Middle Persian and Pahlavi

It is normally understood that the earliest accessible manifestations of the language are the early Sasanian inscriptions of Shapur I (240–272 AD), particularly his inscription at Ka'ba-i Zardusht (hereafter ŠKZ), and the famous *mowbed*, Kirdēr (active prior to 290 AD). These are inscribed in what is commonly called "Inscription Pahlavi", a rather clear script with individual letter types, which except in a few cases, do not resemble each other and thus allow for relatively easy transliteration. This script, however, does use heterograms (or Arameo-grams; MP *Huzwarish*) to render the most common words, as well as the stems of the common verbs, which are then pronounced in Middle Persian, although actually written in Aramaic. Soon after, Middle Persian appears as one of the languages used for writing the teachings of Mani, the third-century Partho-Babylonian religious leader who established the famous gnostic religion of Manicheism. The Manichean script, as it is called, is itself a development of Aramaic, although it is not clear in what relation to Inscription Pahlavi, and takes advantage of clear, distinct letter types and is devoid of the use of heterograms.

* I am greatly indebted to Dr Vesta Sarkhosh Curtis of the British Museum's Department of Coins and Medals for allowing me access to their great collection of coins, of which some pictures are included here, and for guiding me through them. Unless otherwise stated, the British Museum holds the copyright of all pictures used in this article and they are reproduced by the kind permission of the BM. I am additionally grateful to Dr Michael Alram of the Austrian Academy of Science/Kunsthistorisches Museum, Vienna, for introducing me to numismatics, particularly the coinage of Persis.

The most common manifestation of Middle Persian, however, is in a script called "Book Pahlavi", or Pahlavi in the strict sense. This is used for writing the secular and, more commonly, religious literature of the Sasanians and the early Islamic period. In fact, the evidence of the script that we have from manuscripts is often much later than the Sasanian period and starts in the twelfth century AD and continues, in the form of commentaries, until the nineteenth century. This script has the disadvantage of using eleven to twelve signs to represent over twenty sounds. Because many of the letter shapes have merged into one, the Book Pahlavi script uses the same sign to render /n/, /w/, /u/, /o/, and even /r/ on occasions. It is further complicated by the very active use of heterograms, whereby most common words and verbal stems, as well as specific concepts such as the word for daemons, are rendered in Aramaic.

A script termed "cursive Pahlavi" is found on earlier documents, even though it most likely developed from Book Pahlavi. These documents comprise various papyri and parchments dated mostly to the seventh century and found in Egypt and various locations on the Iranian Plateau.[6] This script, besides having all the disadvantages of Book Pahlavi, also presents the researcher with the additional challenge of missing, carelessly written – and thus easily confused – words, and wrong spelling. The decipherment of these documents has been the task of only a few very patient scholars.

Another derivative of Book Pahlavi is the famous Avestan script, used to write the sacred hymns and later ritual texts of Zoroastrianism sometime in the late Sasanian period.[7] Constructed specifically to record religious texts, and one of the clearest scripts ever created, it employs carefully distinguished signs that sometimes manage to render even the variants on a nasal sound. Nonetheless, Avestan, like Book Pahlavi, has reached us in much younger manuscripts dating from the thirteenth century or later.

It is worth mentioning here that based on the testimony of early Islamic historians (e.g. Mas'udi), seven different scripts were used in the Sasanian period to render various concepts, probably a reference to the varieties of Pahlavi and associated scripts such as the Avestan.

Origins of Pahlavi?

Here, however, we are most concerned with what preceded the earliest manifestations of Pahlavi. Although the ŠKZ represents the earliest substantial appearance of Inscription Pahlavi and the Middle Persian language, the script in which it is written is actually attested from the evidence of coin inscriptions of Shapur (*c.* 200–210 BC) and Ardashir V, the sons of Pābag. These were the last two kings of Persis before Ardashir V established the Sasanian empire in 223–224 AD and thus became Ardashir I, the founder of the new dynasty. The coins of these two kings show a formula that in a way anticipates parts of the canonical formula on Sasanian coins up to the early fifth century. The inscription on the coin of Shapur reads:

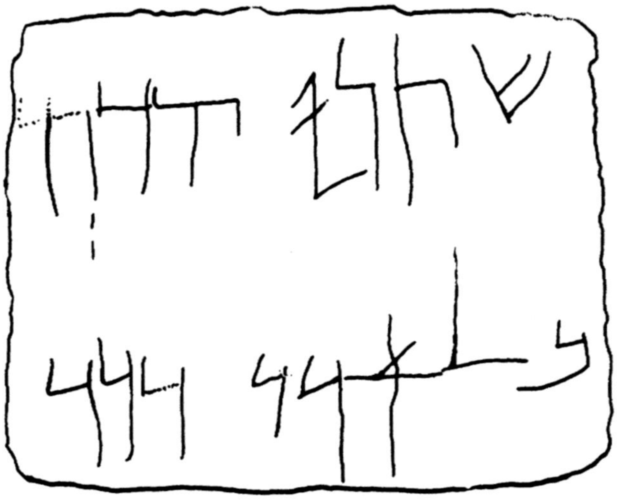

Figure 9.1: The inscription of Failaka (after Naveh, 1995).

šhpwhly MLKA BRH bgy p'pky MLKA

Shapur the King, son of Lord Pābag the King

The use of the term *bgy* (MP *bag*/*bay*, from Old Iranian *baga* "God") is one of the most obvious points of departure from the inscriptions of previous kings of Persis, which usually followed the formula of "X the King", occasionally followed by "son of Y the King".[8] But what is most important is the dramatic way in which the shapes of the letters on Shapur's coin inscriptions, and those of Ardashir V, differ from those used for the coin inscriptions of the rulers who preceded them.

The earliest coin inscriptions of the Persis series (e.g. Baydād) present a famous formula for designating the king. This is as follows:

bgdt prtrk' zy 'lhy' br bgwrt[9]

Baydād, the *frataraka* of the gods, son of Bagawart (Bayward?)

The script used for the inscription is quite close to what is termed "Lapidary Aramaic Script"[10] and the letter forms seem to have been adopted from those designed for being carved on stone (see Fig. 9.1).

The inscription of Baydād on his coins in fact shows a remarkable similarity to the Lapidary Aramaic inscription: see Fig. 9.2.

The shape of the letters "b" 𐡁, "d" 𐡃, "k", and "r" are almost exactly the same as the ones on the Lapidary Aramaic inscription. This simply suggests a close affinity between the Persis script and the type of script used to write Imperial Aramaic, which is close to the inscription above. Similarity of surfaces used for inscribing the lapidary inscription and

Figure 9.2: Line drawing of inscription on coins of Baydād. From M. Alram, Iranisches Personennamenbuch: Nomina Propria Iranica in Nummis, *p.165.*

the coin die is an easy explanation for the preference in using this script.

The general shape of the letters stays the same under the immediate successors of Baydād and no major shift is seen, although in order to meet particular circumstances (i.e. the name of the king) more letters are introduced, specifically "s" and "š" used in the name of Ardashir I. This remains the case until the reign of Dārāyān I (perhaps early second century BC), the first ruler of Persis, who uses the title *MLKA* or "King" instead of *frataraka*, "governor".[11]

On the coins of Dārāyān I (see Fig. 9.3), the shape of the letter "d" has become greatly simplified to a simple vertical line (), and "l" () is similarly simplified, with only a small additional half-circle attached to the bottom of the vertical line to distinguish it from the "d", and eventually even "r" and sometimes "k". The letter "a", which previously appeared on the coins of Baydād and his descendants in a shape close to the later Pahlavi form, seems on the coins of Dārāyān to become more similar to the Aramaic form. The most important feature of the coins of Dārāyān is the introduction of the letter "m" (), which becomes quite a prominent feature on the subsequent coins of Persis because of the constant appearance of the word *MLKA*.

The coins of Dārāyān II (mid to late second century BC), the son of Vadfradād (Autophradates) IV, display the first instance of the appearance of the ligature used to express the Aramaic word *BRH*, "son [of]"(see Fig. 9.4, 9.5).

These coins also display a different type of the letter "t" (), now more rounded in its right-hand hook. Additionally, the letter "p"(), previously written as a vertical line with a rounded bend on top, is now made into the semi-circle with a bend at the top, anticipating a development into a full "Pahlavi" letter "p".

On the coins of Ardashir II (*c.* mid first century BC), the letter "h" develops from the type on the coins of Baydād () to a new, open letter resembling a capital Latin "N" (). Also remarkable is the new shape of the letter "š", previously seen as on the coins of Ardashir I, but by the time of Ardashir II written as . It would soon, during the reign of Vahšīr, the successor and brother of Ardashir II, come to be written as , which is closer to the shape we are used to in Pahlavi (see Fig. 9.6).

One of the letters that changes its shape most frequently is "k", with nine different forms throughout the Persis series. Among the most interesting is that found on the coins of Pākor II (*c.* first half of the first century AD). Here, the letter has a more "inscriptional" or lapidary shape, with the main part of the letter formed by a single vertical line with two small extensions on either side of the line, one pointing left and the other pointing right. In general, the letters on the coins of Pakor II appear to be straighter and less curved, which seems to be the direction in which the whole series is moving.

Figure 9.3: MLKA as it appears on a coin of Dārāyān I (Alram type 558).

Figure 9.4: Reverse of a coin of Dārāyān II (photo by the author).

Figure 9.5: The ligature BRH on a coin of Dārāyān II (Alram type 564).

Figure 9.6: Reverse of a coin of Vahšīr (photo: CoinArchives.com).

Figure 9.7: Reverse of a coin of Napād (late first century AD).

Figure 9.8: Reverse of a coin of Ardashir V/I (c. 210–215 AD).

On the coins of Mančihr I (*c.* first half of the second century AD), we are introduced to the letter "č", which was previously unknown in the series. The basic shape of the letter appears to have been copied from Aramaic *sade* (Hebrew צ) and given the value of "č", which is common in later Middle Iranian.

The most interesting change in the shape of a letter happens on the coins of Mančihr II and concerns the letter "m". Previously this had been written with three strokes, either crossing each other () or forming a square without the side at the bottom (). But now the letter is written as a circle, produced in one continuous stroke that starts at the top, creates a loop, and then ends at the bottom left, with a slightly flattened top right side of the letter ().

The letters stay largely the same, with only slight changes, for the rest of the Persis series. However, under Shapur and Ardashir V/I, the coin inscriptions begin to differ significantly from the previous versions. A simple comparison will demonstrate the case: see Fig. 9.7 and 9.8.

A comparison of certain letter shapes from Fig. 9.8 shows a dramatic departure from the script of previous coins of Persis. The shape of the letter "p", in particular, will demonstrate this. From the lapidary to the "normal" Persis form, the semicircular, the letter on the coins of Ardashir I takes the shape most recognisable in the Pahlavi inscriptions: . The same can be argued for the letters "h" and "k" (which receives an unprecedented shape and additional stroke at the bottom), as well as the letter "b", which takes its full "Pahlavi" form, with very little resemblance to the established "Persis" form.

Eastern and western influences?

In the light of the suggested departure of Pahlavi, as seen on the coins of Shapur and Ardashir I/V, from the previous letter forms found on Persis coins (Persis "Aramaic"?), it seems necessary to try to find some alternative path of development for Pahlavi, possibly via comparison with non-Persis scripts. This might in some cases be unusual, or even unnecessary, but equally it might prove to be a useful avenue of study.

In his study of the Mandaean script, Coxon follows Macuch in suggesting that it appears to have certain affinities with that of the Nabataeans, although he dismisses Macuch's idea that this would prove the presence of Mandaeans in southern Mesopotamia as early as second century AD.[12] Cox refers to a passage from 'Ishodad,[13] where the latter suggests that the Pahlavi script, particularly its use of heterograms, was created by a servant of the king of "Assyria" and where he calls the Syriac alphabet "Mesene". On this basis, Coxon argues for an eastern Syriac origin of the Pahlavi alphabet.

A comparison of letter types from the coins of Characene (early second century BC to early third century AD) shows interesting similarities between letters used in Persis and Characene, as well as certain similarities between the scripts of Persis and Elymais. The basic letter shapes in Elymais (mid second century BC to early third century AD, see Fig. 9.9) – most importantly "š", "m" and "r" – appear to be quite similar to those found in Persis, except for the unusual shape of the letter "a", which also has parallels from the inscriptions of Tang-i Sarvak[14] and Shimbar.[15] Letter "b" too, on the coins of Kamnaskires-Orodes III (*c.* early second century AD), has a shape that is unique. Not only is it dissimilar to the Persis shape, it also exhibits a dramatic shift from the Aramaic script.

The coins of Characene (see Fig. 9.10) likewise show similar letter shapes to those of Persis, including the letter "m", as well as "g", "l" and "z". The shapes of the letter "y", which is reduced to a single dot, and that of "a", a full circle, are both innovations and seem to bear little resemblance either to the scripts that surround them, or to the Aramaic script from which they are derived. Both of these scripts, despite their similarities to the script of Persis, are quite dissimilar to the Pahlavi script that is used

Figure 9.9: Reverse of a coin of Orodes II (c. 50–70 AD) of Elymais.

Figure 9.10: Reverse of a coin of Maga of Characene (195–210 AD).

for the inscriptions on the coins of Shapur and Ardashir V/I. The development of the Aramaic script used for writing the occasional inscription on the coins of Elymais and Characene seems to be independent both from the Persis script and that of the later Pahlavi.

Eastern dynasty, eastern script?

An examination of the inscriptions on the coinage of the Indo-Saka kingdom (first two centuries AD) highlights the similarities between the letter shapes from this region and those of the terminal Persis/early Sasanian coins. While letters such as "m" and "b" appear to have kept their original, Aramaic-style shapes on the coins of Abdagases (first half of the first century AD) and Sanabares (second century AD?), more variable letters such as "y", "n" and "t" have clearly developed further from their Aramaic origins.[16] Most significantly, the shape of the letter "a", a commonly occurring letter on the coinage of the Indo-Sakas, appears strikingly similar to that on the coins of Shapur and Ardashir V. Another example is the letter "t", which appears on the coins of Shapur and Ardashir almost exactly the same way as it does on the coins of the Indo-Saka ruler Prahata (Alram's "Pahlava", perhaps late second century AD).

Still more recently, the last king of the Indo-Saka line, who was defeated and replaced by Ardashir during his eastern campaigns, uses on his coins a script quite similar to that of Ardashir. Farn-Sāsān (*c.* 210–223?), as he is called, uses an "r" that is very similar to the "Pahlavi" letter of the same value, and his letter "s" is entirely different from what one sees on the Persis coins, although it is fair to say that it is not a Pahlavi "s" either. Sadly, the letter "s" does not appear on the coins of Shapur or on the early coins of Ardashir as king of Persis. However, its occurrence on Ardashir's coins after he founded the Sasanian dynasty shows that the letter is indeed similar to the shape used by Farn-Sāsān (see Fig. 9.11).

Michael Alram has previously argued that Ardashir's eastern campaigns followed those in the west of Iran and Mesopotamia, and took place after his issuing of coins in Hamedan and Ctesiphon (mints B and C).[17] Alram thus suggests that Ardashir already had a well-developed coinage before he reached Sakastan and the territory of the Indo-Sakas, specifically that of Farn-Sāsān.[18] This is specifically argued based on the appearance of a fire-altar on the back of Farn-Sāsān's coins, which Alram attributes to the influence of Ardashir's coinage, and sign of the former's submission to the latter (see Fig. 9.12).

However, it has also been suggested by some, including Marek Jan Olbrycht,[19] that the "Sasanian" dynasty itself might have originated from further east than Persis, indeed from the territory of the Indo-Sakas in Sakastan. This is an intriguing suggestion, considering the mysterious origins of the name Sāsān, the eponymous ancestor of the Sasanians, and its apparent abundance in the Indo-Saka territory,[20]

Figure 9.11: Obverse of a coin of Farn-Sāsān, showing part of the inscription; on the reverse, an altar (photo courtesy of T. Mallon/ Grifterrec*).*

Figure 9.12: Gold issue of Ardashir V/I as the Sasanian King of Kings, including the standard Sasanian obverse formula and the altar on the reverse.

including its appearance as part of the names of Farn-Sāsān and his father Adur-Sāsān. In view of the remarkable similarities between the script used for the coinage of Shapur and Ardashir V and those of the Indo-Saka kings such as Farn-Sāsān, or even Sanabares, an investigation into the eastern origins of the Sasanian family might prove fruitful. Detailed observation of the development of the fire altar, which appears to be an important part of the suggestion that the coins of Farn-Sāsān copied the motif from the issues of Ardashir – instead of the other way round – might eventually be useful in establishing the chronology of the coinage of Ardashir.

It also remains to be seen how the script of the coinage of the Indo-Saka could have influenced the local issues of Ardashir and his older brother. What implications this might have, and in what way the comparison of the scripts might help us in deciphering the inscription of coins such as Ardashir's so-called "successor" issue,[21] which were minted in Sakastan, remain to be seen.

Notes

1 See M. Alram 1986.
2 For the argument that Baydād was not in fact the first issuer of the coins in the series, see Curtis 2010, p. 379–396; also Hoover 2008.
3 Recently, experts including Rika Gyselen and Philippe Gignoux appear to prefer the term Parsig for the script. See the introduction to the new volume of *Res Orientales*: Gyselen 2012; and in this volume. Here, I use the terms Inscription Pahlavi or simply Pahlavi to denote the form of the script that appears in early Sasanian inscriptions and is most prominent on Sasanian coin issues.
4 See Frye 2006: p. 57–60, who has a rather straightforward, if not always very insightful, narrative of this development.
5 Weber 2007a, p. 185; also see footnote 3 above.
6 For an introduction to the Pahlavi documents of the Bancroft Library, UC Berkeley, see Azarpay, Martin, Schwartz and Weber 2003, p. 17–29. For their publications, see Gignoux 2010. A newer collection, the so-called "Tabaristan Archive", has also been published: Gignoux 2012.
7 Weber 2010, p. 255–263.
8 For example, the case of Napād and Nāmbed: see Alram 2008 for the full list of inscriptions.
9 Klose and Müseler 2008, p. 34 (plate 2/3a, where the name *bgwrt* is visible).
10 Naveh 1995, p. 1–4.
11 Wiesehöfer 2001. For alternative readings of the name, see Naster 1970, p. 74–80. See also Soudavar 2009, p. 422–423.
12 P. Coxon 1970, p. 16–30.
13 *C.S.C.O.* cxxvi (1950), 6,11. 20–27.
14 Henning 1952, p. 151–178.
15 Bivar and Shaked 1964, p. 265–290.
16 For these coins and analysis of their inscriptions, see Alram 1986.
17 Alram 2007, p. 227–242.
18 Nikitin 1994, p. 67–69; see also Alram 2007 for a discussion of the sequence of Ardashir's coinage as it relates to that of Farn-Sāsān.
19 See Olbrycht in this volume.
20 Schwartz 1996, p. 253–257.
21 Alram & Gyselen 2003: Ardashir type VIII/3a.

References

Alram, M. (1986). *Iranisches Personennamenbuch: Nomina Propria Iranica in Nummis,* Vienna.

——— (2007). "Ardashir's eastern campaigns", in J. Cribb, G. Herrmann (eds), *After Alexander: Central Asia Before Islam*, Proceedings of the British Academy, vol. 133, London: p. 227–242.

Alram, M., and Gyselen, R. (2003). *Sylloge Nummorum Sasanidarum, Paris-Berlin-Wien, Bd. 1, Ardashir I. – Shapur I.*, Vienna.

Azarpay, G., Martin, K., Schwartz, M., and Weber, D. (2003). "New information on the date and function of the Berkeley MP Archive", *Bulletin of the Asia Institute* 17: p. 17–29.

Bivar, A.D.H., and Shaked, S. (1964). "The inscriptions at Shimbār", *Bulletin of the School of Oriental and African Studies* 27/2: p. 265–290.

Coxon, P. (1970). "Script analysis and Mandaean Origins", *Journal of Semitic Studies* 15, no. 1: p. 16–30.

Curtis, V.S. (2010). "The Frataraka coins of Persis: bridging the gap between Achaemenid and Sasanian Persia", in J. Curtis, St J. Simpson (eds), *World of Achaemenid Persia,* London and New York: p. 379–396.

Frye, R.N. (2006). "The Aramaic alphabet in the East", *Journal of Inner Asian Art and Archaeology* 1, no. 1: p. 57–60.

Gignoux, P. (2010). "La collection de textes attribuables à Dadenvindad dans l'Archive pehlevie de Berkeley", in R. Gyselen (ed.), *Sources for the History of Sasanian and Post-Sasanian Iran*, Res Orientales 19, Bures-sur-Yvette: p. 11–134.

——— (2012). "Une archive post-sassanide du Tabaristan (1)", in R. Gyselen (ed.), *Objets et documents inscrits en Parsig,* Res Orientales 21, Bures-sur-Yvette.

Gyselen, R. (2012). *Objets et documents inscrits en Parsig,* Res Orientales 21, Bures-sur-Yvette.

Henning, W.B. (1952). "The Monuments and Inscriptions at Tang-i Sarvak", *Asia Major*: p. 151–178.

Hoover, O. (2008) "Appendix 5: Overstruck Seleucid coins", in A. Houghton, C. Lorber, O. Hoover, *Seleucid Coins. A Comprehensive Catalogue, Part 2: Seleucus IV through Antiochus XIII*, New York and Lancaster, PA: p. 209–230.

Klose, D., and Müseler, W. (2008). *Statthalter und Rebellen Könige. Die Münzen aus Persepolis von Alexander dem Grossen zu den Sasaniden*, Munich.

Naster, P. (1970). "Note d'epigraphie monetaire de Perside: fratakara, frataraka, ou fratadara?", *Iranica Antiqua* 8: p. 74–80.

Naveh, J. (1995). "The inscription from Failaka and the Lapidary Aramaic script", *Bulletin of the School of Oriental and African Studies* 297 (Feb. 1995): p. 1–4.

Nikitin, A.K. (1994). "Coins of the last Indo-Parthian King of Sakastan (A farewell to Ardamitra)", *South Asian Studies* 10, no. 1: p. 67–69.

Schwartz, M. (1996). "*Sasm, Sesen, St. Sisinnios, Sesengen Barpharangès, and ... 'Semanglof'", *Bulletin of the Asia*

Institute 10: p. 253–257.

Soudavar, A. (2009). "The vocabulary and syntax of iconography in Sasanian Iran", *Iranica Antiqua* XLIV: p. 422–423.

Weber, D. (2007a). "Remarks on the development of the Pahlavi script in Sasanian times", in *Religious Texts in Iranian Languages: Symposium Held in Copenhagen May 2002*, vol. 98, Copenhagen: p. 185–195.

——— (2007b). "Einige Bemerkungen zur Palaeographie des Pahlavi", in M. Macuch, M. Maggi and W. Sundermann (eds), *Iranian Languages and Texts from Iran and Turan, Ronald E. Emmerick Memorial Volume*, Iranica 13, Wiesbaden: p. 433–442.

——— (2010). "Writing exercises in late Sasanian times: a contribution to the culture of writing Pahlavi", in M. Macuch, D. Weber and D. Durkin-Meisterernst (eds), *Ancient and Middle Iranian Studies,* Iranica 19, Wiesbaden: p. 255–263.

Wiesehöfer, J. (2001). "Frataraka", *Encyclopaedia Iranica X.*

10

Parthian Studies: Two New Notes

Daryoosh Akbarzadeh
Research Institute of the Cultural Heritage and Tourism Organisation (RICHTO), Tehran

The Parthian era is considered one of the most important and under-studied periods in the history of the region that is now Iran. Although the data from texts associated with this period is very small and insignificant, archaeological evidence testifies to the greatness of the culture and art of the Parthian era. The cultural heritage associated with this era has been discovered over a vast expanse, from the borders of China and Central Asia, all the way to Mesopotamia and Syria in the west.[1]

On the other hand, the omission and distortion of the Parthian heritage by the Sasanians is in an important issue.[2] This deliberate omission of the Parthian heritage from Persian history and literature can be traced through Sasanian texts and, even more importantly, through post-Sasanian texts. These include some of the neglected texts of the Parthian period, such as the Master of Tus; Firdowsi in the *Shahnameh* claims only to have heard its name.[3] However, given that the oral tradition has played a significant role in the formation of Persian history and literature, there are certainly avenues for the transmission of data, no matter how meagre, and such data acquires additional importance as there is so little surviving evidence for the Parthians.[4]

In this article, I would like to present two notes discussing points arising from post-Sasanian texts.

Note 1: Ardavan (Artabanus) *Aqdam* (First) or Ardavan *Afdom* (the Final, the Last)

In *Mojmal al-Tawarikh wa al Qasas* we find:[5]

> Ashk ibn Dara ibn Darab, Ashk ibn Ashkan, Shapur ibn Ardavan ibn Ashk, Bahram ibn Shapur ... Ardavan ibn Balashan, the Great Ardavan ibn Ashkanan ... *The younger Ardavan Afdom*; Ardavan has been referred to in *Sayr-al-Moluk* as: *Aqdam, meaning the last.*

And also:[6]

> The first Sasanian king was Ardashir Babakan ... In this period Ardashir fought many kings and killed Ardavan, the last Parthian King of Kings, who was named *Aqdam* = "the First". When he was killed by Ardashir, and when his [Ardavan's] head was kicked by him [Ardashir], at that moment Ardashir was called *Shahanshah* ...

Zayn-al-Akhbar writes:[7]

> Ardavan (is the son of Balash), (nicknamed) *Afdom*. Yazdjerd [Yazdigird] (is the son of Shahriyar), (nicknamed) *Afdom King*. Ardashir-e Babakan killed Ardavan and called himself King of Kings (of Iran).

Tha'labi also writes:[8]

> Tabari has said that their first was King *Aqfur* who reigned for sixty-two years. He (King Aqfur) reigned over Ctesiphon and most parts of the lands of Iraq and Fars and the kings called him king and for him in the name of friendship and not in the name of tribute, they sent gifts.
>
> ... He then went to war with the Romans and took his revenge for Dara ... King Ardavan, son of Bahram, son of Balash: the last king of Parthia. He was called as "*the younger Ardavan*" by the Arabs, as according to some reports, after him another Ardavan became king, who was called by the Persians "*the Great Ardavan*". He is considered the greatest king of the Parthians with larger territory, higher respect and the most famous name.[9]

It is assumed that Muslim scholars not only used the Pahlavi term *"Afdom"* ("last") for Ardavan, but that they also described Ardavan as *"Aqdam"* ("first"). That is to say both the *first* and the *last* Parthian king; in Persian literature, the use of two contrasting terms, such as "the Benefactor

(*Niku-kar*) Ardashir" and "the Offender (*Bezeh-kar*) Ardashir", is common (*cf.* Tabari: 1983, 607, 627). The Sasanian sources, both written and oral, led to the Islamic sources focusing on the "*Afdom* King" of the Parthians; Ardavan being trampled beneath Ardashir Babakan's feet provides clear evidence for Ardavan being "the last".

Here I want to look more closely at the word *Afdom*. According to Nyberg, the term *Afdom* (> OIr *apa-tama, MPrs. 'bdwm, Paz. Awadum, MP II. 1974, 37) in the Sasanian texts has a very specific meaning and has been used as "the *last* and the *final*(ly)" and the like (Mackenzie: 1971, 3). This term, apart from appearing with this meaning in Sasanian texts, is also traceable in Islamic texts.[10]

It is obvious that through copying many errors have occurred in the Persian texts. Using the letter "F" instead of "P"; or "P" instead of "F"; "K" instead of "G"; "P" instead of "B"; L instead of K/B and vice versa – these are common errors in Persian manuscripts. Therefore, it cannot be ignored that in many Persian texts *"Ardavan-e Aqdam"* should be read as *"Ardavan-e Afdom"*. This confusion is the result of the historical problem of scribal error in the Persian language.

It is also obvious that when there is a discussion in Persian texts about *"Ardavan Aqdam"*, it refers to Ardavan, the last Parthian king. It is also clear that in all Islamic sources the Parthian dynasty starts with Ashk (Arsaces) ibn Ashk or Ashk ibn Dara. The existing texts refer back to Sasanian sources, and more precisely to the battle between Ardashir, the first Sasanian king, with the last Parthian king, namely Ardavan. Information about the first Parthian king in Islamic sources is meagre. Furthermore, the geographical extent of the kingdoms of *Ardavan Afdom* and *Ardavan Aqdam* is very similar, and comparable to the geographical extent of the kingdom of Ardavan in *Karnameh Ardashir Babakan* and Firdowsi's *Shahnameh*.[11]

It is not surprising that *Afdom* can be understood with the aid of other literary texts of the Persian language. Early Persian poets use *Afdom* to mean "the last" and "the end", or "final".

Divan-e Rudaki:[12]

> *Finally* (>be *Afdom*): you will be placed in dust upon your death
> As your birth was from dust
> Beware not to be deviated from the right path
> As you will be sent to hell at *last* (>be *Afdom*)

Abu Shokur Balkhi:[13]

> Now what should be done at the *end*? Except for you to sweep the house with your tail ...

Asadi Tusi:[14]

> Do not move with uncertainty, as this would *ultimately* lead you to hell ...

Note 1: Conclusion

Without doubt *Afdom* (*cf.* *bāfdom*) is one of the most recognised words in Middle Persian. Islamic sources provide additional evidence for its interpretation. This term was simply used to convey the concept of "the last" and "the latest". Therefore, it is obvious that "Ardavan *Afdom*" refers to Ardavan (Artabanus) IV, the last Parthian king.

It is also clear that "Ardavan *Aqdam*" or *"āqdam"* is an incorrectly written variant of *Afdom*, which has been introduced through scribal error. The evidence of *Sayr-al-Moluk Azarwan* is an example of this. In several pages of *Majmal-al-Tawarikh* (2009) we witness the correct use of Ardavan *Afdom* but elsewhere (p. 60) we suddenly encounter Ardavan *Aqdam* who was killed by Ardashir Babakan. The probability that in some texts *Aqdam* is no more than a corruption of *Afdom* cannot be ignored.

This case of *Aqdam*/*Afdom* reminds us of the occurrence in Islamic texts of the terms Ardavan *Akbar* and Ardavan *Asghar* ("the older Ardavan" and "the younger Ardavan"). It should be noted that in none of the Islamic texts is there to be found a similar report as the description of Ardavan *Aqdam* and it is not clear to whom the Ardavan *Aqdam* refers. Given that the term *Aqfur* is unusual and not recorded in any Persian glossaries, I would like to put forward the suggestion that *Aqfur*, which occurs in some Islamic texts, could also be a modification of *Afdom*/*Aqdam*.

Note 2: Parthian Genealogy

Firdowsi writes:[15]

> *Konun ay sarayandeh fartut-e mard*
> *suy-e gah* ***Ashkanian*** *baz-gard*
> *Bozorgan ke az tokhm* ***Arash*** *bodand*
> *dalir o sabokbar o sar-kesh bodand*
> (The grandees, who were from the seed of Arash/ were brave and chivalrous)
> *Cho bar takht-eshan shad benshandand*
> *Moluk tavayif hami khandand*
> *Cho kutah shod shakh o bikheshan*
> *naguyad jahan-dideh tarikheshan*
> *Az ishan joz az nam nashnideam*
> *na dar nameh khosravan khandeam*

Tabari writes:[16]

> Ashk son of Ashkan, after whom Shapur, Gudarz, Bijan ... Narsy ... the Parthian Ardavan, Khosrow, Balash, the younger Ardavan and then Ardashir son of Babak became the king.

It is also said[17] that:

> Ashk, son of Ashkan, is one of the children of *Kay-Qobad* ...

Further, it is said:[18]

> From the Parthian, King Aqfur, son of Balash, son of Shapur ...

Tha'labi writes:[19]

> The Parthians reigned over Iraq and near Persia and the Jibal and the Roman Emperor over Mosul and the Hephthalites ruled over Balkh. These kings considered the Parthian kings as great. It has been said that Ashkan was among the children of the great Dara. Also it has been said that he was one of the children of *Ashkan ibn Kay Arash ibn Kay-Qobad* and there is dispute over the Parthian ancestry.[20]

Ma'sudi said:[21]

> Afrasyab was after Nothar, who he was son of Atuj son of Taser son of Rami son of *Aras* son of Burak ...
>
> The first king of Moluk-al-Tavayif was Ashk son of Ardavan son of Ashkan son of the oppressor[22] ... *Siavash, son of King Kay-kavus*. Ardavan, Shapur, Neyzar ... reigned after Khosrow, his son Balash ibn Khosrow, after Balash his son Ardavan ibn Balash.[23]

Maqdasi:[24] in the account of Moluk-al-Tavayif, who are called the Parthians (the Arsacids):

> The Parthian Ashk reigned for ten years ... then Bizhan reigned for twenty-one years, later Jowzar, Narse ... Ardavan for twelve years ... Balash ... then the younger Ardavan for thirteen years and then the Moluk-al-Tavayif kingdom came to an end and the monarchy fell to the Sasanian.

Mojmal al-Tawarikh wa al Qasas:[25]

> Ashk ibn Dara ibn Darab, Ashk ibn Ashkan, Shapur ibn Ardavan ibn Ashk, Bahram ibn Shapur ... Ardavan ibn Balashan, the older Ardavan ibn Ashkanan ... the younger Ardavan *Afdom*.

It seems that for the genealogy of the Parthians we are faced with two lines of tradition. First, one that has a purely historical basis; and a second that incorporates elements of mythology. The question of how the Parthians served the Kayanid kings and found their way into the national epic of Iran[26] has been repeatedly studied. Here I would like to focus on the question of the relationship of the Parthians with the legendary Arash the Archer. Is it accidental or intentional?

It is well known that the Parthians are famous in history for both warfare and archery and that their skills in archery influenced the West. Skillful Parthian archers were able to take the enemy by surprise in the shortest possible time under a shower of arrows. References to Parthian archery can also be found on Parthian coins. Based on both oral and written evidence, Arash is known in Iranian mythology for his skills in archery. The name Arash appears in both the Avestan and Middle Persian texts.[27]

Maqdasi writes:[28]

> Then Manuchehr became king ... Afrasiab was a Turk who aimed to avenge his father and he put Manuchehr under siege for years. Then they agreed that Afrasiab should give him one shot of an arrow from his country. So they told a man named Arash to shoot an arrow, and he was a strong and agile man ...

I would like to conclude by emphasising how the great Khorasan region, which is associated with the birthplace of the Parthians and with the archery of the legendary Arash, is the place of origin of Iranian myths and beliefs. It is the largest and most important region for the recording Iranian history, traditions and culture in the early Islamic period (post-Sasanian texts).

In conclusion, I would like to propose the following as possible solutions to the issues raised in this article.

1. The reputation of the Parthians as skillful archers could have been instrumental in integrating the myth of Arash into Parthian mythology.
2. The sense of national identity created in Iran after the Parthian victory over the Seleucids could then have been used to incorporate Arash as a character who was crucial in establishing the geographical boundaries of Iran.
3. The assumption that Arash might be a corruption of Arshak cannot be valid, as Islamic texts distinguish clearly between the two and do not suggest any confusion.
4. There is no evidence to prove that the Parthians created a genealogy in which they could claim descent from Arash: cf. Sasanian genealogy and their relationship with Daray-e Darayan, the last Achaemenid king. However, the manufacture of such a pedigree was not so unusual in ancient Iran: cf. the tale of Bahram-e Chubineh, *Shahnameh* (2003, p. 1683).

Notes

1 Akbarzadeh 2007, p. 1.
2 Daryaee 2005, p. 202.
3 Shahnameh, 2003 ed., p. 1177.
4 Navabi 1996, p. 7.
5 2009, p. 32.
6 2009, p. 60
7 2006, p. 62–63, 84.
8 1989, p. 284–286.
9 *Ibid.*, p. 299.
10 Cf. Moin 1992, p. 324; Dehkhoda 1346, p. 491, 3076.
11 Cf. *Al-Kamil*, by Ibn Athir 1986, p. 49.
12 1999, p. 73, 88.
13 1991, p. 104.
14 1975, p. 5.
15 2003, p. 1177.
16 1983, p. 498.
17 *Ibid.*, p. 499.
18 *Ibid.*, p. 500.

19 1989, p. 286.
20 Cf. *Al-Kamil*, by Ibn Athir 1986, p. 50.
21 In Moruj-al-Zahhab 2008, p. 221, 229–230.
22 Although this term could be a scribal error for *Arash* (see *ibd.* 221), its adjective ("oppressor") makes me doubtful.
23 Cf. Al-Tanbiyat wa-al-Ashraf 2010, 89; *Al-Kamil*, by Ibn Athir 1986, 50).
24 2007, p. 510.
25 2009, p. 32.
26 Tafazzoli 1996, p. 271.
27 Mazdapur 1999, p. 360–370.
28 2007, p. 504.

References

Abu-Shokur-e Balkhi, see below, Navabi, M.Y.

Akbarzadeh, D. (2007). *Japan in Medieval Persian Manuscripts and Japan–Iran Relation*, Ankara.

Anonymous. (2009). *Mojmal al-Tawarikh wa al Qasas*, edited by M.-T. Bahar, Tehran.

Asadi Tusi, A.M.A.A. (1975). *Garshasb-nameh*, edited by H. Yaghmaee, Tehran.

Ibn al-Athir, A. (1986). *Al-Kamil fi al-tarikh,* edited by A. Halat, Tehran.

Daryaee, T. (2005). *Sasanian Empire*, Persian translation by M. Saqebfar, Tehran.

Dehkhoda, A. (1967). *Loghat-nameh*, introduction by M. Moin, Tehran.

Ferdowsi, A. (2003). *Shahnameh*, Moscow edition, vols. I–II, Tehran.

Gardizi, A.S.Z. (2006). *Zayn al-akhbar*, edited by Rahimzadeh-Malek, Tehran.

Mackenzie, D.N. (1971). *A Concise Pahlavi Dictionary*, London.

Maqdasi, M.T. (2002), *Afarinesh va Tarikh*, translated and with notes by M.R. Shafiee-Kadkani, Tehran.

Mas'udi, A.H. (2008). *Muruj adh-dhahab wa ma'adin al-jawhar,* translated by A. Payandeh, 8th edition, Tehran.

——— (2010), *Kitab altanbih wa al-ishraf,* Persian translation by A. Payandeh, Tehran.

Modaberi, M. (1991). *Sha'eran-e bi Divan* (Poets with No Poetical Works), Tehran.

Mazdapur, K. (1999). *Garshasp, Tahmures and Jamshid Tales*, Tehran.

Mo'in, M. (1992). *Farhang Mo'in*, 8th edition, Tehran (in Persian).

Navabi, M.-Y. (1996). *Yadegar-i Zariran*: translation, notes and comparison with Shahnameh, Tehran.

Nyberg, H.S. (1974). *A Manual of Pahlavi II: Ideograms, Glossary, Abbreviations, Index, Corrigenda to Part I*, Wiesbaden.

Rudaki, (1999). *Divan-e Rudaki* (Rudaki's Poetical Works), edited by N. Emami, Tehran.

Tabari, M.J. (1983). *Tarikh al-Rusul wa al-Muluk*, translated by A. Payanadeh, Tehran.

Tafazzoli, A. (1996). *Tarikh-e Adabiyat-e Iran-e pish az Islam*, edited by J. Amouzegar, Tehran.

Tha'alibi, A.M.A.M.M.I (1989). *Tarikh Tha'alibi*, translated by M. Fezaeli, Tehran (1989).

ARCHAEOLOGICAL

11

A Note on Architectural Traditions in Arsacid Parthia: The Round Hall at Nisa

Antonio Invernizzi
University of Turin

The Round Hall in the Central Ensemble of the citadel of Mithradatkert (Figure 11.1) is perhaps the most peculiar building of Parthian Nisa, in present-day Turkmenistan. Its layout and constructional technique are particularly noteworthy. The interior hall, a grandiose, circular space with a diameter of 17 m, is enclosed by a square perimeter. The latter work is a precinct, as the masonry of the two parts shows independent construction. The inner ring is only two and a half mud bricks thick and is almost literally inscribed within the thicker masonry of the outer square (Figure 11.2). The spaces between the inner corners of that square and the ring are filled with bricks.

Even before the completion of the excavations, G.A. Pugachenkova proposed a reconstruction of the upper parts of the hall, based on the model of the Arsinoeion at Samothrace: a cylindrical drum with a two-tiered wall, covered by a sloping wooden roof.[1] A careful examination of the remains of the walls at Nisa, in combination with the structural analyses carried out in the course of more recent investigations, suggests a very different shape, however, and disconnects the structure from Hellenistic architecture. A Near Eastern taste is apparent in this hypothesis: an oval dome resting directly on the ground below, with its top probably emerging from the outer square block in the way that will become common in Sasanian and Islamic architecture (Figures 11.3 and 11.4).[2] The proposal is certainly audacious – for the Round Hall would be much older than the earliest standing examples – and has met with criticism.[3] Thus it has been questioned whether the attested inclination of the walls can be explained only by the proposed model, especially in the absence of other Parthian evidence for the technique necessary to cover such a large space with a dome.

As for the measurements: they can obviously be only indicative and it is true that, after decades of exposure to the harsh Nisa climate, the state of preservation of the wall surfaces is poor. Yet the figures suggesting a slight inclination of the walls, beginning at floor level, towards the interior were derived from less eroded points on opposite sides and should be counted as objective evidence. The observed convergence can hardly be ascribed to mere chance. By contrast, it has been suggested that the inclination results simply from an earthquake,[4] but in that case one has to assume that this deformation occurred in a surprisingly coherent way all around the hall.

As for the chronological issue, it is true that the date of the Round Hall (150–100 BC) is centuries prior to such technical accomplishments as the brick domes of the Islamic "ice-houses" of Margiana (Figure 11.5),[5] the brick vault of the Sasanian Taq-i Kisra at Ctesiphon, or the grandiose domes of the early Sasanian period like Ardashir's hall in Firuzabad and the cruciform hall in Bishapur. And it is also true that the use of different materials in these later cases required different technical solutions. However, their refined construction was certainly not a sudden innovation: it presupposes a long progress of experience and maturing. General building techniques of Near Eastern origin at Nisa are anything but primitive, and the absence of other large Parthian domes provides an argument from silence. At any rate, the Round Hall was certainly roofed; analyses based on structural calculations prove that the hypothetical model is consistent with the available building techniques of the time and that a dome would match the constructional remains ideally. A wooden roof, as suggested by Pugachenkova, should be ruled out on the basis of the same evidence.

Previously, V.L. Voronina had already observed that the technique required for Pugachenkova's Hellenistic roof is totally foreign to the architectural culture of Central Asia.[6] Though archaeological evidence suggests

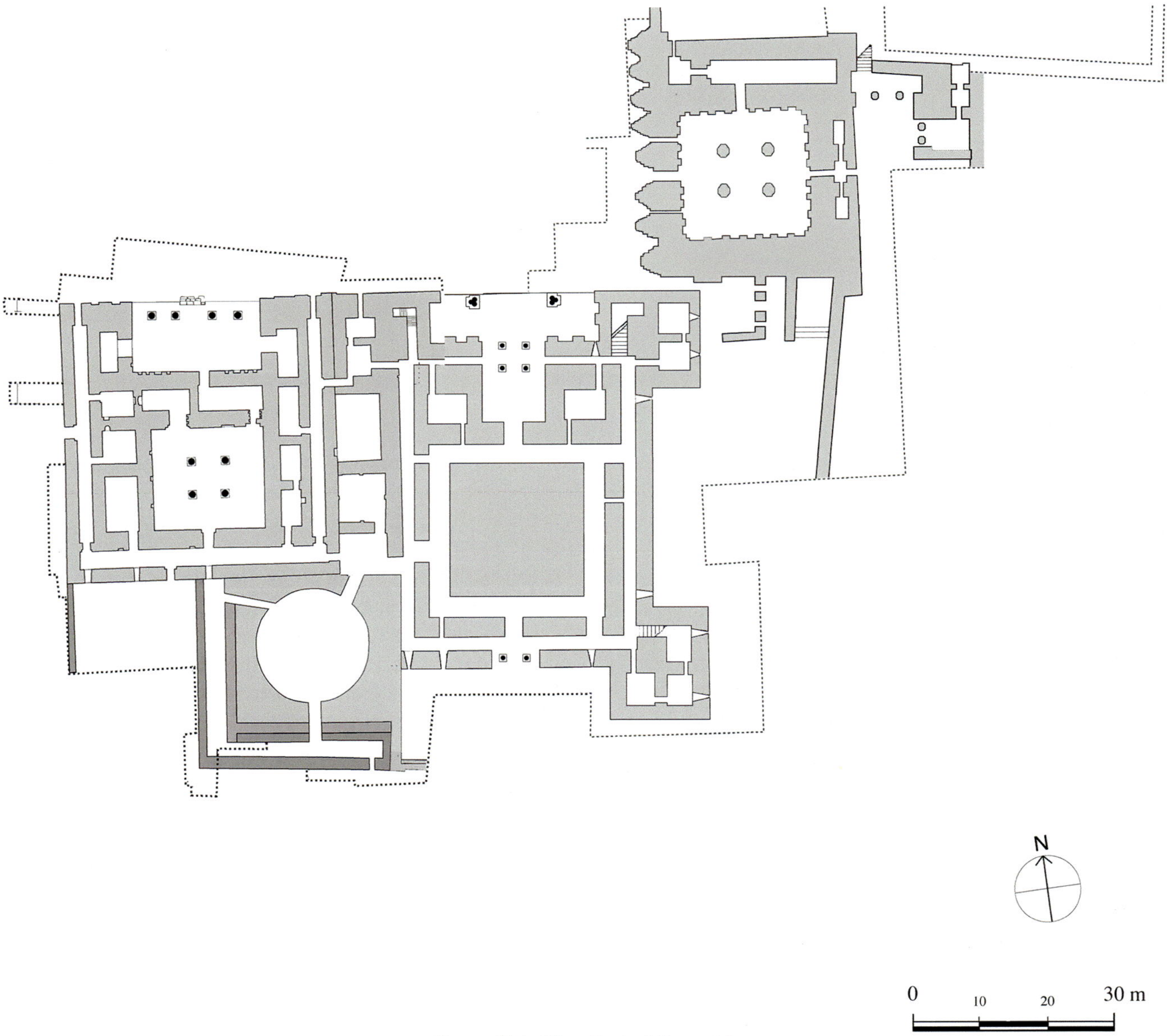

Figure 11.1: Nisa Central Ensemble

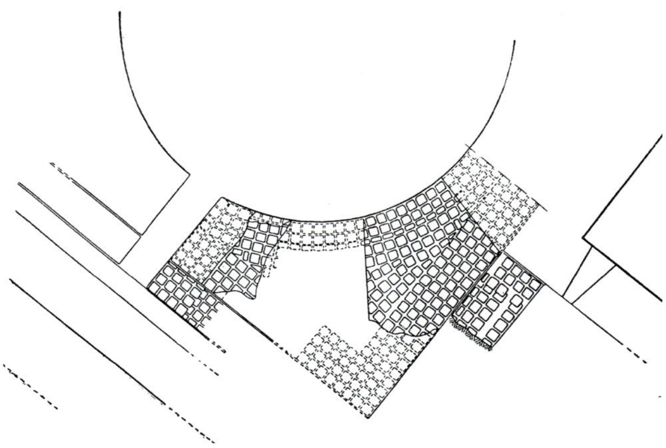

Figure 11.2: Nisa Round Hall constructional scheme

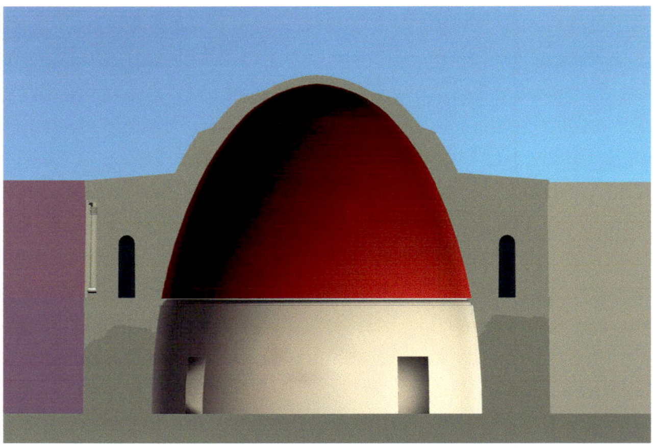

Figure 11.3: Nisa Round Hall

Figure 11.4: Nisa Round Hall

Figure 11.5: Margiana ice house

that wood was used rather frequently in this area, it was in general employed either as a framework for blocks of mud brick masonry, or for roofs of very different shapes based on very different principles. The ideal shape among these was the lantern-roof, which informed the accepted reconstructions of the Square Hall and the Red Building. It may additionally be remarked that, according to the Greek model, an enormous weight would have rested on a very thin ring, thinner than the outer square perimeter walls, which would be deprived of any precise structural function. By contrast, the assumption of a self-standing dome gives the surrounding square the function of containing efficaciously the outward thrust.

The reconstruction of a wooden roof in the Greek style by Pugachenkova results from a simple formal idea, which was not, however, tested against the available data. On the basis of these data, and using the small section drawing published by Pugachenkova (Figure 11.6),[7] the hypothetical roof would consist of two shells: a circular one on the inner hall and a necessarily square one on the outside that would presumably rest on the corners of the square perimeter. This design is technically absolutely unlikely, and in striking contrast not only to Central Asian but also to Greek architectural practice. In addition, the amount of timber necessary would be rather high, thus increasing by a large scale the weight of the roof and the risk of instability. Pugachenkova's model is suitable only for a building that is entirely circular, both on the inside and outside.

The excavators seem to have imagined the Round Hall to be roofed by a dome as well, at an early stage in their thinking. This is borne out by the old scale model of the entire citadel (Figure 11.7) now exhibited in the Ashgabat Museum, which was produced at an early stage of field research. Apparently later reflection and the search for possible parallels occasioned the rejection of the dome thesis and the formulation of alternative solutions. Still, as on-site observations and engineering calculations have clearly shown, a dome ranks first among possible alternatives as the ideal roof for the Round Hall.

Judging from the list of domes in ancient Central Asia recently published by Baimatowa,[8] Central Asian architects were undoubtedly familiar with this type of roof and the principles of the relevant building technique. The evidence is, however, limited to square layouts of much lesser size and to buildings of more modest demand. Dome structures also figure widely in scholarly literature; their use

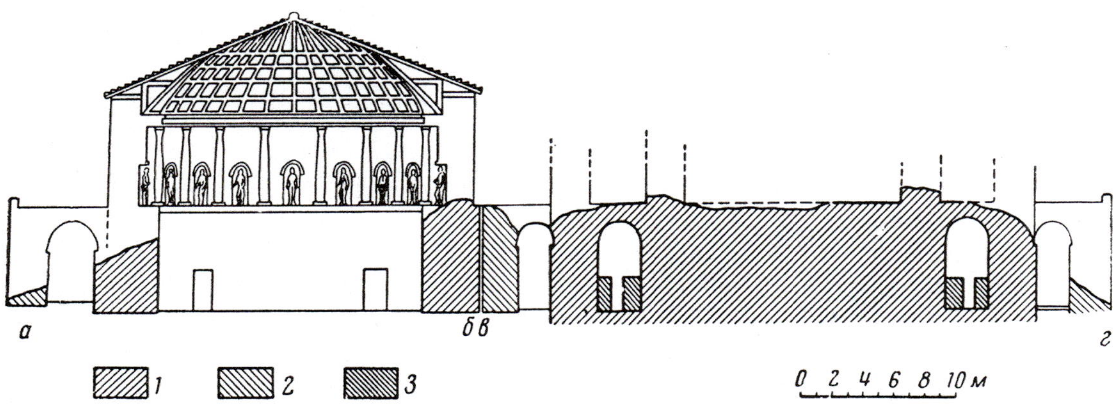

Figure 11.6: Nisa Round Hall section

Figure 11.7: Ashgabat Museum JuTAKE model

has been proposed for a number of imposing ancient Central Asian buildings. Building 2 at Altyn 10 (Figure 11.8)[9] is an example for the Achaemenid period, and a dome of precisely oval section (Figure 11.9) was reconstructed for a funerary building of the first or second century AD at the Bairam-Ali necropolis (Marw).[10]

Archaeological evidence offers additional and more important arguments for domes with square ground plans in ancient Central Asia. The prime structural peculiarity of the Round Hall of Nisa is the structural independence of its inner ring from its outer square. Possibly the idea of inserting a circular room – to commemorate the founder, Mithradates I, and/or other individuals – in the Central Complex was inspired by Macedonian models in its general shape[11] and function.[12] The technique, however, and the architectural principles, as well as in a sense the typology of the building, are firmly rooted in local Central Asian traditions. Buildings like the graves of the Iron Age necropolis at Tagisken (Figure 11.10)[13] provide direct evidence.

Tagisken is situated in Chorasmia, south of the lower course of the Syr-Darya, not far from its mouth on the Aral Sea. The Tagisken necropolis contains several mausoleums.[14] The earliest date to the ninth to the eighth centuries BC; their layouts and structural features can be compared with the Round Hall in Nisa. The larger mausoleums, nos. 4, 5 and 7, consist of a quadrangular or rounded space in the centre, surrounded by two rings of thick mud brick pillars. The outer ring separates two circular corridors, one inside, one outside; this entire construction is set within an outer square precinct, also of mud bricks; small empty spaces occur in the four corners. Rings of wooden poles were set around the interior mud pillar rings. In the larger buildings, these poles were connected with fences of masonry or wickerwork trellis. Having no structural rationale, it is likely that these elements simply reproduce features common in local domestic buildings.

In spite of their evident formal, technical and functional differences, the above structures share with the Round Hall the layout of the inner structure – a circle in a square perimeter – and the building technique based on centric elements. They also have comparable dimensions, the inner circle reaching up to 14 m in diameter, the outside walls of

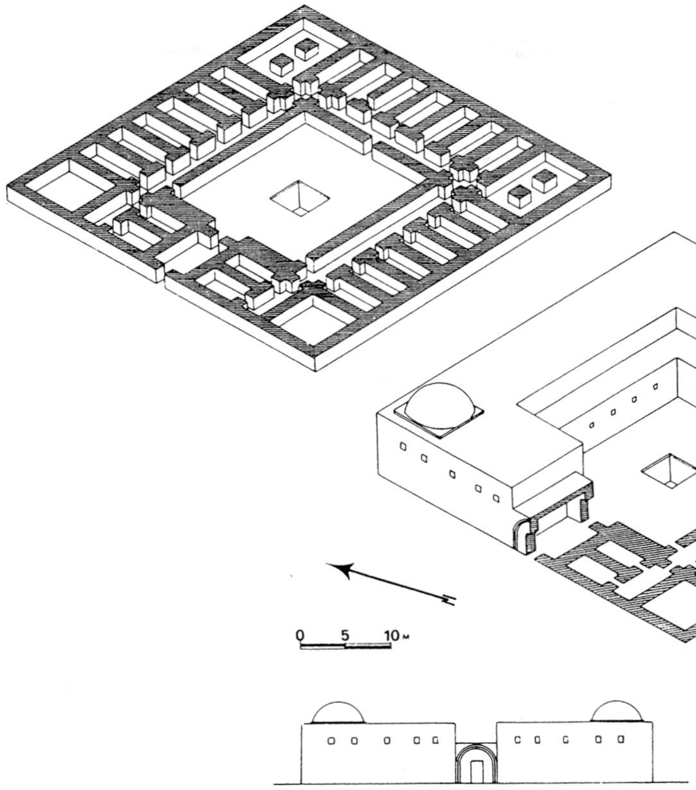

Figure 11.8: Altyn Tepe

Figure 11.9: Merv (Marw) funerary building

the outer square 17.5–18 m. The orientation of the buildings is roughly similar and, finally, the function of the buildings is comparable in a more general sense: funerary at Tagisken, commemorative of ancestors at Nisa.

The Tagisken mausoleums are thought to imitate contemporary common dwellings in their layouts and structural features, with a characteristic alternation of mud brick and wooden elements. Their elevation is never preserved up to a sufficient height, but terracotta ossuaries may be invoked as evidence for roofing; they, too, are unanimously thought to reproduce real buildings, yet on a smaller, simplified scale. Among the ossuaries, those from the fifth to sixth centuries

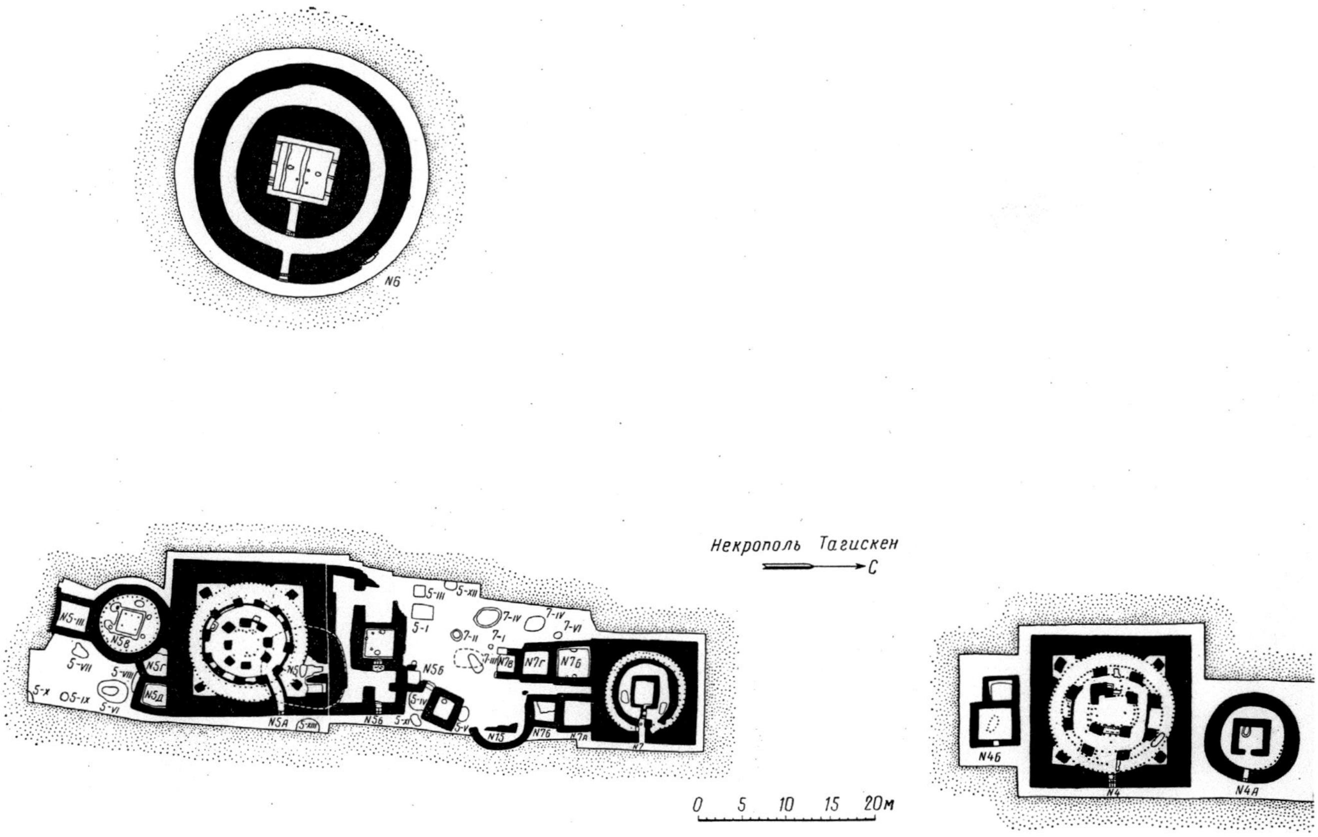

Figure 11.10: Necropolis of Tagisken

Figure 11.11: Ossuaria of Bajram-Ali

from Bairam-Ali (Marw)[15] (Figure 11.11) are particularly significant; they show a dome-shaped inner room set in a perimeter with the shape of either a truncated cone or a square with vertical or slanting walls. The top of the dome of these ossuaries rises over the outer square, exactly in the way that would become typical for Islamic architecture. When the Italian team first proposed the dome hypothesis for the Round Hall, these ossuaries were overlooked, but the typological affinity is so striking that it provides important confirmation for this model. Also, the parallel between mausoleums and ossuaries invites identification of the latter as primarily models of graves rather than being directly inspired by houses. At this point it may be observed once more that the sphere to which the parallels belong is again roughly the same: funerary in the broadest sense for the mausoleums and ossuaries, commemorative for the Nisa Round Hall, a building directly devoted to the memory of deceased kings and the location of certain funerary rituals, hence in a way a cenotaph.

Notes

1 Pugachenkova 1958, colour plate in front of p. 104.
2 Masturzo 2008; Blasi/Coïsson/Ferretti 2008; Invernizzi, in press (a) and in press (b).
3 Pilipko 2008, p. 40.
4 Pilipko 2008, p. 40.
5 Herrmann 1999, p. 56, fig. 49; Blasi/Coïsson/Ferretti 2008, fig. 82.
6 Voronina 1960, p. 45–46; cf. Baimatowa 2008, p. 209.
7 Krasheninnikova/Pugachenkova 1964, p. 132, fig. 10.
8 Baimatowa 2008.
9 Sarianidi 1977, fig. 60; Rapin 1992, pl. 47; Invernizzi 2000, fig. 14.
10 Koshelenko 1977, fig. 27; Usmanova/Filanovich/Koshelenko 1985, p. 239, pl. xcvii: B3.
11 Compare the *tholos* of the Vergina palace, which was a sacred space, a shrine in a ceremonial palace in the vicinity of the necropolis of the Macedonian kings (Hoepfner 1996, fig. 5; Invernizzi 2000, p. 46–47, fig. 23).
12 Philip II erected a *tholos* for displaying a statuary family group in the panhellenic sanctuary of Olympia as an important act of political propaganda towards the Greek cities (Schultz 2009). Similar examples may have inspired the erection of the rulers' statues in the Round Hall (Invernizzi 2011).
13 Tol'stov/Zhdanko/Itina 1963.
14 On the funerary rituals in the Tagisken necropolis see Lelekov 1972.
15 Rapoport 1971, p. 62–63, fig. 20; Cf. Rtveladze 1999, p. 112; *Gosudarstvennyj Muzej Iskusstv Karakalpakskoj ASSR*, Moskva 1976, p. 9, fig. 16 (ossuary from Burly-kala, Kwarezm, 1st–3rd centuries AD).

References

Baimatowa, N.S. (2008). *5000 Jahre Architektur in Mittelasien. Lehmziegelgewölbe vom 4./3. Jt. v. Chr. bis zum Ende des 8. Jhs. n. Chr.*, Archäologie in Iran und Turan 7, Mainz.

Blasi, C., Coïsson, E., Ferretti, D. (2008). "La Sala Rotonda di Nisa Vecchia: ipotesi geometriche di una copertura a cupola e loro validazione statica", in Invernizzi and Lippolis (2008): p. 66–81.

Herrmann, G. (1999). *Monuments of Merv. Traditional Buildings of the Karakum*, London.

Hoepfner, W. (1996). "Zum Typus der Basileia und der königlichen Andrones", in W. Hoepfner, G. Brands (eds), *Basileia. Die Paläste der hellenistischen Könige. Internationales Symposion in Berlin vom 16.12. bis 20.12.1992*, Mainz: p. 1–43.

Invernizzi, A. (2000). "The Square House at Old Nisa", *Parthica* 2: p. 13–53.

——— (2011). "Parthian Art – Arsacid Art", in *Les Parthes d'Est en Ouest: actualité de larecherche sur les Parthes*, Topoi 17: p. 189–207.

——— (in press, a). "Mithradates I and the Round Hall of Nisa", in *Studies in memory of G.A. Pugachenkova*, Ashabad.

——— (in press, b). "Tradizioni architettoniche nella Parthia arsacide", in *Parthische Kunst – Kunst im Partherreich (Proceedings of the Meeting, Basel 9. October 2010)*, Düsseldorf.

Invernizzi, A., and Lippolis C. (eds) (2008). *Nisa Partica. Ricerche nel complesso monumentale arsacide 1990–2006*, Monografie di Mesopotamia IX, Florence.

Koshelenko, G.A. (1977). *Rodina Parfjan*, Moscow.

Krasheninnikova, N.I., and Pugachenkova, G.A. (1964). "Kruglyj zal parfjanskoj Nisy (Arheologičeskie issledovanija i voprosy rekonstrukcii)", *Sovetskaja Arheologija* 4: p.119–135.

Lelekov, L.A. (1972). "K istolkovaniju pogrebal'nogo obrjada v Tagiskene", *Sovetskaja Etnografija* 1: p. 128–131.

Masturzo, N. (2008). "L'architettura della Sala Rotonda di Nisa Vecchia", in Invernizzi and Lippolis (2008): p. 43–65.

Pilipko, V.N. (2008). "The Central Ensemble of the Fortress Mihrdatkirt. Layout and Chronology", *Parthica* 10: p. 33–51.

Pugachenkova, G.A. (1958). *Puti razvitija arhitektury Južnogo Turkmenistana pory rabovladenija i feodalizma*, Trudy Južno-Turkmenistanskoj Arheologičeskoj Kompleksnoj Ekspedicii VI, Moscow.

Rapin, Cl. (1992). *Fouilles d'Aï Khanoum, VIII La trésorerie du palais hellénistique d'Aï Khanoum. L'apogée et la chute du royaume grec de Bactriane*, Mémoires de la Délégation Archéologique Française en Afghanistan XXXIII, Paris.

Rapoport, Ju.A. (1971). *Iz istorii religii drevnego Horezma*, Moscow.

Rtveladze, E. (1999). *Velikij Selkovyj put'. Enciklopedičeskij spravočnik. Drevnost' i rannee srednevekov'e*, Tashkent.

Sarianidi, V.I. (1977). *Drevnie zemledel'cy Afganistana. Materialy sovetsko-afganskoj ekspedicii 1969–1974 gg*, Moscow.

Schultz, P. (2009). "Divine Images and Royal Ideology in the Philippeion at Olympia", in J. Tae Jensen, G. Hinge, P. Schultz, B. Wickkiser, *Aspects of Ancient Greek Cult. Context – Ritual – Iconography*, Aarhus Studies in Mediterranean Antiquity VIII, Aarhus: p. 125–193.

Tol'stov, S.P., Zhdanko, T.A., and Itina, M.A. (1963). "Arheologičeskie raboty na drevnih ruslah Syr-dar'i", in *Polevye issledovanija Horezmskoj Ekspedicii v 1958–1961 gg*, I, Moscow: p. 32–47.

Usmanova, Z.I., Filanovich, M.I., and Koshelenko, G.A. (1985). "Margiana", in Koshelenko, G.A. (ed.), *Drevnejšie gosudarstva Kavkaza i Srednej Azii*, Arheologija SSSR, Moscow: p. 226–242.

Voronina, V.L. (1960). "Doislamskie kul'tovye sooruženija Srednej Azii", *Sovetskaja Arheologija* 2: p. 42–55.

Will, E. (1976). "Banquets et salles de banquet dans les cultes de la Grèce et de l'empire romain", in *Mélanges d'histoire ancienne et d'archéologie offerts à Paul Collart*, Lausanne: p. 353–362.

12

Women, Dance and the Hunt: Splendour and Pleasures of Court Life in Arsacid and Early Sasanian Art

Barbara Kaim
University of Warsaw

Despite the long history of research on ancient Iranian monarchies, scarce sources considerably limit our knowledge of Iranian court life in the past. This is particularly true for the Arsacid and early Sasanian periods. Iranian written sources, including chiefly early Sasanian royal inscriptions, are occasional, while external information is not only incomplete but its scientific value has frequently been questioned. Ancient authors are primarily focused on conspicuous wealth and ceremonial splendour perceived as signs of licentiousness and decadence.[1] However, that consumption-focused approach is employed to describe the dynasties of ancient Iran often enough to raise doubts about the impartiality of the authors and the reliability of their reports. Given the above, even the smallest piece of information available from archaeological sources becomes vital.

The present study is designed to indicate one more, though probably still incompletely exploited, source of information about court life, namely the architectural decoration of palaces. We largely rely on the assumption that wall, floors and ceilings were decorated to prioritise certain chambers in the overall room hierarchy that must have been established based on the nature of activities intended for such chambers. Viewed in this light, the decorative themes that occur in palatial architecture, if carefully examined, are capable of helping to reconstruct at least some aspects of court life. Its epicentre is usually perceived as lying in the royal capitals. Indeed, ancient authors enumerate several chosen by the Arsacid kings as their seasonal abodes.[2] The most frequently mentioned among the Arsacid royal capitals is Ctesiphon or a coronation city and a royal winter residence.[3] Regrettably, neither the palace at Ctesiphon nor royal structures once existing at Ecbatana and Rhagae or at Hecatompylus[4] have been archaeologically ascertained. Thus, the structures revealed at Old Nisa continue to be the only known Arsacid edifices that can be directly linked to royalty. They have implications for our present study as their decoration provides an in-depth look into certain aspects of royal ideology that give us a better understanding of the reasons for the presence of some specific motifs in architectural decoration of the Arsacid period. Although the functions of some of these structures still await identification, it seems evident that Old Nisa became a large ceremonial centre of the Arsacid dynasty after major constructional alterations either in the final years of Mithradates I or soon after his demise.[5] Essential structures of the centre include the Square House, the Red Building, the Square Hall, the Round Hall and the Tower Building.

Unearthed during recent excavations in the central sector of the site, the Red Building represents an earlier phase in this monumental complex. The Red Building is square in plan, with its main entrance from the north, through a deep portico flanked by two small rooms. Both the front wall of the platform on which the Red Building stands and the rear wall of the portico are faced with a frieze of stone slabs decorated by a continuous series of flutings under a bead and reel pattern. The walls of the Red Building used to be plastered red purple. Coloured plaster was also applied over the floors in two rooms of the Building. The practice of applying dark red purple plaster can be traced back to Achaemenid palatial structures. As argued by the excavator, the colour purple might have carried specific meaning for both the Achaemenids and the Arsacids, and its use may be assumed to have pointed to a link between the Red Building's decorations and royal ideology.[6]

In addition to the Red Building, there was also the Square House in the northern sector of the site, built in the early construction phase of Old Nisa. The purpose of the Square House appears clear from the equipment revealed in place.

Invernizzi argues that the Square House was a ceremonial banquet hall in which royal guests rested on banquettes or benches constructed along the walls.[7]

Sumptuous banquets held at the royal courts of ancient Mesopotamia and Iran have a long history and are richly documented by written records and iconographic sources. Whether official or not, banquets were intended to emphasise the wealth and power of the monarch and to express kingship by means of the copious size of portions, extravagant menus and luxurious tableware. An invitation to a royal banquet was an official declaration of royal favour, an acknowledgement of one's high rank and privileges, as well as a method for strengthening alliances and loyalty, and for uniting élites around the monarch.[8] Therefore the ancient authors' view of banquets as providing nothing but entertainment to the monarch can hardly be upheld; in fact, banquets were a crucial element of court rituals designed both to enhance the social prestige of the royal court and to strengthen royal power.

Wine, the large-scale consumption of which is proven by capacious storage vessels and *ostraca*, surely constituted an important component of banquets at Old Nisa. It is supposed that wine was served from ivory rhytons stored in the Square House when it ceased to serve its original purpose and became a treasury.[9] Manassero, following Hoffmann's tracing of changes with regard to the meanings of rhytons with animal foreparts, concludes that, given that rhytons were generally a symbol of Dionysus in the Hellenistic period, the Square House rhytons were used to pour libations in honour of Arsacid heroized ancestors.[10] The acceptance of Manassero's view entails the assumption that the rhytons were not used for this purpose until the fortified residence had been transformed into a memorial and ceremonial centre for the Arsacid dynasty; according to Invernizzi, this change of function occurred during the reign of Mithradates I or his immediate successor.[11]

It was after the reign of Mithradates I that the monumental structures (except the Red Building) of the central complex were built. These included the Round Hall, which is adjacent to the south-eastern corner of the Red Building, and which is interpreted as a mausoleum or *heroon* of an Arsacid ruler. Discovered among surviving fragments of colossal male and female statues once adorning the Round Hall, a fragment of a statue of Mithradates I is deemed by Invernizzi to support the view that it was actually that king for whom the *heroon* was constructed.[12] Similar monumental clay statues were also used to decorate the Square Hall built during the second construction phase at Old Nisa. Invernizzi believes that the statues from the Square Hall and the Round Hall represent mythical or deified ancestors of Mithradates I.[13]

The purpose of the Tower Building remains unclear. This is the tallest structure of Old Nisa, built in the vicinity of the Square Hall and the Round Hall, and which once had remains of a columned building on the top, as mentioned by early excavators. Regrettably the remains were not properly recorded before they became no longer traceable.[14] In addition fragments of wall-paintings, which have been discovered outside their original context during recent excavations, cannot be identified in terms of dating and their precise original location within the columned building. However, several fragments have been successfully matched to reveal a scene depicting a battle between two groups of mounted men dressed in the Iranian style.[15] Whether historical or mythological, the scene was obviously intended to glorify the military achievements of the Arsacids and, as such, sat well within the ideological programme of the ceremonial centre.

If the current initial and still imprecise timeline for Old Nisa's construction[16] proves correct, it appears reasonable to suggest that the process of the creation of a dynastic centre was accompanied by the adoption of Hellenistic patterns of the presentation of royal power and majesty. This was surely not driven by anything other than ideological motives and the need to present an Arsacid ruler as one of the monarchs of the Hellenistic East, and the equal of his peers in terms of power.

The particular nature of the structures at Old Nisa prevents their examination from being truly fruitful and yielding extensive information about court life, except the previously mentioned role of banquets. However, when combined with information from coins datable to the time of Mithradates I, it adds to the reconstruction of some aspects of the Arsacids' royal ideology which was undoubtedly mirrored by court life.

Whether the Round Hall, Tower Building and Square Hall were constructed during or after the reign of Mithradates I, it was at this very time that changes in royal ideology occurred. These changes are traceable chiefly in coins minted under Mithradates I. Prior to the conquest of Media and Mesopotamia, coins already started to bear the legends *basileos theou* or *basileos megalou theopator(os)*, which, according to Dąbrowa, suggests the beginning of a ruler cult inspired by Hellenistic culture.[17] Those coins continued to depict the ruler wearing the traditional satrapal headgear, sometimes referred to as the *bashlyk*; his later drachms and tetradrachms, however, portrayed the ruler wearing a royal diadem.[18] Deemed an attribute of royalty but of debatable origin, the diadem seems to be associated with Dionysus in the Hellenistic period.[19]

The iconography and legends on coins show that some elements of royal ideology were modified by successors of Mithradates I. These modifications generally consisted of a return to Iranian traditions.[20] Regrettably their impact on various aspects of court life cannot be identified with certainty. It seems highly likely that elements such as audiences, banquets and hunts, which were deeply rooted in the Eastern tradition, would have been subject only to qualitative and quantitative changes. Sadly, a paucity of sources prevents any in-depth study.

A similar paucity affects studies of almost every aspect of court life, including royal women, otherwise a rewarding topic that is readily addressed by modern scholars.[21] It is only very infrequently that royal women are treated at any length in Greek or Latin sources. The exception here is Musa, a slave concubine whom we see promoted to royal consort (of Phraates IV) and mother of a royal successor (Phraataces).[22] Usually, however, ancient authors point to a large number of concubines at royal and noble courts. Concubines are normally referred to collectively with other goods, for instance "his treasures and his concubines",[23] and, as a rule (except for the case of Musa), anonymously. Anonymity, however, did not necessarily entail their unimportance for court life, as there were cases when concubines gave birth to rulers.[24]

As for royal consorts, the sources usually record only the queen's name and rarely give her titles. Those that record titles prove that rulers could have several wives, each holding the title of queen.[25] These were chosen from the royal family, sometimes including such close relatives as half-sisters, and probably also from Parthian noble families.[26] And since marriages were traditionally designed to strengthen internal or external alliances, queens of foreign origin were not infrequent: Phraates II (138–127 BC) was married to Laodice, a daughter of Cleopatra Thea and Demetrius II Nikator; Mithradates II (124/123–88/87 BC) to a daughter of Tigranes, king of Armenia; Sinatruces (77 BC) was probably married to a Mesopotamian woman; Orodes II (57–38 BC) to Laodice, a daughter of Antiochos I Theos and Isias Philostorgos of Commagene; and Vonones I (8–9 AD) to a Scythian princess.[27]

Royal women surely formed a part of the ruler's innermost circle and their public appearance was one of the methods to manifest royalty, as suggested by the fact that Tiridates I, the king of Armenia and founder of the Armenian line of the Arsacid dynasty, went to Rome together with his consort in 66 AD. Riding on horseback next to her husband and wearing a helmet instead of a veil, she made an immense impression upon the Romans.[28]

Ancient sources seem to indicate, however, that Arsacid royal women did not play any more prominent role: they lived in the seclusion of the women's chambers or harem, lacking any involvement in court intrigues and not participating in entertainments. Nevertheless, the actions of the royal consort upon the demise of the king of Adiabene,[29] or those of Queen Talasi'asu of Mesene who, upon her husband's death, was able to enthrone her juvenile son,[30] as well as the appearance of a female portrait and the legend "Lady Rangodeme" on the reverse of coins minted by otherwise unknown local ruler of eastern Iran in the first century BC,[31] along with other representations of royal women in art of the Arsacid period, all seem to challenge this view.[32] Although it is beyond question that depictions of men largely outnumber depictions of women and that this is typical for Near Eastern art, we should remember that at Old Nisa, among fragments of clay statues and paintings, there were some female representations.[33] Representations of women occur also in the court art of local Parthian rulers and neighbouring monarchies.[34] There is no need to cite familiar examples from Hatra or Dura Europos. There is, however, a rock relief at Tang-e Sarvak (Khuzestan) that deserves more attention, for it shows a ruler of Elymais seated and most probably accompanied by his consort.[35] Yet other examples worth mentioning are the painting from Kuh-e Khwaja (Sistan), which shows a king and queen seated in three-quarter view on an elaborate throne,[36] and female busts in stucco found with male busts at Qaleh-i Yazdigird (western Iran).

Discovered in the 1970s, the castle at Qaleh-i Yazdigird is chiefly known for its rich architectural stucco decoration.[37] Given the fact that we still have no archaeological record for any royal Arsacid palace (this being understood to mean a structure combining state administrative and royal residential functions), this Parthian noble's seat can serve as a complementary source of information on royal court life. This is valid only on the assumption that nobles mirrored kings as much as possible, including specifically their court life and residential design, but this seems a reasonable assumption, given tendencies throughout history.

Since the excavations at Qaleh-i Yazdigird have not been completed, neither the ground plan of the castle nor the precise function of each of the only partly unearthed rooms can be determined. Nevertheless, a group of three large rooms (nos 1, 5, 11) is striking, the ground plans and layout of which are deemed by the excavators to have echoes of the complex of the northern *eyvan* of the residence at Parthian Assur.[38] These three rooms have yielded the largest quantity of decorated stucco fragments. If indeed one of the rooms (no. 11, according to the excavators) had the form of and served as an *eyvan*, that is the most important and formal part of a castle, then the neighbouring rooms, although separated by corridors, might have been used for less official but still public purposes.

Geometrical and stylised floral patterns lavishly employed for stucco decorations at Qaleh-i Yazdigird resemble those of Parthian Uruk, Assur and Seleucia. For the present study, however, more important are certain figural motifs that are relatively abundant at Qaleh-i Yazdigird but which rarely occur in Mesopotamian residential decoration. A good starting point for the list of the Qaleh-i Yazdigird figural motifs is the male and female busts. These differ from one another in terms of size, hairstyle and clothing. One of three largest busts was found in fill of Room 1. It depicts a man with his hair gathered in two bunches, within a medallion with an egg-and-dart pattern around its border (Figure 12.1). It is enclosed within a square frame, the upper part of which is decorated with vine scrolls and grape clusters. Although his face has been damaged, a diadem round the temples

Figure 12.1: Qaleh-i Yazdigird. Portrait of a Parthian noble in medallion: a) after Keall 1980; b) courtesy of the National Museum of Iran, Tehran.

is still visible, indicating that he was of princely rank, if not higher.

Similar in size and following the same rule of composition, but far more poorly preserved, is a medallion with a female portrait, found in room fill in the western sector of the site (Figure 12.2).[39] A folded garment drapes over her left shoulder to form a V-shaped neckline and leaves her right shoulder uncovered. Similarly dressed is a female depicted within a much less elaborate medallion from Room 11. Unfortunately, her head is not preserved (Figure 12.3).[40] Interestingly, such a garment is not used for other female busts, whether much smaller examples enclosed within rhomboid frames,[41] or those on figured capitals.[42]

Assuming that the busts once decorating the walls at Qaleh-i Yazdigird depicted real people, it is probable that those who enjoyed the highest prestige had their busts set within medallions. Regrettably the lack of any information about either the inhabitants of Qaleh-i Yazdigird or, indeed, general principles for Parthian residential decoration prevents their identification. Of course, the fact that the man is shown wearing the diadem and enclosed within a medallion tempts us to see him as an owner of the castle, and the women as his wives or family members.

Because of the prevailing presence of motifs rooted in Greco-Roman iconography in the decorations of Qaleh-i Yazdigird, a feature which is examined in detail below, the formal similarity between these medallion busts and *imagines clipeatae* ("framed portraits" in Latin) should not escape our attention, although the origin, purpose and meaning of the latter continues to be a matter of debate.[43] The oldest known public building exhibiting portraits within medallions is a monumental structure at Delos dedicated to Mithridates VI of Pontus (120–63 BC) and built *c.* 102/1 BC, that is when the king was still alive. Inscriptions which accompany the busts identify them as friends, courtiers, foreign allies and associates of Mithridates.[44] In the Roman world, this specific type of portraiture was used to honour both living heroes and deceased ancestors.[45]

In terms of chronological and territorial distances, the portraits of Qaleh-i Yazdigird have closer ties with portrait medallions that are painted on the walls and vaults of houses and temples at Dura Europos,[46] which show perhaps deities or actual house owners.[47]

The examples referred to above are strong indicators that in any studies on the meaning and purpose of such portraits, due consideration should be given to the original location where they were displayed. Therefore, if Qaleh-i Yazdigird was indeed a residence of a local noble, it is very likely that the people depicted within the medallions were from its owner's innermost circle but not necessarily from his closest family.

Identification of other male portraits from Qaleh-i Yazdigird, including the one contained within a *medallion*

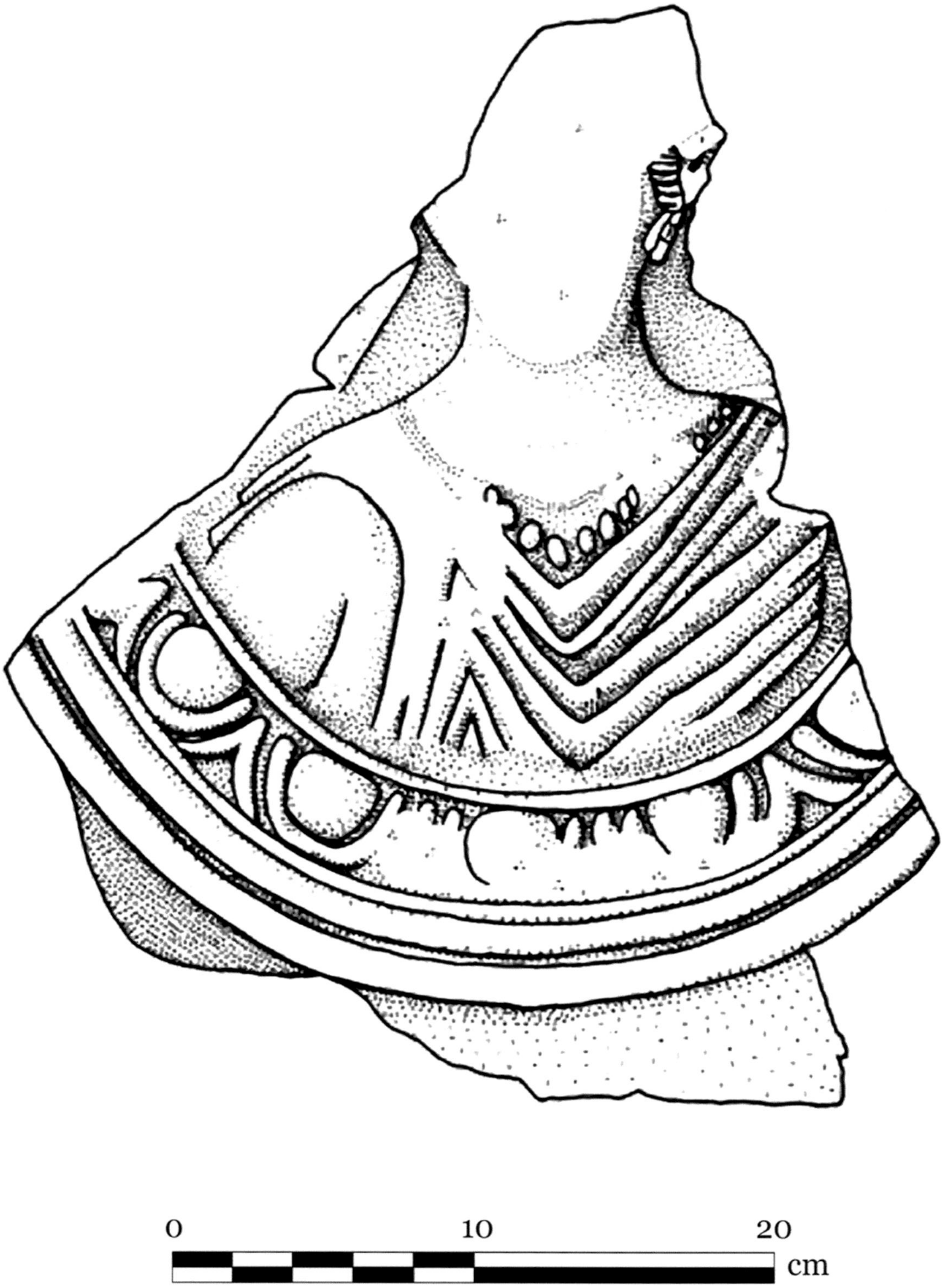

Figure 12.2: Qaleh-i Yazdigird. Female portrait in medallion (after Keall 1980).

or *peopled scroll* (Figure 12.4),[48] is even more difficult, if not impossible.

With its origin traceable back to Late Classical Greek and Hellenistic art, the *peopled scroll* motif gained popularity in Eastern and Western art of the first millennium AD. While the motif seems linked with the cult of Dionysus[49] in Roman culture, it is far from being evidently associated with Dionysus in the Qaleh-i Yazdigird context, for the male portrait enclosed by the peopled scroll shows a typical Parthian hairstyle and bears no Dionysian connotations whatsoever.

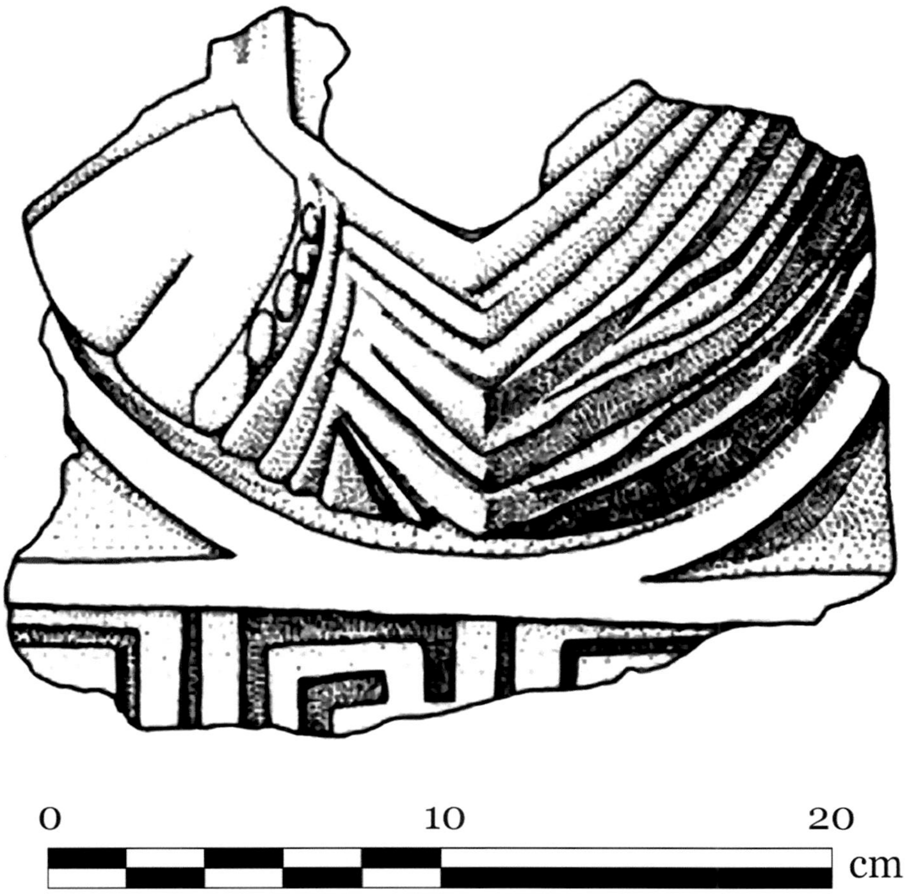

Figure 12.3: Qaleh-i Yazdigird. Female portrait in medallion, head missing (after Keall 1980).

Similar problems of identification are encountered for the female busts emerging from acanthus leaves on stucco engaged column capitals. Common in Hellenistic architecture, human-headed capitals have been found also at Assur, Warka and Seleucia in the Parthian period.[50] However, due to the isolated nature of these Parthian finds, any reconstruction of the decorative programme for the buildings to which they originally belonged is precluded. In Hellenistic and Roman architecture, themes connected with Dionysus were used to decorate such capitals.[51] This is probably also the case for one of the Qaleh-i Yazdigird engaged capitals, which portrays a nude figure holding two dolphins by their tails (Figure 12.5).[52] The Greco-Roman tradition links dolphins with Apollo, Aphrodite or Dionysus. However, the way the figure is holding the dolphins undoubtedly echoes the Near Eastern tradition of representing the Master/Mistress of the Animals.

Deeply rooted in the Near Eastern tradition, including specifically Iranian art, are hunting scenes. These are also present at Qaleh-i Yazdigird. They decorate yet another fragmentary engaged half-column, the surface of which is divided into rectangular panels enclosing a nude hunter or animals in an alternating arrangement.[53]

Outnumbering the scenes with Near Eastern origins, however, is a group of stucco reliefs the theme of which originates within the Western tradition. The reliefs show scenes with clear Dionysian connotations, such as two Erotes playing with a feline animal, a figure picking a grape cluster from a stylised vine, a reclining nude male reaching for a grape cluster with his right hand (Figure 12.6) and dancers.[54]

The decoration of the engaged half-column reconstructed on the basis of fragments discovered in fill of Room no. 11 also without question has its origins in Dionysian iconography. The surface of the half-column is divided into panels separated by guilloche scrollwork (Figure 12.7). The reconstruction shows a central top panel containing a male figure easily identifiable as Pan, because he is holding pipes and has the hindquarters and legs of a goat (Figure 12.8). The Pan panel is flanked by two more panels, each containing a nude female resting her left arm on a high plinth, her left leg flexed across in front of her right, and her right arm held up to her brow. A similar female figure occupies the central panel in the decorative band immediately below, while each side panel contains a male figure shown in Parthian dress. In the lowermost band, a female figure is depicted wearing a draped robe in the central panel, while Pan appears in each side panel. The position of arms and legs leaves no room for doubt that all these personages are

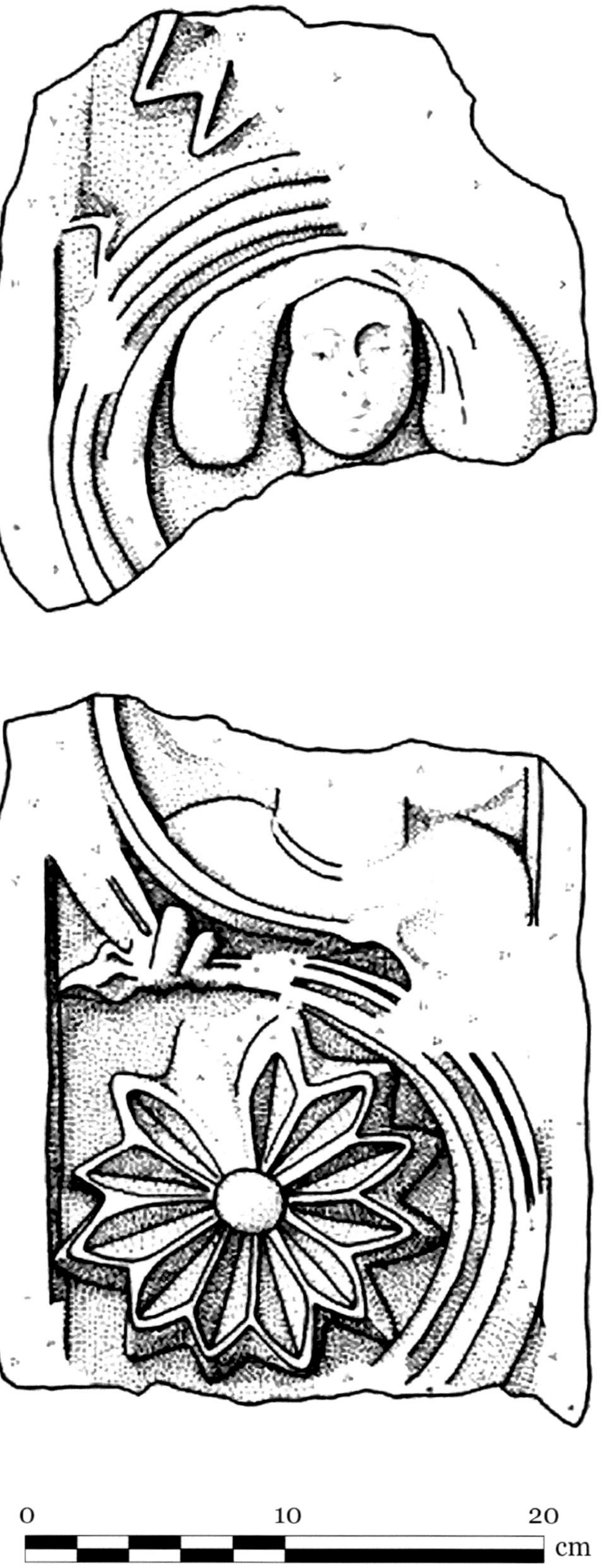

Figure 12.4: Qaleh-i Yazdigird. Male portrait in vine scroll (after Keall 1980).

dancing. And written sources are unanimous in declaring that dancing frequently accompanied banquets and played an important role in the court life of the Achaemenids, Arsacids and Sasanians.[55] Depictions of dance seem quite popular in art of the Arsacid period. Among good examples are bone plaques discovered over one hundred years ago at Olbia in the Crimea, datable to the first to second centuries AD.[56] The object which they originally decorated cannot now be reconstructed. They show a ruler enthroned and accompanied by courtiers, nude female dancers and nude male acrobats. Other examples come from Mele Hairam and Merv (Marw), which yielded two bone plaques showing young male nudes[57] and a terracotta plaque depicting a female dancer, respectively.[58] While female nudes are traditionally identified with goddesses or specifically with Anahita in an Iranian context, nudity itself does not necessarily allude to divinity; this is suggested by another bone object from Mele Hairam which seems to denote nothing but human youth. The object is decorated with a bearded man, a woman clad in a long robe, a beardless man (therefore presumably in his youth), and a young female nude (Figure 12.9). Of course, as far as the Qaleh-i Yazdigird scene is concerned, it is possible, because of the presence of Pan, that the female nude might actually be a maenad.

The presence of personages usually linked to the Dionysiac sphere next to "Parthians" at Qaleh-i Yazdigird shows how Dionysian iconography from the Greco-Roman world was reinvented in the Parthian idiom. This phenomenon is also manifested in another, though perhaps less spectacular way in the Qaleh-i Yazdigird decoration when a Dionysian motif and a traditional Near Eastern symbol of power and authority are combined to form a single decorative motif: a footed kantharos (wine vessel), an attribute of Dionysus, between merlons.[59] In Near Eastern architecture before the Achaemenids, a merlon, that is an element used in fortified structures, served a primarily military purpose and, when used in sacral buildings, denoted power, governance and prestige. But already in the architecture and art of the Achaemenids, merlons lost their defensive role in favour of decorative purposes, while probably continuing to convey their symbolic meaning. This was also the purpose of the terracotta merlons from Old Nisa.

Because of fundamental differences between Zoroastrianism and the cult of Dionysus, it seems quite impossible that Dionysian scenes or elements kept their original religious meaning in residential decorations of the late Arsacid period, when Zoroastrianism was already well established within Iranian society. However, certain general messages underlying the Dionysian iconography might have not been rejected or forgotten. For example, Erotes could be deemed never-aging children, or images of perfect youth, or the grapevine could be construed as a symbol of fertility, plenitude and abundance. It seems that Dionysian scenes and attributes present in the decorations

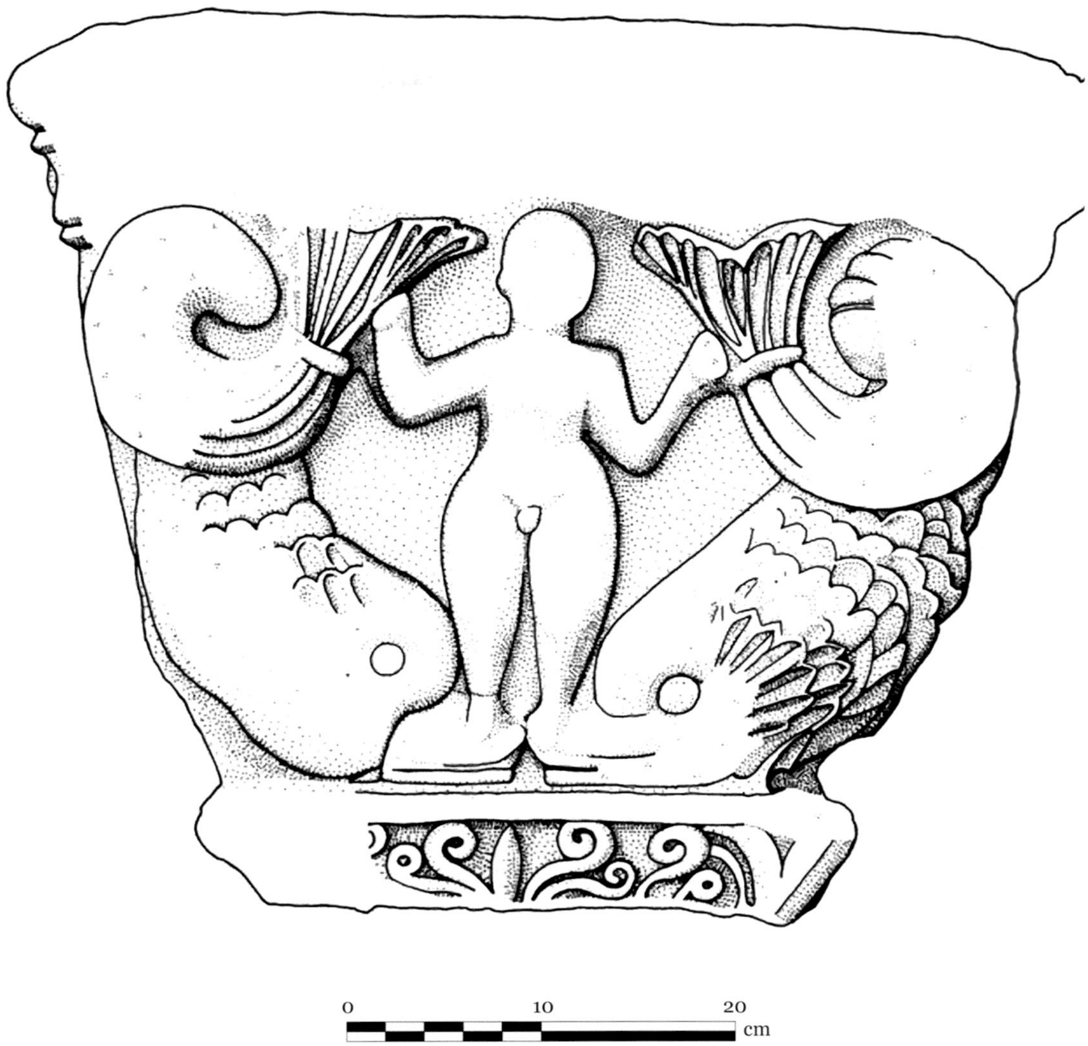

Figure 12.5: Qaleh-i Yazdigird. Nude (female?) figure holding two dolphins by their tails (after Keall 1980).

of Qaleh-i Yazdigird were intended to reflect a banquet, its light-hearted atmosphere and pleasures beefed up with wine and dance, thus alluding at the same time to the prosperity and wealth of the castle's owner.

To understand how and why Dionysian scenes were so favoured at the Arsacid court, it is necessary to refer to Hellenistic royal ideology, which largely drew on the myth of Dionysus's conquests in the East. As argued by Versnel, Dionysus became a model for Hellenistic kings, since he defeated mortal adversaries rather than supernatural opponents and conquered real territory.[60] His mythical achievements made him, like Heracles, a royal god. Alexander the Great regarded Dionysus as his heroic-divine predecessor for the conquest of the East,[61] while some Hellenistic kings openly identified themselves with Dionysus.[62]

In the Hellenistic period, a diadem was a symbol of Dionysus. Mithradates I, who ceased to wear a traditional *bashlyk* in favour of a diadem after his conquest of Media and Mesopotamia, a shift clearly seen on coins minted before and after the campaign, seems to draw on this very aspect of Dionysus as a victorious god. The iconography of coins issued by successors of Mithradates I proves that the diadem was not the only sign that the Arsacids adopted some elements of Hellenistic ideology. This should not, however, be understood to mean that the Near Eastern tradition and Iranian elements of royal ideology were completely abandoned by the Arsacids. Just the opposite: traditional customs were particularly valued by Parthian nobles, who deemed tradition a valid basis for political and cultural identity.[63] After all, the concept of a victorious king was deeply rooted in Iranian ideology. Nevertheless, confronted with powerful neighbours both to the east and west, the Arsacids adopted elements of the Hellenistic tradition, thus putting themselves on the same plane as their neighbours. In the course of time, the Zoroastrian religion and Iranian

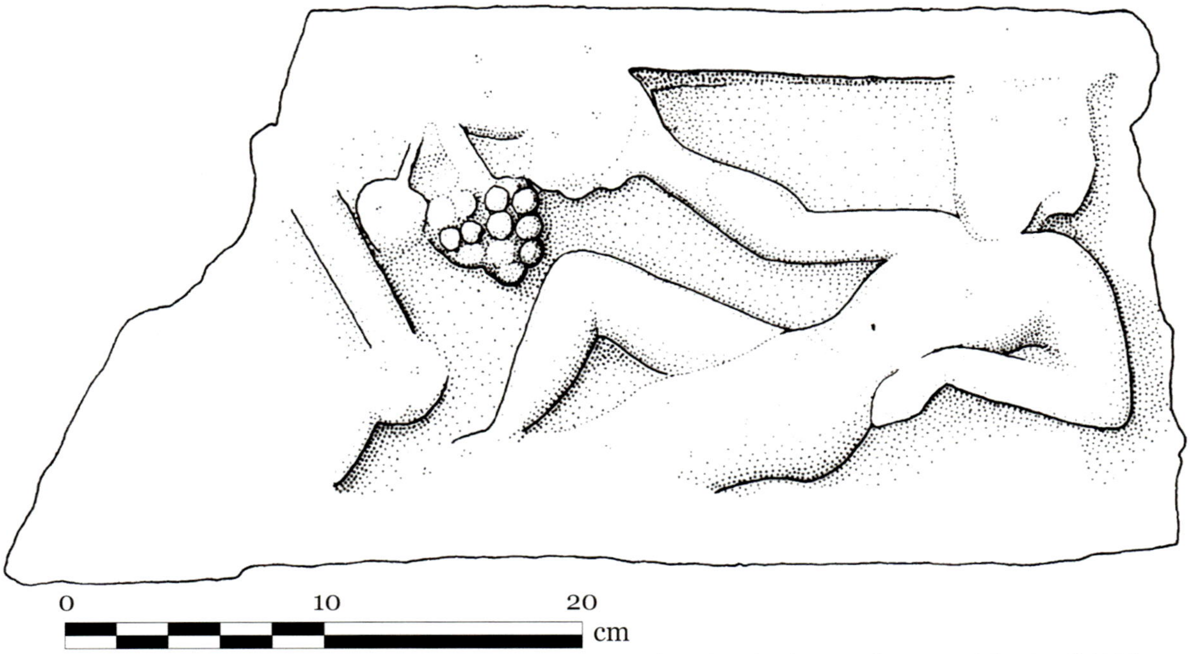

Figure 12.6: Qaleh-i Yazdigird. Reclining nude male reaching for a bunch of grapes from vine (after Keall 1980).

Figure 12.7: Qaleh-i Yazdigird. Fragment of engaged half-column: a) after Keall 1980; b) courtesy of the National Museum of Iran, Tehran.

tradition began to prevail. The latter particularly appreciated hunting and banqueting, which explains why the decoration of Late Arsacid Qaleh-i Yazdigird accommodates so many elements of Dionysian iconography with its wine, joy and revelry, so appropriate to the atmosphere of the banquet.

As no Arsacid royal palace has survived or been discovered to date, we must rely solely on our assumptions or suppositions that their decorations included royal hunting and banqueting scenes, the latter incorporating some Dionysian elements. The suggestion concerning the

Figure 12.8: Qaleh-i Yazdigird. Reconstruction of the decoration of engaged half-column (after Keall 1980).

Figure 12.9: Mele Hairam. Bone hilt decorated with images of a bearded man, a woman wearing a long robe, a beardless man and a nude female.

Figure 12.10: Bishapur. Dionysiac heads (after Ghirshman 1956).

inclusion of a Dionysian component is further strengthened by the fact that motifs for the floor mosaics in two rooms at Bishapur included masks of satyrs, Silenos, Pan and maenads (Figure 12.10) beside half-naked female musicians, dancers and flower bearers (Figure 12.11).

Ghirshman, who first excavated Bishapur, was sure that he had unearthed a sector of a palace of Shapur I, with mosaic rooms serving banqueting purposes.[64] For Lukonin, however, the mosaics echoed Zoroastrian feasts, including specifically Nowruz, that were celebrated in the royal palace.[65] Von Gall, emphasising the Dionysian nature of the mosaic images, argued that they relate to Dionysus as a god of victory and linked them with the triumphal reliefs of Shapur I in the nearby gorge. Such an interpretation

Figure 12.11: Bishapur. Woman playing the harp (after Ghirshman 1956).

was rejected by Balty, who claims that all surviving scenes show a royal banquet.[66] Recently a new interpretation for the mosaics and a new purpose for the mosaic rooms have been proposed.[67] Drawing on Azarnoush's identification of the entire complex as a fire temple, Callieri views the mosaic rooms as a space for the Zoroastrian community to gather for a common ritual meal that included wine. In his attempt to explain the presence of Dionysian motifs in a Zoroastrian fire temple, Callieri concludes that they were picked for their eschatological connotations. As there is no mention in Zoroastrian religious texts of any ritual banquets, their existence here is explained as evidence that common religious practice departed from orthodoxy. However, such a departure appears to us hardly possible, given that the Bishapur complex was almost undoubtedly a royal foundation.

As far as the eschatological dimension of the mosaic motifs is concerned, the Greco-Roman world did indeed use Dionysian iconography in funeral contexts, which saw Dionysus as a lord of death, rebirth and eternal renewal. However, the concept of birth, death, the journey into the underworld and rebirth is foreign to Zoroastrianism. And Zoroastrian meals dedicated to the souls of the departed did not necessarily take place in temples,[68] although it is possible that some ritual community meals were consumed there.[69]

Attention should also be drawn to the fact that Azarnoush's identification of a large cruciform hall at Bishapur as the main room of a fire temple is based on alleged similarities between ground plans of the hall and room no. 104 in the Sasanian residential building at Hajiabad. Azarnoush identified this room at Hajiabad as a temple of Anahita.[70] However, the asserted similarities are in fact superficial: the hall at Bishapur is a *chahar taq*, while the asymmetrical rectangular room at Hajiabad shares common features with another room of the same complex (room no. 175) rather than with the *chahar taq*. Moreover, if it is accepted that the faithful did not have access to the main room of fire temples, the enormous size of the cruciform room at Bishapur (22.75 m x 22.75 m) seems excessive even for a royal foundation (Room A at Takht-e Sulaiman is not larger than 7.65 m x 7.65 m.).[71] First and foremost, however, neither Bishapur nor Hajiabad has yielded any decisive evidence proving the functions of the rooms that are being compared.

Although Muslim authors assure us of the existence of a fire temple at Bishapur, their reports are rather laconic. Al-Mas'ūdī mentions that the city of Sabur (Bishapur) in the province of Fars has a temple founded by Dara, son of Dara.[72] However, the immediately following sentences leave it unclear whether the temple was actually located within the limits of the town of Bishapur. This is because of a certain lack of precision about location in al-Mas'ūdī's writing: while reporting about Firuzabad, he mentions a fire temple in the town, founded by Ardashir, son of Babak (Papak), which he had visited, and which was located one-hour's distance from the town.[73] So if al-Mas'ūdī mentions a structure as being in a town, it is likely he means merely in its vicinity. As far as Bishapur is concerned, the location of the temple outside the town seems to be confirmed by Istahri, Ibn Hauqal, Idrīsī and the anonymous author of *Hudud al-Alam*, who mention two temples, both located near the gates of Bishapur.[74]

Given all these concerns, it is more likely that the structure at Bishapur is a royal palace rather than a temple. If this is indeed the case, the mosaics may be viewed as evidence for the continuation of the tradition of using Dionysian motifs which, in addition to depictions of female musicians and dancers, seem suitable for reflecting the atmosphere of court banquets.

Written sources prove that the pomp, opulence and ceremony of the Sasanian court dazzled the king's subjects and foreign élites. Surrounded by their courts, the members of which are known from royal inscriptions and late or post-Sasanian texts,[75] Sasanian kings travelled between their imperial centres together with their closest family, that is royal consorts, numerous concubines and their offspring. The family and the harem also accompanied the king on war campaigns, sometimes becoming the booty of his enemies.[76] Traditionally, audiences (rather poorly documented for the Arsacid period), banquets and hunts, all reflected in Sasanian literature and art, continued to constitute an important element of court life.[77] Just as in the Arsacid period, royal guests participated in banquets, which, in addition to the pleasures of the table, offered an opportunity to discuss state affairs. Guests were seated according to protocol in a strict hierarchy[78] that symbolically reflected the king's control over the empire. The king himself reclined on the cushions of a banqueting couch[79] large enough to share with an important guest.[80] Royal banquets were organised for various significant occasions, including annual religious feasts.[81]

The presence of female musicians and dancers among mosaic depictions at Bishapur suggests that music and dance were an indispensable part of royal banquets. This is further confirmed by written sources which point to banquets taking place not only in palace rooms but also in royal gardens.[82] It is beyond any doubt that, on the one hand, banquets constituted a royal prerogative, involving the consumption of sophisticated meals and top quality wine,[83] watching female dancers and listening to music and songs. It is also beyond any doubt, however, that on the other hand, with their clear hierarchy of seats, banquets built an image of the king as the central figure within his empire.

The decoration of some rooms at Bishapur also included stone and stucco reliefs which, unfortunately, have not survived to the extent necessary for a complete reconstruction of their scenes. Nevertheless, given the fact the Iranian epic tradition couples royal banquets with hunts to form a symbiotic pair, it is plausible that the fragment of the stone relief from the Eastern Mosaic Hall, which shows a charging horseman, used to be part of a hunting scene. Since Ammianus Marcellinus mentions Persian houses as being richly decorated with scenes representing a king hunting game,[84] it seems reasonable to assume the presence of such scenes in a royal palace, the more so as fragments of hunting reliefs were identified at Ctesiphon.[85]

To sum up, the decoration of both the Arsacid noble residential structure at Qaleh-i Yazdigird and the royal palace at Bishapur does reflect the pleasures of court life: hunts and banquets. Although banquets played an essential role in the court life of ancient Iranian monarchies, they are, however, rarely depicted in art. This is a contrast to the many written sources that describe the wealth and splendour of royal banquets, with their strict rules of protocol and hierarchy.

Two main conclusions can be drawn from this overview of architectural decoration in the Arsacid and early Sasanian periods:

1. There is a clear discrepancy between the programme of interior decoration of palaces and the official art of rock reliefs and coinage as far as decorative themes are concerned, with the former abstaining from scenes of a religious or military nature. Because a similar trend is seen in Achaemenid art, this discrepancy can be deemed a specific element of the Iranian tradition.
2. Elements of Greco-Roman Dionysian iconography that were adopted by the Arsacids survived until Sasanian times, gradually losing their prevalence, as proved by the decoration of the Sasanian manor house at Hajiabad.[86] The house's wall decoration still displays some elements rooted in the Hellenistic world: figures of a nude child with a bunch of grapes in each hand, medallion portraits and portrait busts, among which Azarnoush managed to identify two portraits of the Sasanian king Shapur II, a bust of Shapur II's son Ardashir, and a bust of Shapur II's vassal, Bahram II Kushanshah. Several other busts represent unidentifiable figures from the Sasanian nobility, all of them "most distinguished personalities of the empire".[87] Portrait busts were also used, in addition to depictions of female dancers and musicians, to decorate late Sasanian residential houses at Kish and in the vicinity of Ctesiphon.[88] Having no religious content, these motifs were taken over by early Muslim rulers to accentuate their royal power and prerogatives.

Notes

1 A rather different picture of traditional court life is given by Ferdowsi in the *Shahnameh* where sumptuous banquets and light-hearted revels are, however, interlaced with episodes of battle and heroism.

2 See Jacobs 2010, p. 87–88.
3 Pliny, *N.H.*, 6.122; Strabo, 16.1.16; Josephus, *Ant. Iud.*, 18.48–50; Amm. Marc., 23.6.23.
4 For Ecbatana see Polyb., 10, 27; Strabo 11.13.1, 16.1.16; Curtius Rufus, 5.8.1; Tacitus, *Ann.* 15.3; for Rhagae – Athenaios, 12.513f–14a; for Hecatompylus, see Strabo, 16.1.16.
5 Invernizzi 2001, p. 147; Invernizzi 2001a; Lippolis 2009, p. 54; Lippolis 2010; Pilipko 2007, p. 156.
6 Lippolis 2009, p. 57–59.
7 Invernizzi 2000.
8 Chaumont 1966, p. 471–497.
9 Invernizzi 2001a, p. 301, argues that this might have occurred during the reign of Artabanus III in the first century AD.
10 Manassero 2012.
11 Invernizzi 2001, p. 147.
12 Invernizzi 2001, p. 141–147; 2001a, p. 308–309; 2004.
13 Invernizzi 2001, p. 147–148.
14 Invernizzi 2001a, p. 303; Pilipko 2001, p. 197–198.
15 Pilipko 2000, pl. I:2.
16 See Pilipko 2001, p. 339–352; Pilipko 2007, p. 256.
17 Dąbrowa 2008; Dąbrowa 2011, p. 258.
18 Curtis 2007, p. 62.
19 Fredricksmeyer 1997.
20 Neusner 1963, p. 45–48; Wolski 1990; Wolski 1977, p. 210; Vardanyan 2001; Curtis 2007.
21 Gaslain 2003; Huber, Hartmann 2006; Brossius 2006, p. 106–110; Lerouge 2007, p. 340–341, 344; Dąbrowa 2010, p. 126.
22 Bigwood 2004; Bigwood 2008; Strugnell 2008.
23 Tacitus, *Ann.* 6.43,1.
24 Vonones II and his Greek *concubine* had five sons who held the thrones of *Parthia* and Armenia: see Karras-Klapproth 1988, p. 95–96.
25 Minns 1915, p. 28, 31, 35; Bigwood 2008.
26 Bigwood 2004, p. 44–45; Bigwood 2008.
27 Huber, Hartman 2006: p. 486–487; Bigwood 2008.
28 Dio Cassius, 83.1.2.
29 Josephus, *Ant.Iud.* 20, 26; Gregoratti 2012.
30 Shayegan 2011, p. 113.
31 Alram 1986, nos. 1269 and 1269A.
32 There are also stories of warrior women and heroines such as Gurdafarid, Gurdya and Jarira in Firdausi's *Shahnameh* that give us a picture consistent with ancient Iranian tradition.
33 Pilipko 2001, p. 257, 278.
34 Deams 2001, p. 49–50.
35 Kawami 1987, pl. 45.
36 Kawami 1987a, p. 43.
37 Keall, 1977; 1980; Herrmann 1977, p. 67–72.
38 Keall 1977, p. 5.
39 Keall 1980, fig. 6, 3.
40 Keall 1980, fig. 6, 2.
41 Keall 1980, figs 7, 7–8.
42 Keall 1980, figs 7, 2 and 5.
43 Winkes 1979, p. 481–484.
44 Chapouthier 1935, p. 13–42; Erciyas 2005, p. 134–146.
45 Fejfer 2008, p. 233–235.
46 Rostovtzeff 1936, p. 265–308, pls X–XI.
47 Pollard 2000, p. 55.
48 Keall 1980, fig. 7, 6.
49 Toynbee, Ward-Perkins 1950, p. 1–2, 25.
50 Mercklin 1962, p. 30–33, abb. 152, 91–96.
51 Webb 1996, p. 18.
52 Keall 1980, fig. 12.
53 Keall 1980, fig. 12, 1–2.
54 Keall 1980, fig. 9, la and b; fig. 8, 3; fig. 8, 4, fig. 10, 3; fig. 10, 6; fig. 10, 7.
55 Shahbazi, Friend 1993.
56 Pharmakovsky 1907.
57 Kaim 2010, p. 324, pl. 2.
58 Pugachenkova 1962, p. 123, fig.3.
59 Keall 1980, fig. 10, 1, 2 and 4.
60 Versnel 1970, p. 250–253.
61 Alföldi 1985, p. 125.
62 Tondriau 1953.
63 Lerouge 2007, p. 359; see also Curtis 2007, p. 7–25 for a revival of Iranian traditions in post-Hellenistic Iran.
64 Ghirshman 1956, p. 179.
65 Lukonin 1967, p. 183.
66 Von Gall 1971; Balty 2006, p. 29–44.
67 Callieri 2008; 2009, p. 53–55. This new interpretation was accepted by D. Huff 1993, p. 54, but L. Bier 1993, p. 58, and R. Boucharat 2006, p. 48 seem to remain undecided.
68 See e.g. Boyce 1996; Dhabhar 1932, p. 397.
69 Hultgärd 2004, p. 381.
70 Azarnoush 1987; 1994, p. 81–88.
71 The size of the main room in smaller temples discovered recently in Iran does not exceed 5 × 5 m: see Moradi 2009.
72 *Les prairies d'or*, p. 78.
73 al-Masʿūdī clearly mistook the palace of Ardashir, which lies about 5 km from the city of Ardashir Xwarrah, for a fire temple.
74 See Schippmann 1971, p. 142–143.
75 Wiesehöfer 2007, p. 61–63.
76 Narseh's family was captured by Galerius (Christensen 1936, p. 233) and the harem of Peroz by the Hephthalites (Tabari, I: 877).
77 Daryaee 2009, p. 50–52.
78 *Letter of Tansar*: 44; T. Daryaee 2007.
79 Harper 1979; for reasons of propaganda, the king depicted on Sasanian silver vessels does not lean back on the cushions of his banqueting couch but sits upright in an enthroned pose.
80 Garsoïan 1989, p. 146, 515; 2004.
81 About Khusrau Anushiravan celebrating six Gahambars, see Dhabhar 1932, p. 325.
82 For a Parthian banquet in a garden, see Wardrop 1914, p. 4–5.
83 For different types of wine see *Husraw ud Rēdak* 56–58, trans. Monchi-Zadeh, 75; Daryaee 2006; Daryaee 2009, p. 51.
84 Amm. Marc., 24.6.3.
85 Kröger 1982, p. 22–30, pls. 4–6.
86 Azarnoush 1994, p. 93–182.
87 Azarnoush 1994, p. 238.
88 Kröger 1982, pl. 28.

References

Alföldi, A. (1985). *Caesar in 44 v. Chr. Band 1. Studien zu Caesars Monarchie und ihren Wurzeln*, Bonn.

Alram, M. (1986). *Iranisches Personennamenbuch. Band IV, Nomina propria Iranica in Nummis,* Vienna.

Azarnoush, M. (1987). "Fire Temple and Anahita Temple: A Discussion on Some Iranian Places of Worship", *Mesopotamia* 22: p. 391–401.

——— (1994). *The Sasanian Manor House at Hajiabad, Iran*, Florence.

Balty, J. (2006). "Mosaïques romaines, mosaïques sassanides: Jeux d'influences réciproques", in J. Wiesehöfer, P. Huyse (eds), *Ērān und Anērān. Studien zu den Beziehungen zwischen dem Sasanidenreich und der Mittelmeerwelt*, Stuttgart: p. 29–44.

Bier, L. (1993). "The *Sassanian* Palaces and their Influence in Early Islam", *Ars Orientalis* 23: p. 57–66.

Bigwood, J.M. (2004). "Queen Mousa, Mother and Wife (?) of King Phraatakes of Parthia: A Re-evaluation of the Evidence", *Mouseion* 4: p. 35–70.

——— (2008). "Some Parthian Queens in Greek and Babylonian Documents", *Iranica Antiqua* 43: p. 235–274.

Boucharlat, R. (2006). "L'architecture sassanide", in F. Demange (ed.), *Les Perses sassanides. Fastes d'un empire oublié (224–642)*, Paris: p. 47–50.

Boyce, M. (1996). "Death", *Encyclopaedia Iranica*, Vol. VII/2: p. 179–181, available online at http://www.iranicaonline.org/articles/death-1 (accessed online 23 January 2013).

Brossius, M. (2006). *The Persians*, London.

Callieri, P. (2008). "'Dionysiac' iconographic themes in the context of Sasanian religious architecture", in D. Kennet, P. Luft (eds), *Current Research in Sasanian Archaeology, Art and History*, Oxford: p. 115–125.

——— (2009). "Bishapur: the Palace and the Town", *Cahiers de Studia Iranica* 42: p. 51–65.

Chapouthier, F. (1935). *Exploration archéologique de Delos, le sanctuaire des dieux de Samothrace (Delos XVI)*, Paris.

Chaumont, M.L. (1966). "L'ordre des préséances à la cour des Arsacides d'Arménie", *Journal Asiatique* 254: p. 471–497.

Christensen, A. (1936). *L'Iran sous les Sassanides, Copenhagen.*

Curtis, V.S. (2007). "The Iranian Revival in the Parthian Period", in V.S. Curtis, S. Stewart (eds), *Age of the Parthians*, *The Idea of Iran, vol. 2*, London.

Dąbrowa, E. (2008). "Mithradates I and the Beginning of the Ruler Cult in Parthia", in E. Dąbrowa (ed.), *Orbis Parthicus: Studies in Memory of Professor Józef Wolski*, Electrum 15: p. 41–51.

——— (2010), "The Parthian Kingship", in G.B. Lanfranchi, R. Pollinger (eds), *Concepts of Kingship in Antiquity, Proceedings of the European Science Foundation Exploratory Workshop held in Padova, November 28th–December 1st, 2007*, Padua: p. 123–134.

——— (2011). "ΑΡΣΑΚΗΣ ΘΕΟΣ. Observations on the Nature of the Parthian Ruler-Cult", in C. Lippolis, S. de Martino (eds), *Un impaziente desiderio di scorrere il mondo. Studi in onore di Antonio Invernizzi per il suo settantesimo compleanno*, Monografie di Mesopotamia 14, Florence: p. 247–251.

Daems, A. (2001). "The Iconography of Pre-Islamic Women in Iran", *Iranica Antiqua* 36: p. 1–150.

Daryaee, T. (2006). "The Art of Wine in Ancient Persia", *Hamazor, Publication of the World Zoroastrian Organization* 1: p. 34–36.

——— (2007). "The Middle Persian Text Sūr ī Saxwan and the Late Sasanian Court", in R. Gyselen (ed.), *Des Indo-Grecs aux Sassanides: Données pour l'histoire et la géographie historique*, Res Orientales XVII, Bures-sur-Yvette: p. 65–72.

——— (2009). *Sasanian Persia: The Rise and Fall of an Empire*, London.

Dhabhar, B.N. (1932). *The Persian Rivayats of Hormazyar Framarz and others,* Bombay.

Erciyas, D.B. (2005). *Wealth, Aristocracy and Royal Propaganda under the Hellenistic Kingdom of the Mithradatids in the Central Black Sea Region in Turkey*, Colloquia Pontica 12, Leiden.

Fejfer, J. (2008). *Roman Portraits in Context*, Berlin.

Fredricksmeyer, E.A. (1997). "The Origin of Alexander's Royal Insignia", *Transactions of the American Philological Association* 127: p. 97–109.

Gall, H. von (1971). "Die Mosaiken von Bishapur", *Archäologische Mitteilungen aus Iran* N.F. 4: p. 193–205.

Garsoïan, N.G. (1989). *The Epic Histories (Buzandaran Patmut'iwnk')*, Harvard.

——— (2004). "Armeno-Iranian relations in the pre-Islamic period", *Encyclopaedia Iranica* online edition, 2004, available at http://www.iranicaonline.org/articles/armeno-iranian-relations-in-the-pre-islamic-period (accessed online 16 December 2012).

Gaslain, J. (2003). "De l'esclave à la reine : remarques sur la présence feminine dans le monde parthe", in *de Kêmi à Birit Nari: revue internationale de l'orient ancien*, Paris: p. 100–111.

Ghirshman, R. (1956). *Fouilles de Chapour. Bîchâpour. Vol. II: Les mosaïques sassanides*, Paris.

Gregoratti, L. (2012). "Parthian Women in Flavius Josephus", in M. Hirschberger (ed.), *Jüdisch-hellenistische Literatur in ihrem interkulturellen Kontext, Düsseldorf, 10.-11. Februar 2011*, Frankfurt am Main: p. 183–192.

Harper, P.O. (1979). "Thrones and Enthronement Scenes in Sasanian Art", *Iran* 17: p. 49–64.

Herrmann, G. (1977). *The Iranian Revival*, Oxford.

Huber, I., and Hartmann, U. (2006), "'Denn ihren Diktat vermochte der König nicht zu widersprechen ...'. Die Position der Frauen am Hof der Arsakiden", in A. Panaino, A. Piras (eds), *Proceedings of the 5th Conference of the Societas Iranologica Europaea, held in Ravenna, 6–11 October 2003*, Milan: p. 485–517.

Huff, D. (1994). "Architecture sassanide", in L. Vanden Berghe, B. Overlaet (eds), *Splendeur des Sassanides: l'empire perse entre Rome et la Chine (224–642)*, Brussels: p. 45–61.

Hultgård, A. (2004). "Ritual Community Meals in Ancient Iranian Religion", in M. Strausberg (ed.), *Zoroastrian Rituals in Context*, Leiden: p. 367–388.

Invernizzi, A. (2000). "The Square House at Old Nisa", *Parthica* 2: p. 13–53.

——— (2001). "Arsacid Dynastic Art", *Parthica* 3: p. 133–157.

——— (2001a). "Arsacid Palaces", in I. Nielsen (ed.), *The Royal Palace Institution in the 1st Millennium BC*, Athens: p. 295–312.

——— (2004). "Thoughts on Parthian Nisa", *Parthica* 6: p. 133–143.

Invernizzi, A., and Lippolis, C. (2008). "Nisa Partica. Ricerche nel complesso monumentale arsacide 1990–2006", Monografie di Mesopotamia IX, Florence.

Jacobs, B. (2010). "Die inneren Verhältnisse im Partherreich", in U. Hackl, B. Jacobs, D. Weber (eds), *Quellen zur Geschichte des Partherreiches. Textsammlung mit Übersetzungen und Kommentaren*, Göttingen: p. 77–166.

Kaim, B. (2010), "Bone Reliefs from Fire Temple at Mele Hairam, South-West Turkmenistan", *Iranica Antiqua* 45: p. 321–335.

Karras-Klapproth, M. (1988). *Prosopographische Studien zur Geschichte des Partherreiches auf der Grundlage antiker literarischer Überlieferung*, Bonn.

Kawami, T.S. (1987). "Monumental Art of the Parthian Period in Iran", *Acta Iranica* 13, Leiden.

——— (1987a). "Kuh-e Khwaja, Iran, and its Wall Paintings: The Records of Ernst Herzfeld", *Metropolitan Museum Journal* 22: p. 13–52.

Keall, E.J. (1977). "Qal'eh-i Yazdigird: the Question of its Date", *Iran* 15: p. 1–9.

Keall, E.J., *et al.* (1980). "Qal'eh-i Yazdigird: its Architectural Decorations", *Iran* 18: p. 1–42.

Kröger, J. (1982). *Sasanidischer Stuckdekor*, Mainz.

Lerouge, Ch. (2007). *L'image des Parthes dans le monde gréco-romain. Du début du Ier siècle av. J.-C. jusqu'à la fin du Haut-Empire romain*, Oriens et Occidens 17, Stuttgart.

Lippolis, C. (2009). "Notes on the Iranian Traditions in the Architecture of Old Nisa", E. Dąbrowa (ed.), *Orbis Parthicus: Studies in Memory of Professor Józef Wolski*, Electrum 15: p. 53–72.

——— (2010). "Parthian Nisa. Some Considerations Based on New Research", in *South Asian Archaeology 2007: Proceedings of the 19th Meeting of the European Association of South Asian Archaeology in Ravenna, Italy, July 2007. Volume II: Historic Periods*: p. 165–177.

Lukonin, V.G. (1967). *Persia II: From the Seleucids to the Sassanids*, Geneva, Cleveland, New York.

Manassero, N. (2012). "Meanings of rhyta and meanings of Old Nisa", in R. Muradov (ed.) *Traces of Empires: Ancient and Medieval Culture of Central Asia* (Festschrift Galina A. Pugachenkova), available online at http://www.academia.edu/1207356/_Meanings_of_rhyta_and_meanings_of_Old_Nisa (accessed online 2 January 2013).

Melikian-Chirvani, A.S. (1992). "The Iranian Bazm in Early Persian Sources", in R. Gyselen (ed.), *Banquets d'Orient*, Res Orientales IV, Bures-sur-Yvette: p. 95–120.

Mercklin, E. (1962). *Antike Figuralkapitelle*, Berlin.

Minns, E.H. (1915). "Parchments of the Parthian Period from Avroman in Kurdistan", *Journal of Hellenic Studies* 35: p. 22–65.

Monchi-Zadeh, D. (1982). *Xusröv I Kavatan ut retak. Pahlavi Text, Transcription and Translation, Monumentum Georg Morgenstierne*, Acta Iranica 22, Leiden: p. 47–91.

Moradi, Y. (1388/2009). "The Chahartaq of Mile Mihehgeh: A Fire Temple of the Sasanian Period, *Motāle'āt-e Bāstānshenāsi, Journal of the College of Literature and Human Science*, University of Tehran, Vol. 1, No. 1, 1388: p. 155–185 (in Persian).

Neusner, J. (1963). "Parthian Political Ideology", *Iranica Antiqua* 3: p. 40–59.

Pharnakovsky, B. (1907). "Archäologische Funde im Jahre 1906: Südrussland", *Archäologischer Anzeiger:* p. 126–153.

Pilipko, V.N. (2000). "On the Wall-Paintings from the Tower-Building of Old Nisa", *Parthica* 2: p. 69–86.

——— (2001). *Staraya Nisa: osnovnye itogi arkheologicheskogo izucheniia v sovetskii period*, Moscow.

——— (2007). "Nekotorye itogi arkheologicheskih issledovanii na Staroy Nise", *Rossiyskaya Arkheologia* 1: p. 150–158.

Pollard, N. (2000). *Soldiers, Cities and Civilians in Roman Syria*, Ann Arbor.

Pugachenkova, G. (1962). "Koroplastika drevnego Merva", *TJuTAKE* XI, Ashhabad: p. 117–173.

Rostovtzeff, M., *et al.* (eds.) (1936). *The Excavations at Dura-Europos conducted by Yale University and the French Academy of Inscriptions and Letters: Preliminary Report of Sixth Season of Work, October 1932–March 1933*, New Haven.

Schippmann, K. (1971). *Die iranischen Feuerheiligtümer*, Berlin, New York.

Shahbazi, A. Sh., and Friend, R.C. (1993). "Dance", *Encyclopaedia Iranica*, Vol. VI, Fasc. 6: p. 640–645.

Shayegan, M.R. (2011). *Arsacids and Sasanians: Political Ideology in Post-Hellenistic and Late Antique Persia*, Cambridge.

Strugnell, E. (2008), "Thea Musa, Roman Queen of Parthia", *Iranica Antiqua* 43: p. 275–298.

Tondriau, J. (1953). "Dionysos, dieu royale. Du Bacchos tauromorphe primitif aux souverains hellénistiques Neoi Dionysoi", in Παγκάρπεια, *Mélanges Henri Grégoire*, vol. 4, Brussels: p. 441–466.

Toynbee, J.M.C., and Ward-Perkins, J.B. (1950). "Peopled Scrolls: A Hellenistic Motif in Imperial Art", *Papers of the British School at Rome* 18: p. 1–43.

Vardanyan, R. (2001). "Tendenze culturali e ideologiche nell'impero partico riflesse dalla monetazione", *Parthica* 3: p. 25–132.

Versnel, H.S. (1970). *Triumphus: An Inquiry into the Origin, Development and Meaning of the Roman Triumph*, Leiden.

Wardrop, O. (1914). *Visramiani. The Story of the Loves of Vis and Ramin*, Royal Asiatic Society, London.

Webb, P.A. (1996). *Hellenistic Architectural Sculpture. Figural Motifs in Western Anatolia and the Aegean Islands*, Los Angeles.

Wiesehöfer, J. (2007). "King, court and royal representation in the Sasanian empire", in A.J.S. Spawforth (ed.), *The Court and Court Society in Ancient Monarchies*, New York: p. 58–79.

Winkes, R. (1979). "Pliny's Chapter on Roman Funeral Customs in the Light of Clipeatae Imagines", *AJA* 83, 4: p. 481–484.

Wolski, J. (1997). "L'idéologie monarchique chez les Arsacides", in *Studi vari di storia greca, ellenistica e romana: Atti VIII, 1976–1977,* Ce.R.D.A.C., Milan: p. 223–236.

——— (1990). "Le titre 'Roi des Rois' dans l'idéologie monarchique des Arsacides", in J. Harmatta (ed.), *From Alexander the Great to Kül Tegin*, Budapest: p. 11–18.

NUMISMATICS

13

Quantifying Monetary Production: Ecbatana and Media in Parthian Times

Pierre-Yves Boillet

Lycée Cézanne, Aix-en-Provence

Around 148/147 BC, Parthian rulers took possession of Ecbatana, the capital of Media, until then in the hands of the Seleucid dynasty. Although there was no real upheaval, monetary practice undeniably evolved as a result of this change of ruler. The use of money became less frequent and monetary practice seems to have been lost.

This article aims to quantify monetary production in Parthian times and to study the evolution between Seleucid and Arsacid periods.

Introduction

Polybius used the most glowing terms to depict the land of Media. He stressed in turn the strategic role of the region between east and west, the vast economic resources "worthy of that of a kingdom",[1] and the quality of livestock.[2]

Ancient Media seems to have occupied a unique place in the organisation of the Iranian region.[3] Ecbatana, the regional centre, was successively a royal capital of the Achaemenid kings, the seat of a military command in Seleucid times, and then a royal residence under the Parthians. These statuses proceeded from its geographical position at the intersection of the various empires and kingdoms of the first millennium BC, to say nothing of its crucial legacy of a history marked by the construction of organised states, prior to the Achaemenid period.[4]

Despite this historical importance, and the fact that Hamadan must be considered one of the major sites of ancient Iran,[5] ancient Media remains a *terra incognita*; literary and archaeological sources are far too thin to trace the history of the region, so much so that Heleen Sancisi-Weerdenburg says about an earlier era, "it is not even clear what precisely should be called Media".[6] There are two explanations for this: first, excavations have been few[7] but, more importantly, most of the material attributed to Ecbatana is in fact of uncertain origin and therefore cannot be used.[8]

Moreover, the available sources are quite limited. The literary sources, mainly Greek and Roman, should be viewed with caution due not only to the geographical but also to the cultural distance. Concerning the Parthian period, only Justin gives us a continuous narrative of events from the origins of the Parthians until the reign of Augustus. But we have no equivalent for the early Roman empire, so we must often content ourselves with information "*exposant, du point de vue de Rome, les exploits des armées romaines, des empereurs romains et où on ne tient compte que très rarement et de façon très sporadique des conditions socio-économiques en vigueur dans l'État des Arsacides*".[9]

That said, there are many references to the site and the region: Ecbatana and Susa are the two Achaemenid capitals most frequently cited in the Greek and Roman sources, and are often mentioned together elsewhere.[10] But, in reality, only two Greek authors evoke with any precision the splendour of ancient Ecbatana (Herodotus I, 98 and Polybius X, 27). Other references appear only as supplements; without any attempt at being comprehensive, this is partly the case for Ctesias, Berosus, Plutarch and Isidorus of Charax.

Finally, only coins and their cross-operation with other types of sources can help us detect as accurately as possible the situation in Media from the late fourth century BC to the first third of the third century AD.

Activity of the Ecbatana mint in Parthian times

The numismatic material

The corpus of Parthian coins to which we refer here consists of 5,832 coins. The following public collections have been consulted directly:[11] the Coin Cabinet of the Bibliothèque nationale of France (Paris); the Department of Coins and Medals of the British Museum (London); the Department of Coins and Medals of the Fitzwilliam Museum (Cambridge); the Department of Coins and Medals of the Ashmolean Museum (Oxford); the Numismatic Museum of Athens; the Coin Cabinet of Berlin (Staatliche Museum); the Coin Cabinet of Vienna (Kunsthistorisches Museum); the collections of the National Museum of Iran (Tehran) and the Museum of Khorramabad (Iran); and finally the American Numismatic Society (New York).

The catalogues held by the Cabinet des médailles, Paris (more than 8,000 public sales catalogues) have been systematically studied through September 2005. Only the illustrated catalogues have been taken into account.[12]

Representatives in the various collections

With regard to the Parthians, the silver denominations (overwhelmingly drachms) are most frequently included

Table 13.1. Representatives in the Parthian sample

Kings	*n/O*[1] *(drachms)*	*Kings*	*n/O (drachms)*
Mithradates I	1.45	*Vologases I*	3.84
Phraates II	1.25	*Vardanes II*	2.75
Darius	1.89	*Pacorus II*	5
Phraates III	2.52	*Vologases II*	2.14
Mithradates III	3.41	*Artabanus III*	3.46
Orodes II	2.10	*Vologases III*	4.78
Pacorus I	1	*Osroes I*	16.75
Phraates IV	3.48	*Parthamaspates*	8.90
Phraataces	2.39	*Mithradates IV*	3.58
Phr. & Musa	3.96	*Vologases IV*	4.49
Vonones I	14.63	*Osroes II*	5.71
Artabanus II	4.23	*Vologases V*	3.56
Vardanes I	3.14	*Vologases VI*	4.81
Gotarzes II	7.37	*Artabanus IV*	3.31
Vonones II	12.73		

Table 13.2. Activity of the Ecbatana mint in Parthian times

Kings	*Estimated number of original dies*[1]		*Estimated number of original dies per year of reign (average)*	*Kings*	*Estimated number of original dies*		*Estimated number of original dies per year of reign (average)*
	Guilbaud	*Good*			*Guilbaud*	*Good*	
Mithradates I	7.657	8.439	0.242	*Vologases I*	13.05	12.73	0.477
Phraates II	2.37	2.812	0.235	*Vardanes II*	3.41	3.3	1.115
Darius	6.226	8.167	7.196	*Pacorus II*	14.12	12.519	0.492
Phraates III	5.68	5.9	0.444	*Vologases II*	2.086	2.187	0.712
Mithradates III	3.415	3.322	1.122	*Artabanus III*	4.278	4.239	0.425
Orodes II	43.58	46.47	2.269	*Vologases III*	23.047	21.02	0.524
Pacorus I	?	?	?	*Osroes I*	2.482	1	0.087
Phraates IV	30.67	29.877	0.84	*Parthamaspates*	8.873	5.702	7.287
Phraataces	6.74	6.452	1.649	*Mithradates IV*	16.63	16.48	1.505
Phr. & Musa	7.86	7.522	3.845	*Vologases IV*	13.039	14.45	0.312
Vonones I	6.133	2.782	1.114	*Osroes II*	10.878	11.3	11.089
Artabanus II	16.28	15.36	0.564	*Vologases V*	9.381	8.627	0.529
Vardanes I	9.39	9.972	1.382	*Vologases VI*	18.64	16.66	0.882
Gotarzes II	10.38	7.68	0.82	*Artabanus IV*	6.257	6.922	0.823
Vonones II	9.594	4.809	7.201				

[1] W.W. Esty, "Estimation of the Size of a Coinage: a Survey and Comparison of Methods", *NC* 146, 1986, p. 185–215.

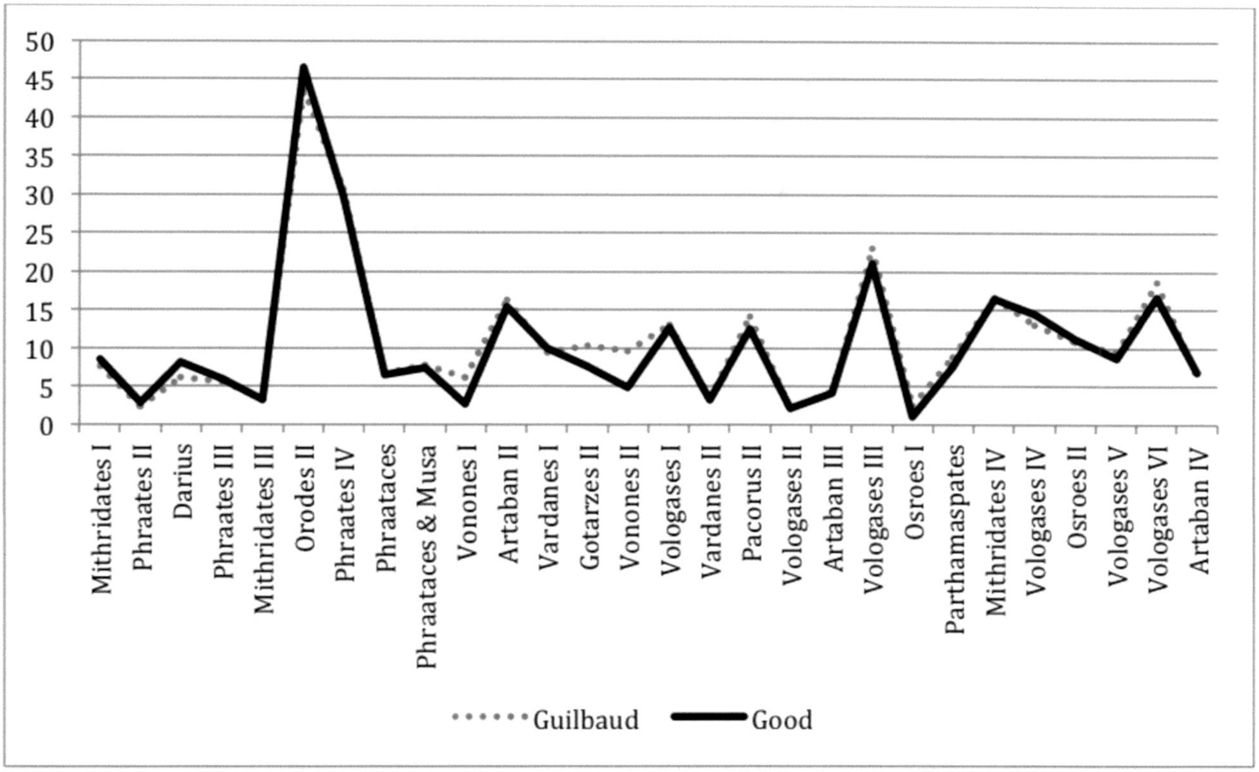

Figure 13.1: Estimated number of original dies (equivalent tetradrachms).

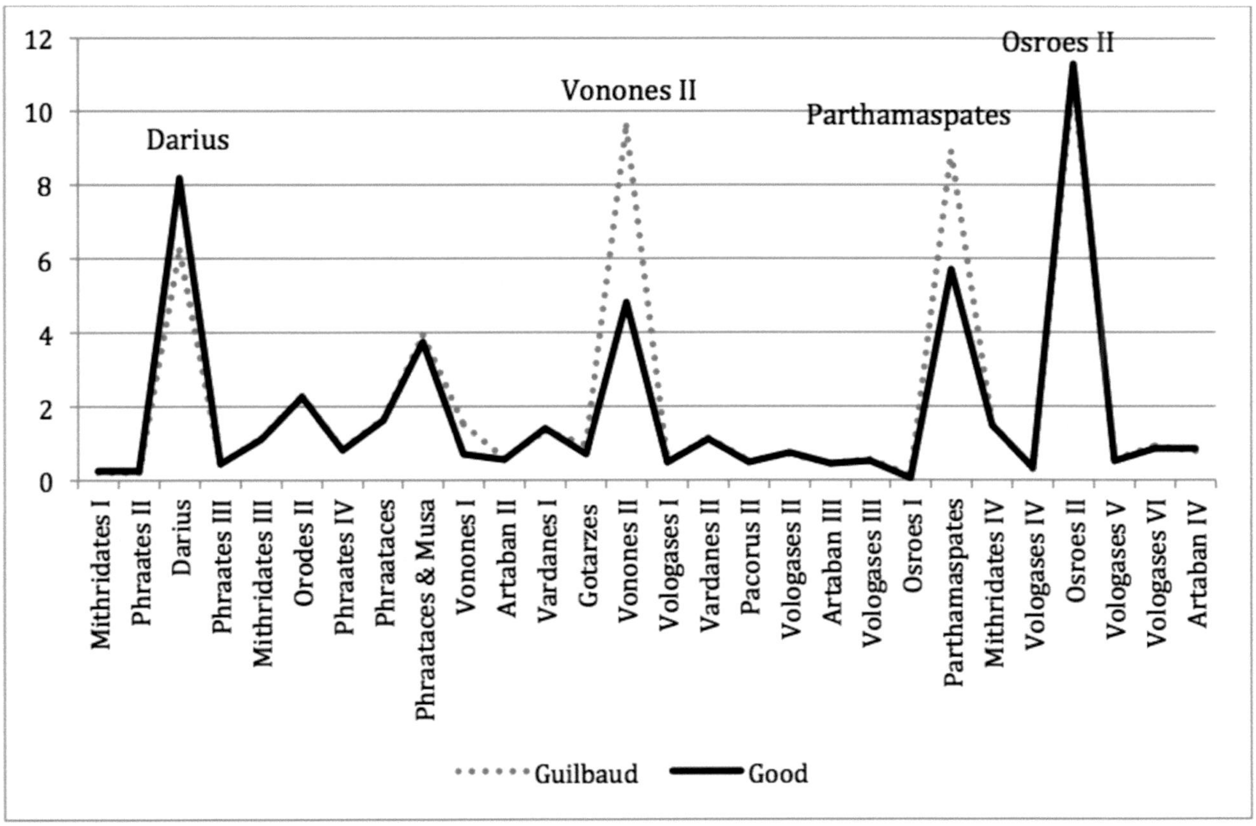

Figure 13.2: Estimated number of original dies per year of reign (equivalent tetradrachms – average).

in the sales catalogues, while the bronzes are mostly or exclusively represented in the cabinets. Parthian bronzes, usually of poor quality, have a negligible impact. The collections in Paris, Berlin and Vienna are in this respect very well represented, more so than the Seleucids.

When reading the tables and figures above, two observations are obvious:

- First, Orodes II is the Arsacid king who struck the most coins, with the equivalent of about forty dies for tetradrachms throughout his reign.
- Second, if one focuses on the study of the number of dies used by regnal year, we see that the rulers or usurpers who reigned only one year, or at least for only a short time, stand out quite significantly, since their annual average emissions are about eight or nine times higher than for other kings.

A decline in the use of money in Media

Nothing indicates that the urban network of Media or the nature of trade in the region had changed dramatically compared to what it had been under the Seleucids. However, the use of money seems to be reduced in the Arsacid period. Indeed, while in Media the Seleucids (between 311 and 148 BC) used an average of 1.17 tetradrachm dies per year, the Parthians between 148 BC and 222 AD did not use more than 0.80. The findings are similar if one studies coinages issued in peacetime: 0.58 tetradrachm dies were necessary to supply market money under Seleucus IV, while 0.44 was sufficient under Phraates III.[13]

However, the population of ancient Media is estimated between 1 and 1.25 million people[14] and we therefore arrive at a ratio of 0.4496 to 0.608 tetradrachm dies per year per million inhabitants. At the same time, the data show double the dies for Mesopotamia (1 die per year per million inhabitants[15]). Keep in mind that ancient Media is defined by a macro- or even monocephalic system: the urban network was not very dense, and therefore the need for coins small.[16]

Parthian bronze coinage and the minting of drachms in Ecbatana

Until the reign of Vardanes I (40–47 AD), the Parthian kings regularly minted bronze, principally in either two denominations (chalkous and dichalkous) or four

Table 13.3: Percentage of use of metals (mint of Ecbatana)

Kings	*AR*	*AE*	*Kings*	*AR*	*AE*
Mithradates I	45.16%	54.84%	*Vologases I*	86.5%	13.5%
Phraates II	45.45%	54.55%	*Vardanes II*	100%	-
Darius	80%	20%	*Pacorus II*	100%	-
Phraates III	42.24%	57.76%	*Vologases II*	100%	-
Mithradates III	97.61%	2.39%	*Artabanus III*	100%	-
Orodes II	31.14%	68.86%	*Vologases III*	100%	-
Pacorus I	10%	90%	*Osroes I*	100%	-
Phraates IV	40.82%	59.18%	*Parthamaspates*	100%	-
Phraataces	72%	28%	*Mithradates IV*	98.57	1.43%
Phr. & Musa	96.11%	3.89%	*Vologases IV*	100%	-
Vonones I	71.875%	28.125%	*Osroes II*	100%	-
Artabanus II	67.14%	32.86%	*Vologases V*	100%	-
Vardanes I	100%	-	*Vologases VI*	100%	-
Gotarzes II	100%	-	*Artabanus IV*	100%	-
Vonones II	100%	-			

Table 13.4: Percentage of use of metals (mints of Ecbatana and Seleucia on the Tigris from Mithradates I to Artabanus IV)

	Tetradrachms		*Drachms*		*AE*	
	Ecbatana	*Seleucia*	*Ecbatana*	*Seleucia*	*Ecbatana*	*Seleucia*
c. *148 BC* – c. *226 AD*	0%	60%	93%	6%	7%	34%
until Vardanes I	0%	93.93%	82%	0%	18%	6.07%
from Vardanes I	0%	61.49%	97.94%	9.62%	2.06%	28.89%

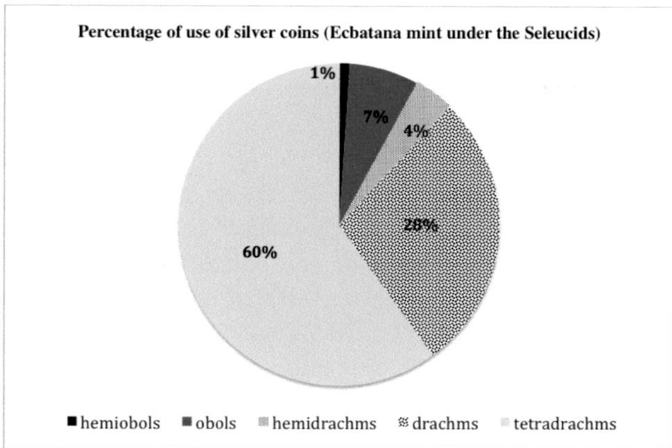

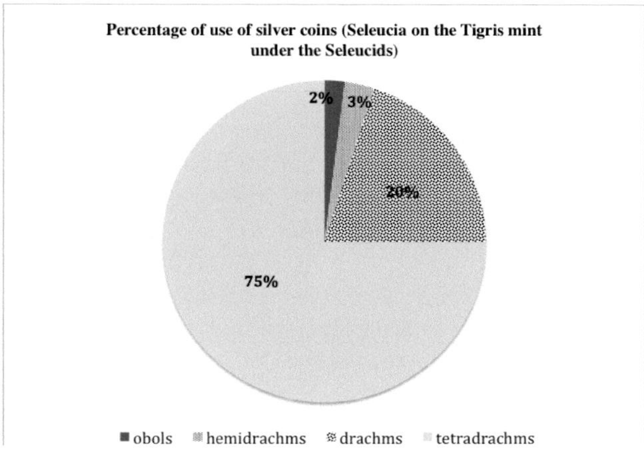

Figure 13.3: Percentage of use of silver coins.

denominations (the same plus the tetrachalkous and octochalkous under Mithradates I). Then from the middle of the first century AD, bronze strikes suddenly disappear, apart from a few rare exceptions. Thus, two major periods are needed to differentiate Parthian monetary practice in Media: until about 38–40 AD, the mint is diverse and denominations of low value are common, while later on monometallism based on the drachm becomes the almost exclusive practice.

The comparison with the coinage of Seleucia on the Tigris is illuminating in this regard.

The Parthians thus modified the monetary practice that the Seleucids had introduced into Media: while the Greek sovereigns widely struck tetradrachms, their Parthian successors, in the mint of Ecbatana at least, ceased their production.[17]

Moreover, with the advent of Vardanes I the workshop of Ecbatana specialised in striking drachms. This is new: indeed, the Seleucids struck most of their metal in the form of tetradrachms (60% of emissions[18]) and the Parthian predecessors of Vardanes struck nearly 20% in bronze coins. Perhaps the facts will help us understand the situation at the mint of Seleucia on the Tigris: while emissions of bronze nearly ceased at Ecbatana with Vardanes I (2% of total production), the workshop at Seleucia in the same time period dramatically increased the striking of bronze (29% of the monetary production, versus approximately 6% from Mithradates I to Vardanes I).

The workshops of Ecbatana and Seleucia on the Tigris thus appear to have issued two coinages complementary to each other, so should we infer a reorganisation of the satrapies inherited from Seleucids? The question is worth asking; indeed, since the Greek era, each royal residence struck various emissions to provide for all requirements, whether daily needs (small denominations and bronze) or high intrinsic value (drachms and tetradrachms to finance military campaigns). After the reign of Vardanes I, Ecbatana exclusively issued drachms, while Seleucia's priority was to issue tetradrachms and bronzes. This would seem to suggest a monetary area larger than the strict boundaries of each satrapy. Nothing really can completely confirm this hypothesis, but the circulation of money is a strong indicator; the data on the Parthians in this area remain very thin and are therefore difficult to interpret.

Chronic political instability

Parthian kings regularly faced revolts, conspiracies or external threats. The history of the dynasty is marked by parricide and fratricide. The question is whether this instability might explain the volume of some strikes under a few of the kings.

The singular case of Orodes II is interesting: after killing his father Phraates III with the help of his brother Mithradates III, Orodes turned against his brother when he (Orodes) occupied Babylon and Seleucia on the Tigris. Subsequently, in 53 BC, he faced the threat of the triumvir Crassus, who was then defeated by the Parthian general Surena at the battle of Carrhae. Does this succession of events explain why Orodes II used about 2.3 dies per year of his reign, compared to Mithradates III who used about 1.1, and Mithradates IV who used 1.5?

One last element may finally support this idea of war coinage: the contemporaneity of the various series that emerges from the die-links analysis would fit with the idea that some of the series were produced in a short time to answer special needs.

Die-Links

The Parthian drachms die-links chart (see Appendix) shows a strike density even more intense than it was for the connections of Seleucid tetradrachms. Obverses are almost always associated with many reverses, which are themselves coupled to many other obverses. This finding is somewhat surprising, since we have just seen that Media was a region much less monetised under the Parthians than under the Seleucids. The technical study of the coinage of Osroes II can enlighten us in this regard. This coinage offers one of the most revealing examples of the density of the Parthian strikes; that of Vologases VI has the same characteristics.

Osroes II in about 190 AD struck (simultaneously?) drachms using about thirty dies. Such an issue is truly amazing. A decline in the quality of the dies can be seen, which would suggest that it was necessary to use many more dies. It is quite clear that the coins minted are of poor quality:[19]

1. Double strikes are much more common than for other kings (New York, American Numismatic Society, tray 971, n° 1944.100.83558[20]).

2. Strikes irregularly dispersed the metal on the surface of the flan (for example, New York, American Numismatic Society, tray 971, n°1944.100.83558).
3. The metal used for the flans is poor; oxidation (unusually common on these silver coins) is almost the rule (Vienna, Münzkabinett, Cabinet 12, n°23160,[21] n° 23161;[22] London, British Museum, Cabinet 162, tray 22, n°1894,0506.2289,[23] n°1900,0101.23;[24] also New York, American Numismatic Society, tray 971, n°1923.150.408[25] and especially n°1973.56.1718[26]).
4. Coins show frequent die cracks, a surprising finding for a brief period of use, as for Osroes: for example Vienna, Münzkabinett, Cabinet 12, n°23163,[27] n°23162;[28] London, British Museum, Cabinet 162, tray 22, n°1930,0812,69,[29] n°1877,1202.1;[30] or finally Berlin, Münzkabinett, Cabinet 14/58, n°18408, and 4/10,[31] n°18410, 5/2.[32]

If the technical assumption is correct, fewer coins than usual were produced from each die. However, the coin characteroscopy for drachms of Osroes II is rather high (5.71). Nevertheless, more than 40% of dies are represented by a single surviving coin, the high characteroscopic index being obtained through some dies being especially well represented.[33] The technical criteria may partly explain the high number of dies found for Osroes II, but it apparently cannot be extended to explain the emissions, almost all also consistent, of Darius and of Vonones II or even Parthamaspates. The quality of their coinage does not specifically differ from other contemporary Parthian kings; characteroscopic indices relating to their coinages are high, while the number of dies represented by a single specimen is rather low compared to other Parthian rulers.[34]

The rhythm of multiple pairs of dies could then, in this case, be explained in two ways:

1. First, the rulers were faced with external pressures that forced them to strike drachms from between 30 and 40 dies almost simultaneously. Coin production appears to have been characterized by the greatest inconsistency[35] as shown elsewhere by the die-links of Osroes II.[36]

Table 13.5: The most populous weight

Kings	*The most populous weight*	*Kings*	*The most populous weight*
Mithradates I	3.75–3.79g and 3.80–3.84g (28.57% each)	*Vologases I*	3.65–3.69g (12.25%)
Darius	4.05–4.09g (23.33%)	*Vardanes II*	3.70–3.74g (20%)
Phraates III	4.05–4.09g (21.73%)	*Pacorus II*	3.65–3.69g (16.17%)
Mithradates III	4.05–4.09g (36.11%)	*Vologases II*	3.60–3.64g (30.76%)
Orodes II	3.75-3.79g (10.80%)	*Artabanus III*	3.75–3.79g (23.404%)
Pacorus I	A single example: 3.86g	*Vologases III*	3.75–3.79g (19.55%)
Phraates IV	3.80–3.84g (12.093%)	*Osroes I*	3.70–3.74g and 3.80–3.84g (13.33% each)
Phraataces	3.70–3.74g (18.51%)	*Parthamaspates*	3.75–3.79g (28.97%)
Phr. & Musa	3.65–3.69g and 3.70–3.74g (14.14% each)	*Mithradates IV*	3.70–3.74g (16.16%)
Vonones I	3.85–3.89 (19.28%)	*Vologases IV*	3.65–3.69g and 3.70–3.74g (13.87%)
Artabanus II	3.70–3.74g and 3.80–3.84g (13.42% each)	*Osroes II*	3.65–3.69g (15.78%)
Vardanes I	3.70–3.74g (18%)	*Vologases V*	3.70–3.74g (14.28%)
Gotarzes II	3.60–3.64g (11.41%)	*Vologases VI*	3.60–3.64g (15.84%)
Vonones II	3.70–3.74g (17.53%)	*Artabanus IV*	3.65–3.69g (24.28%)

Table 13.6: Theoretical weight of Parthian drachms

Kings	*Theoretical weight*	*Kings*	*Theoretical weight*
Mithradates I	3.82–3.87g	*Vologases I*	3.64–3.66g
Darius	4.06–4.08g	*Vardanes II*	3.73–3.75g
Phraates III	4.01–4.03g	*Pacorus II*	3.65–3.67g
Mithradates III	4.11–4.13g	*Vologases II*	3.65–3.67g
Orodes II	3.85–3.87g	*Artabanus III*	3.80–3.82g
Pacorus I	A single example: 3.86g (3.90–3.92g)	*Vologases III*	3.73–3.75g
Phraates IV	3.83–3.85g	*Osroes I*	3.69–3.71g
Phraataces	3.76–3.78g	*Parthamaspates*	3.79–3.81g
Phr. & Musa	3.75–3.77g	*Mithradates IV*	3.69–3.71g
Vonones I	3.85–3.87g	*Vologases IV*	3.69–3.71g
Artabanus II	3.75–3.77g	*Osroes II*	3.66–3.68g
Vardanes I	3.71–3.73g	*Vologases V*	3.71–3.73g
Gotarzes II	3.64–3.66g	*Vologases VI*	3.66–3.68g
Vonones II	3.71–3.73g	*Artabanus IV*	3.71–3.73g

2. The second hypothesis: having reigned only a short time, the kings began issuing their own coins massively and rapidly to legitimize their rule in a period of rebellion against the ruling regime;[37] the usurpers would then have chosen to monetise silver in large amounts (unrelated to their needs) rather than bronze. Was this with the help of Rome? A metallurgical analysis of coins in this regard would be of interest to know the origin of the metal.

Putting obverse dies into service under the Parthians

Striking coins with about thirty obverse dies simultaneously (or almost so) is somewhat surprising, since it presupposes also the commissioning of several of these synchronous obverse dies simultaneously rather than as required. The finding remains unexplained: "*cette idée [la mise en service simultanée de plusieurs coins de droit] soulève une réticence naturelle. C'est que, quoiqu'il faille se méfier de l'anachronisme, on a un certain mal à imaginer un responsable de la production donnant l'ordre de graver en série un nombre important de coins de droit, avant même de savoir si ceux-ci seront nécessaires…*"[38] Maybe we should explain this phenomenon by the poor quality of the dies requiring the use of a large number.

Another explanation could be a technical issue proposed by J. Bingen[39] and G. Le Rider:[40] several contiguous obverse dies were engraved on the same anvil, thereby facilitating their simultaneous use. This explanation does not seem to be supported by the evidence: "*aucun bout de gravure appartenant à un autre coin*"[41] could be distinguished on the obverse.

Maybe in the final analysis, if the technical criteria do not appear to be supported, we should see the die usage as offering evidence of the unstable political context of the time, that required the new ruler to issue a substantial coinage early in his reign in an attempt to prevent the sort of the troubles that were likely to arise under such uncertain circumstances.

Observations on the weight of Parthian coins

The coinage of Mithradates I faithfully follows that of his Seleucid predecessor Alexander I Balas. The magistrate AOY ⚲ remained in office (see below) and the technical aspects of striking remain unchanged. The weights confirm this view. Alexander Balas had struck drachms of very light weight, far from the Attic or Euboeo-Attic standards. The median weight of the last Seleucid drachms from the workshop of Ecbatana is 3.88g.[42] The median weight of the first Parthian drachms is about 3.78g.[43] This is a significant difference, but the drachms are still light. Conversely, from the reign of Darius until the end of that of Mithradates III, the weights are aligned on much higher bases, since the theoretical modal weight of drachms for a 24-year period (*c.* 70–*c.* 54 BC) is about 4.06g to 4.08g, or about 6.30% heavier than under Mithradates I. But, presumably as with Orodes II, and permanently under Pacorus I, the weight fluctuates again to return to the standard employed in the late Seleucid and early Parthian periods, and finally staggers, with some exceptions, to between 3.65g and 3.75g. We certainly should not see in this any reform but rather trial and error in monetary practice.

The essential point is that, as with the axis (12h on all coins, with some errors at 11h and 1h), Parthian coins are characterised by a stable weight for more than three centuries.

Bronze

The first Parthian bronze coins issued at Ecbatana also follow the reforms introduced by Alexander I Balas. Indeed, chalkous, dichalkous and tetrachalkous are given the same marks of value as under Alexander Balas, applied to coins of almost identical weight. No changes occur, other than a continuous shift of the weight; however, the slow and steady evolution in weight cannot allow us to imagine a monetary reform.

Notes on control marks

Control marks give rise to some comments. Monograms used by Molon in the Seleucid period shed light for us on his policy. He rebelled against royal power, but maintained the magistrate in charge (or one of the magistrates) at the workshop of Ecbatana. In turn, Antiochus III subsequently confirmed that same magistrate in office. This is similar to the case found at the end of the Seleucid and the beginning of the Parthian dynasty: the magistrate AOY [monogram] who was responsible for the mint under Alexander I Balas continued his supervisory work at the workshop of Ecbatana during the reign of Mithradates I. The case is interesting because the other mint officer seems to have departed for the monetary workshop of Seleucia on the Tigris.

The invasion of Media and the capture of Ecbatana by the Parthians could indeed mark a break in the tenure of the monetary magistrates. G. Le Rider dates the Seleucids' loss of the capital of Media to 148 or 147 BC.[44] A magistrate with the monogram [monogram] remains in place. However, another control mark, [monogram], attested during the reign of Alexander I Balas, now disappeared from the workshop. A link can possibly be established with Seleucia on the Tigris, where the monogram [monogram] appears on coins issued between 150 and 145 BC[45] (for which we could propose a new dating between 148/7 and 145 BC to reflect the assumed transfer of the magistrate). Moreover, it is when Ecbatana passed under Parthian control that Seleucia started to issue drachms, which it had not struck since the reign of Seleucus II.[46]

Nevertheless, the hypothesis cannot be confirmed as a definitive conclusion for two reasons:

1. First, while links between the workshops at Seleucia on the Tigris and Ecbatana can be identified, no other source corroborates the hypothesis of the transfer of a magistrate after the fall of Ecbatana.
2. More importantly, the monogram in question is so simple that it may have been used simultaneously by many magistrates in many workshops of the empire.

Much work lies ahead before we can trace with certainty the monetary history of the Parthians.

Notes

1 Polybius V, 44–45. See also Briant 1966, p. 758.
2 Polybius X, 27.
3 Boucharlat 1990, p. 149.
4 Sancisi-Weerdenburg 1988, p. 197–212.
5 Brown 1998.
6 Sancisi-Weerdenburg 1988, p. 203.
7 Sarraf 1997; Knapton, Sarraf and Curtis 2001.
8 Muscarella 1980.
9 Wolski 1980.
10 Weissbach 1905.
11 Boillet 2009.
12 *Ibid.*
13 Boillet 2009.
14 Aperghis 2004, p. 240
15 *Ibid.*
16 Aperghis, *id.*, p. 240: "One may also consider Ekbatana, serving Media, with an output of half a die per year on average. In terms of population, Seleukid Media should have possessed about a quarter of Mesopotamia's population and one would have expected roughly one die per year at Ekbatana. The smaller number, if not a statistical error, might simply be an indication of the lesser need for coinage in a region not so heavily urbanized, where much payment, taxation and exchange were still being conducted in kind."
17 McDowell 1935.
18 *Ibid.*
19 Comparison of the monetary emissions of Vologases IV and Vologases V is illuminating in this regard.
20 A21-P1.
21 A1-P1.
22 A37-P10.
23 A23-P30.
24 A21-P2
25 A21-P2
26 A19-P1
27 A12-P24
28 A4-P5.
29 A21-P18.
30 A4-P11.
31 A1-P1
32 A21-P1
33 Especially dies A1, A3, A4, A5, A6, A9, A10, A14, A19 and A21, all represented by more than ten specimens.
34 Except for Darius.
35 This inconsistency is characterised by die axes or by the unusually poor quality of the strikes, as is the case for the coins of Osroes: orientations are still 12h, but less well adjusted, with significant alignments to 11h or 1h.
36 Appendix 1.
37 This is the case with Osroes II against Vologases IV, and then during the armed conflict that pitted him against Vologases V.
38 Callataÿ 1999.
39 Bingen 1969, p. 16.
40 Le Rider 1977, p. 419–420.
41 Callataÿ 1999, p. 93.

42 That is a theoretical weight of 3.92–3.94g. See Boillet 2009.
43 That is a theoretical weight of 3.82–3.84g.
44 Le Rider 1965, p. 339–340.
45 Houghton and Lorber 2008, p. 249.
46 *Ibid.*

References

Aperghis, G.G. (2004). *The Seleukid royal economy: the finances and financial administration of the Seleukid Empire*, Cambridge.

Bingen, J. (1969). "Le trésor monétaire de Thorikos 1969", in Thorikos VI, s.l.

Boillet, P.-Y. (2009). Ecbatane et la Médie d'Alexandre aux Arsacides, Unpublished PhD thesis, Bordeaux, n.p.

Boucharlat, R. (1990). "Suse et la Susiane à l'époque achéménide. Données archéologiques", in H. Sancisi-Weerdenburg, A. Kuhrt (eds), *Achaemenid History IV: Center and Periphery*, Leiden: p. 149–175.

Brown, S.C. (1998). "Ecbatana", in *Encyclopaedia Iranica* VIII, 1: p. 80–84.

Callataÿ, F. de (1999). "Étude de technique monétaire: le rapport 'nombre de coins de revers/nombre de coins de droit' à l'époque hellénistique", in *Revue des Archéologues et Historiens de l'Art de Louvain* XXXII: p. 91–102.

Houghton, A., and Lorber, C. (2008). *Seleucid Coins: A Comprehensive Catalogue*, New York and Lancaster, PA.

Knapton, P., Sarraf, M.R., and Curtis, J. (2001). "Inscribed column bases from Hamadan", *Iran* XXXIX: p. 99–117.

Le Rider, G. (1965). "Suse sous les Séleucides et les Parthes: Les Trouvailles monétaires et l'histoire de la ville", in Mémoires de la Mission archéologique en Iran XXXVIII, Paris.

— (1977). *Le monnayage d'argent et d'or de Philippe II frappé en Macédoine de 359 à 294*, Paris.

McDowell, R. (1935). *Coins from Seleucia*, Ann Arbor.

Muscarella, O.W. (1980). "Excavated and unexcavated Achaemenian Art", in D. Schmandt-Besserat (ed.), *Ancient Persia: the Art of an Empire*, Undena Malibu: p. 23–42.

Sancisi-Weerdenburg, H. (1988). "Was there ever a Median Empire?", in H. Sancisi-Weerdenburg, A. Kuhrt (eds), *Achaemenid History, III, Method and Theory*, Leiden: p. 197–212.

Sarraf, M.R. (1997). "Neue architektonische und städtbauliche Funde von Ekbatana-Tepe (Hamadan)", in *Archäologische Mitteilungen aus Iran und Turan* XXIX: p. 321–339.

Sellwood, D. (1980, 2nd ed.). *An Introduction to the Coinage of Parthia*, London.

Weissbach, F.H. (1905). "Ekbatana", in Pauly-Wissowa 5: p. 2155–2158.

Wolski, J. (1980). "Les Sources de l'époque hellénistique et parthe de l'histoire de l'Iran", in *Acta Antiqua* 28: p. 137–145.

Appendix

The drachm die-links of Osroes II

c. 190 AD

Osroes II is known to us only by his coins; the magnitude of his mintage takes us by surprise. His coins are very similar to those of his predecessor, Vologases IV; differences relate only to details such as tiara and beard, as well as some variants of letters on the reverse.

Osroes II struck coins only at Ecbatana. This suggests that he controlled only the region of Media during his short reign.

Characteroscopic index

Denominations	*n*	*d*	*n/d*
Drachms	240	42	5.71

Monograms, letters and symbols on Parthian coins (reverse)

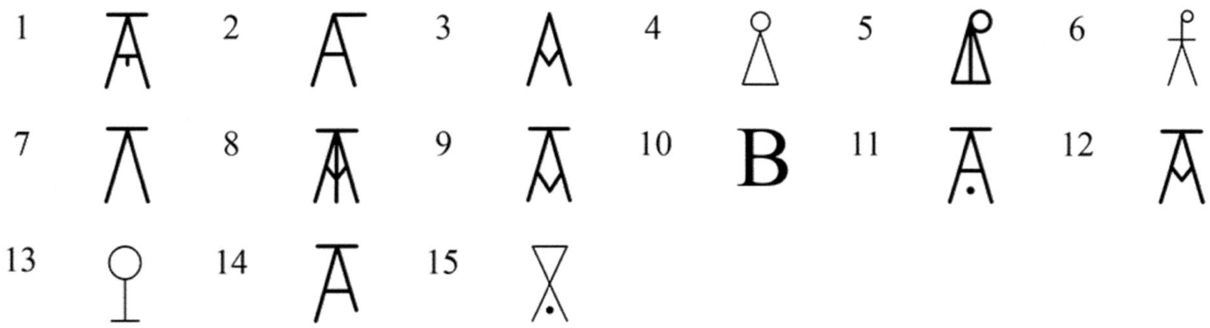

Series I

Obverse: Bust left, long beard, wearing tiara.

Reverse: Archer seated right. In the field, variant letters (A). Around the king, in two lines: ΒΑΣΙΛΕΩΣ ΒΑΣΙΛΕΩΝ ΑΡΣΑΚΟΥ ΔΙΚΑΙΟΥ ΕΥΕΡΓΕΤΟΥ ΕΠΙΦΑΝΟΥΣ [ΦΙΛΕΛΛΗΝΟΣ]. The Greek of the legend is too corrupt to make sense.

Group 1: No pellet over the bow on the reverse

References: Sellwood, *Coinage of Parthia*, 85/1 & 3.

Letter A (14)

Note: The legends are unreadable.

1. A1^{1}-P1(a) London, British Museum, Cabinet 162, tray 22, n° 1900,0706.118. 3.53g, 18ø, 12h.
2. A1^{1}-P2^{1}(a) London, British Museum, Cabinet 162, tray 22, n° 1930,0812.67. 3.67g, 19ø, 12h.
3. A1^{1}-P3^{1}(a) London, British Museum, Cabinet 162, tray 22, n° 1894,0506.2285. 3.80g, 18ø, 12h.
4. A1^{1}-P4(a) London, British Museum, Cabinet 162, tray 22, n° 1889,0105.1582. 3.74g, 18ø, 12h.
5. A2^{1}-P5^{1}(a) Oxford, Ashmolean Museum, n.c. 3.83g, 19ø, 12h.
6. A3^{1}-P5^{1}(a) Berlin, Münzkabinett, Cabinet 14/58, n° 258/1882, 4/7. 3.11g, 19ø, 12h.
7. A3^{1}-P5^{1}(b) London, British Museum, Cabinet 162, tray 22, n° 1894,0506.2287. 3.80g, 19ø, 12h.
8. A3^{1}-P6^{1}(a) Jacques et Pierre Stivin, November 1987, n° 38. ?g, 27ø, 12h.
9. A3^{1}-P6^{1}(b) Albrecht-Hoffmann, June 1984, n° 118. ?g, 19ø, ?h.
10. A3^{1}-P7$^{1?}$(a) Peus 349, 30 October - 1st November 1996, n° 221. 3.48g, 20ø, ?h.
11. A3^{1}-P8^{1}(a) Hirsch 220, 21–22 February 2002, n° 1487. 3.84g, 19ø, ?h.
12. A3^{1}-P8^{1}(b) Hirsch 231, 26–28 November 2003, n° 460. 3.83g, 19ø, ?h.
13. A3^{1}-P9^{1}(a) Ritter, November 1998, n° 451 = Ritter, December 1997, n° 430. ?g, 19ø, ?h.
14. A3^{1}-P10^{1}(a) Künker 23, 30 September - 1st October 1992, n° 158. 3.39g, 18ø, ?h.
15. A3^{1}-P10^{1}(b) Rauch, 24-25 February 1977, n° 21. ?g, 18ø, ?h.
16. A4^{1}-P5^{1}(a) Vienna, Münzkabinett, Cabinet 12, n° 23162. 3.725g, 19ø, 12h.
17. A4^{1}-P5^{1}(b) Berlin, Münzkabinett, Imhoof-Blumer collection, Cabinet 14/58, n° 4/3. 3.78g, 19ø, 12h.
18. A4^{1}-P6^{1}(a) Berlin, Münzkabinett, Guthrie collection, Cabinet 14/58, n° 5/9. 3.45g, 18ø, 12h.
19. A4^{1}-P11^{1}(a) London, British Museum, Cabinet 162, tray 22, n° 1877,1202.1. 3.26g, 19ø, 12h.
20. A4^{1}-P11^{1}(b) Paris, Cabinet des Médailles, n.c. 1308. 3.55g, 21ø, 12h.
21. A4^{1}-P11^{1}(c) London, British Museum, Cabinet 162, tray 22, n° 1894,0506.2286. 3.61g, 20ø, 12h.
22. A4^{1}-P11^{1}(d) London, British Museum, Cabinet 162, tray 22, n° 1889,0105.1583. 3.57g, 20ø, 12h.
23. A4^{1}-P11^{1}(e) London, British Museum, Cabinet 162, tray 22, n° 10. 3.67g, 19ø, 12h.
24. A4^{1}-P12(a) Oxford, Ashmolean Museum, n.c. 3.53g, 18ø, 12h.
25. A4^{1}-P13(a) Berlin, Münzkabinett, Löbbecke collection, Cabinet 14/58, n° 4/6. 3.64g, 18ø, 12h.
26. A5^{1}-P6^{1}(a) Sternberg, 16-17 November 1978, n° 342. 3.62g, 18ø, ?h.
27. A5^{1}-P7^{1}(a) Schenk-Behrens, 13-15 June 1996, n° 235. 3.58g, 19ø, ?h.
28. A5^{1}-P7^{1}(b) Schulman, 27-29 March 1890, n° 475. 3.43g, 18ø, ?h.
29. A5^{1}-P14^{1}(a) Elsen, List 202, January - February 1999, n° 165. 3.89g, 19ø, ?h.
30. A6^{1}-P6^{1}(a) Schulman, 22-24 October 1985, n° 191. 3.22g, 17ø, ?h.
31. A6^{1}-P14^{1}(a) Peus 333, 6-11 May 1992, n° 461. 3.39g, 18ø, ?h.
32. A6^{1}-P15^{1}(a) Elsen, List 190, April 1997, n° 59. 3.74g, 20ø, ?h.
33. A6^{1}-P16(a) Emporium Hamburg, 18-19 May 1994, n° 115. 3.70g, 17ø, ?h.
34. A6^{1}-P17^{1}(a) Schulman, 8-9 November 1982, n° 60. 3.29g, 18ø, ?h.
35. A7^{1}-P6$^{?}$ (a) CGF, 18 June 2004, n° 74. 3.69g, 17ø, ?h.
36. A7^{1}-P14^{1}(a) Elsen, List 196, December 1997 - January 1998, n° 46. 3.50g, 20ø, ?h.
37. A7^{1}-P17^{1}(a) Rauch, 16-19 January 1984, n° 346. ?g, 18ø, ?h.
38. A7^{1}-P18(a) Jean-Marie Defranoux, 29 June 1985, n° 157. 3.55g, 19ø, ?h.
39. A7^{1}-P19^{1}(a) Peus 324, 5-7 April 1989, n° 315. 3.51g, 20ø, ?h.
40. A8^{1}-P6^{1}(a) Hirsch 178, 12-14 May 1993, n° 525. 3.42g, 18ø, ?h.
41. A8^{1}-P14^{1}(a) Gadoury, 3-5 October 1982, n° 441. 3.64g, 20ø, ?h.
42. A8^{1}-P20(a) Hirsch 185, 15-18 February 1995, n° 501. 3.58g, 18ø, ?h.
43. A9^{1}-P6^{1}(a) CGF, 31 December 2002, n° 121. 3.69g, 20ø, 12h.
44. A9^{1}-P6^{1}(b) Rauch, 8-9 November 1974, n° 32. ?g, 19ø, ?h.
45. A9^{1}-P9^{1}(a) Peus 309, 2-4 May 1984, n° 90. 3.23g, 19ø, ?h.
46. A9^{1}-P19^{1}(a) Peus 303, 20-22 October 1981, n° 210. 3.04g, 19ø, ?h.
47. A9^{1}-P21(a) Freeman & Sear, 14 January 1998, n° 215. 3.88g, 20ø, ?h.
48. A9^{1}-P22(a) Schenk-Behrens, 23-24 May 2002, n° 139. 3.58g, 21ø, ?h.
49. A9^{1}-P23(a) Schulman, 19-21 March 1986, n° 196. 3.34g, 19ø, ?h.
50. A10^{1}-P7^{1}(a) SKAZ, Autumn 1991, n° 131 = SKAZ, Spring 1987, n° 57. 3.63g, 19ø, ?h.
51. A11-P7^{1}(a) Peus 363, 26 April 2000, n° 5197. 3.69g, 18ø, ?h.
52. A12^{1}-P7$^{1?}$ (a) SKAZ, Spring 1986, n° 65. 3.63g, 18ø, ?h.
53. A12^{1}-P14^{1}(a) Spink Taisei Zürich 49, 27–28 October 1993, n° 23. 3.65g, 19ø, ?h.
54. A12^{1}-P24^{1}(a) Vienna, Münzkabinett, Cabinet 12, n° 23163. 3.79g, 19ø, 12h.
55. A13^{1}-P7^{1}(a) Malloy, 23 March 2000, n° 173. ?g, 18ø, ?h.
56. A13^{1}-P24^{1}(a) Elsen, List 193, September 1997, n° 101. 3.66g, 17ø, ?h.
57. A14^{1}-P7^{1}(a) Peus 303, 20–22 October 1981, n° 211. 3.53g, 20ø, ?h.
58. A14^{1}-P9^{1}(a) Schulman, 20–21 October 1988, n° 506. 3.74g, 21ø, ?h.
59. A14^{1}-P19^{1}(a) Davissons Ltd, 18 November 1994, n° 113. 3.70g, 20ø, ?h.

60. A14^{1}-P25(a) Hirsch 182, 4–6 May1994, n° 439. 3.60g, 19ø, ?h.
61. A15^{1}-P8^{1}(a) Albrecht-Hoffmann 73, 22–24 April 1992, n° 392. 3.57g, 19ø, ?h.
62. A15^{1}-P9^{1}(a) G. Henzen, 159, May 2005, n° 243. 3.74g, 19ø,. ?h.
63. A15^{1}-P11^{1}(a) Berlin, Münzkabinett, Cabinet 14/58, n° 10195, 4/9. 3.59g, 20ø, 12h.
64. A16^{1}-P9^{1}(a) Gorny & Mosch 126, October 2003, n° 1468. 3.16g, 20ø, ?h.
65. A16^{1}-P9?^{1}(b) CNG 14, 20 March 1991, n° 225. 3.35g, 17ø, ?h.
66. A17^{1}-P9^{1}(a) Giessener Münzhandlung Dieter Gorny 79, 11 October 1996, n° 310. 3.92g, 22ø, ?h.
67. A17^{1}-P15^{1}(a) Harlan J. Berk, 22 July 2003, n° 167. 3.47g, 18ø, ?h.
68. A17^{1}-P17^{1}(a) Kovacs, 18 May 1990, n° 194. 3.47g, 19ø, ?h.
69. A17^{1}-P26(a) Lanz 5, 1 December 1975, n° 275. 3.73g, 20ø, ?h.
70. A18-P9^{1}(a) Hirsch 176, 19-20 November 1992, n° 417. 3.61g, 20ø, ?h
71. A19^{1}-P11^{1}(a) Paris, Cabinet des Médailles, n° H3351. 3.65g, 20ø, 12h.
72. A19^{1}-P27(a) Oxford, Ashmolean Museum, n.c. 3.63g, 20ø, 12h.
73. A19^{1}-P28(a) Oxford, Ashmolean Museum, n.c. 3.50g, 18ø, 12h.
74. A20^{1}-P11^{1}(a) London, British Museum, Cabinet 162, tray 22, n° 1894,0506.2283. 3.34g, 19ø, 12h.
75. A21^{1}-P11^{1}(a) London, British Museum, Cabinet 162, tray 22, cat. 1. 3.62g, 20ø, 12h.
76. A21^{1}-P29(a) New York, American Numismatic Society, tray 971, n° 1973.56.1717. 3.05g, 21ø, 12h.
77. A22^{1}-P15^{1}(a) Freeman & Sear, 10 March 1995, n° 248. 3.50g, 19ø, ?h.
78. A23^{1}-P30(a) London, British Museum, Cabinet 162, tray 22, n° 1894,0506.2289. 3.40g, 17ø, 12h.
79. A24-P31(a) London, British Museum, Cabinet 162, tray 22, n° 1894,0506.2284. 3.57g, 20ø, 12h.
80. A25-P32(a) New York, American Numismatic Society, tray 971, n° 1977.158.808. 3.50g, 22ø, 12h.
81. A26^{1}-P33(a) Schenk-Behrens, 23-24 May 2002, n° 138. 3.74g, 19ø, ?h.
82. A26^{1}-P34(a) Albrecht-Hoffmann 72, 2–4 December 1991, n° 940. ?g, 19ø, ?h.
83. A27-P35(a) Albrecht-Hoffmann 50, 23–25 November 1983, n° 238. 3.55g, 17ø, ?h.
84. A28^{1}-P17^{1}(a) Künker 21, 16–18 March 1992, n° 352. 3.38g, 20ø, ?h.
85. A28^{1}-P36(a) CNG 39, 18 September 1996, n° 822. 3.41g, 19ø, ?h.
86. A29^{1}-P37^{1}(a) Emporium Hamburg, 17-18 May 2001, n° 149. ?g, 19ø, ?h.

Letter A (7)

Note: The legends are unreadable.

87. A1^{1}-P1^{1}(a) Vienna, Münzkabinett, Cabinet 12, n° 23160. ?g, 18ø, 12h.
88. A1^{1}-P1^{1}(b) Berlin, Münzkabinett, Cabinet 14/58, n° 18408, 4/10. 3.80g, 18ø, 12h.
89. A1^{1}-P2^{1}(a) Berlin, Münzkabinett, Löbbecke collection, Cabinet 14/58, n° 4/5. 3.24g, 17ø, 12h.
90. A1^{1}-P3^{1}(a) Numismatica Wien, 22–23 June 1977, n° 129. 3.23g, 18ø, ?h.
91. A1^{1}-P3^{1}(b) Schulman, 19–21 March 1986, n° 195. 3.66g, 18ø, ?h.
92. A1^{1}-P3^{1}(c) Rauch, 5 November 2001, n° 153. 3.64g, 17ø, 12h.
93. A1^{1}-P3^{1}(d) Peus 338, 27–29 April 1994, n° 240. 3.72g, 18ø, ?h.
94. A1^{1}-P3^{1}(e) Numismatica Wien, 22-23 June 1977, n° 130. 3.35g, 19ø, ?h.
95. A1^{1}-P3^{1}(f) Numismatic Fine Arts, 18 December 1987, n° 489. 3.72g, 16ø, ?h.
96. A1^{1}-P3^{1}(g) Elsen, List 191, May-June 1997, n° 113. 3.61g, 18ø, ?h.
97. A1^{1}-P4^{1}(a) Rauch, 24–25 February 1977, n° 20. ?g, 16ø, ?h.
98. A1^{1}-P5^{1}(a) Peus 345, 1-3 November 1995, n° 263. 3.78g, 18ø, ?h.
99. A1^{1}-P5^{1}(b) Numismatic Fine Arts, 20 October 1978, n° 104. ?g, 16ø, ?h.
100. A1^{1}-P6^{1}(a) Schulman, 19-21 April 1989, n° 215 = Schulman, 11-12 April 1988, n° 260. 3.35g, 18ø, ?h.
101. A1^{1}-P7^{1}(a) Numismatica Wien, 20–21 November 1975, n° 148. 3.51g, 18ø, 6h.
102. A4^{1}-P8(a) Berlin, Münzkabinett, Cabinet 14/58, n° 18409, 5/1. 3.53g, 19ø, 12h.
103. A4^{1}-P9(a) Berlin, Münzkabinett, Cabinet 14/58, n° 5/6. 3.49g, 20ø, 12h.
104. A5^{1}-P1^{1}(a) CGF, 31 December 2002, n° 122. 3.69g, 20ø, 12h.
105. A5^{1}-P1^{1}(b) Elsen, 14 November 1984, n° 66. 3.71g, 17ø, ?h.
106. A5^{1}-P1^{1}(c) Albrecht-Hoffmann 74, 11–13 November 1992, n° 477. 3.66g, 18ø, ?h.
107. A5^{1}-P1^{1}(d) CNG 12, 26 September 1990, n° 532. 3.70g, 16ø, ?h.
108. A5^{1}-P1^{1}(e) Numismatica Wien, March 1975, n° 39. ?g, 18ø, ?h.
109. A5^{1}-P1^{1}(f) CNG 45, 18 March 1998, n° 678. 3.74g, 19ø, ?h.
110. A5^{1}-P1^{1}(g) Albrecht-Hoffmann 59, 29–31 October 1986, n° 1274. 3.66g, 18ø, ?h.
111. A5$^{1?}$-P1^{1}(h) CNG 10, 21 March 1990, n° 162. 3.27g, 21ø, ?h.
112. A5^{1}-P1^{1}(i) Albrecht-Hoffmann 39, 16–17 April 1980, n° 715. 3.57g, 20ø, ?h.
113. A5^{1}-P1^{1}(j) Numismatica Wien, March 1975, n° 38. ?g, 18ø, ?h.
114. A5^{1}-P10^{1}(a) Peus 326, 1–3 November 1989, n° 410. 3.71g, 19ø, ?h.
115. A5^{1}-P10^{1}(b) Dorotheum, 3–5 May 1981, n° 54. ?g, 18ø, ?h.
116. A5^{1}-P11^{1}(a) Rauch, 7–8 June 1977, n° 97. ?g, 19ø, ?h.
117. A5^{1}-P11^{1}(b) Ritter, November 1998, n° 450 = Ritter, List December 1997, n° 429. ?g, 18ø, ?h.
118. A5^{1}-P11^{1}(c) Numismatica Wien, 20–21 November 1975, n° 149. 3.72g, 18ø, 12h.
119. A5^{1}-P11^{1}(d) Lanz 66, 22 November 1993, n° 343. 3.65g, 19ø, ?h.
120. A5^{1}-P12^{1}(a) Emporium Hamburg, 17–18 May 1995, n° 74. ?g, 18ø, ?h.
121. A5^{1}-P13^{1}(a) Rauch, 22–24 April 1987, n° 100. ?g, 19ø, ?h.
122. A6^{1}-P1^{1}(a) Rauch, 8-9 November 1974, n° 31. ?g, 18ø, ?h.

123. A6^1-P14^1(a) New York, American Numismatic Society, tray 971, n° 1923.150.407. 3.56g, 21ø, 12h.
124. A8^1-P1^1(a) CNG 6, 1 March 1989, n° 148. 3.60g, 21ø, ?h.
125. A8^1-P1^1(b) Müller (Münz Zentrum) 78, 7–9 September 1994, n° 113. 3.30g, 18ø, ?h.
126. A8^1-P6^1(a) CNG 3, 29 April 1988, n° 207. 3.79g, 20ø, ?h.
127. A8^1-P14^1(a) Numismatica Wien, 11–14 May 1976, n° 114. 3.64g, 18ø, 11h.
128. A8^1-P? (a) Albrecht-Hoffmann 39, 16–17 April 1980, n° 716. 2.36g, 17ø, ?h.
129. A10^1-P1^1(a) TKA, 15-16 April 1985, n° 119. 3.52g, 17ø, ?h.
130. A10^1-P1^1(b) Burgan, 25 November 1991, n° 311. 3.58g, 19ø, ?h.
131. A10^1-P1^1(c) CNG 18, 3 December 1991, n° 233. 3.52g, 18ø, ?h.
132. A10^1-P1^1(d) CNG 37, 20 March 1996, n° 764. 3.65g, 17ø, ?h.
133. A10^1-P1^1(e) Schenk-Behrens, 2 April 2004, n° 95. 2.92g, 17ø, ?h.
134. A10^1-P1^1(f) Platt, December 1994, n° 198. 3.65g, 16ø, ?h.
135. A10^1-P1^1(g) Peus 326, 1–3 November 1989, n° 411. 3.49g, 18ø, ?h.
136. A10^1-P1$^?$(h) Albrecht-Hoffmann 65, 9–12 November 1988, n° 407. 3.54g, 19ø, ?h.
137. A101-P101(a) Müller (Münz Zentrum) 106, 28–29 March 2001, n° 245. 3.45g, 20ø, ?h.
138. A101-P151(a) Schulman, 15-16 October 1990, n° 396. 3.65g, 18ø, 12h.
139. A101-P151(b) SKAB, 27-28 October 1987, n° 905. 3.65g, 18ø, ?h.
140. A101-P161(a) Rauch, 5 November 2001, n° 152. 3.77g, 18ø, 12h.
141. A101-P161(b) TKA, 14-15 April 1986, n° 186. 3.71g, 18ø, ?h.
142. A101?-P17(a) Schulman 28–29 September 1976, n° 273. 3.83g, 19ø, ?h.
143. A141-P11(a) Hirsch 183, 20–24 September 1994, n° 720. 3.75g, 17ø, ?h.
144. A141-P111(a) Albrecht-Hoffmann 68, 25–27 April 1990, n° 540. 3.68g, 18ø, ?h.
145. A141-P131(a) Ritter, List December 1998, n° 369. ?g, 19ø, ?h.
146. A141-P131(b) CGF, 16 June 2000, n° 116. 3.70g, 19ø, 12h.
147. A191?-P11(a) New York, American Numismatic Society, tray 971, n° 1973.56.1718. 3.39g, 20ø, 12h.
148. A191-P11(b) New York, American Numismatic Society, tray 971, n° 1944.100.83557. 3.78g, 20ø, 12h.
149. A191-P21(a) Berlin, Münzkabinett, Prokesch-Osten collection, Cabinet 14/58, n° 5/10. 3.55g, 19ø, 12h.
150. A191-P181(a) Oxford, Ashmolean Museum, n.c. 3.68g, 16ø, 12h.
151. A191-P191(a) Oxford, Ashmolean Museum, n.c. 3.35g, 18ø, 12h.
152. A191-P201(a) Oxford, Ashmolean Museum, n.c. 3.60g, 18ø, 12h.
153. A191-P211(a) Berlin, Münzkabinett, Imhoof-Blumer collection, Cabinet 14/58, n° 4/2. 3.82g, 19ø, 12h.
154. A191-P211(b) New York, American Numismatic Society, tray 971, n° 1938.50.230. 3.43g, 19ø, 12h.
155. A191-P221(a) Noble Numismatics 49, 22–24 November 1995, n° 2070. 3.66g, 17ø, ?h.
156. A211-P21(a) Berlin, Münzkabinett, Prokesch-Osten collection, Cabinet 14/58, n° 5/4. 3.70g, 19ø, 12h.
157. A21^1-P15^1(a) CGF, 27 November 2004, n° 169. 3.52g, 20ø, 12h.
158. A21^1-P23^1(a) Albrecht-Hoffmann 59, 29–31 October 1986, n° 1275. 3.71g, 18ø, ?h.
159. A21^1-P24^1(a) Peus 343, 26-28 April 1995, n° 272. 3.57g, 19ø, ?h.
160. A23^1-P1^1(a) Hirsch 229, 17–20 September 2003, n° 2032. 3.74g, 18ø, ?h.
161. A23^1-P1^1(b) Numismatic Fine Arts, 24–25 March 1977, n° 406. 3.43g, 18ø, ?h.
162. A23^1-P15^1(a) Numismatic Fine Arts, List, 20 October 1978, n° 105. ?g, 17ø, ?h.
163. A23^1-P?(a) Harlan J. Berk, 22 July 2003, n° 168. 3.67g, 17ø, ?h.
164. A26^1-P25^1(a) Peus 326, 1-3 November 1989, n° 409. 3.56g, 20ø, ?h.
165. A30^1-P1^1(a) Rauch, 30 October-1 November 1975, n° 37. ?g, 19ø, ?h.

Note: The coin is overstruck.

166. A31^1-P1^1(b) Ponterio & Associates, 1 November 1994, n° 394. 3.81g, 18ø, ?h.
167. A31^1-P26^1(a) Ponterio & Associates, 1 November 1994, n° 393. 3.66g, 19ø, ?h.
168. A31^1-P27(a) Dorotheum, 1-4 December 1981, n° 77. ?g, 18ø, ?h.

Letter A (11)

Note: The legends are unreadable.

169. A30^1-P1(a) Oxford, Ashmolean Museum, n.c. 3.67g, 17ø, 12h.
170. A32^1-P2(a) Gorny & Mosch 130, March 2004, n°1506. 3.66g, 17ø, ?h.
171. A33-P3(a) Oxford, Ashmolean Museum, n.c. 3.78g, 18ø, 12h.

Group 2: Pellet over the bow on the reverse

References: Sellwood, *Coinage of Parthia*, 85/2.

Letter A (14)

Note: The legends are unreadable.

172. A1^1-P1(a) London, British Museum, Cabinet 162, tray 22, n° 19. 3.68g, 18ø, 12h.
173. A2^1-P2^1(a) Paris, Cabinet des Médailles, J. de Morgan collection, n° 1002. 3.75g, 21ø, 12h.
174. A2^1-P3(a) New York, American Numismatic Society, tray 971, n° 1944.100.83568. 3.46g, 21ø, 1h.
175. A3^1-P4^1(a) London, British Museum, Cabinet 162, tray 22, 1850,0412.55. 3.50g, 20ø, 12h.
176. A4^1-P5(a) Berlin, Münzkabinett, Cabinet 14/58, n° 259/1882, 4/8. 3.31g, 20ø, 12h.
177. A5^1-P6^1(a) SKAZ, Spring 1982, n° 73. 3.77g, 20ø, ?h.
178. A5^1-P7^1(a) SKAZ, Spring 1980, n° 68. 3.69g, 20ø, ?h.
179. A6^1-P8^1(a) Peus 348, 2–4 May 1996, n° 341. 3.54g, 18ø, ?h.
180. A6^1-P9^1(a) Albrecht-Hoffmann 58, 23-25 April 1986, n° 1606. 3.73g, 18ø, ?h.
181. A6^1-P9^1(b) CNG 35, 20 September 1995, n° 415. 3.67g, 20ø, ?h.

182. A7^1-P6^1(a) Numismatic Fine Arts, List, 20 October 1978, n° 103. ?g, 19ø, ?h.
183. A9^1-P6^1(a) Schenk-Behrens, 13-15 June 1996, n° 234. 3.48g, 21ø, ?h.
184. A9^1-P6^1(b) Rauch, 18–20 January 1988, n° 190. ?g, 23ø, ?h.
185. A9^1-P8^1(a) Gorny & Mosch 130, March 2004, n° 1493. 3.75g, 20ø, ?h.
186. A14^1-P8^1(a) Elsen, List 192, July-August 1997, n° 107. 3.89g, 19ø, ?h.
187. A14^1-P8^1(b) Peus 301, 25–27 May 1981, n° 539. 3.45g, 21ø, ?h.

Note: The coin is overstruck.

188. A14^1-P10^1(a) Numismatica Wien, 22–23 June 1977, n° 128. 3.69g, 21ø, ?h.
189. A14^1-P11^1(a) Ponterio & Associates, 12 July 1994, n° 330. 3.80g, 20ø, 12h.
190. A15^1-P8^1(a) Paris, Cabinet des Médailles, n.c. 1305. 3.49g, 20ø, 12h.
191. A16^1-P8^1(a) CNG 39, 18 September 1996, n° 823. 3.81g, 19ø, ?h.
192. A17^1-P10^1(a) Gilles Blançon, List 50, 2005, n° 293. ?g, 20ø, ?h.
193. A19^1-P11^1(a) London, British Museum, Cabinet 162, tray 22, n° 1894,0506.2290. 3.27g, 19ø, 12h.
194. A19$^{1?}$-P12^1(a) London, British Museum, Cabinet 162, tray 22, n° 1891,0603.193. 3.77g, 21ø, 12h.
195. A19^1-P13^1(a) London, British Museum, Cabinet 162, tray 22, n° 5. 3.53g, 18ø, 12h.
196. A19^1-P14(a) Paris, Cabinet des Médailles, J. de Morgan collection, n° 1004. 3.59g, 19ø, 12h.
197. A19^1-P15^1(a) Van der Dussen, 19–20 April 1993, n° 122. 3.71g, 20ø, ?h.
198. A20^1-P15^1(a) London, British Museum, Cabinet 162, tray 22, n° 1865,0805.20. 3.65g, 19ø, 12h.
199. A20^1-P16(a) New York, American Numismatic Society, tray 971, n° 1944.100.83555. 3.73g, 20ø, 12h.
200. A21$^{1?}$-P2^1(a) London, British Museum, Cabinet 162, tray 22, n° 1930,0812.68. 3.65g, 20ø, 12h.
201. A21^1-P2$^{1?}$ (b) London, British Museum, Cabinet 162, tray 22, n° 1900,0101.23. 3.70g, 19ø, 12h.
202. A21^1-P17(a) London, British Museum, Cabinet 162, tray 22, n° 1900,0101.24. 3.48g, 17ø, 12h.
203. A21^1-P18(a) London, British Museum, Cabinet 162, tray 22, n° 1930,0812.69. 3.60g, 18ø, 12h.
204. A21^1-P19(a) London, British Museum, Cabinet 162, tray 22, n° 1917,0204.148. 3.66g, 20ø, 12h.
205. A21^1-P20(a) Athens, Numismatic Museum, Cabinet 54, n° 411. 3.58g, 18ø, 12h.
206. A21^1-P21(a) New York, American Numismatic Society, tray 971, n° 1944.100.83554. 3.29g, 19ø, 1h.
207. A22^1-P6^1(a) Schenk-Behrens, 5–6 December 1996, n° 193. 3.72g, 20ø, ?h.
208. A22^1-P6^1(b) Peus 318, 7-8 May 1987, n° 1348. 3.58g, 21ø, ?h.
209. A22^1-P6^1(c) Dorotheum, 14 October 1983, n° 216. 3.80g, 19ø, ?h.
210. A22^1-P8^1(a) Hirsch 231, 26-28 November 2003, n° 461. 3.84g, 18ø, ?h.
211. A23^1-P22(a) Berlin, Münzkabinett, Löbbecke collection, Cabinet 14/58, n° 4/4. 3.76g, 18ø, 12h.
212. A31^1-P7^1(a) Birkler & Waddell, 9 December 1982, n° 144. 3.14g, 20ø, ?h.
213. A31^1-P8^1(a) Ponterio & Associates, 1 August 1995, n° 358. 3.59g, 21ø, ?h.
214. A34-P4$^{1?}$ (a) London, British Museum, Cabinet 162, tray 22, n° 1917,0204.146. 3.44g, 23ø, 12h.
215. A35^1-P6^1(a) Superior Stamp & Coin Co., Inc., World Coin List Summer, n° 61. 3.50g, 19ø, ?h.
216. A35^1-P6^1(b) Lanz 97, 22 May 2000, n° 354. 3.74g, 20ø, ?h.
217. A35^1-P8^1(a) CNG 31, 9-10 September 1994, n° 497. 3.63g, 19ø, ?h.
218. A35^1-P8^1(b) Schulman, 2–4 June 1982, n° 320. 3.64g, 20ø, ?h.
219. A35^1-P10^1(a) Rauch, 7–8 June 1977, n° 96 = Numismatica Wien, 9-11 November 1976, n° 469. ?g, 20ø, ?h.
220. A35$^{1?}$-P24(a) CNG 37, 20 March 1996, n° 763. 3.55g, 19ø, ?h.
221. A36-P8^1(a) Peus 372, 30 October 2002, n° 712. 3.85g, 24ø, ?h.
222. A37-P10^1(a) Vienna, Münzkabinett, Cabinet 12, n° 23161. ?g, 19ø, 12h.
223. A38^1-P12^1(a) Paris, Cabinet des Médailles, n.c. 1307. 3.39g, 19ø, 12h.
224. A38^1-P15^1(a) Berlin, Münzkabinett, Cabinet 14/58, n° ? 3.73g, ?ø, 12h.
225. A39-P23^1(a) New York, American Numismatic Society, tray 971, n° 1944.100.83556. 3.45g, 22ø, 12h.
226. A40-P23^1(a) Paris, Cabinet des Médailles, J. de Morgan collection, n° 1003. 3.03g, 20ø, 12h.
227. A41^1-P24(a) Berlin, Münzkabinett, Prokesch-Osten collection, Cabinet 14/58, n° ? 3.53g, ?ø, 12h.

Letter A (7)

Note: The legends are unreadable.

228. A4^1-P1^1(a) Berlin, Münzkabinett, Cabinet 14/58, n° 30/1873, 5/7. 3.75g, 19ø, 12h.
229. A19^1-P2^1(a) Berlin, Münzkabinett, Cabinet 14/58, n° 18412, 5/5. 3.53g, 17ø, 12h.
230. A19^1-P3(a) Paris, Cabinet des Médailles, n.c. 1306. 3.53g, 17ø, 12h.
231. A19^1-P4(a) New York, American Numismatic Society, tray 971, n° 1974.52.31. 3.75g, 19ø, 1h.
232. A19$^{1?}$-P? (a) Berlin, Münzkabinett, Cabinet 14/58, n° 18411, 5/3. 3.71g, 17ø, 12h.
233. A21^1-P1^1(a) Berlin, Münzkabinett, Cabinet 14/58, n° 18410, 5/2. 3.51g, 17ø, 12h.
234. A21^1-P2^1(a) New York, American Numismatic Society, tray 971, n° 1944.100.83558. 3.50g, 21ø, 12h.
235. A21^1-P2^1(b) New York, American Numismatic Society, tray 971, n° 1923.150.408. 3.49g, 19ø, 12h.
236. A21^1-P5(a) Berlin, Münzkabinett, Guthrie collection, Cabinet 14/58, n° 5/8. 3.65g, 17ø, 12h.
237. A38^1-P6(a) Paris, Cabinet des Médailles, n.c. 1304. 3.66g, 19ø, 12h.
238. A42-P7(a) Schenk-Behrens, 12-13 September 2000, n° 119. 3.30g, 19ø, ?h.

Series II

Obverse: *id.*

Reverse: No archer and no letter. Legend only.

New type/*unicum*

Note: The legend is unreadable.

239. A1[1]-P1(a) Gorny & Mosch 130, March 2004, n° 1492 = CNG 36, 1995, n° 440. 3.80g, 18ø, ?h.

NB: Unicum for the reverse.

New type/*unicum* or photographic error?

Note: The legend is unreadable.

240. A6[1]-P1(a) CNG 51, 15 September 1999, n° 642. 3.37g, 20ø, ?h.

Series III

Obverse: *id.*

Reverse: Archer seated left (photographic error in the catalogue?). Letter A (7) in right field.

Die-links

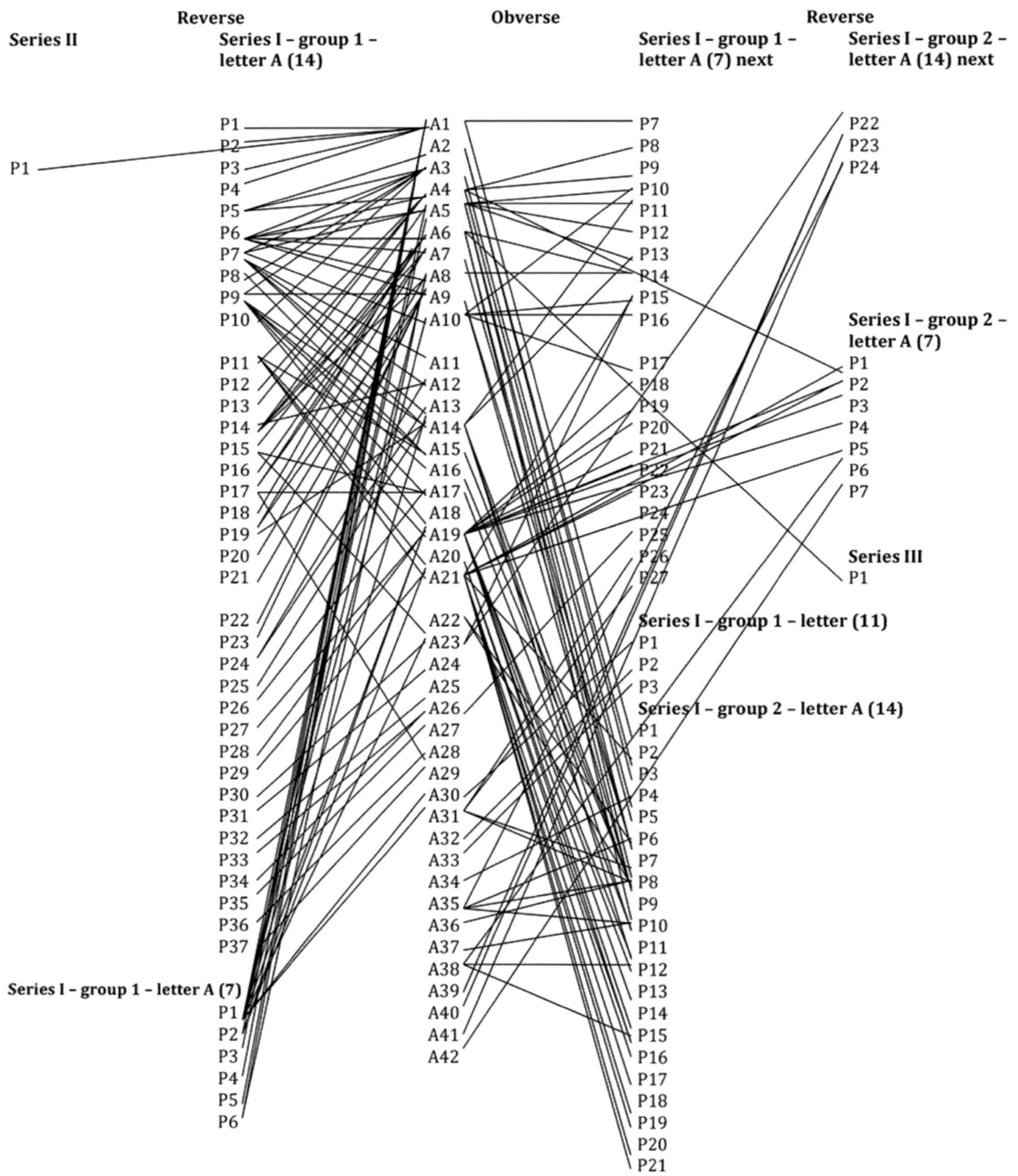

14

The Coinages of Paradan and Sind in the Context of Kushan and Kushano-Sasanian Numismatics

Nikolaus Schindel

Institut für Kulturgeschichte der Antike, Österreichische Akademie der Wissenschaften

---

It is a well-known fact that the absolute chronology of the history of Central Asia and northern India during the Kushan period still offers some disputed problems. Even if nowadays the majority of researchers prefer a starting date of the Kanishka Era in 127 AD,[1] the question still cannot be regarded as having been solved once and for all – too many problems, especially of a methodological nature, remain. It should also be emphasised that a degree of consensus is no proof of anything – after all, truth (or at least the highest degree of probability) in academic questions does not necessarily follow democratic principles. I have stated on several occasions[2] that I do not believe the current theory that regal year one of Kanishka equals 127 AD to be correct.

It should be remembered that even if some of Robert Göbl's ideas have proved flawed, many of his suggestions are still worthy of consideration. After all, his work is of pivotal importance for our understanding of Kushan and Kushano-Sasanian coinage, especially when it comes to the uniquely important topic of the reconstruction of numismatic systems. It is superfluous to underline the importance of coins for the reconstruction of Kushan history.[3] While it is essential to re-evaluate ideas articulated in earlier research, new scientific developments must also be incorporated. In this paper I will on the one hand re-examine a very important idea of Göbl concerning ribbed ribbons on Kushan coinage in the light of new developments in research on Paradan coinage. On the other hand, I will briefly discuss the gold coinage of Sind modelled after Sasanian prototypes and draw some comparisons with the Kushano-Sasanian coin series.

The coinage of Paradan and ribbed ribbons on Kushan coinage

Göbl repeatedly claimed that the use of ribbed ribbons on gold issues of the Kushan King Huvishka must have been influenced by Sasanian imperial coins (Figures 14.1, 14.2).[4] Since Ardashir I (224–240 AD), the first Sasanian King of Kings, whose absolute chronology can be established beyond doubt, was also the first to use this feature on his coinage – mostly (Figures 14.3, 14.5), but not always (Figure 14.4) – it follows according to Göbl that the respective Huvishka coins must be later than 224 AD. It has to be emphasised that Huvishka's first emission in mint A already shows ribbed ribbons.[5] If this feature was really taken over from the Sasanians, then Huvishka's accession to the throne must be dated later than that of Ardashir I, which means that it is not possible to let the two reigns overlap in such a way that Huvishka became king earlier than 224 AD. One argument in favour of Göbl's interpretation is the fact that both in Huvishka's mint A[6] as well as under Ardashir I (Figures 14.3, 14.4),[7] coins with ribbed ribbons occur alongside specimens with plain ribbons; the patterns of their use is thus very similar. In mint B, the common occurrence of ribbed ribbons commences later than in A.[8] According to the current *communis opinio*, however, combining the alleged starting date of the Kanishka Era of 127 AD with the date range for Huvishka provided by the inscriptions (years 26 to 64 of the Kanishka Era)[9] results in a chronological frame for his reign of *c.* 153 to 191 AD, that is to say, at least thirty-three years earlier than the accession to the throne of the Sasanian king Ardashir I, and thus the earliest possible date for the introduction of ribbed ribbons in Sasanian coinage.

A B

Figure 14.1: Kushan. Huvishka, dinar, Mint A. Göbl 1984, no. 154. CNG, Auction 87 (18 May 2011), lot 771.

A B

Figure 14.2: Kushan. Huvishka, dinar, Mint B. Göbl 1984, no. 342. CNG, Auction 91 (19 Sept. 2012), lot 457.

A B

Figure 14.3: Sasanian. Ardashir I, drachm, Mint B/"Hamadan". Alram/Gyselen 2003, type IIIb/3b. CNG, Auction 91 (19 Sept. 2012), lot 466.

A B

Figure 14.4: Sasanian. Ardashir I, drachm, Mint B/"Hamadan". Alram/Gyselen 2003, type IIIb/3b. CNG, e-auction 272 (25 Jan. 2012), lot 184.

A B

Figure 14.5: Sasanian. Ardashir I, tetradrachm, Mint C/"Ctesiphon". Alram/Gyselen 2003, type IIe/3a. Schaaf coll.

If one accepts the 127 AD starting date for the Kanishka Era, one must then assume that Huvishka invented the ribbed ribbons independently of Ardashir I. Since they occur only on coins of this single Kushan king, while they represent a major and typical feature of Sasanian art in all different media – not only coins – it seems highly improbable to me that the ribbed ribbons were taken over from these Kushan coins by Ardashir I. But even the idea that this treatment of the ribbons was invented independently by Huvishka before the emergence of the Sasanian empire is very unlikely: after all, ribbed ribbons were never used on any coin issue at all before Ardashir I. True, ribbed ribbons can be seen on a few rock reliefs attributed to the Parthian period.[10] But if we limit ourselves to numismatics, they cannot be found in the Arsacid coin series. With a symbol of power as important as the diadem,[11] we can safely assume that the rendering of the diadem ribbons had a religious and political meaning, even if it is difficult for us nowadays to specify it. The parallel depiction in Sasanian and Kushan coinage thus in all probability is not due to some chance contacts between different die cutters and thus devoid of any deeper meaning, but rather relates to imperial propaganda. Considering the natural opposition between a western Iranian and an eastern Iranian empire, it might be more than guesswork to assume that the use of the ribbed ribbons is connected with a religio-political position in the world of Iran to which both Ardashir I and his successors, as well as Huvishka, aspired. It should be remembered that both the Sasanian and the Kushan ruler bore the title "King of Kings".

New and potentially important evidence can be brought into this discussion by taking into account the coin series of the kings of Paradan (*Pāratarājas*),[12] a principality in what is today south-western Pakistan.[13] It has been studied in a series of articles by Tandon.[14] In the famous inscription at Naqsh-i Rustam,[15] Shapur I (240–272 AD) claims to have been lord of Paradan. But this assertion of direct Sasanian rule is seriously invalidated by the independent coinage of the kings of Paradan. I agree with Tandon that the numismatic evidence strongly implies that Paradan "may never really have been a province of the Sasanian empire at all".[16] In the inscription of Narseh (293–302/3 AD) at Paikuli, the king of Paradan is mentioned among the rulers who "stayed by my (Narseh's) advice and counsel",[17] which tells us nothing about the status of Paradan. It should be stressed that even if some elements of the coinage are Indian rather than Iranian, other evidence, especially from onomastics, proves that the kings of Paradan were Iranians.[18]

Now to my main point: in discussing the numismatic evidence, Tandon claims that "One surprise in the Pārata coinage is that it betrays no Sasanian influence whatsoever. Neither the fabric nor any of the design elements on the coins seem to have any similarity with Sasanian coinage"; "the coins (*sc.* the Paradan issues) show no Sasanian influence in terms of design, fabric or denomination".[19]

I think that this is not entirely accurate. Without doubt, the main parameters of Paradan coinage are independent of Sasanian traditions. Their style is different; they show a typical Parthian weight standard;[20] the legends are written in either Brahmi or Kharoshthi; the reverse symbol is much more Indian than Iranian. But there is one very important feature which connects some Paradan issues with Sasanian coins: the last kings (according to Tandon) employ ribbed ribbons on their issues (Figures 14.6, 14.7, 14.8).

A B

Figure 14.6: Paratarajas. Koziya. CNG, e-auction 268 (16 Nov. 2011), lot 168.

A B

Figure 14.7: Paratarajas. Koziya. CNG, e-auction 212 (17 June 2009), lot 154.

A B

Figure 14.8: Paratarajas. Datayola II. http://coinindia.com/galleries-parata-rajas.html, coin no. 23.

A B

Figure 14.9: Paratarajas. Datayola II. Tandon 2009, fig. 18.

A B

Figure 14.10: Kushano-Sasanian. Ohrmazd 1/Kavad. Göbl 1984, type 1124. Kunsthistorisches Museum Wien, Münzkabinett.

As in the case of the Kushan kings, there is no explicit information regarding the absolute chronology of the rulers of Paradan. There are, however, several glimpses which allow us some insights. From a numismatic point of view, the most important piece of evidence is the overstrike of two Paradan coins of Datayola II (Figure 14.8), dated by Tandon to *c.* 275–300 or *c.* 300–325 AD,[21] on Kushano-Sasanian issues of Ohrmazd 1 and the "satrap" Kavad (Figure 14.10).[22] Based on the evidence from imperial Sasanian coinage, the former's reign started after 300 AD.[23] Independently of my approach, Tandon thus arrives at a very similar absolute date for Datayola II. The uncertainty of a mere twenty-five years, it should be borne in mind, is not so much when one considers that as regards Year One of Kanishka I, we are still uncertain about the century, let alone the decade. Still, this certain and reliable numismatic link between Kushano-Sasanian and Paradan coinage can definitely serve as a chronological anchor, so to speak, with which to moor the last Paradan kings. I basically agree with Tandon, bearing in mind that even these absolute dates must remain hypothetical since we have no direct information for the individual durations of the reigns. The absolute dating by Tandon is as follows:[24]

Yolamira:	*c.* 125–150 or *c.* 150–175 AD
Bagamira:	*c.* 150–155 or *c.* 175–180 AD
Arjuna:	*c.* 155–165 or *c.* 180–190 AD
Hvaramira:	*c.* 165–175 or *c.* 190–200 AD
Mirahvara:	*c.* 175–185 or *c.* 200–210 AD
Miratakhma:	*c.* 185–200 or *c.* 210–225 AD
Kozana:	*c.* 200–215 or *c.* 225–240 AD
Bhimarjuna:	*c.* 215–225 or *c.* 240–250 AD
Koziya:	*c.* 225–250 or *c.* 250–275 AD
Datavharna:	*c.* 250–275 or *c.* 275–300 AD
Datayola II:	*c.* 275–300 or *c.* 300–325 AD

Judging from the evidence of the overstrikes cited above and my own chronology of the Kushano-Sasanian rulers, the second, slightly later variant seems more likely to me. This actually opens a quite fascinating, if highly speculative possibility. In the Paradan series, there is a marked deterioration in metal quality from silver or rather good billon to bronze under Bhimarjuna.[25] Accepting the later dating for him, and bearing in mind that these dates are all approximate, one can hardly avoid the impression that there is a connection between the metrological developments in Paradan and the dramatic fall from billon to copper in the Roman empire in 260 AD under the Emperor Gallienus (sole reign 260–268 AD). Tandon himself has raised the possibility that there might have been a connection between economic decline in Rome and the deterioration in metal quality in Paradan.[26] This minor adjustment in absolute chronology might help explain the phenomenon even better, despite the fact that no Roman elements are recognisable in the Paradan series.

One point needs to be addressed here: Tandon has compared the way the tunic is rendered on the large copper coins from Koziya onwards (Figure 14.7) to the rendering of the king's costume on Kushan coins from the time of Kanishka II.[27] However, there are basic differences in dress and attributes: the Kushan king wears a kaftan over a shirt,[28] while the kings of Paradan wear a tunic with a girdle. If the king wears body armour rather than a kaftan, under Kanishka II the hem is still straight,[29] thus the detail concerns different types of garment rather than necessarily different chronological layers. One might also add that some reverses of Huvishka show the tunic with a slightly curved hem rather than a completely straight one, which clearly proves that this variant existed well before Kanishka II.[30] While the sword at the waist is common to both series, the gesture of the left hand resting on the scabbard is purely Sasanian, and has no models in Kushan coinage.

By the way, there might be another connection in a matter of detail between Sasanian and Paradan coinage. In both series, an object resembling a lily sceptre is very occasionally encountered. While the Paradan ruler Datayola II holds it in his hand (Figure 14.11),[31] on the Sasanian issues of Narseh it is simply placed in the right obverse field (Figure 14.12).[32] Which way the influence worked is uncertain in this case. Once again, however, some type of interaction between Sasanian and Paradan coinage is probable.

Let us now return to the ribbed ribbons. As long as the basic chronological approximation of Tandon is accepted, it follows that the first king of Paradan to employ ribbed ribbons, Koziya, has to be dated after 224 AD, i.e. after the accession to power of Ardashir I. It seems once again obvious that the introduction of ribbed ribbons was directly influenced by Sasanian coinage; in the Paradan series, there are no chronological problems comparable to those concerning the use of the ribbed design in Kushan coinage. If one does not want to go to extremes and claim that the rulers of Paradan also invented the ribbed ribbons independently of the Sasanians, then we have here a clear example of a basically self-contained eastern Iranian coin series taking over an important and typical feature from western Iran. If one accepts the now commonly agreed dating for the reign of Huvishka (*c.* 153–191 AD), this would mean that Koziya's issues are at least a quarter of century later than those of Huvishka. If one were to track the model for Koziya's ribbed ribbons to the Kushan issues of Huvishka, then first and foremost it is very strange that they were used so late after the original models were minted.

Another argument against this possible, but unlikely alternative explanation is the fact that Huvishka uses the ribbed ribbons only on his gold dinars, never on his bronze coinage, whereas all Paradan coins featuring this detail are made of copper.

But even if this is so, there is a strong argument for assuming direct connections between Kushan and Paradan coins. The object held by Koziya or Datayola II (Figures 14.7, 14.8) very much resembles the sceptre – called *Kolbenszepter* by Göbl[33] – held by Huvishka on many dinar issues (Figures 14.1, 14.2). However, while this element certainly has no Sasanian parallels, the way the ribbed ribbons are shown is certainly much more closely related to Ardashir's issues such as Figure 14.5, so one cannot simply use the evidence of this sceptre to explain away the ribbed ribbons in Paradan as adopted from an independent Kushan innovation pre-dating Ardashir I. Thus, I would claim that there exists a certain "triangle" between Sasanian, Kushan and Paradan coinage which belongs to the second to the fourth quarters of the third century AD.

It goes without saying that one single pictorial detail in itself cannot solve a question as complex as that of Year One of Kanishka I. Still, I feel confident that we have here clear evidence that the typical Sasanian ribbed ribbons were taken over in an eastern Iranian petty kingdom, definitely after their introduction in Sasanian Iran, and equally certainly, I believe, using Sasanian coins as a model. I think that this parallel can be of importance also for the question of Kushan chronology. If the ribbed ribbons were taken over from the Sasanians by the kings of Paradan, the same process becomes more likely also in the case of Huvishka's ribbons. This, in turn, would – as Göbl has repeatedly claimed – mean that the currently accepted date of Huvishka is incorrect, and that he must be dated after the accession to the throne of Ardashir I, i.e. after 224 AD.

A B

Figure 14.11: Paratarajas. Datayola II. Tandon 2009, fig. 15.

A B

Figure 14.12: Sasanian. Narseh, drachm, style J = Sistan. Alram/Gyselen 2012, type Ia/2a. Schaaf coll.

The coinage of Sind

The second coin series which has so far never been studied in the context of Kushan or Kushano-Sasanian coinage is the Sind series. The plain reason is that this is another relatively obscure series. Even though these coins have been known for quite some time,[34] the first somewhat comprehensive treatments were published by Robert Senior about twenty years ago.[35] For the sake of completeness, it should be noted that one specimen was published by that great scholar of Sasanian numismatics, Robert Göbl, who, however, failed to make sense of it.[36] Based on Senior's remarks especially as regards the find spots, I addressed the question of these Sind issues briefly in SNS 3.[37] At that time, I was able to catalogue altogether eighteen gold dinars ranging chronologically from Shapur II's (309–379 AD) SNS type 2 to the third crown of Peroz (457–484 AD).[38] A quick look at the internet database *www.coinarchives.com*[39] shows how much more material is available today:

Table 14.1: Gold dinars of Sind

King	*SNS 3*	*coinarchives*	*types*
Shapur II	2	5	5
Ardashir II	3	-	2
Shapur III	4	5	3
Wahram IV	1	-	1
Yazdigird I	1	1	1
Wahram V	4	9	6
Yazdigird II	-	-	-
Peroz	3	35	5
1st crown	1	2	3
2nd crown	-[1]	-	-
3rd crown	2	33	2

1 Schindel 2004, vol. 2, pl. 145, no. C17 also seems to bear the third crown of Peroz, and not his second variant.

If a coin already catalogued in SNS 3 also turned up in *www.coinarchives.com*, I did not count it twice. "Types" means variants in legends or symbols, especially in front of the bust on the obverse.

The localisation of the series is based on provenances from coins in trade, from Sind itself,[40] as well as from Baluchistan and Kutch.[41] However, these coins prove that Sind was not a Sasanian province in the same way as, for instance, Asuristan or Fars. The local peculiarities in typology, style and – especially important – denominations strongly imply that Sind was not under direct Sasanian control, but was rather a region where Persian rule was exercised in a more indirect way. Sasanian rule over Sind (if this is the correct interpretation of the more generic term "Hindustan")[42] is mentioned in two Sasanian inscriptions. Shapur I claims in his inscription at Naqsh-i Rustam to be *inter alia* lord of "Hindustan";[43] and Shapur King of the Sakas lists apart from Sakastan and Tiran also Hindustan (*hndy*) as being under his rule.[44] However, we have seen above that in the case of Paradan, Shapur's claim and the historical reality as mirrored by the coins are not necessarily always in accord. On rare Sasanian seals, the term *snd* is used, which definitely refers to Sind.[45] The fact that there seem to have been no attempts to introduce the silver drachm as the main currency in Sind, I believe, strongly argues against direct Sasanian rule. The drachms attributed by Göbl[46] to the same mint as the dinars with the alleged mint signature LYHC in fact belong to an eastern mint which I would locate much farther to the north-east, and which is attested until Wahram IV (388–399 AD).[47] Its style shows no connections with Sind. It must also be emphasised that while some dies might have been produced by western Iranian craftsmen, or at least under their guidance,[48] the "heavy" dinar weight had already been abandoned under Peroz's father Yazdigird II (438–457 AD) in the Sasanian series,[49] although it remained in use in Sind, albeit with some weight reductions. The "light" Sasanian dinar of *c.* 4.25 g[50] left no mark in the Sind series. In addition, anachronistic typological details like the attendants holding barsom bundles under Peroz should be mentioned.[51]

A B

Figure 14.13: Sasanian. Shapur II, dinar. Mint VI = Marw. Schindel 2004, type Ia/1b. British Museum, Department of Coins and Medals.

A B

Figure 14.14: Sasanian. Shapur II, dinar, Mint IX = "Kabul". Schindel 2004, type Ib1/3a. Goldberg, Auction 62 (1 Feb. 2011), lot 3151.

A B

Figure 14.15: Sind. Shapur II, dinar. CNG, Mail Bid Sale 66 (19 Apr. 2004), lot 874.

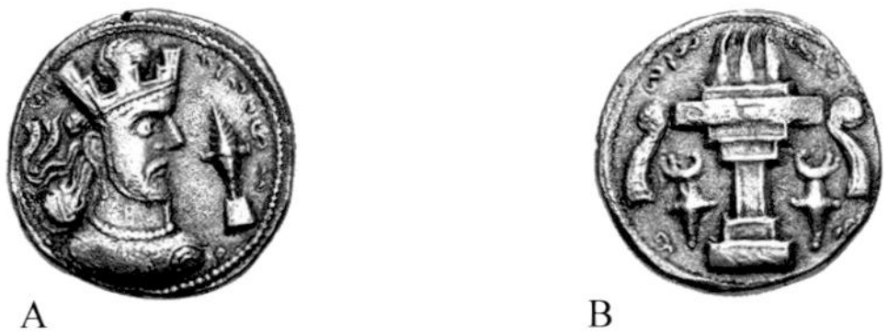

A B

Figure 14.16: Sind. Shapur II, dinar. Triton XV (3 Jan. 2012), lot 1374.

The starting point of the Sind series is under Shapur II, more specifically, his second reverse type (Figure 14.14), which served as the model for all Sind coins featuring his crown known to me (Figures 14.15, 14.16). Some of these Shapur II Sind dinars have been attributed by Göbl to an alleged mint "Rīhc" (Figure 14.15).[52] It is mildly amusing that he stated that the reading of the word in the right obverse field as Pahlavi LYHC is "*eindeutig*". In reality, it is not Pahlavi at all, but Brahmi. It simply says *sri*, "lord",[53] and is attested on issues from Shapur II to Wahram V (420–438 AD), that is to say, to the last king in the series but one.[54] My idea is that *sri* refers to the Sasanian King of Kings depicted on the obverses as overlord, but hardly on the same semantic level as the regular imperial titulature on undoubtedly official Sasanian coins from regular mints within the Sasanian realm. It is also under Wahram V that for the last time very degenerate remains of a circular Pahlavi legend can be observed. *Sri* is not always encountered, however, since there are some variants which bear either a symbol in front of the bust or else nothing at all. Only under Peroz are the remains of the Pahlavi inscriptions finally dropped, and instead of the rather general word *sri* the legend *Rana Datasatya*[55], sometimes read as *Ranaditya Satya*,[56] is added on the reverse (Figure 14.21).[57]

It is fascinating that even today, with a remarkable increase in traceable specimens, the most commonly attested rulers apart from Peroz (Figures 14.20, 14.21) are Shapur III (383–388 AD) (Figures 14.17, 14.18) and Wahram V (Figure 14.19). As of today, I know of five dinars for each from regular mints within Sasanian Iran,[58] which is markedly fewer than the nine and thirteen Sind gold coins respectively. It must also be emphasised that at the same time that I found on *coinarchives.com* the total of fifty-five Sind dinars listed above, I also found ninety Kushano-Sasanian gold pieces. That is to say that in sheer numbers these obscure Sind gold coins are about half as common as the much better studied Kushano-Sasanian dinars (Figure 14.22), which is in itself an important piece of information. Admittedly, the duration of the Kushano-Sasanian coin series is shorter. I believe that it began after 300 AD,[59] and that the regular coinage up to Wahram 6 did not extend beyond *c.* 360 AD. The Sind series, on the other hand, can be dated from the SNS type 2 of Shapur II,[60] which I believe was introduced after 325 AD, down into the later reign of Peroz, that is to say, in

A B

Figure 14.17. Sind. Shapur III, dinar. Triton VI (14 Jan. 2003), lot 524.

A B

Figure 14.18: Sind. Shapur III, dinar. Schaaf coll.

A B

Figure 14.19: Sind. Wahram V, dinar. Schaaf coll.

A B

Figure 14.20: Sind. Peroz, dinar, 1st crown. CNG, e-auction 154 (13 Dec. 2006), lot 100.

A B

Figure 14.21: Sind. Peroz, dinar, 3rd crown. Schaaf coll.

the 480s AD, as *terminus post quem* for the use of the third crown. Thus, while the Kushano-Sasanian coins of the "main series" were produced over a period of not much more than half a century, the period of production of the Sind dinars was approximately three times longer. The real numerical relationship between the two series therefore should be given as *c.* one to six, but still, it must be emphasised that the Sind coinage is a rather substantial phenomenon, and not just an obscure and rare oddity.

A B

Figure 14.22: Kushano-Sasanian. Ohrmazd 1, dinar, Balkh. Göbl 1984, type 707. Goldberg, Auction 44 (10 Feb. 2008), lot 3679.

As regards Peroz, there are two remarkable features. While his rare first crown, for which I was able to collect only twelve drachms back in 2004,[61] is attested by no less than three Sind dinars, his much more common second crown is still missing from the Sind series. As a reminder, it should be stated that in SNS 3, I was able to list twelve coins with the first crown, 143 with the second and 419 with the third.[62] The patterns of minting in the Sind series clearly do not follow the imperial model, but I am unable to provide an explanation. However, Peroz dinars from Sind with his third and last crown are very common, as can be seen from Table 14.1, but there are only two variants. The vast majority show a sun symbol in front of the bust on the obverse and employ the Brahmi legend most commonly read as *Rana Datasatya* to each side of the fire altar on the reverse (Figure 14.21). This inscription replaces the attendants to the left and right of the altar and thus places this type at the end of the series. Maybe the commonness of this particular type is due to the dispersal of a large coin hoard in trade, since the low number of variants is by comparison with the other kings quite untypical for the series.

Let us now have a look at the metrology of the Sind coins. The earliest issues cluster around 7.20 g and 7.30 g. This is the same area where the weight peak of the old, "heavy" Sasanian dinar lies; due to the rather small number of attested coins, it is not easy to define it with the utmost accuracy.[63] In any case, the weights of the Kushano-Sasanian dinars up to Wahram 6 are almost always heavier than 7.50 g, and their ideal weight seems to have been *c.* 7.80 g.[64] They certainly cannot have been the inspiration for the Sind series, which follows rather the weight of the imperial Sasanian dinar. Under Peroz at the latest, but maybe already during the reign of Wahram V, the ideal weight of the Sind dinars was lowered from the old Sasanian value of *c.* 7.20 g to a new, local standard of *c.* 6.90 g – a minor reduction of about 5%. This new weight standard can be observed very clearly under Peroz. The gold quality declined too, since several specimens are of a pale and sometimes even silverish appearance. Without accurate measurements, the details of these developments remain obscure to us. The deterioration in gold purity in the Sind series and in Late Kushan and Kushano-Sasanian coinage is certainly a parallel phenomenon.[65] But we should not forget that in the Sind series, the decline in gold purity becomes easily traceable only in the second quarter of the fifth century, at a time when a low gold content had been the rule in Bactria and northern India for at least half a century. The decline in

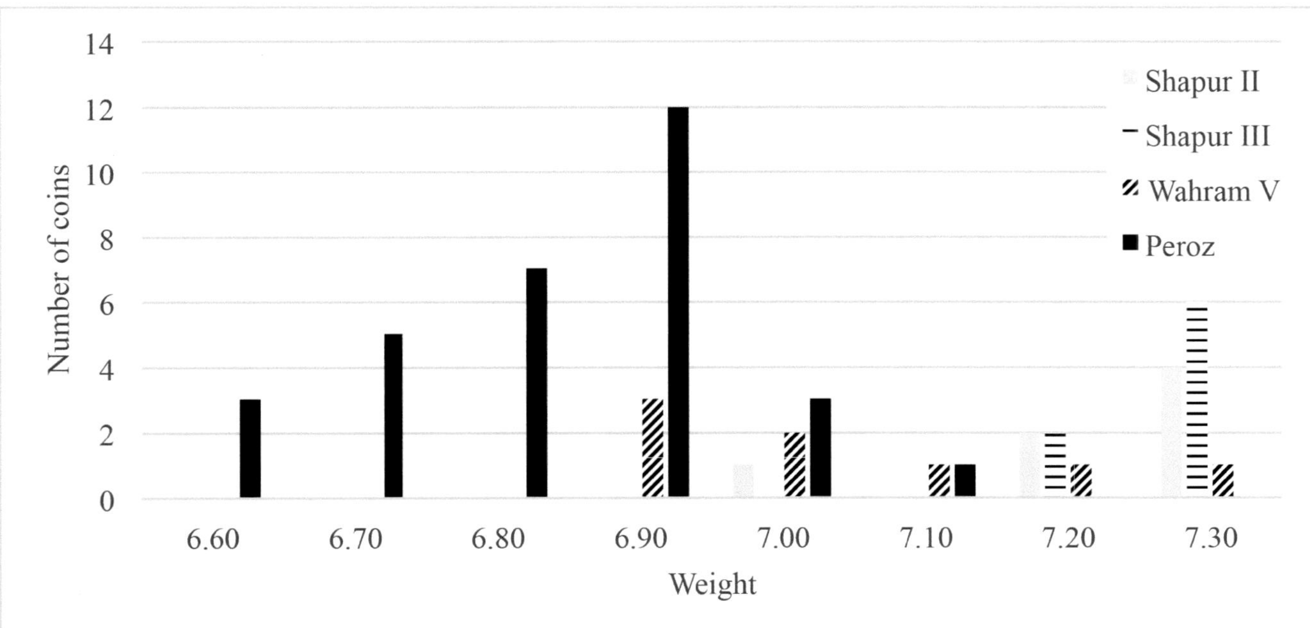

Figure 14.23: Metrology of the Sind coins

gold purity is thus not a simultaneous phenomenon in the Kushan world on the one hand and Sind on the other, even if the underlying economic reasons might easily have been interrelated.

What information do the Sind issues convey for our understanding of Kushano-Sasanian coinage? On the one hand, they show that a kind of Sasanian "provincial" coinage was also struck in areas other than Bactria and northern India. Without overlooking the basic differences, the mixture of imperial Sasanian and local, indigenous elements in typology, style, legends, denominations and so on of the Kushano-Sasanian series is therefore not unique.

On the other hand, although discussing the style of the Sind series is certainly difficult, it seems to me that the Shapur II Sind dinars show more similarities with eastern issues such as those from Marw and Herat than with western mints.[66] One Shapur III dinar (Figure 14.17) with a very clear *sri* in front of the bust shows on the reverse to the right and left of the bust in flames some Pahlavi letters which might represent MLWY, i.e. the mint name Marw. There are no Shapur III dinars from that city bearing the mint signature; his Marw issues lack the mint name and are of a markedly different style.[67] This position of the mint name is encountered on rare early Marw dinars of Shapur II which lack, however, the bust in flames (Figure 14.13). Even if the typological developments are thus somewhat complicated, it seems quite probable that the rather plentiful Sasanian gold coinage minted in Marw stimulated the Sind issues. After all, Marw is the most productive Sasanian gold mint in the fourth and early fifth centuries; additionally, it should be remembered that Kushano-Sasanian gold coins bearing this mint name also exist.[68] While this important mint might have originally influenced both the Kushano-Sasanian as well as the Sind gold coinage, these two series later on developed in different directions.

If we are to evaluate the historical information these two coin series can possibly convey, we need to be cautious because of the general lack of sources. However, it seems that in Sind the Sasanians did not encounter a monetary system as well developed as that of the Kushans, and therefore had more freedom of manoeuvre than in Bactria and Gandhara. They did not, however, try to introduce the silver drachm in Sind. While the various names of the Kushano-Sasanian rulers up to Wahram 6 most probably represent various governors sent to Kushanshahr by the Sasanian central government,[69] there can be no doubt that the person cited on the majority of Peroz's Sind dinars was not a functionary of the Sasanian Empire. The different historical development of Kushanshahr and Sind can also be deduced from the fact that by the third quarter of the fourth century at the latest, the Sasanian Kings of Kings and their Kushano-Sasanian governors ceased to exercise any direct control in Bactria and most of Gandhara, while the Sasanian presence in Sind continued well into the reign of Peroz. The absence of coins of Yazdigird II might be explained by military setbacks in the east during his reign.[70] The temporary successes of Peroz's eastern campaigns[71] are most probably mirrored in the resumption of the issue of Sind dinars, despite the enigmatic lack of known coins with his second crown. If the introduction of his third crown was occasioned by his first defeat of the Hephthalites,[72] then the presence of the legend *Rana Datasatya* could be easily explained by assuming that the Sasanians had to acknowledge local rulers and cooperate with them in order to retain some influence in the area. After all, this Indian inscription replaces the generic term *sri* which I believe refers to the Sasanian king depicted on the obverse. Even before, the dinars were certainly not struck by regular Sasanian governors, but rather have to be seen in the context of much more indirect and less effective Iranian rule. The mention of an Indian – whatever his exact position might have been – is certainly quite a different matter. After the final defeat and death of Peroz in 484 AD,[73] Khurasan was lost,[74] and in the context of this catastrophe, the Sasanian position in Sind also collapsed.

Notes

1 Errington and Curtis 2007, p. 71 (with literature).
2 Schindel 2005a, Schindel 2009, p. 12–14; Schindel (in press).
3 For the coinage, cf. the only fully comprehensive study, Göbl 1984, with important additions and corrections in Göbl 1993; furthermore, Alram and Klimburg-Salter 1999; Errington and Curtis 2007.
4 Göbl 1984, pl. 179; Göbl 1999, p. 158, pl. 3.
5 Göbl 1984, pl. 11.
6 Göbl 1984, pl. 11–21.
7 Alram and Gyselen 2003, p. 95, pl. 1–19.
8 Göbl 1984, pl. 21–27.
9 Cribb 1999, p. 188.
10 For example, Bard-i Nishandeh (Kawami 1987, pl. 26), even if the similarities with reliefs from the undoubtedly Sasanian site of Bishapur (Bier 2009, p. 31, 36) might possibly advocate a date very close to that of Ardashir I.
11 Schindel 2004, vol. 1, p. 64 f.
12 On the equation of the writing variants Pārata and Pārada, see Tandon 2012, p. 32 f.
13 Tandon 2012, p. 27.
14 Tandon 2006; Tandon 2009; Tandon 2010; Tandon 2012.
15 Back 1978, p. 287.
16 Tandon 2012, p. 27.
17 Skjærvø 1983, p. 54.
18 Tandon 2012, p. 36.
19 Tandon 2012, p. 22.
20 Tandon 2012, p. 34; Alram and Gyselen 2003, p. 162, 167.
21 Tandon 2009, fig. 18; Tandon 2012, p. 35.
22 Göbl 1984, type 1124.
23 Schindel 2005; Schindel 2012.
24 Tandon 2009, p. 155; in Tandon 2012, p. 49–54 he uses the earlier chronology with some minor modifications.
25 Tandon 2009, p. 146.
26 Tandon 2012, p. 38.

27 Tandon 2012, p. 35 f.; cf. Göbl 1984, pl. 33–51.
28 Göbl 1984, p. 37 f., pl. 160.
29 Göbl 1984, pl. 33, no. 538, pl. 34, no. 547 f.
30 For example, Göbl 1984, pl. 19, no. 265, pl. 26, no. 351, pl. 27, no. 382.
31 Tandon 2009, p. 151.
32 Alram and Gyselen 2012, p. 330.
33 Göbl 1984, p. 36 f.
34 Paruck depicts four Sind coins on his plates: one Shapur II dinar (Paruck 1924, vol. 2, pl. 11, no. 253), two pieces of Ardashir II (Paruck 1924, vol. 2, pl. 12, no. 258 f.), and one of Shapur III (Paruck 1924, vol. 2, pl. 12, no. 262).
35 Senior 1996; Senior 1990; Senior 1991a; Senior 1991b; Senior 2002.
36 Göbl 1987, p. 215, no. E28, pl. 31, fig. 31, in reality an early Peroz issue from Sind.
37 Schindel 2004, vol. 1, p. 507–509, vol. 2, pl. 145.
38 Schindel 2004, vol. 2, pl. 145.
39 As at October 5th, 2012.
40 Senior 1990, p. 15.
41 Senior 1990, p. 15; Senior 1991a, p. 42.
42 Gyselen 1989, p. 87 f.; more strongly for this equation, Gyselen 2002, p. 193.
43 Back 1978, p. 287 (Pahlavi *hndstn,* Greek INΔIA).
44 Back 1978, p. 492.
45 Gyselen 1989, p. 112; Gyselen 2002, p. 42.
46 Göbl 1984, pl. 143, no. 1353.
47 Schindel 2004, vol. 1, p. 238.
48 Schindel 2004, vol. 1, p. 509.
49 Schindel 2004, vol. 1, p. 375.
50 Schindel 2004, vol. 1, p. 99 f.
51 Schindel 2204, vol. 1, p. 508.
52 Göbl 1984, p. 54, pl. 143, no. 1352.
53 Senior 1991, on the authority of G. von Mitterwallner.
54 Schindel 2004, vol. 2, p. 145.
55 Senior 1996.
56 Tandon 2008, p. 21, note 28.
57 Senior 1996; Nelson 2011, p. 424, no. 1042.
58 Schindel 2004, Bd. 2, pl. 25, nos. A6 f.; pl. 59, nos. A4, A5; pl. 64, no. A29; SNS Schaaf (in press).
59 Schindel 2012.
60 Schindel 2004, vol. 1, p. 216 f.
61 Schindel 2004, vol. 1, p. 402.
62 Schindel 2004, vol. 1, p. 402, tab. 34.
63 Schindel 2004, vol. 1, p. 99 f.
64 Göbl 1984, p. 115 f.
65 Blet-Lemarquand 2006.
66 Göbl 1984, pls. 133 f., 136–138.
67 Schindel 2004, vol. 2, pl. 32, no. N2.
68 Göbl 1984, pl. 114, nos. 1026 f.
69 Schindel (in preparation).
70 Schindel 2004, vol. 1, p. 386.
71 Schindel 2004, vol. 1, p. 414 f.
72 Schindel 2004, vol. 1, p. 390–399.
73 Schindel 2004, vol. 1, p. 418.
74 Schindel 2004, vol. 1, p. 435, 448, 490 f.

References

Alram, M., and Gyselen, R. (2003). *Sylloge Nummorum Sasanidarum Paris – Berlin – Wien, Band I: Ardashir I. – Shapur I.*, Vienna.

—— (2012). *Sylloge Nummorum Sasanidarum Paris – Berlin – Wien, Band II: Ohrmazd I – Ohrmazd II.*, Vienna.

Alram, M., and Klimburg-Salter, D.E. (eds) (1999). *Coins, Art and Chronology. Essays on the pre-Islamic History of the Indo-Iranian Borderlands*, Vienna.

Back, M. (1978). *Die sassanidischen Staatsinschriften. Studien zur Orthographie und Phonologie des Mittelpersischen der Inschriften zusammen mit einem etymologischen Index des mittelpersischen Wortguts und einem Textcorpus der behandelten Inschriften*, Leiden.

Bier, L. (2009). "Palais B at Bishapur and its Sasanian Reliefs", in R. Gyselen (ed.), *Sources pour l'histoire et la géographie du monde iranien (224–710)*, Res Orientales 18, Bures-sur-Yvette: p. 11–40.

Blet-Lemarquand, M. (2006). "Analysis of Kushana Gold coins: Debasement and Provenance Study", in F.De Romanis and S. Sorda (eds), *Dal denarius al dinar: l'oriente e la moneta romana, Atti dell'incontro di studio, Roma 16–18 Settembre 2004*, Rome: p. 155–171.

Errington, E., and Curtis, V.S. (2007). *From Persepolis to the Punjab. Exploring Ancient Iran, Afghanistan and Pakistan*, London.

Falk, H. (2007). "The Names of the Pāratarājas Issuing Coins with Kharoshthī Legends", *Numismatic Chronicle* 167: p. 171–178.

Göbl, R. (1984). *Münzprägung des Kušānreiches*, Vienna.

—— (1987). "Supplementa Orientalia II", *Litterae Numismaticae Vindobonenses* 3: p. 203-216.

Gyselen, R. (1989). *La géographie administrative de l'empire sassanide. Les témoignages sigillographiques*, Paris.

—— (2002). *Nouveaux matériaux pour la géographie historique de l'empire sassanide: Sceaux administratifs de la collection Ahmad Saeedi*, Paris.

Kawami, T.S. (1987). *Monumental Art of the Parthian Period in Iran*, Acta Iranica 26, Leiden.

Nelson, B.R. (ed.) (2011). *Numismatic Art of Persia. The Sunrise Collection. Part I: Ancient – 650 BC to AD 650*, Lancaster, PA.

Paruck, F.D.J. (1924). *Sāsānian Coins*, 2 vols, Bombay.

Schindel, N. (2004). *Sylloge Nummorum Sasanidarum Paris – Berlin – Wien, Band III: Shapur II. – Kawad I. / 2. Regierung*, 2 vols, Vienna.

—— (2005a). "Adhuc sub iudice lis est? Zur Datierung der kushanosasanidischen Münzen", in H. Emmerig (ed.), *Vindobona docet. 40 Jahre Institut für Numismatik und Geldgeschichte der Universität Wien, 1965–2005*, Vienna *Numismatische Zeitschrift* 113/114: p. 217–242.

—— (2005b). "The Sasanian Coinage in Merw during the 5th century A.D.", *Simposio Simone Assemani sulla monetazione Islamica*, Padua: p. 43–54.

—— (2006). "Sasanian Gold Coinage: An Overview", in *Dal denarius al dinar: l'oriente e la moneta Romana*, Rome: p. 105–129.

—— (2008). "Die Münzstätte Marw von Ardashir II. bis zur Mitte des 5. Jahrhunderts n. Chr.: Ein Nachtrag", *Numismatische Zeitschrift* 116/117: p. 249–251.

—— (2009). "Ardashir 2 Kushanshah and Huvishka the Kushan: Numismatic Evidence for the Date of the Kushan King Kanishka I", *Journal of the Oriental Numismatic Society* 198: p. 12–14.

—— (2012). "The Beginning of Kushano-Sasanian Coinage", in M. Alram and R. Gyselen, *Sylloge Nummorum Sasanidarum Paris – Berlin – Wien, Band II: Ohrmazd I. – Ohrmazd II.*, Vienna: p. 65–73.

—— (in press). "The Era of the Bactrian Documents: A Reassessment", *Gandharan Studies* 5.

—— (in preparation). *Fundmünzen aus Usbekistan Band 1. Schatzfunde spätkushanischer und kushano-sasanidischer Kupfermünzen und ihr Beitrag zur Kenntnis von Prägesystem und Geldumlauf im kushano-sasanidischen Herrschaftsbereich.*

Senior, R.C. (1991a). "Coin of Vahran V indicates earlier mint activity at Sind than was previously thought", *The Celator* 5/2: p. 42 f.

—— (1991b). "The Coinage of Sind from 250 AD up to the Arab Conquest", *Oriental Numismatic Society Newsletter* 129: without pagination.

—— (1996). "Sind region, new coins", *Oriental Numismatic Society Newsletter* 149: p. 6.

—— (2002). "Some Unpublished Ancient Coins", *Oriental Numismatic Society Newsletter* 170: p. 14–19.

Skjærvø, P.O. (1983). *The Sassanian Inscription of Paikuli. Part 3.1 Restored text and translation*, online at: http://www.humanities.uci.edu/sasanika/pdf/Paikuli.pdf (accessed 23 January 2013)

Tandon, P. (2008). "More early medieval silver portrait coins of the Yashaaditya series", *Oriental Numismatic Society Newsletter* 195: p. 17–23.

—— (2006). "New Light on the Pāratarājas", *Numismatic Chronicle* 166: p. 173–209.

—— (2009). "Further Light on the Pāratarājas", *Numismatic Chronicle* 169: p. 137–171.

—— (2010). "The Coins of the Pāratarājas: A Synthesis", *Supplement to Journal of the Oriental Numismatic Society* 205: p. 15–31.

—— (2012). "The Location and Kings of Pāradāan", Studia Iranica 41/1: p. 25–56.